THE HOUSE OF HANOVER

THE HOUSE OF HANOVER

GEORGE I
(1714-1727)

GEORGE II
(1727-1760)

GEORGE III
(1760-1820)

WILLIAM IV
(1830-1837)

GEORGE IV
(1820-1830)

QUEEN VICTORIA
(1837-1901)

THE HOUSE OF HANOVER

by Alvin Redman

COWARD-McCANN, Inc.
New York

"*Nor is it always in the most distinguished achievements that men's virtues or vices may be best discerned; but very often an action of small note, a short saying, or a jest, will distinguish a person's real character more than the greatest sieges or the most important battles.*"

PLUTARCH

CONTENTS

ACKNOWLEDGMENT

Figures 7, 10, 11, 19, 25, 26, 27, 28, 29, 30, 32, 35, 36, 37 and 38 are reproduced by gracious permission of Her Majesty The Queen.

Figure 5 is reproduced by kind permission of the Hon. Robin Neville and the Ministry of Works (Crown Copyright).

Figure 16 which is Crown Copyright is reproduced by kind permission of the National Trust.

Figure 33 is reproduced by kind permission of the Earl Peel.

Figures 1, 3, 4, 9, 13, 15, 20, 21, 22, 23, 24, 31, 34, 39, 40 and 41 are reproduced by kind permission of the National Portrait Gallery.

Figure 6 is reproduced by kind permission of the Trustees of the Wallace Collection.

I wish to acknowledge also, the assistance of Mr. G. Norman Knight, M.A., Barrister-at-Law, who has read the proofs and made many helpful suggestions, as well as compiling the index.

LIST OF ILLUSTRATIONS

GENEALOGICAL TREE OF THE HOUSE OF HANOVER

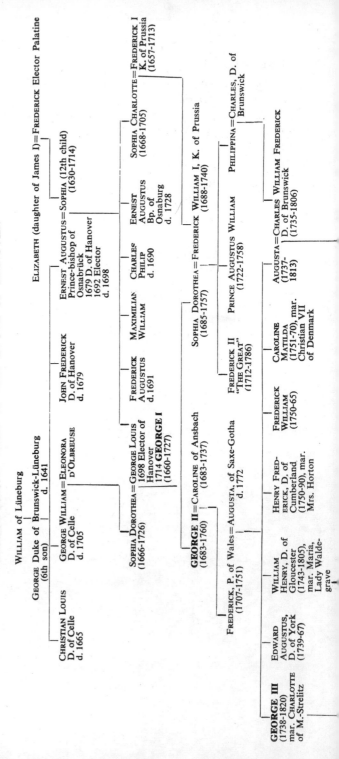

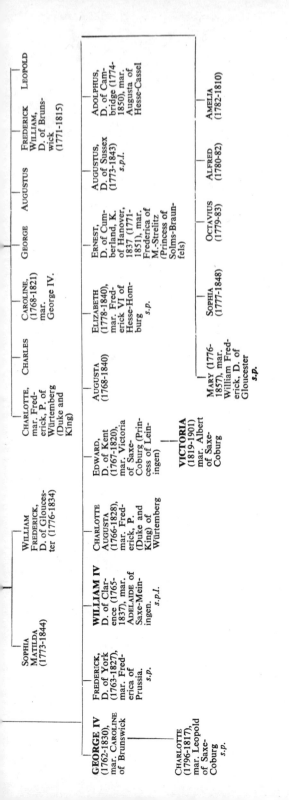

THE HOUSE OF HANOVER

CHAPTER ONE

ANCESTRY

I

THE PATH of events that led a German prince, who could not speak a word of English, to the throne of Great Britain was a devious one. It began in Celle, a town of ten thousand people, upon the fast-flowing River Aller, in the midst of the vast Lüneburg plains between Hamburg and Hanover. In those days, it was a town of wooden dwellings dominated by a great brick church. Here ruled, as his father Ernest of Celle had done before him, Duke William of Lüneburg, the progenitor of the House of Hanover.

William of Lüneberg, or "William the Pious" as he was known to his subjects, governed his people with a rigid, religious discipline. He had fifteen children, seven sons and eight daughters, and a macabre spectacle is presented of Duke William on his death-bed, old, sightless and insane, surrounded by his family, with the sons drawing lots to decide which one shall inherit the none-too-large property and marry to propagate the race of the Guelphs. The winning lot fell to the sixth brother, Duke George.

The routine of life instituted by the old Duke continued. The rules were rather those of a monastery than a minor European court. The trumpeter sounded for the two meals of the day at nine in the morning and four o'clock in the afternoon. Swearing, rudeness and boisterous conduct were forbidden, and the time-table, interspersed with hymns and sermons, was observed by all; except the marrying Duke George. The mundane life bored him and before long he set out on the Grand Tour of Europe, including incidentally in his itinerary the Court of Queen Elizabeth.

He did not return however until 1617 when he found himself a wife and held his court at Zell. Here in the interests of economy he was joined by his brothers, who were still single or had contracted left-hand marriages. The orderly religious way of life was resumed.

Duke George was again stirred by his restlessness and set out to seek his fortune wherever the prize was richest. First, he served as a general in the Protestant Army in Lower Saxony, then with the Emperor in Germany and Italy, and later as a general in the Swedish Army. The belligerent Duke was successful, and in his last destructive sortie he took the Abbey of Heldesheim as his share of the loot. He liked it so much he decided to live there, and settled down to a peaceful existence. Once more the simple, religious routine was the order of the day. So the belligerent Duke George became the quiet sedate man of wealth and substantial property.

The quiet ways of Zell were not the ways of the rest of Europe, for a picture of the day is one of a desert of starving peasantry, gathering meagre crops from the scanty soil; a devastated, plundered landscape, with the courts as oases of wealth, splendour, immorality and ruthlessness, linked together by roads of wheel-rutted mud. Along these roads the carriages of the courts jolted and swayed while the occupants living in a separate world, were oblivious to the poverty and starvation outside their carriage doors. As we look back, the figures emerging from the mists of time are bejewelled, bewigged, well-fed, dissolute and elegant. These, with their noble gestures to dissolute acts are the ones that history notes, not the starving peasantry, obscure, featureless, suffering the customs of their times, herded together by floggings and threats into the service of their lords. For these poor souls the gigantic roulette wheel of Life spun and they were the counters. A regiment of soldiery gaily changes hands on the spin of the wheel or the turn of a card; on the whim of a mistress or for the caresses of a harlot.

In the year 1641 Duke George died in the Abbey of Heldesheim and joined his brothers and forebears in the great brick church on the sandy banks of the Aller. He left four sons to forge further links in the chain that leads to Great Britain's House of Hanover.

The four sons, like their father when young, were restless. The second brother, George William, spent a great deal of his time visiting Venice which was the pleasure-centre of Europe, crowded with victorious men of war savouring the licentious pleasures as their reward. It was the capital of vice and gaiety in Europe and the Prince was enchanted. He brought back to the quiet sedate life of Zell, Italian dancers and singers and companions of his debaucheries, so that the atmosphere was transformed. To cap it all he married a commoner, a French one at that—Eleanor d'Olbreuse, and in the eyes of his subjects thus degraded the family name. This was an ironic trick of fate, for Eleanor's daughter, the inheritor of great wealth, and beauty besides, was, as time shewed, to marry George the First of England.

The eldest and third brothers are unimportant to this story. Of the first brother Christian Louis there is little record. He died in 1665 and George William succeeded him; whilst it is sufficient to say of the third brother, John Frederick, that he too became enamoured with the pleasures of Italy. He was so impressed indeed that he was converted to Roman Catholicism and Mass was said where once " William the Pious " sang his hymns.

The brothers George William and Ernest Augustus were very close to each other. They had from early youth been inseparable companions, sharing their travels, adventures and pleasures; living in the dissolute manner of the fashionable *élite* of France and Italy. Their tastes were similar and they enjoyed amorous escapades, which were many, for they were both handsome and had dashing reputations.

When their father died the three brothers divided the territories of Brunswich-Lüneburg (which came to be known as Hanover in English usage from the capital city) between themselves. The eldest brother Duke George William claimed the biggest area with the capital of Celle; John Frederick was given the area around Hanover, and Ernest Augustus, the youngest, became Bishop of Osnabruck and on John Frederick's death in 1679 took over his brother's territory of Hanover. Thus the two brothers who had shared so much also shared the inheritance.

But they were to be linked even closer for their children were destined to become the founders of England's House of Hanover.

It is the youngest of the four brothers who now holds the stage. Ernest Augustus of Brunswick, after the brothers had divided between themselves the territories of Duke George, " the Marrying George ", eventually became the holder of the entire possessions. But more important than his heritage is the fact that he married Sophia, daughter of Frederick the winter King of Bohemia, granddaughter of James I and the niece of Charles Stuart. In 1658, nine years after the head of Charles I had dropped into the basket at Whitehall, she brought as her dowry, unknowingly and unpredictably, the reversion of the Crown of Great Britain.

She was a handsome woman, shrewd and accomplished, and fortunately for the Hanoverian succession she was the only daughter of the luckless Elizabeth Stuart who was a Protestant. The others became Catholics. Sensible and understanding, Sophia was fully aware of her husband's faults, which were many for he was a true man of his times, and she closed her eyes to his drinking bouts and licentious habits. Her husband, now Bishop of Osnaburg and Duke of Hanover, was a jovial prince. He loved the bottle, his stomach and women, not necessarily in that order. He loved them together, and like his brothers before him he often sought them in Italy. This is not to indicate that he neglected the pleasures of life in Hanover; far from it. The Electoral Court of Hanover was a sumptuous affair, modelled, as was the custom of the many European courts, on Versailles, the French Court of Louis XIV, and the language and manners were French. The retinue of Duke Ernest of Hanover, like that of Louis, was numerous and well-paid. Amongst the throng ministering to the needs and whims of the Elector were High Marshals, High Masters of the Horse; and incidentally there were no fewer than six hundred horses in the royal stables with twenty coachmen, and another hundred assorted helpers such as postilions, ostlers, smiths, horse-doctors, grooms and the like; chamberlains, ushers, pages, gentlemen of the bed-chamber, fencing-masters, dancing masters, court physicians, barbers, organists, twenty assorted cooks, bakers, scullions, officers of the wine cellars and a host of others. Strangely enough, only two washerwomen are listed for the entire court.

The entertainments were lavish and frequent and to pay for them and the wages of his retainers the jovial, happy Duke sold by the thousand his Hanoverian soldiers. They were driven off in herds like cattle to fight the battles of the highest bidder. This was the general custom in Europe but was a favourite indulgence of the German princes. To lead these bands of troops there were adventurous nobles who travelled from court to court offering their services. Their successes were handsomely rewarded from the spoils of battle. This was the day of the opportunists and inevitably the feminine beauties of the time played their part. They too travelled the courts weaving their intrigues as favourites and mistresses. They earned their rewards in jewels, wealth and titles.

Duke Ernest Augustus had six children and the five sons in turn fought and loved in the service of other courts. Two of his sons were killed in campaigns, two other rebelled against their father and fled. His daughter was married to the Elector of Brandenburg, whilst the eldest son George Louis married Princess Sophia Dorothea, his beautiful cousin of Zell, the daughter of George William, Duke of Celle.

2

Princess Sophia Dorothea, the daughter of Duke George William, was his only child to survive infancy and consequently she was spoiled by her indulgent parents. She was born at the castle of Celle in 1666, the year the Great Fire destroyed the half-timbered Elizabethan city of London. She was a pretty and attractive child, brought up in an atmosphere of love.

The families of the ducal brothers at Celle and Hanover, thirty miles apart, used to exchange visits and Sophia Dorothea as she grew older noticed that she was treated with slightly less dignity and respect than were her cousins. The reason was that her mother, Eleanor d'Olbreuse, although descended from the ancient Huguenot nobility of France, was not recognized by German rules to be her father's wife. She was a commoner and by law a prince could only marry a person of equal rank; thus the children of a "morganatic marriage" were treated as illegitimate. The Emperor was the only one able to raise Eleanor to princely rank and so make the union legal, but George William was prevented from using his influence with the Emperor to arrange this adjustment by circumstances of his own making.

Years earlier it had been George William, and not his brother, who had proposed to the beautiful Princess Sophia. Formal consent had been given by the Elector Palatine and the marriage settlement arranged. As the date of the wedding approached, however, George William had misgivings about the advantages of matrimony. He decided that he could not go through with the marriage; yet he dared not insult the Palatine family. He evolved a simple plan to suit both courts.

The plan was that his brother Ernest Augustus should take his place and marry Princess Sophia. But the only way he could persuade his astute and calculating brother to agree was to settle upon him a very liberal settlement, and to promise that he himself would never marry, so that in due course the succession of the dukedoms of the two elder brothers, for John Frederick was then alive, should devolve upon Ernest Augustus and his descendants. Accommodatingly Princess Sophia said she did not mind which brother went with the inheritance. Thus the exchange was effected and George William went off to Italy to enjoy his bachelordom.

When he returned from Venice with the beautiful and charming Eleanor d'Olbreuse, however, there was considerable consternation in the household of Duke Ernest Augustus, for there was nothing to guarantee that George William would keep his word, except his honour.

For years afterwards George William tried to cajole and bribe them to release him from his promise, but they refused to do so and it was not until it became obvious that Sophia Dorothea would be the only child that they agreed; the succession being through the male line. Even for this release Ernest Augustus insisted upon a further settlement and in this manner the estates of George William dwindled. The Emperor duly created Eleanor "Countess of the Empire" and declared the marriage legal in 1675. In the following year she became the Duchess of Celle.

Sophia Dorothea was therefore nine years old before she became the legitimate daughter of the Duke of Celle, although when she was eight her father had persuaded the Emperor to grant her princely rank and thus ensured her marriage rights, together with a dowry of 15,000 crowns (equal to £30,000 sterling at the time).

There were many suitors, even at this early age, amongst them George of Denmark, who later married Anne of England; but George William had other ideas. His ambition was for the daughter he treasured so much to become the reigning Duchess of Celle and he realized that the way to this prize was through his brother's heir, George Louis. The boy had already been sent to England speculatively as a possible suitor for the hand of the young Princess Anne, but he had not been accepted and was now available as a tempting marriage prospect. On the death of his father Ernest Augustus he would become heir to the Dukedom of Hanover, for his uncle John Frederick was unmarried, and eventually he would succeed also to the Dukedom of Celle. Thus by marrying her cousin Sophia Dorothea would become the Duchess of both domains. It was a tempting prospect.

George William lost no time in putting the proposition before his brother. Unfortunately the idea did not appeal to the boy's parents, nor indeed did it appeal to the young George Louis, now sixteen years of age. Sophia Dorothea was eleven and the two children were hostile to each other. The Duchess Sophia was at first vehement in her disagreement for she had not forgotten her rejection by George William and she couldn't stand her sister-in-law the Duchess of Celle. Sophia said: "The boy is averse from the marriage and we to the alliance with d'Olbreuse." However the idea of consolidating the two duchies into one was certainly a proposition to be considered carefully and "if it is gilded with 100,000 crowns a year in our full control we may shut our eyes to take it," she added after reflection.

The Estates of Calenberg, who met like a Parliament, were of the same opinion and said they would agree to the fusing of the two duchies; indeed they would add some financial inducements, which was an important incentive to Ernest Augustus. Thus the two brothers overcame the reluctance of their respective wives, George William by his enthusiasm and Ernest Augustus by his greed.

The negotiations had continued intermittently for two years and in 1682 the Duke and Duchess of Celle paid a " state visit " to the Court of Hanover to settle the terms of the marriage agreement; Baron Bernstorff the Minister of Celle and Count Platen the Minister of Hanover drew up the contract with the help of the two Duchesses, who were now compliant.

The bargain was struck with the Duke of Celle paying to his brother, and not to the young couple, the sum of 150,000 thaler (equal to £30,000 in English money at the time) together with an annual sum of 50,000 thaler for six years. The dowry of 15,000 crowns was handed to George Louis personally so that Sophia Dorothea would be completely dependent on her husband, and after the death of her parents all their possessions and revenues would pass to her husband. It was a hard bargain.

However, despite the generous settlement the young Prince George was not happy about the marriage. His mother said : " He did not like it, but the money tempted him as it would anybody else." His first reaction when the union had been mentioned to him had been : " No Frenchwoman !" and Sophia Dorothea was indeed French, for her father had obtained her naturalization as a Frenchwoman in the hope of protecting her should he die prematurely. French was her natural tongue, and as her parents prided themselves on their French tastes, which were the most polished and fastidious of the day, she was indoctrinated from birth with Versailles's manners and sympathies. George Louis, however, was essentially German and although, of course, he spoke French and dressed in the French style (the cocked hat worn with a peruke was the new fashion), he resented the French influence.

The wedding was a quiet one and took place on the 21st of November, 1682, in the Princess's apartments with a minimum of ceremony. She was sixteen and he was twenty-one.

Ten days later the young couple were escorted to Hanover in magnificent style and with fanfares of trumpets attended by a regiment of cavalry, pages, officers and officials, all in bright costumes. Their carriage was the centre-piece of a triumphant procession of a hundred state-coaches, each drawn by eight horses bedecked with red velvet trappings and red twisted silk reins, accompanied by footmen dressed in red and blue uniforms with silver buttons. In all it was a spectacle to gladden the heart of the pomp-loving, military-minded young Prince George.

Hanover, untouched by the Thirty Years' War, was a prosperous city with high pointed gable-fronted houses, red tiled roofs, and elaborately carved signs. There were crowds lining the wide streets to welcome the wedding procession and the spectacle must have dwarfed the little Princess from the smaller, poorer, more spartan town of Celle. In Hanover the citizens were better dressed and during celebrations even the servants wore frizzled wigs and gay costumes. Indeed the Duke had some misgivings about the way in which the townspeople aped their betters and he issued a decree restricting the height of women's head-dresses, forbidding the too extravagant wearing of silk and silver and restricting the carrying of swords, for in those days people were supposed to dress in accordance with their rank.

Mingled with the awe Sophia Dorothea must also have felt many misgivings, for George was a taciturn, selfish, unfriendly husband and his mother made no pretence of hiding her hostility to her new daughter-in-law.

Another person at the Court of Hanover who hated the arrival of the young bride was Countess Platen the mistress of Duke Ernest Augustus, which was a much coveted, semi-official position. She was a conniving woman and to consolidate her own security for the future she had encouraged the young George Louis to have an affair with her young sister, but he had soon grown tired of her affections. As an alternative Countess Platen had replaced her sister with her own daughter Frau von Kielmannsegge (Ernest Augustus was the father and gave permission for this illegitimate child to bear the same names, Sophia Charlotte, as his only legitimate daughter) as a mistress to her half-brother the young Prince George. The Countess therefore looked upon Sophia Dorothea as a threat to her future position. She also resented the contrast between her own be-daubed, vice-lined appearance and the fresh-complexioned beauty of the young Princess, who was gay, charming and accomplished.

Despite the prejudice shown towards her, Sophia Dorothea must have found life at court a gay one, if drunken and dissolute, for it was almost a continuous round of vicious, un-licensed pleasure. There were also performances in the Court Theatre and the Opera House; entertainments in the town's Guild Hall intermingled with balls and masquerades and torch-dances, in which the couples danced hand-in-hand, each holding a blazing torch six feet in length. The dances were from six in the evening until supper and then went on until daybreak, con-tinuing night after night for a week at a time; inevitably they involved love-making.

Countess Platen was a prominent figure in this mad round of gaiety and when, as often happened, a long string of coaches conveyed the revellers to the country palace or one of the mag-nificent hunting-boxes she took the leading role; whilst the Duchess for obvious reasons stayed behind. So for a time, amongst the crowd of irresponsible pleasure-seekers, the young Princess found happiness. Her husband was often absent on military duties or seeking entertainment elsewhere.

When she had been married two years she gave birth to a son. He was born in October 1683, and was named George Augustus. This providing of an heir to the duchy pleased her father-in-law, who became very friendly towards her, but the Duchess seemed to resent the birth for she was even more antago-nistic. Perhaps she was jealous, for in 1685 the Duke when he was in Venice with Countess Platen sent for Sophia Dorothea to join them, and the Duchess had already noticed the growing affection between them.

Ernest Augustus allowed his daughter-in-law complete free-dom when the party entered wholeheartedly into the social rounds of Venice and later of Rome, then the two most brilliant and unlicensed pleasure-centres in Europe, and the morally-lax way of life in these gay cities must have had an unfortunate influence upon the capricious and volatile girl of twenty.

Just before he had left the Court for Italy the Duke had quarrelled with his second son, Augustus, and as a result he had ordered him to leave Hanover to earn his own keep in the Emperor's army engaged in the war with the Turks. Reduced to the level of a penniless nobleman, Augustus had been forced by lack of money and influence to become a junior officer existing only on his pay. This " turning-out " of his son however did not affect the Duke's enjoyment in Italy for he squandered money recklessly in the pursuit of pleasure without giving a thought to his son's penniless plight.

The Duchess had been shocked and very unhappy about the affair but she was powerless to intervene on her son's behalf in the face of her husband's implacability. She said that at night she shed tears but treated the matter as one of amusement during the day. In her frustration she built up further hatred against her daughter-in-law to whom she attributed some of the blame for the Duke's unfeeling attitude.

After a year in Italy the Duke's party returned to Hanover and Sophia Dorothea found herself in a worse position than before. Her husband, who had returned from the war during her absence in Italy, had found himself a mistress, Melusina von Schulenburg, and installed her in an apartment in the palace. This was the beginning of the estrangement between the Duke and the Duchess and the birth of a second child, named Sophia Dorothea after the mother, caused the gap to become even wider.

The atmosphere of acrimony provoked Sophia Dorothea to such wild outbursts of indignation and sarcasm that she was likened by the court to a wildcat in her attacks on her husband and his family. They were probably astonished at her displays of indignation for they must have seen nothing amiss in a situation that was quite the accepted rule of conduct in all the European courts of that time.

They were an ill-assorted pair, even in those days when compatability was considered to be an unimportant part of marriage. Sophia Dorothea was beautiful, talented, vivacious and witty. George Louis was selfish, taciturn, and cruel. Both were immoral and the young Princess was to pay for this fault in the coinage of tragedy.

3

The splendid Court of Hanover was now nicknamed " the German Venice " for the wealthy Duke Ernest Augustus had organized festivities to rival even those of the Italian pleasure-cities. He had rebuilt his palace, added a new wide street to the town, built an opera house in the Italian style, where the performances equalled those in Vienna, and his famous Carnival which lasted from December to the Spring attracted the wealthy pleasure-seekers from all over Europe.

The way of welcoming the visitors to Hanover was a ceremonial in itself. The Duke's carriages and a guard of honour awaited them; the nobles being accommodated in the palace and their retinues in the town, thus the citizens of Hanover were also encouraged to enter into the festivities and dissipations of the day and the entertainments of the night.

During the fête of 1688 Prince Charles, the fourth son of Duke Ernest Augustus, was told by his father to join the Emperor's army, but luckily for him he did not suffer the fate of his brother for on this occasion the Duke bought him the command of a regiment.

In the summer he was to leave for service in Hungary and the gay young Prince intended to enjoy this farewell Carnival to the full. He invited a friend to share his pleasures. He was a wealthy nobleman and his name was Count Philip Christopher von Königsmarck.

Count Königsmarck was a typical example of the young noblemen who travelled around war-stricken Europe seeking adventure and fortune where they could find them. He was a scion of an ancient Swedish family from whom he had inherited good looks and a noble name. He possessed all the attractions of the rake that so often appeal to the feminine heart and his daring, wit and courtly manners gained him an entrée into fashionable circles everywhere. His dashing repuation and sheer audacity had become a legend.

He attended the final masquerade and as became his rank he was given a place at the most important table. Here he met Sophia Dorothea. This was not the first time they had met for as a child he had accompanied his parents on a visit to the court at Celle. On that occasion his mother had been discussing the suitability of a marriage between her eldest son Carl Johann*

---

* Years later the elder Königsmarck was expelled from England when he became involved in a brutal murder that shocked even the London of Charles II. His bravos murdered a man named Tom Thynne. The young Philip who had accompanied his brother to London also left England as some of the antagonism was also directed towards him.

and Sophia Dorothea. Whilst the discussions were taking place
Philip himself had formed a childish attachment to the young
Princess and they imagined themselves to be in love. Now when
he again met Sophia Dorothea she had become a beautiful young
woman and he felt the reawakening of his early romantic feelings. The next year, 1689, again saw him at the court at Hanover. This time he brought with him his beautiful sister Aurora
and an impressive retinue, for in the ensuing months he had
inherited great wealth on the death of a relative. He had decided
to settle in Hanover.

His brother-in-law, General Lowenhaupt, was already in the
service of the Duke and it was a simple matter to arrange a
colonelcy for Philip. Indeed the Duke was delighted that such
an important and wealthy nobleman had joined his court. But
when he again entered Sophia Dorothea's life it was not as an
innocent youth, but as a libertine, a rake, an adventurer, handsome and unscrupulous. Their love affair was resumed but this
time passion replaced innocence.

It is likely that their interest in each other might have passed
unnoticed in the general behaviour at court, particularly as 1689
was an anxious year when military and political events were the
topics on everyone's lips. The flames of war were spreading
throughout Europe and the hot breath of danger was everywhere.

Duke Ernest Augustus found himself drawn irrevocably into
that Grand Alliance organized by the Emperor and William of
Orange, of which his brother George William was already an
enthusiastic member. Now events were moving with disquieting
speed; Louis XIV had invaded Germany and Holland, whilst
William had arrived in England. The fortunes of William of
Orange were of particular importance to Ernest Augustus, since
William's acquisition of the crown of England undoubtedly
brought the House of Hanover into the reckoning as it seemed
probable that neither Mary nor Anne would leave children. The
next in line would then be Sophia, the only descendant eligible
under the conditions of the Bill of Rights.

Within a few months war began to drain away the manhood
of Hanover and at the head of the marching regiments went the
Duke of Hanover himself and his sons; with Prince Charles

went Count Königsmarck to the war against the Turks, the others went to the Netherlands.

The Carnival of 1690 took place as usual but apprehension dulled the sparkle. The merriment was marred even more when the news arrived that the detachment under the command of Prince Charles had been annihilated by the Turks. Anxiously confirmation was awaited from Constantinople and when it came there could be no doubt that the Prince had been killed. Königsmarck however had escaped.

To Sophia Dorothea the suspense, and then relief at her lover's escape, must have set the seal of sincerity on what had been an amorous escapade and when he returned her heart was already pledged to him, whilst her husband had become even more repugnant in consequence. She welcomed Königsmarck with a new warmth that must have touched even the heart of this handsome practitioner of romance and vice.

Practitioner he was indeed, for at some time during his visits to Hanover he had also commenced an affair with the Countess of Platen, the court favourite of Ernest Augustus. She was a painted, sin-raddled harridan, ruthless, scheming and well-versed in court machinations, so that it was obviously not her beauty that had attracted Königsmarck but her influence, which was boundless. The handsome, gay cavalier appealed to the Countess, for she was greedy of everything, and at times she exerted herself to a point of ridicule to gain his attentions.

The old Countess of Platen was as willing a victim to his audacious charms as was the young Princess. Each was aware of the other's rivalry, and so were many others, for Königsmarck often boasted in his drunkenness of the intimacies he enjoyed with the two court ladies, and the rival mistresses hated each other with thinly veiled hostility.

Philip lived in a street close to the palace and as he was now in command of the guard had ample opportunities of meeting Sophia Dorothea, dangerous though it may have been. But he was never the one to take account of danger. This was an age of letter-writing and although they met frequently they also engaged in a voluminous correspondence. In their letters they reveal their growing infatuation and apparent disregard of the consequences. They even reproached each other for happenings

that caused jealousy, and lovers' quarrels and reunions appear
at regular intervals, interspersed with a coarseness and debauched
outspokenness that are unquotable today. In the hope of preventing identification of characters they used ciphers and numbers to
indicate individuals but some of the names are so obvious as to
appear naïve in their deception. Naturally Sophia Dorothea's
marital associations with George Louis aroused Philip at times
to indignation and as these occur in their letters we can imagine
the frenzied outbursts that must have taken place when they met.

At this time there was an incident at court which should
surely have warned the two lovers of the risks they were running
and of the dreadful penalties they would incur if their deception
was discovered. The second son Augustus whom Ernest Augustus
had disinherited was killed in battle and Max, the third son,
became the second in line. He became involved in an ambitious
plot to circumvent the existing rule of primogeniture made by his
father in 1682. By making a protest to the Imperial Court he
hoped to establish his claims in the future and to this end invoked the assistance of his father's rivals among the minor courts.
His sister Charlotte, the Electress of Brandenburg, heard of the
plot and told her father.

The Duke of Hanover allowed the scheming to continue, until
in December, 1691, he had his son Max and his accomplice, von
Moltke, arrested and thrown into prison at the fortress of
Hamlen. It then came to light that the Duke's other younger
sons, Augustus and Charles who had both been killed in battle,
had also been involved and the Duke's anger against his son
Max bore the bitterness of the discovery. Fortunately the Duke
of Celle interceded on the son's behalf and Max was not executed
but only banished. His confidant von Moltke did not escape
punishment for he suffered the agonising fate of being " broken
on the wheel ", a barbarous custom; and one that Königsmarck
might himself suffer.

Sophia Dorothea also seemed to be oblivious of the ruin she
was inviting, for her father and mother learnt of her behaviour
and pleaded with her without success to discontinue her association with Königsmarck. In moments of clear-sightedness she
feared Countess Platen and warned Philip not to stop paying his
attentions to her hated antagonist. But too often the young

Princess, mendacious and witty, allowed her feelings to overcome her caution and she sparked her tongue in the court circles
with tales and comments, always detrimental to her older rival,
that goaded the Countess into moods of impotent fury. The
passionate infatuation of Sophia Dorothea grew uncurbed, despite the repeated warnings and remonstrances from her parents
and friends. The strength of her feelings destroyed her prudence
particularly when her lover was absent on his military duties, for
then she made no pretence of hiding her feelings and sometimes
wept openly.

From one of these campaigns Königsmarck had recently
returned when he was forced to witness a ceremony which caused
a lovers' quarrel and threw him into a jealous rage. The ceremony was to confer upon the Duke and Duchess the dignity of
Elector and Electress and in turn their son George Louis and
their daughter-in-law Sophia Dorothea became Electoral Prince
and Princess.

A few days before the ceremony the party had paid a state
visit to Brandenburg, from which journey Sophia Dorothea had
contrived to absent herself by pleading indisposition. Instead she
had arranged a clandestine meeting with her newly-returned
lover.

The ceremony of installation was a magnificent affair for the
Electorship was the realization of an ambition the Duke had long
cherished. The whole court was assembled, together with guests
from the neighbouring duchies, to witness the ceremony and
afterwards there was a magnificent banquet to signal the beginning of a festival lasting nearly three months. During this series
of ceremonies Sophia Dorothea had to play an official part with
her husband which drove Königsmarck to express his blind
jealousy in a stream of abusive letters to Sophia Dorothea.

In this mood of bitterness it was inevitable that he should
neglect Countess Platen and a quarrel arose between them, the
exact cause of which is not known, but it marked the beginning
of a campaign of vindictiveness that was to reach a tragic
climax.

Königsmarck threw aside his caution and blamed "Le
Platen" for all his recent misfortunes (his family affairs had
suffered a setback and his finances had been depleted). He even

threatened to pick a quarrel with Countess Platen's son and to challenge him to a duel, which would have meant almost certain death to his opponent, for Königsmarck was a brilliant swordsman. His anger spurred the impulsive Sophia Dorothea to endanger their position even more by also finding cause to quarrel openly with Countess Platen.

The vindictive Countess was not one to endure insults without retaliation, and she had suffered the greatest insult of all in the scorn of Königsmarck. Spies were now watching every move the young lovers made and from their reports the Countess relentlessly built up her dossier of revenge. The pyre of tragedy was ready and it needed only the spark.

The lovers had prepared a desperate scheme of flight. They intended to seek refuge with Duke Antony Ulric of Brunswick-Wolfenbüttel who was antagonistic towards Hanover.

The dark hour of reckoning was near, for on the night of Sunday, the 1st of July 1694, the escape was planned. George Louis was safely absent in Berlin. The Princess was ready for flight with her belongings and jewels stowed in her carriage, and Philip of Königsmarck was on his way to meet her. He was never to reach the tryst, for the spies of Countess Platen served her well. She stirred the complacent Ernest Augustus to anger and he gave the order for the immediate arrest of Königsmarck. On the lonely road he was waylaid by a party of the Elector's guards and in the encounter he was slain. The carriage of the Countess Platen was in the shadows of the roadside and as he lay dying she stood over him and exulted, her heart torn with revenge, anger and rejected passion. He cursed her with his dying breath and as he died she ground her heel into his mouth to stem the flow of vituperation. She had loved him with all the bitterness of her twisted soul. The body of Königsmarck was disposed of by the guards and never found.*

4

The Königsmarck affair aroused a storm of indignation and became the gossip of Europe. Rumours were rife and diffused as

* Another version of his murder records that he was still alive when carried from the roadside and was thrust into a red-hot oven.

to the manner of his end, but everyone was convinced that it was a case of murder. Letters found at Königsmarck's house proved the truth of the intrigue. They were shown to the Duke of Celle, the highly indignant father of Sophia Dorothea, who said that he " would never have believed her so guilty had it not been for the letters."

George Louis was still in Berlin and Sophia Dorothea was filled with bitter hatred towards him, believing he had played a part in the murder of her lover. To avoid meeting her husband on his return the official reports said she had asked her father for permission to return to Celle but her father had refused her request, therefore she had " withdrawn for the present to the magistrate's house at Ahlden, which lay on the way ". In truth she was a prisoner in the bleak castle of Ahlden.

The Electress issued an official account in an attempt to quieten the voice of scandal :

" The Königsmarck affair was like this : he was gloomy in the evening and pretended he was going to bed, but his secretary saw that he went out all alone, and when he did not return for four days they went to Marshal Podewils and told him their master was lost. They hunted for him everywhere but could not find him. The Duke had his things sealed up, so that nothing should be taken, but they took his correspondence . . . We must take comfort in thinking that God does all for the best. If the wife cannot endure her husband she is better from him than with him."

Sophia Dorothea confessed that she had been indiscreet, but persisted in her denials that she had committed adultery although she agreed the evidence appeared to be against her. She begged to be parted from her husband as " she despaired of ever overcoming the aversion the prince has for several years evinced towards her," and she asked " to be allowed to withdraw from the world ".

A divorce was inevitable, for the affair had cast a stigma on the House of Hanover and consequently jeopardized the line of succession in England. Already in London they were referring to the young George Augustus as " Young Königsmarck " Count Platen was given the conduct of the case and his own invidious position at the court which Sophia Dorothea viewed with undisguised contempt added venom to his attitude towards her. She could expect no mercy from him: and she received none.

Count Platen co-opted the assistance of Baron Bernstorff, who had ambitions of becoming George Louis's minister when the son succeeded to the dukedom. They had already found Sophia Dorothea guilty and together they settled the terms which would guarantee her inheritance passing to her husband and at the same time remove her from the scene.

But the superficial processes of the law must first be observed and they set up a Tribunal of a President and eight members; four lawyers and four Protestant clergymen.

The sentence had already been decided upon and it was a matter of formality for the tribunal to pronounce it. But first the cunning Bernstorff persuaded Sophia Dorothea to sign a declaration stating that she wished to be separated from her husband. By signing the document the unhappy Princess was led to believe that she would be allowed to retire from the court life to live as a private individual.

On December 28th, 1694, the decree of divorce was pronounced; the Prince was permitted to remarry but the Princess was forbidden to make a second marriage. The punishment to be inflicted upon the Princess was not mentioned in the pronouncement. Beneath the thin veil of legal formalities despotism defied justice and no appeal was allowed. The Princess was sentenced to imprisonment in the fortress of Ahlden, her existence was to be forgotten and her children were never to see her again. To the world she was dead.

She was twenty-eight years of age and was to remain a prisoner for the rest of her life. The portraits of her children, George then twelve and his sister, Sophia Dorothea, were to be her only consolation in her solitude until her death thirty-two years later.

In 1726 she became ill and in her fevered ravings she cursed her cruel husband. Then she relapsed into a state of coma from which even the portraits of her children could not rouse her. On the 13th of November she died and her misery was ended.

The possible succession to the crown of Great Britain was a topic of vital interest in Hanover but Duke Ernest Augustus was only interested in Germany. Queen Anne's delicate little son, the Duke of Gloucester, was still alive and the Duchess Eleanor suggested that a match might be arranged between the young Duke and the seven-year old Sophia Dorothea.

George Louis, like his father, was completely indifferent to the possibility of the English succession and coldly rejected the ambitious plan.

The other grandmother, the Electress Sophia, for once agreed with the Duchess Eleanor, and as she had care of the children of George Louis she was determined that they should speak the language which her son had always obstinately refused to learn.

George Louis himself took very little interest in his two children and in fact he made it quite plain that he actively disliked them; his son in particular, because he had inherited his mother's looks.

The little boy was rather feminine in appearance, with delicate features and the fair skin and light brown hair of Sophia Dorothea.

As he grew older he became more masculine and developed a great interest in troops and military matters, but as his father saw mirrored in him so many characteristics of the imprisoned " Princess of Ahlden " dislike turned into hatred. The mother's name was never mentioned in Hanover and was deleted from the State Prayers. Her portraits were destroyed, although the young Prince George Augustus managed to obtain two which he kept hidden from his father.

In 1698 the Elector Ernest Augustus died and George Louis became the new Elector. The inevitable new ministerial appointments and changes included the removal from the court of the Platens and their influence. The son was a very different man from his father and the court assumed the tone of his sombre and taciturn character. A contemporary record reveals the change : " It is no wonder that pleasure is no longer to be seen in Hanover, as in the last régime, for this Elector is so cold he turns everything to ice, which his father and uncle were not. It will get worse with time if the Elector has the settling of it, for he knows nothing of what is princely as I have seen in all his doings."*

Sophia Dorothea wrote to her husband begging his forgiveness and imploring him to "permit me to see and embrace our beloved children, my gratitude for this boon, so ardently longed for, will be infinite since I desire nothing else to enable me to die content."

She also wrote to the Electress: "I beseech once more your Electoral Highness to forgive all I have done which may have offended you and to speak a little on my behalf to your son the Elector. I implore him to grant me the forgiveness which I desire so intensely and to allow me to embrace my children. It would also be my passionate desire, Madame, to kiss the hands of your Electoral Highness before I die."

Both letters were unanswered for George Louis was implacable in his revenge.

Seven years later, when she had been imprisoned for eleven years, her last hope of release vanished when her father George William died. He had not seen his daughter since her incarceration, although he had several times expressed a desire to do so. Bernstorff, whom he had consulted, had warned him that if he did approach the Elector, the inevitable anger might seal her fate for ever. George Louis was now all-powerful, the sole ruler of both territories and the plight of the "Princess of Ahlden" was hopeless.

The Elector made a triumphant entry into Celle and the occasion was celebrated by a tremendous banquet. It was held in the castle that had been built by George William for his wife and daughter, but George Louis was not a man of sentiment and the Duchess of Celle was evicted without ceremony. She went to live in her dower-house at Lüneburg, with a few French friends to keep her company.

Apart from taking control of the castle George Louis also took possession of his father-in-law's will, which he destroyed, as the old Duke had left his personal property to his grandson.

---

* The Duchess of Orleans in a letter.

Shortly before the death of the Duke of Celle in 1705, the Elector's son George Augustus was married to Caroline of Ansbach, one of the most eligible of the German princesses. She was born at Ansbach, in 1683, and was therefore twenty-two, the same age as her husband who was fulsomely described at the time as being "middle-sized like his Father, well made and of manly Aspect and Deportment, he speaks very gracefully and with the Greatest Easiness imaginable, nor does his great vivacity let him be ignorant of anything."

Her father, the Margrave of Ansbach, had died when she was four years old and five years later her mother had been re-married to the Elector John George IV of Saxony, taking her young daughter with her to the court of Dresden. Tragedy again entered Caroline's young life for the Elector died in 1694 and two years later her mother died, so that she became an orphan at thirteen.

Frederick III, Elector of Brandenburg (he became King Frederick I of Prussia in 1701) who was married to Sophia Charlotte, the daughter of the old Elector Ernest Augustus, now became her guardian and she was taken to Berlin. Frederick and his wife were very fond of the high-spirited Caroline and regarded her as a daughter, for they had no daughter of their own. In turn Sophia Charlotte's mother, the old Electress Sophia, also became very attached to Caroline and treated her as a favourite granddaughter. Quite naturally she met George Augustus, the real grandchild of the Electress Sophia.

Even at this early stage the Electress Sophia already had hopes for the eventual marriage of the two children, "but I do not think God will let me be so happy," she said at the time, and her influence was probably one of the reasons why Caroline had rejected the earlier marriage proposal of one eminently eligible suitor, the Emperor's second son, the Archduke Charles.

This match had first been discussed when Caroline was fifteen, then a beautiful and attractive child, but the formal proposal was not made until 1704. Another reason for the rejection was the possible succession to the crown of England, for in 1701 the Act of Settlement had named the descendants of Sophia as being in line to the throne.

Another more important, yet somewhat unusual reason in

those days, was that George Augustus was actually in love with Caroline. He had chosen her himself.

Caroline arrived in Hanover on the 2nd of September and the marriage took place the same evening. The old Electress Sophia was delighted, whilst the Elector George Louis was indifferent to what happened to the garrulous son he detested; except that the wedding ceremony should be a quiet one. It was; for this reason and also because the recent death of Duke George William had cast a cloud of grief over the court. Significantly a number of English official guests led by the Marquis of Hertford were present and the Electress Sophia gave a special ball in their honour.

Caroline was particularly attentive to the visitors from England and they, in reciprocation, expressed their appreciation of " her winning, easy, affable behaviour and sweet good temper to all our countrymen."*

Judiciously she began to learn English and persuaded her husband to join her in her studies; she " showing that she had a decided turn for the language " and he " getting on pretty well ", for the old Electress had already ensured that he had had a " grounding " in the subject.

With the grudging permission of the Elector, Caroline now had an English instructress so that she could also make herself familiar with the history and literature of England. The lady employed was the beautiful Mrs. Howard, a sister-in-law of the Earl of Suffolk, who had come to Hanover with her spendthrift husband in search of just such a position. Caroline and her husband were also desperately short of money and a story has been recorded of how Mrs. Howard, who was then on terms of personal friendship with Caroline, cut off her hair to help them find the money to entertain the English Ministers. As wigs, of course, were worn in those days the lack of hair would not be noticed.

It was known in England that Queen Anne was relenting in her jealous attitude to the Hanoverians and later in the year the Duke of Marlborough himself visited Hanover, to be received with great ceremony. During his stay he interested himself in the

---

* They also presented her with some tea which, even in those days, English travellers used to take abroad with them.

discussions concerning the impending marriage (which took place the following year) of Caroline's cousins, her sister-in-law the young Sophia Dorothea and the Crown Prince of Prussia (afterwards King Frederick William I of Prussia). The effect of the cordial treatment of the English visitors to Hanover was soon evident for Queen Anne deigned to bestow the important honour of the Garter upon the Electoral Prince.

The ceremony of the Garter was celebrated with wild enthusiasm, which was not appreciated by George Louis, for the elevation of his son to a position of consequence infuriated the Elector. He was even more annoyed when soon afterwards Queen Anne followed the honour with an English peerage and George Augustus became the Duke of Cambridge, a title held only by royalty. This time, the Elector told General Howe, the English Envoy, that a special function would not be held to celebrate the occasion, as he thought the expense involved was a waste of money. Diplomatically the son and his wife told General Howe that they would prefer to receive the honour from the hands of the General himself, whom they knew, instead of receiving it at a special ceremony, from the hands of some nobleman, whom they did not know.

Before the actual patent arrived the Elector found an opportunity of insulting both his son and also the English Envoy at the same time. In January 1707 Caroline was expecting her first child and there was a great deal of anxiety felt at court when the child did not arrive on the expected date. The baby was a fortnight overdue when it was born on the 1st of February.

Despite the acute anxiety the Elector had unpredictably issued instructions that no one was to enter the Princess's apartments except the doctor and the nurse. The ban even applied to the worried father and the Electress Sophia, who was extremely concerned about her beloved granddaughter.

A few days later the birth of a prince was announced, but no official notification was made to the English Envoy (which was a calculated breach of etiquette), and still no one was allowed to see either the mother or the child. About a week later the Elector sent a message to his mother telling her that her great-grandson was to be christened* that same evening, with the Elector, the

* Frederick Louis

Electress, and the King of Prussia, as sponsors. This brief glimpse of Caroline and her baby was all that was permitted and two days later the Elector took the entire court to the Brunswick Fair for three weeks, leaving Caroline alone with only the serving women.

During this time the patent of the Dukedom duly arrived from England, together with a letter in Queen Anne's own handwriting. General Howe, whose duty it was to present the letter, was astonished when the Elector would not allow him to see the Prince. It was not until two months had elapsed that the English Envoy was able to obtain an audience with George Augustus and deliver the patent. Obviously the incident created an unfortunate impression in England.

In 1709 Caroline was again expecting a child and on the 2nd of November a princess was born. This time the Elector did not appear to be interested as the baby was a girl, but the Prince made sure that the due etiquette was observed and also wrote to Queen Anne asking for the favour of being allowed to name the child after her. He also requested permission to name the Queen as godmother.

Two more children were born to the Electoral Prince and Princess, Emily in 1711 and Caroline in 1713, and on these occasions the Elector was again indifferent, to the intense relief of the parents. They now withdrew from court life and by this means they lessened the aggravations forced upon them by the spite of the Elector. Nevertheless he periodically frustrated and tormented them by his refusals and petty indignities; particularly in the case of the Prince by restricting the military activities which he enjoyed so much.

Caroline still found pleasure in the companionship and love of the old Electress Sophia but soon this consolation was to be denied her. On the 8th of June 1714, they were taking an evening stroll together in the beautiful gardens of the Electress's favourite home, Herrenhausen, when suddenly the old lady was taken ill. Caroline assisted her to a nearby arbour where she collapsed on the floor and died in the arms of the granddaughter she loved so much.

A few weeks later news arrived of another death. The message came from England and it was delivered by special messenger.

It told of the death of Queen Anne on the 1st of August 1714. The turn of the House of Hanover had come.

The crown of England was thus forced upon the Elector George Louis for he did not wish to leave Hanover and it was a month before he was ready to depart. He was taking his son, the Electoral Prince, with him and was leaving his only grandson, the seven years old Frederick, who was to be brought up in Hanover under tutors selected by himself.

Crowds lined the streets on the day of the departure of the Elector and there were many sad faces to bid him farewell. He was popular with his subjects, and true to the lachrymose tendencies of the Hanoverians, he shed generous tears when he left them to become George the First of England, King of Great Britain, France, and Ireland, Defender of the Faith. He was fifty-four years of age.

6

In England the line of succession that was broken to bring the House of Hanover into being began with the execution of Charles I at Whitehall on January 30th, 1649. It was the act not of the people, nor their Parliament but of the Puritan Army. The army, having beheaded the King, abolished the House of Lords and conquered Scotland and Ireland by force, ruled for eleven years. This was the only period of military dictatorship in Britain and Cromwell was the dictator. But only he was strong enough to hold the kingdom together, and when he died in 1658 there was no successor. For two years the Military Government struggled to maintain control, until in 1660, Charles II was asked to return to England.

The following year a new Parliament was elected, which was found to be, in the words of Macaulay, " more royalist than the King and more episcopalian than the Bishops ". This was proved to be true by the harsh measures passed against the Noncomformists in the years 1661 and 1665. The King with his strong Roman Catholic sympathies regarded the measures as too severe.

Two years later Charles introduced a set of Ministers, known as the Cabal Ministry, who like himself were tolerant on questions of religion. Parliament retaliated by holding only occasional sessions, thus causing Charles to make the Secret Treaty of Dover with Louis XIV to obtain supplies from France. His part of the bargain was that he would take the first step towards making England a Roman Catholic country by issuing in 1672 the Declaration of Indulgence, offering freedom of worship to Protestants, Nonconformists and Catholics alike. This act suspended by Crown prerogative more than forty Parliamentary statutes, and Charles was forced to withdraw the Declaration. In turn he was made to agree to the Test Act which stipulated that all holding Crown office must receive the Sacrament according to the rites of the Church of England. This meant the immediate resignation of the King's brother, James, Duke of York, from holding office as Lord High Admiral. The Act was also made to apply to the two houses of Parliament and a Bill was introduced, known as the Exclusion Bill which excluded James as a Roman Catholic from succession to the Throne.

In three years there was great dissension, those in favour became known as the Petitioners because of their persistent petitions to Charles, whilst the dissenters earned, by reason of their resolutions stating their abhorrence of the Bill, the name Abhorrers. These names were soon shortened and the Petitioners became known as Whigs after a clan of Scottish Covenanters, and the Abhorrers were called Tories after some outlawed Roman Catholic robbers in Ireland; names that were to be used for almost a century and a half until during Peel's administration in 1828 when the Whigs became Liberals and the Tories Conservatives.

Three times the Exclusion Bill was introduced but on each occasion it was defeated. In 1685, the accession of James II represented the Tory victory over the Whig policy of exclusion, yet less than four years later James was an exile in France. The reason was not only the fact that James was a Roman Catholic but because he abused the constitution in the interests of Roman Catholicism. In 1686 the judges decreed it lawful for the King to decide individual cases himself and henceforth James introduced Roman Catholics into the Army, the Ministry and into the two Universities where all clergymen graduated. Two years later the King issued a Declaration of Indulgence suspending the Penal Laws. On the 10th of June 1688 a son was born to

James II, destroying the patience of those who were prepared to wait until the accession of Mary, his daughter who was married to the Protestant William of Orange. It was enough, and seven Parliamentary members from both parties sent a message to William of Orange asking him to come to England to save the cause of Protestantism. On November 5th William landed at Torbay. The King's supporters deserted (including John Churchill, afterwards the great Duke of Marlborough) and the Queen and Prince fled to France, to be followed by James himself in December 1688.

The Revolution was successful but the power had merely been transferred to the nobles, for the House of Commons was chosen by only the few great and important families. Despite this the new Parliament was successful in welding together England and Scotland into a united Kingdom.

The Convention which met after James had fled the country passed two resolutions. Firstly that it was not in the interests of a Protestant Kingdom to be governed by a Popish King, and secondly that the throne was vacant. The Crown was offered to Mary jointly with William of Orange, conditional on a Declaration of Rights, which reduced the power of the Throne.

Mary died in 1694 and in 1700 the young Duke of Gloucester, the last of Queen Anne's seventeen children, also died. When it was evident that William would not remarry, the line of Protestant succession was again in jeopardy. Parliament therefore passed in 1701 the Act of Settlement which settled the succession to the Throne on the heirs of the Electress Sophia of Hanover, by reason of the fact that as the granddaughter of James I, she was the next in line to the Stuart Kings, excluding Roman Catholics. Her grandson was created Duke of Cambridge and delegations were despatched to Germany to cement the relationship.

When the tragic Queen Anne died in 1714 the way was clear for the Hanoverians and a messenger was sent to convey the news to George Louis, the descendant of Sophia, late Electress of Hanover.

CHAPTER TWO

GEORGE THE FIRST

I

A DENSE FOG shrouded London's river as George I arrived on the 29th September 1714, to claim "the throne of his ancestors", as he called it. His journey had been a leisurely one for he was in no hurry to reach England. He loved Hanover too much. After his tearful farewell fourteen days earlier he had set out on a route that was to take him through Holland, where he attended numerous receptions in his honour.

George loathed leaving the gay life of Hanover for the unpredictable one of London. With him, to assuage the discomfort of the change of scene, he brought his German retinue and personal friends, also his two elderly favourites Ehrengard Melusina von Schulenburg and Sophia Charlotte Kielmansegge, daughter of his father's mistress, the Countess of Platen. Later he created them Duchess of Kendall and Countess Darlington respectively. It is apparent that he inherited his father's taste in mistresses for they were both old and ugly, their cheeks liberally bedaubed with crimson and of an appearance likely to incite ribald comment, which indeed they did. Schulenburg was gargantuan, an immense wobble of flesh—appropriately she was nicknamed "The Elephant"—whilst Keilmansegge was tall, lean and angular. In turn, and no less appropriately, she was nicknamed "The Maypole". Included in his party were his chamberlains and his secretaries, and making his assembly even more eccentric were a band of dark-skinned retainers, captives from his Turkish wars.

They presented a strange, bizarre picture, this motley band of followers, and the crowd waiting to welcome their king at Greenwich must have been open-mouthed as the royal barge emerged from the fog. The fog was so dense that it was considered unsafe for the royal yacht and the escorting vessels, English and Dutch men-of-war, to progress up the river. Instead, a barge was used for the last stage of the journey and the cheers of the waiting crowd drowned the lap of the oars as the barge drew alongside the quay of Greenwich.

It was a strange meeting, this welcoming of the new Defender of the Faith by his wondering subjects; and in turn the royal party must have conjectured as to what awaited them in this London of grey-misted outlines silhouetted behind the torch-lit quay.

As George I stepped ashore, for the first time on England's soil, the waiting crowd fell to their knees in homage. Prominent in the forefront was the Archbishop of Canterbury and the great gentlemen of England, among them the noble lords, Marlborough, Bolingbroke and Oxford; all voicing their welcomes. And George could not understand one word of English.

He stood there before the crowd, a short, rotund, fair-skinned, defiant figure, with the features of the Guelphs, the bulging blue eyes, the heavy jowl and cynical mouth. By nature he was indolent, aggressive, coarse and selfish. These were his faults and many more besides. He had heard tales of the brawling, intriguing English and their insurgent way with monarchs, but he did not fear them. Among all his faults a lack of courage was not one. He was a true Guelph. His reply to the words of welcome was in French, a language he spoke as fluently as his native German, and his bulbous blue eyes were calculating as he surveyed the prostrating Parliamentarians. They were playing their game, he would play his—and take what he could.

2

The England of 1714 was an agricultural country with a scattered population of only six millions.*

* Before 1801, there existed no official return of the population of the British Isles. The estimate formed of the population calculated from the numbers of baptisms, burials and marriages in 1700 was 6,045,008. By 1801 the population had more than doubled.

They were widely dispersed in the towns, villages and hamlets, where they were born, lived, and died, without once leaving their own small community.

This was an age of violence, and the English male was probably the most bloodthirsty man in Europe. Riots and looting mobs were commonplace, and highwaymen and footpads roamed the highways. Disease, dirt, cruelty and death stalked hand-in-hand over the whole country. Public hangings, stonings to death in the pillory, blackened heads on turnpike gates, the whipping of naked women, these were the entertainments of all, and the fate of men, women and children alike. These were the days of bull-baiting, cock-fighting, bare-knuckle fighting, child prostitution, drinking, whoring, raping. These were the sports; together, of course, with cricket and horse-racing, whilst coarseness, foul language and revolting habits were normal conduct both in the elegant drawing-rooms and in the cellars of the filthy slums.

The rich were elegant and exquisitely dressed, against a background of tasteful furnishings and imposing architecture. The men were theatrical in gesture and the women were graceful in movement. Both sexes used foul language and their uninhibited conduct and manners would have shocked us today. They were a strange combination of supreme elegance and revolting earthiness. To George I they were not shocking for to a lesser degree their manners were those of all Europe, and George himself was coarse and crude, with a turn of phrase in French and German to equal the worst of his English subjects.

The London to which he came was a stew of foul smells, slums, cobbled streets, muddy and open drained; Cheapside, Fleet Street, Ludgate Hill, Holborn, all with their swinging signs, the Black Swan, the Blue Boar, the Red Lion, the King's Head; presenting a bawdy, brawling scene. The streets were alive with the cries of the tradesmen, the shouting of the footmen as they cleared the way for the swaying chairmen, the noisy soldiery in bright scarlet indulging in horseplay, the jolting coaches with their straining, clattering horses and the livestock, sheep, cows, hens, and barking dogs; while picking their way delicately through the noisy throng to meet at the coffee-houses and chocolate-houses were the powdered, periwigged *beaux* and gentry of the City.

The Theatre, the Opera, puppet-shows, the cockpits, the gardens, and gambling, which had become an obsession with the whole populace, rich and poor alike—these were the amusements.

The new sovereign and his son were accepted in England without disturbance and it was apparent that the nation as a whole was in favour of the Hanoverian succession. It seemed safe therefore to send a message for Caroline, now the Princess of Wales, to come to England with her little daughters. The youngest child Caroline was ill and was left in Hanover, but the other two children, Anne five years old and Emily three, were sent to the Hague in easy stages under the care of an English tutor, whilst Caroline herself followed three days later. They sailed on Sunday morning the 10th of October and arrived at Margate on Monday night. They were in London on the following Wednesday, the Prince having met them on the way.

The happy young family made a great impression on the crowd in London and they were greeted with cheers all the way to St. James's. They were astounded at the size of London with its one hundred thousand houses, which dwarfed Hanover with only one thousand eight hundred houses and made even Berlin with its five thousand seem small. The Thames too had surprised them with its immense sweep—so charmingly depicted a few years later by Canaletto. The only bridge was London Bridge which was still lined with antique houses. The air was clear and smokeless and from the top of Somerset House, with its gardens stretching to the river frontage, one had a view of the city, from which ran winding roads dotted with trees and farmsteads; Piccadilly fields were the beginning of the open country and all around the town was a mass of green. When Lord Burlington selected a site here he said "he was quite safe from anybody ever building beyond him."

The young couple strolled with their children in St. James's Park observed by inquisitive crowds to whom they inclined their heads in acknowledgment. They intended to please their new subjects, whose houses in Pall Mall, the narrow street adjoining St. James's Palace, encroached almost up to the palace walls.

The royal couple lived in a wing of the palace and recruited only English men and women to their staff. In every way they intended to ingratiate themselves, and they made a point of being affable. The fact that they could speak English gave them the opportunity of an intimacy and understanding that was denied to George I.

Caroline thoroughly enjoyed their influential position particularly as a handsome income of £100,000 had been given to them by the Government. She was treated as a Queen Consort and as London was *en fête* for the six months following their arrival the unhappy days of Hanover became a memory; made poignant only by the absence of her young son Frederick.

They were unaware of the robbers, thieves, and ruffians who haunted the dark streets, where the carrying of weapons was essential to one's safety, unlike quiet Hanover where for fifty years they had only been carried as a mark of rank. In England, highwaymen and footpads were the scourge of the roads leading from London and almost every day private carriages and mail-coaches were held up and rifled.

The dangers of London were soon brought home to them when they saw the wild mobs rioting in the streets, loudly shouting their political opinions. There was a Jacobite rising in Scotland but in London they were burning the effigy of the Pretender and the leaders of the Jacobite rebels were brought to the capital to be convicted of high treason. Thus the first year for the Hanoverians in England was a tumultuous one, for there were mobs in London in September, and in Oxford a few weeks later shouting for King James.

The short, red-faced King George was unperturbed. He was himself by nature belligerent and they could not frighten him. He refused even to consider the petitions for mercy from the relatives and friends of the condemned Jacobite leaders and the prisoners were duly executed. George did not court popularity nor did he fear reprisals. He walked among his subjects, quite unconcerned.

The Mall was the fashionable promenade and George, with members of his family, could often be seen there taking a stroll in the mornings and evenings. His pleaures were simple, though often coarse, and he had little time for the social life of the Court. Indeed the Court of George I would have been a very dull affair had it not been for his son and daughter-in-law, the Princes of Wales and his Princess, Caroline of Ansbach. They loved the social round.

George now hated his son with even greater venom and the mere sight of him was sufficient to put him into an evil temper. He never missed an opportunity of snubbing or annoying the Prince and needless to say the hatred engendered was mutual. The Prince felt an added bitterness towards his father for the treatment of his mother after the Königsmarck affair.

For his daughter-in-law, the Princess, the King had more time. He was attracted by her buxom, bosomy beauty and indeed she often rebuked him for taking liberties with her.

George, of course, spoke French which was the accepted language of Europe, the lingua franca of diplomacy and culture, but it is a curious example of the insularity of the English that scarcely any of the English Ministers and Members of Parliament had taken the trouble to learn French. Thus they were forced to approach their Monarch through the Hanoverian Ministers he had brought with him, notably Bernstorff, Bothmer, and Robethon, or through his mistresses Baroness (a recent elevation) Schulenburg and Madame Kielmansegge.

In consequence, the Hanoverians formed themselves into an inner cabinet and in matters that were wholly of English importance or did not affect their personal interests they were quite willing to sell their favours and influence. Baron Bernstorff and the Schulenburg were particularly grasping in their demands.

The Act of Settlement did not permit the King to bestow titles on foreigners in England but George evaded the restrictions by using the titles of Ireland, which had its own parliament, to reward his favourites. Melusina von der Schulenburg, for example, had been created Baroness, Countess and Duchess of Munster with a heavy revenue from the Irish coffers. In June 1716, she was naturalized and then became Duchess of Kendall.

In the case of his German Ministers the King circumvented the Act by giving them Household appointments and paying their salaries privately. Naturally these evasions caused antagonism and rivalry between the English and German Ministers, for there were not enough lucrative posts to satisfy every claimant; in fact, every nobleman expected to be in the

Government and so did half his relatives. The result was an atmosphere of intrigue and machinations.

The King himself cared little for the politics and affairs of England. He was only concerned with the money he could lay his hands on. There is a story that illustrates this attitude of mind : One of his Hanoverian servants with an honest disposition asked to be allowed to return to Hanover—" Because they steal here too badly; we were so careful in Hanover." George refused to allow him to return home, saying quite irascibly : " Bah ! It is only English money—steal like the rest ! " Thus his Hanoverians, mistresses, favourites, ministers and servants reaped the benefit in titles, lucrative sinecures, and handfuls of English gold.

Early in July 1716 the King felt he needed a rest from the intrigues and political bickerings in England and decided to return to Hanover for a while. He left later in the month, taking with him Lord Stanhope, the Secretary of State, who could speak French and had ingratiated himself with George.

The Prince of Wales was left behind as " Guardian of the Realm and Lieutenant ", which title the King preferred to Regent. In fact it was only due to the insistence of the English Ministers that he left his son in any position of authority at all. He had wished to leave a Council, of which the Prince would not be a member, but the Ministers pressed for the Prince's appointment as Regent to maintain the confidence of the people. Reluctantly George had consented, with the proviso that the Prince should not be allowed to make any decisions whatever; and he must be watched.

Before he left for Hanover George made Sir Robert Walpole and Lord Townshend personally responsible for the good conduct of the Prince of Wales in his absence.

As soon as the King was out of England the intrigues began. Sunderland, encouraged by the powerful and wealthy Duke of Marlborough and his energetic Duchess, followed the King to Hanover with the intention of maligning certain Ministers by saying that they were plotting with the Prince; a certain way of discrediting them. But first he had to visit the Prince, who was at Hampton Court, to obtain his formal permission to travel, without of course in any way disclosing his intentions.

At Hanover Sunderland joined forces with Stanhope and together they played upon the King's hatred of his son to the detriment of their rivals in London. The King lent a willing ear for the stories confirmed the premonitions that they were already firmly rooted in his mind about his son and the Princess of Wales, " cette diablesse Madame la Princesse " as he called her.

Meanwhile in London, the Prince was enjoying his role of " Regent " and was paying meticulous attention to the minor affairs that he was permitted to handle. His good humour made him generally agreeable to everyone; whilst his Princess was making full use of her charming personality to please the ladies of consequence. It was said that they " gained the hearts of all that had the happiness to see them ".

Walpole and Townshend played their allotted parts by always being close to the Prince or by having him kept under observation, whilst watching them on the King's behalf was Baron Bothmer, who reported to Hanover that the two Ministers were actually involved with the Prince. This confirmed the information that was being dripped into the King's ear by Stanhope and Sunderland, busy stoking the fires of hatred.

On the 28th of October the Court left Hampton Court. The Prince and Princess returned to London by barge and they were happy on this beautifully sunny day because the birth of another child was almost due. A week later, after a very difficult confinement, the baby was born dead and Caroline's own life was in great danger.

Walpole and Townshend had not at this time realized that Caroline was the influence behind the Prince. Instead they believed the best channels of approach were through Mrs. Howard, generally believed to be his mistress, and Mary Bellenden, a Maid-of-Honour to the Princess, to whom the Prince was attracted. Caroline they misjudged and discounted as being of no importance. Their attentions to Mrs. Howard and Mary Bellenden were calculatingly noted by the resentful Caroline. In private she referred to Townshend as " the sneeringest falsest knave that ever was!" Walpole, she found aggressive and uncouth, with a habit of using coarse language in front of her that was shocking even in those days.

The first indication that the insinuations of the two Ministers in Hanover were taking effect was the arrival of orders from the King instructing his son to dismiss Lord Townshend. He was given the appointment of Lord-Lieutenant of Ireland, a method known to be the sugar used to coat the pill of disgrace.

In the new year, 1717, the King returned to England and one of his first acts was to dismiss Townshend from the Irish post. Walpole saw in this action the danger signal and immediately resigned to forestall his own disgrace. Sunderland and Stanhope were now in command of the situation and filled the Governments posts with their own sycophants.

The Prince and Princess of Wales also saw the red light of danger and unobtrusively withdrew from the centre of the stage to lead a quiet family life with their children.

One day the Duchess of Marlborough visited them and told the story of how she found one of the children screaming after having received a thrashing. When she made a fuss of the weeping child the Prince clicked his tongue saying: " You English are none of you well-bred, because you was not whipped when you was young!"

At that very moment the Prince himself would probably have been receiving a whipping if his father George I had been able to arrange it, for during his sojourn in Hanover the King's anger and indignation against his son had grown to maniacal intensity. To find, when he returned to London, that the Prince and " cette diablesse " had in the meanwhile contrived to become popular was almost more than he could bear; he was now only waiting for the opportunity to inflict pain and revenge upon his son and daughter-in-law.

A few months later the opportunity occurred, and it was a cruel one. The Prince and his wife had returned in the autumn to their wing at St. James's Palace, as Caroline was again expecting a child. On November 13th the child was born and to everyone's delight it was a prince.

The jubilant father was beside himself with joy and immediately sent the good news to his father, at the same time begging him to stand as one godparent and also requesting that the uncle, Bishop of Osnabruck and Duke of York, should by proxy be the other one.

The King attended the christening which was held in the

Princess's bedroom, but named the Duke of Newcastle, whom he knew his son hated, as the other godparent. After the ceremony as soon as his father had left the room the Prince shook his fist under the nose of Newcastle saying angrily, "You are a rascal; but I shall find you!" (i.e. I shall get even with you).

The Duke of Newcastle immediately told the King of the incident and no doubt the tale was duly embellished. It was the opportunity George had been waiting for. He chose to regard his son's annoyance as a challenge to a duel, which in the royal palace constituted a serious offence. Three dukes were ordered to tell the Prince that he was under arrest and was to remain in the bedroom.

The Prince was indignant and his abrupt treatment of the arresting dukes caused them to report his conduct to their master. The next morning however saw a change of attitude in the Prince and he wrote an explanatory and conciliatory letter to his father; a few hours later, as the result of further thought, he wrote another one of an even more submissive nature.

The letters had absolutely no effect upon the implacable George. Instead, "not finding them satisfactory, and having besides other reasons of discontent at several steps the Prince had taken," he turned the screw of his hatred by sending a letter with Vice-Chamberlain Coke, ordering the Prince and his wife to leave the palace before nightfall. The only concession he would permit was that if the Princess was too ill to be moved she might stay until her condition enabled her to be removed without risk; a judicious step this one and probably advised by one of his Ministers. The most cruel and unfeeling part of the message appeared at the end of his letter: "But you are further charged to say to the Princess from me that it is my will and my grandson and granddaughters stay at St. James's."

Caroline was distraught with grief at this terrible pronouncement and, weak as she was, she fainted several times within the hour; her ladies in attendance became hysterical for they thought she was dying. When she recovered sufficiently to collect her thoughts together the desperately unhappy Princess refused to remain in the palace and said she would go with her husband.

Then followed a heart-rending scene as the newly-born baby was literally torn from his mother's arms and her trio of tearful young daughters, aged five, seven and nine, came to say "good-bye." Caroline was carried, almost in a state of collapse, to the nearby home of Lord Grantham, the Prince's Chamberlain.

The next day the four children were removed even farther from their mother's reach for they were taken to Kensington to be placed in the care of the widowed Countess of Portland.

An even worse blow was to come, for a few weeks later on the 17th of February, the baby died. The death certificate signed by four court physicians is preserved in the British Museum. It certifies that the baby would have died in any event, but the catastrophe is tinged with suspicion.

This terrible blow retarded the recovery of the grief-stricken Princess, but the other children were still not permitted to visit their mother, whilst the anguished father was forbidden to enter Kensington Palace to see them.

Remorselessly the King pressed home his vengeance and he issued orders that all who were in the joint service of the King and the Prince must resign from the employment of one or the other. He added that anyone who called upon the Prince and the Princess would be barred from the King's Court. The royal rank of the Prince of Wales was to be ignored and he and his wife were to be regarded as private citizens.

Inevitably, a scandal of such magnitude soon became the talk of London, then Paris, then Berlin, until it became the gossip of all the courts of Europe; and perhaps it even reached the ears of the tragic " Princess of Ahlden ", to add even greater torment to her misery.

The King was relentless and he now added insult to injury by ordering the Prince to pay the £19,000, which had been allocated for the upkeep of the children he was unable to visit. The Prince had been forced to obey the King's orders to give up his children, but now he sought legal advice to avoid being made to pay the cost of the unhappy separation.

George I had already forced his Lord Chancellor Cowper to resign when he would not agree to the withdrawal of the children from their parents unless flagrant misconduct was involved, and replaced him with the more amenable Chief Justice Parker.* He was now faced with a fresh point of law. This time he was

* A favourite of the King and later created Earl of Macclesfield.

unable to evade the issue and was forced to pay the money himself for the upkeep of the children's establishment. George I now decided that strict economies were necessary and immediately reduced the amount involved considerably.

Again the Prince wrote to his father begging for the return of his children and in his letter he said: "If the detaining of my children from me is meant only as a punishment I confess it is of itself a very severe method of expressing Your Majesty's resentment. Pity the Princess and suffer her not to think that the children which she shall with labour and sorrow bring into the world, if the hand of heaven shall spare them, are immediately to be torn from her, and instead of comforts and blessings be made an occasion of grief and affliction to her."

This letter, reasonable though it was, suffered the same fate as the other letters the Prince had sent to his father. In speaking of this, Caroline said that her husband had written " as humbly as he could have done to the Almighty Himself " but they had not received a reply. She herself had sent the King a letter that had evoked an answering one, but it had been so abusive in blaming her for setting the Prince against " Lord " Newcastle, that she had not dared to write another one.

The only consolation left to the unhappy parents was that they were now in full control of their official income. They bought Leicester House* in Leicester Fields as their London residence and they took Richmond Lodge, on the riverside in the beautiful Richmond Gardens, as their country house. Their existence, living between their two houses, would have been happy if their children had been allowed to live with them. As it was they settled down to a quiet peaceful way of life highlighted for Caroline by a weekly visit (now permitted after six months) to her children; travelling from Leicester House to Kensington, as any private lady would have done, in a sedan-chair carried by common chairmen.

3

There were now two factions in the social and political world of London, for Leicester House competed with St. James's and

* The site of the present Empire Cinema.

Richmond Lodge with Hampton Court, each with their supporters; the King's safeguarding their present positions, whilst
those of the Prince looked to the future. The court of the Prince,
on the side of opposition and ambition, was gayer and freer
than the King's court.

London was divided and sometimes even families were split.
One interesting example was the Howards. This couple had
returned to England from Hanover, the husband as a Groom-of-
the-Bedchamber to George I, whilst his wife Henrietta Howard
(the one who had sold her hair in Hanover) was a dresser and
personal servant to the Princess.

Mrs. Howard lived apart from her husband, who was noted
for his brutality and meanness, and she was treated by Caroline
as a valued servant on terms of intimacy. She was beautiful and
charming and was a general favourite at the court of the Prince.
To the Prince she was more, she was his mistress.

In those days it was considered unmanly and rather odd in
the fashionable world for a man not to have a mistress. The
Prince, although in love with his wife, saw no reason, if he ever
gave it a thought, to depart from the current custom. He had
been unsuccessful in his efforts with Mary Bellenden, a Lady-
in-Waiting to his wife, and had turned for consolation to Mrs.
Howard.

An incident is recorded of his attempt to persuade Mary
Bellenden to become his mistress—how he sat with her discoursing on the advantages of such an association, whilst at the
same time to lend substance to his persuasions he played significantly with a handful of gold coins. She listened with growing
impatience until she was forced to cry out: " Sir, I can bear it
no longer; if you count your money any more I shall go out
of the room."

The Prince was not put out, and so to explain her conduct
she confessed that she was in love with a gentleman in his own
service, Colonel John Campbell. Generously the Prince said that
if she did not marry without his permission he would treat her
husband with favour. A few months later she broke her promise
and married the handsome colonel secretly. She misjudged the
Prince for he did not bear any resentment when the news leaked
out and the colonel was in his service for many years afterwards.

Caroline regarded her husband's affair with Mrs. Howard
quite complacently, indeed she now became more intimate and
confiding to " my good Howard " as she called her. At times
she found the Prince rather tiresome and it was a relief to have
him taken off her hands for a while, particularly by such a
pleasant person as Mrs. Howard, who was uninterested in
political intrigues.

In due course the Prince's affair with Mrs. Howard came to
the ears of the King who sent his Bedchamber official, Mr.
Howard, to call at Leicester House in the role of an injured
husband to raise a rumpus. Howard duly did as he was told
and stood outside the gate of Leicester House demanding his
wife, watched by an amused crowd. This sudden interest in a
wife he had neglected and his own vicious character prevented
anyone from taking his complaints seriously.* It was guessed
quite correctly that the King was behind the action of the
" jealous " husband.

Leicester House was becoming more popular than ever, whilst
to the lucky few who were invited to spend a few days in the
country at Richmond Lodge (the accommodation was very
limited as the lodge was small) it was a holiday full of gaiety and
pranks and the journey by river, which was the customary means
of reaching Richmond, was very pleasant.

It must have been very galling to the King to discover that
the banishment of his hated son had not in any way reduced
the Prince's popularity or affected his enjoyment of life. He therefore decided to curtail his pleasures by taking away his income
and he asked his Ministers to have the income of £100,000 paid
direct to the King by an Act of Parliament. He would then pay
to his son whatever amount he considered essential. It was no
trouble whatever to persuade Stanhope and Sunderland to draw
up the Bill, but after that he met resistance and the plan had
to be abandoned.

His next step was to deprive his son of the inheritance of
Hanover when he succeeded to the throne. The new Lord
Chancellor Parker (now Earl of Macclesfield) was willing enough

* When George I died Howard accepted a sum of money to give her
an official separation, which proved the real extent of the injury to his
damaged feelings.

54

but pointed out that the proposal was not feasible under the Act of Settlement.

Instead the King devised a scheme in the form of the Peerage Bill, which restricted the number of Peers and prevented the appointment of new ones. Thus the Prince would be unable to reward his present supporters in the future in the manner they coveted most. The Bill, drawn up by Stanhope and Sunderland, passed the House of Lords but was defeated in the Commons by Walpole (the King was absent in Hanover at this time).

When the King returned after six months in Hanover he forbade Walpole and Townshend ever to appear in his presence, even forbidding them to visit Newmarket races if he himself was present. To Walpole this was merely a temporary eclipse. He was an opportunist and his chance would come.

It was a period of tremendous financial activity and Walpole had a brilliant financial brain. Finance was the King's department most ineptly served and he missed the ability of Walpole.

The Civil List was £700,000 annually plus several other sources of revenue, but despite this huge income the King's finances were in a sorry plight. He and his Ministers had amassed a huge debt of £600,000 in three years and Stanhope was at a loss to deal with the situation. Together the King and Stanhope decided to co-opt the services of Walpole, the Minister who had behind him the confidence of the all-powerful City of London merchants and financiers.

Walpole had gained the friendship of the Prince and Princess by giving them sound and very profitable advice and he did not wish to lose this recently gained support. Now he had the opportunity for combining in his support both spheres of influence.

Obviously the first stipulation that Caroline made for the suggested reconciliation with the King was the return of her children. The Prince was prepared to accept Walpole's scheme without this proviso, for he accepted the reasoning that they must proceed slowly and wait until they had the King in the right humour before making demands. Reluctantly Caroline acquiesced saying quite determinedly : " Mr. Walpole, this will be no jesting matter to me; you will hear of me and my complaints every day and hour, and in every place, if I have not my children again ! "

Having prepared one hand of the bargain Walpole now turned his attention to the other. His approach was through the Duchess of Kendall, " who," he said, " was in effect as much Queen of England as ever any was, though she would sell the King's honour for a shilling advance to the highest bidder." It was merely a question of price.

Skilfully Walpole conducted the negotiations by making both sides appear to have gained their point; for instance the Prince did not wish to leave Leicester House and the King did not want him at St. James's.

During the discussions the news reached Caroline that Princess Anne was ill and the illness was feared to be smallpox. She immediately sent a message to the King begging to be allowed to visit her sick daughter. The King agreed provided she came alone.

In the meanwhile, a letter from the Prince couched in conciliatory terms was delivered to the King. He sent back a message and the Prince immediately went to St. James's. Here, on his knees, he made a suitable apology and the reconciliation was effected. The Prince was allowed to see his children who were now at St. James's and he returned " red-eyed ", yet triumphant, to Leicester House, with Beefeaters escorting his chair as a mark of restored rank.

The news of the reconciliation was announced officially and the next day a state procession was seen by the London crowds entering the Royal Chapel, where a thanksgiving service was held. The King and the Prince then kissed and embraced each other and to all intents and purposes the quarrel was over. Throughout the country there were celebrations, bells were rung, cannons were fired and in drunken revelry the nation rejoiced.

At the next official gathering, a Drawing-Room, great interest was evinced in seeing how the principals would react to each other. The veiled hostility was obvious for all to see and it was plain that this was not peace but only a truce. The Prince was never allowed to act as Regent in the King's absence.

The children also still remained in the care of Lady Portland, although the Princess was now permitted to visit them as and when she wished. She made a great point of speaking to the

King whenever they met officially so that the public would be convinced that the quarrel was ended, but they were both playing parts in which they did not believe.

This was in April 1720 and it coincided with the peak of the share-boom in that fantastic financial phenomenon the " South Sea Bubble ". This was a period of financial speculations wilder than anything England had ever seen before. The South Sea Company was so great that the National Debt was merged into the Company by a guileless Government.

4

At the beginning of 1720, Walpole had sensed that a financial storm was about to break in the City. Earlier he had spoken in the House warning the Government against speculative investment in this Company but his advice had been ignored.

For three years he had appeared to be wrong in his judgment for the Company had expanded with staggering speed. The Prince of Wales had been invited to become a Director, but had cautiously refused, and when the Company had assumed gigantic proportions even the King himself had been approached to become a Governor. He had accepted a large sum of money from the Directors and was made a Governor, with two deputies to sit in at Board Meetings on his behalf. Wildly shares were bought in this stupendous project that was going to make a fortune for everyone.

Astutely, Walpole had foreseen that a rise in the value of the shares was certain, but he had also seen that a fall was inevitable. In the early stages he had bought them himself and had also obtained £30,000 worth for the Prince and Princess of Wales, at a time when the entire nation was hysterical with the fever of speculation; indeed " the whole world was buying shares ".

For example, the shares of one Company, a Copper Company, in which the Prince was interested rose from £4 to £96. When he sold out on Walpole's advice he made a profit of £40,000.

Schemes by the score were being promoted by " Public Companies ", some genuine, some outlandish. At one time one hundred and forty Companies were being advertised in London alone, and the shares found a ready market.

Then in June 1720 the storm broke. The Government prosecuted the Copper Company of which the Prince was a Director. Fortunately for him, his father was away in Hanover at this time and the Commission sent him a warning of the impending prosecution to enable him to resign his directorship and avoid the scandal.

The attack upon the Copper Company had been instigated by the South Sea Company, and others were to follow for the Company was intent on wiping out its rivals. The Bubbles began to burst, and continued to burst, so that the inflated credit of the South Sea Company also suddenly collapsed; leaving only the debris of ruined speculators.

The few who had sold out were rich but the others suffered terrible losses. A report in the *Survey of London* records the scene: "Many a man of reputation and distinction was undone* and obliged to walk on foot; while other, who the year before could scarcely purchase a dinner, were exalted in their coaches and fine equipages, and possessed enormous estates; and such a scene of misery appeared among traders that it was almost unfashionable not to be a bankrupt".

The pillars of commerce were toppling and the number of suicides mounted daily, shops were closing, looms were idle, and people were starving.

In the Government the catastrophe struck down many of its members and the Ministers who had been bribed to exert their influence in connection with the South Sea Company found themselves facing charges of corruption.

The Chancellor of the Exchequer was sent to the Tower; Sunderland resigned and died within a few months; Lord Stanhope, although not accused, became so disturbed by the events that he collapsed and died soon afterwards; others committed suicide to avoid the inquiry. In the flood tide of disaster, Walpole, and behind him Townshend, stood like a rock whilst the rushing waters of abuse, criticism and calumny, swept others to oblivion. The turn of Walpole had come.

He took his chance with both hands and within twelve months

* **The Duke of Portland was one.**

he was First Lord and Head of the Ministry. The measures he had planned for the country's recovery from the disaster of the " South Sea Bubble " were found to be unnecessary. The economy of the country was basically sound; with Walpole at the helm, confidence was restored and the ship of State righted itself.

Walpole had now taken the place of Stanhope in the King's confidence and wisely he took no steps to aid the Prince and Princess, except to foster in the King's mind the impression that they were harmless in obscurity. The children, however, were never returned to their parents and it was a subject upon which Walpole avoided discussion.

It was still the custom for the sovereign to preside at Cabinet Meetings and meetings of the Privy Council, and the Ministers were considered to be personal servants of the King. As George did not understand the English language, and was often away in Hanover, he ceased to attend the meetings and so unwittingly brought about the elimination of the sovereign's personality from political affairs. A Minister was deputed to act as President at the meetings, and thus it was Robert Walpole who became the first Prime Minister of England,* although he shunned the actual title. His position was strengthened by the fact that the King refused to depute his authority to his son, and the Prince of Wales, who understood English and could have been useful, was powerless.

On April the 15th 1721, Caroline's unhappiness was softened slightly when she gave birth to a prince.† The baby was born at Leicester House, and this time the King was more reasonable. He agreed to the Prince's suggestions that the godparents should be his father the King, his sister the Queen of Prussia, and the Duke of York. But infinitely more important to Caroline was that the King, for the first time, allowed her to keep her baby.

For the next seven years the King kept his son in the shadows permitting him no duties and only allowing him to make rare official appearances. In enforced obscurity the Prince became

---

* The position of Prime Minister was not officially recognized until 1905. Up to then the Prime Minister always held some other Cabinet post, usually that of First Lord of the Treasury.
† William Augustus, later Duke of Cumberland.

fussy, critical and carping, and justly came to be regarded as a
dull, ill-natured German.

Two more children, Mary and Louisa, were born in 1723
and 1724. They were also allowed to remain with their mother
and completed the pattern of their parents' quiet life as private
gentlefolk. The Prince and Princess kept themselves aloof from
politics and royal affairs for they had learnt a bitter lesson from
crossing the path of the implacable, vindictive George the First.
In their quiet retreat they waited patiently for the crown to
fall into their grasp.

The turn of the Prince was to come, for on the 10th of June
1727, George I had a stroke in his coach when passing through
Holland. As he sprawled in pain he gasped " Osnaburg, Osnaburg," but he was never to reach it, for he died on the way. He
was sixty-seven years of age and had ruled for thirteen years.

George I was buried at Hanover and was the last English
sovereign to die abroad.

He and his German followers were not liked in England.
They had stolen and plundered where and when they could.
They had been laughed at, sneered at, and ridiculed, but the
Protestant succession had been established.

In his personal life he was vindictive, coarse, cynical, selfish
and avaricious. The records of his actions speak in condemnation of his character and pathological cruelty.

CHAPTER THREE

GEORGE THE SECOND

I

Tʜᴇ ɴᴇᴡs of his father's death was brought to the Prince on the afternoon of the 14th of June 1727. It had taken three days to come from Osnabruck. He and Caroline had eaten well and were in bed together at Richmond Lodge. The jack-booted messenger who brought the news was Sir Robert Walpole himself and he had foundered two horses in reaching Richmond. At first, the servants refused to disturb the royal pair, but Walpole brushed them aside and entered the bedroom. Here, kneeling, he told them of the death of George I.

" *Dat is one big lie,*" bellowed the new king, half-asleep and furious at being disturbed. Walpole repeated the message and from that day George II was to rule over England for thirty-three years, whilst Walpole was to be his Prime Minister for fifteen of them.

The new King and his Queen immediately returned to Leicester House to receive the congratulations of their friends and supporters. George then hung up the two portraits of his mother, Sophia Dorothea, which he had kept hidden during his father's lifetime.

It was generally anticipated that on the death of George I his favourite, Walpole, would fall with him, for it was well-known that George II was antagonistic towards Walpole. However, the guiding influence in the new King's life was Caroline, his wife, and she liked the astute Walpole, who lost no time in declaring that he was ready to serve the son with the same loyalty that he had shown to the father. He added confidently that he would certainly be able to obtain an increase in the amount of the Royal Civil List. This was an argument of a very tempting nature for the King and Queen were already planning how to spend their inheritance. Caroline had soon detected the alert brain behind Walpole's bluff exterior, but this quality was not yet apparent to her more obtuse husband.

The short, bumptious George was an odd mixture; courageous in battle, and even then sometimes an object of ridicule, yet unable to stand alone, relying on the opinions of his wife. The short, plump Queen, with the milk-and-roses complexion and ample bosom, knew well how to control the choleric, turbulent George in his tantrums and rages; for he loved her and she understood him as no one else did.

Caroline soon convinced her husband that Walpole was the Minister most capable of handling their affairs and of ensuring the continued security of the Hanoverian succession.

At their first Drawing-Room she took the opportunity of demonstrating to the unsuspecting politicians the direction of the royal intentions. The royal pair were surrounded by a crowd greater than usual for these occasions. Suddenly the Queen saw Lady Walpole, unimportant and ignored, standing discreetly in the rear. In a loud voice, Caroline said : " There, I am sure, I see a friend !" Everyone turned in the direction of her gaze and taking the obvious hint parted to allow the delighted Lady Walpole to come forward.

Walpole's continuance in office destroyed in one blow all the hopes of the conniving cliques, with their schemes for personal advancement, and when Walpole succeeded in increasing the Civil List to £800,000, plus additional grants from Government funds, he set the seal on his favour with the royal couple.

They were an ill-assorted pair, yet well-matched. George was stupid, blustering and brave, with no other interests in life outside his debauchery, his drinking and his guards, whom he loved to have around him, and music.

He never read a book, indeed the mere sight of a book sent him into a rage; and the Queen, who loved reading, was forced to enjoy her books in the privacy of her closet. Caroline was clever and accomplished, with a wide range of interests, including music which was their only artistic link. They were both coarse, with the same crude sense of humour.

The Queen became very attached to Walpole, who was a short, fat, powerful aggresssive figure, with a clever brain and a subtlety beneath his bluster that appealed to Caroline. She very soon completely reconciled George with his bold Prime Minister, and it was well she did, for Walpole served them and his country ably and successfully. The first opportunity for Walpole to demonstrate his organizing ability was the Coronation and it was a memorable occasion.

At seven o'clock in the morning the Queen was taken in her chair, attended by Mrs. Howard and two other ladies, to an apartment in Westminster, where her servants awaited her. She was dressed in her State robes and was ready to meet the peeresses at nine o'clock.

The Coronation was the most magnificent yet seen in England's history and it formed the pattern for future occasions. A raised gangway had been built between Westminster Hall and the Abbey and soldiers lined the sides to keep the crowd in check. Along this herb-scented platform the procession of Peers, Peeresses, Bishops and Knights, walking in pairs, provided a blaze of colour, scintillating jewellery and ornamentation. It is said that the jewellers of London had been besieged for days before to meet the demand for precious jewels.

Their Majesties walked under a canopy, the Queen thrusting herself forward to display her " petty-coat " which was adorned with £2,400,000 worth of precious stones, bought, borrowed and hired, for only a single pearl necklace of Queen Anne's collection had escaped the plundering hands of George I's German followers. The Queen also carried a sceptre and an Ivory Rod, but she herself declared that " the weight of the jewelled dress was the worst thing I had to bear."

Her train-bearers were her three daughters, Anne, the Princess Royal, Princess Caroline and Princess Amelia, and with her flaxen hair, fair skin and ample bosom the Queen was a regal figure amongst the procession of glittering pageantry.

The church service in the Abbey lasted until three o'clock when the procession returned to Westminster Hall, which was

illuminated by two thousand candles in chandeliers,* and a
magnificent cold luncheon of one hundred and twenty-nine
dishes awaited them.

The Hall was crowded and the official guests who had not
taken part in the procession were packed in the galleries round
the Hall. They were supplied with food from below by drawing
up baskets with ropes. After the Royal Champion had made the
challenge the royal family returned to St. James's; the Queen
first being taken to her apartment to change her dress, afterwards leaving unnoticed in her sedan-chair.

For weeks afterwards State ceremonies were held and the
winter passed in a succession of feasts, levees, Drawing-Rooms
and masquerades, an innovation from Germany. They became
quite the fashion although considered by some to be evil since
they invariably provided bawdy spectacles when the libertines
took the opportunity of indulging in licentious conduct behind
the masks of anonymity.

The popularity of the new King was firmly established and he
increased the good feelings by dismissing his father's German
favourites and appointing English ones in their places.

The King found it a particularly gay season for he had found
a new mistress in the Duchess of Bedford, whilst Caroline viewed
his sexual exploits with indulgent complacency and consoled
Mrs. Howard in her temporary displacement. Mrs. Howard
had been his mistress for ten years and he had visited her at
precisely the same time every evening, often pacing up and
down with watch in hand waiting for the exact hour. Yet he
loved his wife. They both shared a coarse, pathological interest
in sex and he usually described to his curious wife the most
intimate details of his conduct with his mistresses.

Caroline, despite her husband's lustful interest in other
women, exercised a ruling influence over his mind and this fact
was the subject of gossip. Coarse ballads were published in the
" very free " press without any royal action being taken and
the following is a sample of the milder kind but it illustrates the
resentment of the Queen's ascendancy :

---

* A Swiss, Mr. Heidegger, had invented a very complicated system by
which the 2,000 candles were lighted almost at once. Later, Heidegger
was made His Majesty's Master of the Revels.

" You may strut, dapper George, but 'twill all be in vain,
We know 'tis Queen Caroline, not you, that reign,
You govern no more than Don Philip of Spain.
Then if you would us fall down and adore you
Lock up your fat spouse, as your Dad did before you."

The Queen's support of Sir Robert Walpole kept him in office, for no Minister could hold his position against the King's wishes, and this personal power resulted in " back-stairs " court intrigue. There was, in fact, a private staircase to the Queen's apartments which was actually called the " Back Stairs " and Walpole used it almost every day. His approach to the King was invariably through the Queen.

Whatever he had discussed with the Queen was promptly passed on to the King, so that when Walpole saw his master officially the mind of George had already been prepared. If the Queen happened to be present when this happened she would make a show of being surprised so that the King who was, according to Hervey, " infinitely jealous of being governed " was led to believe that he had made the decision.

Lord Hervey had an apartment at the foot of the Queen's private staircase and Walpole used the pretext of visiting him to allay the suspicion that he was " lobbying " Queen Caroline. Even when George saw the jibes in the press concerning his wife's influence he still did not suspect that they were really true. He trusted her implicitly and relied, without question, on her judgment.

The greatest difficulty experienced in influencing the King was in restraining him from going to war. He was keenly interested in military matters and was very eager to lead his beloved Guards into battle. Walpole and the Queen did succeed in preventing his participation in the Polish Succession War and Walpole made his famous remark to the Queen : " Madam, there are 50,000 men slain in Europe this year, and not one Englishman." George had to be content with following the course of the war by studying the reports in conjunction with his map.

During the early part of the reign of George II the power of Walpole was unchallenged. The arrival of the Prince of

Wales in England in December 1728 gave the opposition their much needed fulcrum upon which to exert pressure. The Prince, Frederick Louis, was twenty-one when he came to England and his selfish and unsavoury reputation had delayed his parents in reaching their decision to send for him. They only did so in 1728 because they had heard he was planning to run away to Berlin to marry the Princess Wilhelmina of Prussia, a match to which they were strongly opposed.

2

Frederick Louis was born in 1707 and was " the image of George William of Celle " his great-grandfather. It is said he inherited all the licentious, brutal, and selfish characteristics of his father but only his mother's charming manner. If his grandfather, who arranged Frederick's upbringing, had planned it to instil hatred in the boy towards his parents he could not have achieved a better result.

From the beginning his tutors, appointed by the grandfather, had imbued their selfish pupil with animosity against his father and mother, and whenever George I visited Hanover he exercised his influence on his young grandson's mind. Apparently the boy was allowed to do just as he wished and no restraint was placed upon his activities and extravagances, with the result that he participated freely in the vices and debaucheries of the Hanoverian Court. When he was sixteen he had already set himself up with a mistress.

His father's sister the younger Sophia Dorothea, the Queen of Prussia, had plans for the marriages of her children; her son (he became Frederick II) she wished to see married to the English Princess, Anne; whilst the young Prince Frederick seemed a good match for her daughter Wilhelmina. She had discussed the double marriage with her father George I and he had expressed his approval of the scheme, despite the fact that his son-in-law King Frederick William I and George Augustus hated the sight of each other. This was another way of annoying his son who was against the whole affair.

It had been easy to persuade the young Frederick that he should marry his cousin, plain though she was, and he was encouraged to resent his father's objections to the marriage. After his grandfather's death he still persisted in his intention of marrying Wilhelmina and when the news of his secret marriage plan leaked out it caused his father to summon him to London.

George II was, of course, by now well aware of Frederick's unruly nature and he freely expressed his dislike of the Prince, with the result that in England there was a wave of sympathy for the " forgotten " son and heir.

It was thirteen years since the royal pair had seen Frederick and they must have often wondered what he looked like. At twenty-one he was small and frail, with bulbous eyes. He had his mother's fair hair, and a thin pointed nose. From the painting of Frederick and his sisters by Nollekens one can detect in him a bird-like sharpness, like an alert owl about to pounce. He was not bad-looking in a boyish way, and it was said of him when he arrived in England that he had a pleasant expression and was noticeably polite and respectful to the parents he had not seen for so many years.

This attitude of " excellent regard " was merely a pose as later events proved. He came to England determined to win popularity and to further his own selfish ends, for he had already learnt of the importance of the heir to the throne in the English political system. Behind a façade of exemplary filial conduct the meretricious Prince began almost immediately to conduct a campaign of insults and provocations against his parents.

In public he was always the dutiful son but Hervey reveals that in private he took delight in being rude to his parents. The real cause of the feud is not known, although it is said that Hervey did record the true facts but that the pages containing this information were extracted from his " Memoirs ". Caroline often said that " the King had very grave ground of displeasure against the Prince which people did not know of."

Frederick found he liked London. He was lavish in his spending and soon found himself in debt, but this did not worry him unduly for the settling was done by his father. George II was receiving from Parliament the £50,000 granted by Parliament as the allowance of the Prince of Wales. The King himself paid the Prince's expenses and allowed his son £2,000 a month for his personal needs. He had taken this attitude because the Prince had left behind in Hanover a mountain of unpaid debts and the King hoped, by handling his son's financial affairs himself, to avoid the same things happening in England.

Frederick was reckless with his money and bought himself popularity by paying much more for his purchases than the prices asked. He used to visit the shops on foot and rode about London in an ordinary hackney coach. By mixing freely with the people he undoubtedly courted popularity, which was observed with rancour by his mother the astute Caroline. In her outspoken fashion she said: " My God! popularity always makes me feel sick, but Fritz's popularity makes me vomit."

The antagonism became much stronger when the Prince surrounded himself with the opponents of Walpole and the people who were out of favour at Court. His open criticisms of his father found their way home and Hervey has recorded the bitterness that ensued.

No doubt these constant aggravations decided the King to return to Hanover for a pleasure trip. He had been finding England an unhappy place and he missed the pleasures of the Hanoverian Court where the women were big-bosomed and big-bottomed and spoke his own tongue. The affairs of England did not interest him very much and he knew he could safely leave everything in the capable hands of Caroline and Walpole. The Queen was therefore appointed Regent, to the disgust and mortification of the Prince who had expected to be given the honour.

In retaliation for being overlooked, and there is no doubt that the King never even considered his son for the position of Regent, Frederick began to harass and annoy his mother in every possible way and even insinuated quite openly that she was enjoying her new-found freedom. That she enjoyed the power of her position was true but she was uncompromisingly loyal to her husband in word and deed. Hervey, who was well qualified to speak, said:

" Her predominant passion was pride, and the darling pleasure of her soul was power . . . She was at least seven or eight hours tête-à-tête with the King every day, during which time she was generally saying what she did not think, assenting to what she did not believe, and praising what she did not approve; for they were seldom of the same opinion. Her every thought, word and act was calculated to preserve her influence; to him she sacrificed her time, for him she mortified her inclination : she looked, spoke and breathed but for him, like a weathercock to every capricious blast of his uncertain temper."

3

Meanwhile in Hanover George was enjoying himself and he stayed for several months. Regularly he wrote long letters, often of thirty pages and more, to his wife in England. In his graphic descriptions of his doings he included his love affairs and crudely described his sexual activities with other women in intimate detail. George enjoyed himself so much that he returned to Hanover every two or three years. In his absences a large portrait of the King was placed in his chair in the assembly-room to which the members of the Court made their obeisances.

Always the Queen was left in charge as Regent and thus for many months at a time, over many years, Caroline of Ansbach was virtually the sovereign of England. The capable Caroline showed far greater ability than her strutting irascible, lustful husband (for whom " no woman came amiss to him, if she were but very willing and very fat "), although at the time it was resentfully considered that she interfered too much with politics and there was considerable public animosity towards her.

At this time the power of the Sovereign in politics was still very strong and the bestowal of offices, titles, and pensions, was dependent on the personal wishes of the King. The office of Prime Minister, or the King's Minister as he was called, was as yet a nominal one. The system of Parties and majorities was still in embryo and there was no " King's Opposition ".

The Queen, however, does not seem to have interfered with Walpole's process of elimination of those Ministers he believed might jeopardize his own position. It has been suggested that she was a little in love with him and it is certain that she admired him tremendously.

Sir Robert Walpole was a thickset, stocky man scaling more than twenty stone, with a bull neck, coarse features, heavy black eyebrows and a sensual mouth; a brutal face, yet it was enlivened with intelligence and humour and alert brown eyes. His subtle cleverness, masked by his bluff exterior, and his ruthless ambition made him a formidable opponent for anyone. He was the first Minister to refuse a peerage so that he could retain his position in the House of Commons. This was part of his policy for he liked to present himself as a jovial, bluff, hard-swearing, coarse country squire. By this apparent lack of sophistication he attracted the support of the influential country gentry, whilst he relied upon his skill in debate to win support in London.

His morals were those of the farmyard but he lived in ostentatious splendour in beautiful houses, surrounded by paintings and furniture for which he had paid fabulous sums. Openly he kept a mistress, Molly Skerratt, and made no secret of the fact that he had lost interest in his wife. Nevertheless, he was loyal to those who were loyal to him, rewarding his friends with power and positions. Undoubtedly he possessed financial skill but he was not above bribery, providing the price was large enough.

In 1733 he almost engineered his own downfall, by the introduction of what he called the Excise Bill. The object of the Bill was to prevent the wholesale evasion of duties on wine and tobacco at the ports by having the retailers pay the duties before the goods were delivered from the warehouses. Bulk imports would be free of duty and thus smuggling would be unprofitable. The merchants were against the Bill and stirred up the London mob by spreading stories that the Bill was an attack upon the freedom and liberty of the citizen. The mob, unable to read or write, were easy prey to the rumours and expressed their opinions in the only way they knew—by rioting. Indecent effigies of the Queen and Walpole were publicly burnt, lampoons, cruel caricatures and ballads, added fuel to the fire of hate and Walpole faced a storm of criticism. The Queen wept and Walpole withdrew the Bill.

The withdrawal was hailed as a victory for the people, and for several nights the mob caroused in the streets shouting " King James III ". The City was wild with delight and the Lord Mayor led the celebrations. Similar jubilations took place up and down the country and the Opposition and the Prince were delighted, for they thought these wild scenes meant the end of Walpole. Indeed Walpole had only avoided being lynched by the courage of one of his Ministers who had held the mob at bay with his sword whilst Walpole escaped. The Prime Minister had realized the growing danger of the Jacobites and had begged the Queen to dismiss him from office to preserve the Hanoverian succession.

To the intense disappointment of the Prince and the Opposition the Queen had insisted upon Walpole remaining in office. But the widespread agitation and rioting made the Prince feel he was now in a much stronger position. He began to agitate at Court for his own establishment.

In 1734 another event took place that revealed the growing unpopularity of the King. It was the occasion of the marriage of the Princess Royal to the repulsive looking Prince of Orange. The mob cheered the Prince wildly, for they remembered that a previous Prince of Orange had expelled an unpopular king from England. The allusion was not lost on George II. The King regretted having arranged the marriage, for earlier he had been hesitant when he saw the ugly appearance of the future bridegroom. Then he had asked his daughter if she was still prepared to go through with the marriage. Her reply had been that she would marry him if he were a baboon. Frederick took the opportunity of airing his old and not unreasonable grievance concerning his own marriage.

Unknown to the Prince however there was a bride in store for him. George II had found himself a buxom young mistress in Hanover, Madame de Walmoden, and together they had selected a bride for Frederick. The choice was Princess Augusta of Saxe-Gotha, a big, gangling girl of seventeen, and the King lost no time in writing to Caroline telling her to instruct their son to prepare for his impending marriage. In the same letter he told Caroline of the sexual delights of his mistress Madame de Walmoden. He had called in some painters to portray her nude charms and he would be bringing home the pictorial proof of his revels, to show to his beloved wife.

Frederick was perturbed when he received the news. At the time he was amorously engaged with Lady Archibald Hamilton, who had ten children already. She was old enough to be his mother, but he found her favours too entertaining to be given up.

On the 25th of April 1736 the King returned to England with his improper paintings of his " gigantick fat Venus " and also the Princess Augusta of Saxe-Gotha. Frederick called to examine his prize in the marriage lottery the same evening she arrived at Greenwich Palace. The next day he dined with her and from the royal barge showed her London as far as the Tower. Their engagement was a short one for on the third day they were married.

Princess Augusta was brought in state to St. James's, travelling by coach to Lambeth then by the royal barge across the river to Whitehall; the last stage of the journey through St. James's Park was by sedan chair. The wedding took place the same evening, followed by a splendid banquet. Then came the ceremonious undressing after which the guests filed through the bedroom to see the bride and bridegroom in bed together.

The bride was an awkward, docile creature, and she accepted everything that happened to her with a quiet resignation. Her tranquillity was said to be an indication of good breeding, whilst some said it was due to stupidity; whatever the reason, the King had obviously chosen her because of her harmless disposition. She had had little education and could speak only German. However, this would not be a handicap her mother had told her, for the Hanoverians had been on the throne of England for more than twenty years and in consequence she supposed practically everyone in England spoke German.

Frederick, now that he was married, was given a country house at Kew and a wing at St. James's Palace as a town house. His favourite, Lord Bute, was appointed as his wife's major-domo and his mistress, Lady Archibald Hamilton, became her Lady-of-the-Robes. Queen Caroline had refused to agree to this appointment but Frederick had easily persuaded his wife to ask for Lady Archibald Hamilton, saying that she herself desired it. Apart from the insult to his wife, the Prince had annoyed his parents, and he realized that in the malleable Princess, who towered above him, he had another weapon of aggravation. That very often acute embarrassment was caused to his wife as a result was of no consequence.

The Queen did not show any animosity to her daughter-in-law for the part she played in the family feud. She knew her malicious son was always to blame; the Princess was by nature inoffensive and very young. She was also stupid. The old Duchess of Marlborough, who was out of favour with the Queen at the time, said of Augusta that her conversation " was much more proper and decent for a drawing-room than the wise Queen Caroline's was, who never was half an hour without saying something shocking to somebody or other even when she intended to oblige."

4

After a few months in England the King again returned to the fleshpots of Hanover, and in his absence the Queen, despite Frederick's recent insults, tried to create a more friendly feeling with her son and daughter-in-law. After her morning Drawing-Rooms she often invited them to stay to listen to music or to play cards in the evening. Apparently she found their company very trying, for she said to Lord Hervey with a yawn that she was more tired with Fritz's silliness and Augusta's stupidity than if she had carried them around the garden on her back.

Caroline had more than boredom to contend with, for the strain of politics was beginning to become burdensome and she was a sick woman. For some considerable time she had been experiencing acute internal pains, but she herself did not suspect the seriousness of her illness and she had not consulted her doctor. Stoically she had concealed her sufferings from the King, for she knew that complaints of illness always annoyed him, and when she found herself in too much pain to take part in functions or to walk in the gardens with him, she made the excuse that she was suffering from gout, a fashionable complaint.

To make matters worse, there was open hostility being shown towards the King, owing to his continued absences in Hanover. In the City a notice was nailed at the entrance to the Exchange : " It is reported that His Hanoverian Majesty designs to visit his British dominions for three months in the spring "; whilst on the gate of St. James's someone even dared to pin a notice : " Lost or strayed out of this house a man who has left a wife and six children on the parish ". The reward was four shillings and sixpence, " nobody judging him to deserve a crown."

The news had reached London of the King's affair with Madame de Walmoden and the tales did not need embellishment. The public feeling was symbolized when a decrepit old horse, emaciated and sore-ridden was turned loose in the streets bearing a placard: " Let nobody stop me—I am the King's Hanover Equipage going to fetch His Majesty and his Whore to England ".

Caroline herself for the first time felt some trepidation about his latest amour. In fact she had been unsettled since the retirement from Court of Mrs. Howard (now Lady Suffolk) in 1734. George had become bored with her and when her husband had died in 1733 Lady Suffolk had felt that there was nothing to keep her at Court. Caroline, however, had refused to allow her to resign saying: " Oh, my dear Lady Suffolk, you don't know when you are out how different people will behave."

The King wanted to be rid of her and he grumbled to his wife—" Why will you not let me part with an old deaf woman of whom I am tired?" He showed his feelings to Lady Suffolk by insulting her in public and it was obvious to everyone that her twenty years reign was finished. She pleaded with the Queen that she could not face such harsh treatment and begged to be allowed to resign. Caroline replied: " Child, you know the King; leave it to me. I will answer for it that all will be as well with you as with any of the ladys." But the King had made up his mind and for once the Queen could do nothing about it.

The Queen was upset by her husband's determination and in his new mistress, Madame de Walmoden, she saw for the first time in her marriage a rival to be reckoned with. The situation was beyond her and she felt beset on all sides by troubles; her illness, her son's aggravations, Madame de Walmoden, politics. Everywhere there was unrest and her crown was a burden upon her head.

The Prince of Wales was now more popular than ever, having gained many supporters in the City, Walpole's own territory and normally in favour of the King. The Prime Minister as a counter-measure formed a plan to inveigle the King back to England and lost no time in consulting the Queen.

Walpole reasoned that as it was Madame de Walmoden who kept the King in Hanover then if she came to London the King would not want to go abroad. He begged the Queen to invite her to England, where very soon he assured her she would have

Walmoden in the same situation as that recently occupied by Lady Suffolk. Reluctantly the Queen consented, though it is said she wept at the time, and she wrote to George asking him to invite his friend Madame de Walmoden to come to London.

Much as the idea must have appealed to George, common sense prevailed and he did not take advantage of his wife's offer. But in his letters to Caroline he expressed his appreciation of her thoughtfulness for his welfare.

5

Had George decided to bring his mistress to England there is no doubt that she would have had a very hot reception for discontent was in the air and there were riots up and down the country; the most notable being the " Porteous Riot " in Edinburgh, which was a triumph of mob rule. It began with the arrest of two smugglers who were sentenced to execution. Their daring exploits had captured the public imagination and to the mob they were heroes. On the day of the execution a Captain Porteous was in command of the town guard and his men had been issued with ammunition.

The mob surrounded the gallows, shouting and jeering, and after the first smuggler had been executed they attacked the executioner and the guards with stones. In the *mêlée* the other smuggler escaped and some of the troops fired on the crowd, wounding a number of the rioters. It was only after a tremendous struggle that Porteous and his soldiers were able to escape.

The captain led his men through the narrow winding streets to the tavern where he had arranged to meet the magistrates after the execution. He had intended to give his version of the affray but some of the mob had forestalled him, and when he arrived the magistrates had already received an account of the incident. They ordered his arrest as a murderer.

Porteous was unpopular in Edinburgh because of the violent methods he used to quell rioting, often wading into the crowd, lashing out right and left with his cane. Consequently when he was tried before a jury of townsmen his guilt was a foregone conclusion. He was condemned to execution.

The injustice of the affair stirred the gentry of Edinburgh to anger and they forwarded a signed petition for mercy to Queen Caroline. The Queen's answer was that " though her natural disposition was all mercy, yet would not rashly pardon the criminal, but was graciously pleased to grant a reprieve for six weeks that in the interim she might have the opportunity to inquire more narrowly how far the prisoner was a proper object for royal clemency." It was anticipated that the unfortunate Porteous would have his sentence reduced to transportation, but the mob decided otherwise. On the 7th of September they stormed the prison, Porteous was dragged from his cell and hanged before sufficient troops could be mustered to save him.

The Queen was furious at this usurpation of authority by the mob and it was indeed a precedent of great danger. The rioting spread unchecked for those in authority were reluctant to call out troops in the face of a similar penalty. Walpole was in a quandary. The magistracy of Edinburgh came under Lord Islay whom he did not consider it wise to offend, yet authority must be vindicated.

In the House of Peers there was a strong feeling that action should be taken against the city of Edinburgh and there was an official inquiry into the whole affair. It came to nothing, for the King returned from Hanover before the inquiry and the Queen suddenly changed her views. She said to the Duke of Newcastle, one of the chief agitators for vindication : " You hate Lord Islay and you want to take this occasion to do disagreeable things to him and make it impossible for him to carry on the King's business in Scotland." It was imperative that the King should not be worried, for she said it is " the business of princes to make the whole go on, and not to encourage or suffer little silly, impertinent personal piques between their servants to hinder the business of the government being done." Porteous's widow was given a pension and the incident was closed.

6

George II had experienced a very stormy passage across the Channel in his journey from Hanover. In December 1736 the royal yacht and the attendant warships awaited the King in the Dutch harbour of Helvoetsluys. Admiral Sir Charles Wager was in command and as there was a storm blowing he decided to remain in harbour until it had blown itself out. The King, with his usual personal disregard for danger, ordered the Admiral against his better judgment to set sail.

In the meanwhile the storm increased in violence. The warships sailed into the gale but the royal yacht was unable to leave the harbour, although several attempts were made. It was believed in London that the whole fleet was at sea at the mercy of the tempest. The Queen and the Ministers were alarmed, the Prince and his supporters were delighted; and the populace of London were amused.

For the next few days Caroline preserved a calm exterior despite the panic she felt, for she believed that the succession of Frederick meant the end of the House of Hanover. She herself intended retiring to Somerset House.

At last news arrived of the King, but Caroline's hands were shaking so much that she was unable to open the message. The Duke of Grafton opened it for her and announced in a loud voice that the King was safe. The fortunate messenger received sixty guineas as a reward and the speculations concerning the succession came to an end.

They were revived when the royal yatch put to sea, for a second storm arose and anxiety was felt by the Queen until the King was on firm land again. Even then he was ill having caught a chill and was confined to bed for a few weeks.

Parliament met in the February and Frederick, who had judged the lack of general concern in the King's safety to be to his advantage, took the opportunity of making a personal attack on the King by having a motion moved in the House about his allowance. The income was now £100,000 and it was still being paid to the King on behalf of the Prince of Wales.

Now that the Prince was married and had his own establishments he could quite justifiably claim that the income should be paid direct. To have this matter openly discussed, Frederick calculated, would bring the King to a point of apoplexy and as his father was already ill, and it was believed seriously ill, the time was particularly opportune.

Unaccountably George was quite calm about the matter

although he bitterly resented his son's action. He promised to increase the supplies to his son's household and also to arrange a jointure for the Princess. The motion for direct payment of the income was defeated by thirty votes but the King had to fulfil his promise, which implied he had been stinting his son. By the public airing of the Prince's grievance the King's reputation had suffered a severe blow, for the affair had even displaced in the public's interest the pending Porteous Inquiry.

The King and Queen swallowed their bitterness and Frederick was still permitted to attend their levees and Drawing-Rooms : " But the King never seemed to know when he was in the room, and the Queen, though she gave him her hand* on all these public occasions, never gave him a single word in public or private."

This armed truce did not last long however for the summer saw the final break. In July 1737 the Prince and Princess and their household were staying at Hampton Court with the King and Queen, where they occupied a separate wing.

Frederick had spread the information that the Princess was expecting the birth of a child in October. In fact, this was not the correct date, but whether the wrong information was given to mislead his parents or owing to his wife's stupidity is a matter of conjecture.

During the early evening of the 31st of July it was obvious that the birth was imminent and Frederick hurried his wife into a coach and forced her to endure a jolting journey to St. James's. It is likely that the Prince had made up his mind to insult his parents by disregarding the correct etiquette of having official witnesses present, but was himself mistaken in the dates. Thus he was forced on the spur of the moment to subject his wife to a miserable journey of agony and suspense.

The other theory that has been advanced is that he planned the whole affair, including the secret journey on the very evening of the birth, to prevent his parents being present.

When they arrived at the Palace nothing had been prepared in readiness and it was even necessary to use two table-cloths as sheets, other necessaries being borrowed from houses in Pall Mall. The baby, a girl, was born at eleven o'clock when the

* A point of etiquette being that he should hand the Queen to her seat.

grandparents were retiring to bed at Hampton Court quite unaware of the event.

At half past one in the morning a messenger arrived at Hampton Court with the news that the Princess was about to be delivered of a child. Mrs. Tichborne, the Bedchamber-woman wakened the Queen and gave her the message.

"My God, my nightgown! I'll go to her this moment," cried the Queen.

"Your nightgown, Madam," replied Mrs. Tichborne, "and your coaches too; the Princess is at St. James's."

When Caroline had recovered from her amazement she told the King, who flew into a rage: "You see now with all your wisdom how they have outwitted you. This is all your fault. *There is a false child will be put upon you,* and how will you answer it to all your children? This has been fine care and fine management for your son William; he is mightily obliged to you, and for Anne, I hope she will come over and scold you herself; I am sure you deserve anything she can say to you!"

The Queen dressed hurriedly and set out with her two eldest daughters, two Ladies-in-Waiting and three noblemen for St. James's Palace. They arrived at four o'clock and as they rushed up the staircase they were met at the top by the Prince in nightgown and nightcap. He told them of the birth of a little princess.

It was inevitable that a happening of this importance should soon be common gossip and the affair assumed the importance of a revolt against the King, although Frederick displayed an air of injured innocence. But this time public opinion was against him.

George II was furious and in a letter forbade his son ever to enter his house again. "Thank God," said the King, "tomorrow night the puppy will be out of my house." The Queen added vehemently: "I hope in God I shall never see him again." She never did; although the Prince took up residence close to the Palace at Norfolk House in St. James's Square. For the rest of his life the Prince's Court was the centre of political intrigue against his father.

Hervey records in his *Memoirs* the hatred that George II felt towards Frederick by quoting him as saying that his son was "a monster and the greatest villain that ever was born". Caroline is quoted as saying, " If I was to see him in hell I should feel no more for him than I should for any other rogue that ever went there." She also said to Lord Hervey: " My dear firstborn is the greatest ass and the greatest liar and the greatest canaille and the greatest beast in the whole world and I most heartily wish he was out of it."

7

The year 1737 had been an unhappy and troubled one for the Queen and it was to be her last. On the morning of the 9th of November she was violently ill and suffered agonizing pains. She was forced to take to her bed.

The King proposed cancelling the Court for the day but Caroline insisted on struggling out of bed. She managed to get dressed and entered the reception-room looking like a ghost. As soon as the King had left the drawing-room she again retired to her bed.

Always she had insisted that her illness was due to gout when in truth she was suffering from a ruptured womb which had become malignant. She was suffering extreme pain and begged to be given something to alleviate her agony: " Give me what you will, I will take it " she urged Lord Hervey. She was given large doses of neat whisky.

On the third day of her illness George sent for the surgeon, Ranby, and even then Caroline begged him not to do so. A strange pride, mixed with the fear of humiliation, had prevented her revealing the true nature of her illness until it was too late.

Ranby called in other surgeons and they performed a number of painful operations in a desperate attempt to rectify the damage. The Queen endured their futile efforts with a stoic fortitude, although she seemed to realize the hopelessness of her condition. She had already made terms with death, but she still refused to allow her son Frederick Louis to visit her and sent for the Lord Chancellor to make sure her son did not inherit her private property.

The King was frantic with anxiety and paced up and down the ante-room in agitation. He refused to believe that the death of the Queen was near and worked himself into a rage at any suggestion that she would not recover.

On Sunday the 13th of November the physicians decided she was nearing the end. Calmly she said farewell to her husband and her children, whilst George was shaken with sobs and almost collapsed.

But for six days longer Caroline clung to life during which time she was concerned only with putting her affairs in order. She sent for Walpole: " I have nothing to say to you but to recommend the King, my children, and the kingdom to your care," were her last words to the Prime Minister.

Caroline did not leave a will, saying " all I had was from the King so I will leave it all to him."

In the outer ante-room an anxious crowd waited and among them were supporters of the Prince ill-concealing their morbid delight as the Queen's condition deteriorated.

On the evening of Sunday the 20th of November Caroline's life began to ebb away. George who had been lying down on the floor at the foot of the bed came to her side and began to pray and rant as though to force her to cling to life.

In his selfish fashion he was devoted to Caroline. She well-understood her red-faced, bulky, buffoon of a husband and she loved him for what he was. She still saw in him the ardent lover of years ago who had chosen her of his own free will. They had endured a great deal together and despite his many peccadillos he had never humiliated her. She knew he had always loved her.

The sardonic Hervey in his *Memoirs* has preserved for all time the cruel, macabre death-bed scene with the Queen dying in agony and George grief-stricken by the bedside, hysterical, with tears streaming down his cheeks; and the Queen urging him to marry again and the King's oft-quoted reply, in keeping with the mood of the grotesque pantomime : " *Non, non, j'aurai des maîtresses.*" Hervey's satire was brilliantly malicious but he caricatured, for the sake of effect, what was surely a true, if strange, devotion, that at the time it was the fashion to treat with derision.

After her death the King was pitiful in his grief and at the mention of her name collapsed in a welter of tears. He locked himself in his bedroom for hours at a time, alone with a portrait of Caroline.

As his grief abated he talked incessantly of his wife and his favourite expression, which he repeated time and time again, was: " I never knew a woman fit to buckle her shoe." In her memory he rewarded all her servants by ordering that they should be paid their salaries for life, unless they were able to be found other remunerative positions, and the surgeons and physicians were given £500 each for their services. The salaries and gifts were paid from the King's Privy Purse.

The Palace of St. James's held too much sadness for him and he chose to live at Kensington Palace where the memories were happy ones. But for months he was inconsolable.

Caroline's death was not followed by the customary eulogies although she had been the most able Queen of England since Elizabeth. First and foremost in her mind was her duty to her husband and her children, but everything she did was, to use her own words, " for the sake of the whole "; the " whole " being the Hanoverian succession.

She enjoyed her position of power and during her many regencies she displayed commendable statecraft. By recognizing the ability of Walpole and maintaining him in office she showed good judgment, for between them they kept the ship of State on an even keel during times of great political storms. Together they firmly established the House of Hanover on the throne of England.

At times she was crude in her sense of humour and enjoyed coarse jokes, but she was not a humbug and she hated hypocrisy. Her life was happy, apart from the tribulations caused by her eldest son, for through the husband she loved above all else she achieved her ambition—power. She knew that her influence decided foreign policy, and in England prompted the appointments and dismissals of Ministers and Bishops. Caroline of Ansbach is an important figure in the pageant of England's history.

To Lord Hervey, " with his deadly smile, and ghastly painted face " posterity is indebted for a dramatized portrayal of Caroline and the Court of George II. His *Memoirs* are a masterpiece of cynical observation. They were written in secret and he left instructions that the box in which he deposited them was not to be opened until a considerable number of years had elapsed after his death. Thus he avoided the label of sycophancy. His pen however was dipped in malice and in death he revenged himself on those he hated in life, particularly the King and the Prince of Wales, although Caroline, who was very fond of him, also suffered to a lesser degree the venom of his satire.

John Hervey was a member of the King's Household when he was the Prince of Wales and continued in his service after the coronation. Some months later, whilst on a pleasure trip to Hanover, he met Frederick Louis and when they again met in England he became a member of the Prince's suite.

They were on intimate terms until they quarrelled and he rejoined the King's Court in 1730 (as Vice-Chamberlain) where his hatred of Frederick made him a welcome addition.

His cleverness and handsome appearance (although he used cosmetics like a lady of fashion to hide his pallor) gained him important favour. Thus he was in a position to observe the intimate details of the royal lives. He served them well although in his *Memoirs* he reveals his resentment of the inadequacy of his reward. His wonderful prose record is therefore in parts biased and unfair, sacrificing truth for artistic effect and personal spite.

8

Walpole viewed with concern the King's condition, which alternated between abjection and blustering rages. He decided the best way to assuage the King's grief was to bring his German mistress, Madame de Walmoden, to England. Sir Robert cynically explained the situation to the two elder princesses, who were grown women of twenty-seven and twenty-four.

At first, quite naturally, they did not like the idea but Walpole in his bluff way played on their broadmindedness and they agreed. Madame de Walmoden came to England in June 1738 and was given an apartment at Kensington. Soon afterwards she was created Countess of Yarmouth.

In her arms the King's sorrow abated but he still suffered periods of melancholy and no one dared to mention the possibility of his remarrying, although Court circles buzzed with speculation.

The Prince and Princess of Wales were quite unconcerned. They did not observe the normal period of mourning and conducted themselves in London and at Kew, where they were now living, as though the death of the Queen had never occurred.

Their daily life was dull and uneventful. The family feud still continued but with the Queen gone the Prince had fewer opportunities of venting his spite.

The Princess, in the meanwhile, was busy fulfilling her marital obligations by giving birth to a succession of royal babies. The next child after the Hampton Court episode had been the most important one, for he was the first prince. In anticipation he had been christened George with the additional names William Frederick.

Despite being occupied with her children, Princess Augusta still considered it her duty to engage in the intrigues against her father-in-law. Nevertheless, she accepted with docility her husband's string of mistresses, many of whom were chosen from her own circle of acquaintances. In this respect she followed the example of the late Queen's attitude of mind.

The death of Queen Caroline and the unpopularity of the royal conflict marked the beginning of the end for Sir Robert Walpole, for without her support he was unable to press his policy upon the King. The burning question of the day was whether England should declare war on Spain and Walpole, against public feeling, was for peace.

For many years there had been trouble in the West Indies between the English merchants who smuggled, and the Spanish officials who when they caught the smugglers punished them with sadistic tortures. England was inflamed with indignation. Walpole's policy was unpopular and bravely though he fought, his was a losing battle. The Opposition had found in William Pitt a violent, brilliant orator, whose speeches in the Commons were more stirring than any the members had heard for generations. Inevitably, in 1742, Walpole resigned.*

During his long term of office Walpole had gained Parlia-

* He was created Earl of Orford on his resignation and died three years later.

mentary unity by ruthlessly dismissing those members who disagreed with his views. Carteret had gone for intriguing against his foreign policy, the Earl of Chesterfield and Lord Stair for opposing the Excise Bill, and the Duke of Argyll for pressing for the declaration of war against Spain. Thus when Walpole resigned in 1742 the Prime Minister had become recognized as the ruler of the Cabinet, but he was not able to enjoy for long the achievement of his ambition.

In 1741 the War of the Austrian Succession had broken out and as it spread across Europe, inevitably England became involved. Walpole, who had kept the country at peace for eighteen years, was against any participation, warning sternly that war meant an increased burden of taxation and poverty. He had been forced into a profitless war with Spain in 1739 and he had pursued it half-heartedly. Now a greater issue was involved—the supremacy of Europe.

Pitt in the Commons had stirred the House with his fierce eloquence. Behind his eyes there was a burning ambition and the nation saw his vision of a glorious destiny. He had warned them of the alternative: " When Trade is at stake, you must defend it or perish."*

A new element had been introduced, the merchants in the City. England was prosperous and the merchants realized that the growing affluence of France was endangering England's trade. They recollected the rich gains of Marlborough's war and shouted for a declaration of war against France. With the coming of war Walpole had been swept aside and Carteret, whom the King always liked because he supported his foreign policy wholeheartedly, came back into power with Lord Wilmington as the nominal leader of the Government. The ruling party earned the derisive title of " The Drunken Administration " and the political system became riddled with corruption.

Again the figure of Pitt loomed large on the side of the Opposition. He was against the wholesale employment of troops on the Continent. His idea was that as England was a maritime nation her contribution to the war should be by the use of the

* When he died in 1778 a monument was erected at the Guildhall in the City of London. It was inscribed with the words of Edmund Burke: " A statesman by whom commerce was united and made to flourish by war."

Navy. By sporadic raids on the French coast troops would be drawn away from the main French Army and the Navy could control the Channel, taking rich plunder from the French merchant ships.

He was not concerned with military glory or the safety of Continental powers and in his speeches he continually attacked the policy of defending Hanover—" this formidable Kingdom is considered only as a province of a despicable electorate."

This was in effect an attack upon the King himself, for George II as the Elector of Hanover felt he owed a responsibility to the Emperor and to Prussia; indeed he always regarded his native land as being more important than England. The protection of Hanover was therefore the first concern of his military strategy. His Ministers, anxious to please him, were only too willing to fall in with his plans and England had been committed to land warfare.

George viewed the European scene through what he thought were the eyes of a military strategist as full of enthusiasm he left England to take personal command of his Army.

As Commander-in-Chief he was a ludicrous figure, but in the true Hanoverian tradition he was well-endowed with courage. In June 1743 he led his troops at the battle of Dettingen. The battle took place on the 27th and in the early morning the troops of Britain and Hanover advanced into a French trap with a river on one side and thickly wooded hills on the other. As they moved towards the French Army, another mass of French troops closed upon their rear. The Commander of the French Forces, de Noailles, congratulated himself as he waited for the pincers to close which meant the annihilation of the Allies.

At this vital stage a French commander, de Grammont, made an unaccountable error of strategy. Instead of waiting at Dettingen for the Allies to reach the bottle-neck he ordered his troops to advance. Lord Stair, the Allied Commander, deployed his forces along the left bank of the river with the result that the two armies met on a single front.

With the little, red-faced, middle-aged George at the head the Allied troops advanced and by a great deal of shouting and sword-waving George exhorted his men to attack. Amid the crackle of musketry and booming of cannons he was everywhere, bellowing and swearing, thoroughly enjoying himself. The troops were delighted by the foolhardy bravery of their Commander-in-Chief, but his horse found the excitement too much and bolted to the rear with the wildly gesticulating George struggling to halt its flight.

When at last he succeeded in pulling his horse to a standstill he was at the rear of his forces. He dismounted and ran back through the ranks to the front of the battle. " I can be sure of my legs, they would not run away with me," he said.

By four o'clock in the afternoon the battle was over and George had led his men to victory. Elated with his success he held a ceremony and honoured a number of his officers on the field of battle; among them was the Earl of Stair. His wildly cheering troops called their King " The Little Captain ", and on that day he created history by being the last King of England to lead an army in the field. In November he returned to London to be met by a wildly enthusiastic mob welcoming their courageous Sovereign.

The war dragged on fitfully and the ill-chosen Carteret was deposed. He was succeeded by Henry Pelham, the brother of Lord Newcastle, who had taken part in the battle of Dettingen. But the change made little improvement and the Opposition, with the support of the Prince of Wales, began to exert pressure and spread alarm in the Government ranks. The next year, 1745, was a troubled one both at home and abroad.

On the 11th of May the Allied troops, under the nominal command of the Duke of Cumberland, were defeated in the battle of Fontenoy; a disaster that spread gloom and despondency.

At home on the 25th of July the Young Pretender landed in Scotland to marshal his supporters. In September they met and defeated the King's forces at Prestonpans. The winter saw the Jacobite Army threatening England and the throne of the Hanoverians began to wobble.

The King viewed the progress of the marching Jacobites with customary courage. When the Pretender was at Derby George was still not dismayed and when flight was suggested he said : " Pooh ! don't talk to me that stuff."

The situation was becoming desperate however when the

young Duke of Cumberland (he was twenty-four) returned with his army. The Jacobites were forced to retreat before the onslaught of the Duke's men and were trapped and butchered in the battle of Culloden Moor. It was the end of the Jacobite cause and George II was safe on his throne.

On the Continent the war tailed off to an indecisive conclusion with the peace of Aix-la-Chapelle and England and France settled down like two fighting dogs to lick their wounds.

9

During the Jacobite rising the Pelhams in the face of royal disapproval resigned to avoid dismissal. But a few months earlier they had forged two further links in the chain of constitutional Government, by insisting that the Cabinet should receive the support of the King, and by establishing that the King must accept the nominees of the Prime Minister for positions in the Cabinet.

After a brief spell of twenty-four hours when Carteret and Pulteney failed to form a Government the King was forced to accept the appointment of Pitt to office in the Government. The appointment, despite the King's opposition (he disliked Pitt intensely for his attacks on the electorate of Hanover) was a symbol of the King's diminished prestige and influence.

Any setback to the King delighted the Prince of Wales and already Frederick was making his plans for when he became the Sovereign. The Prince was assisted by his chief adviser, Bubb Dodington, who quite naturally reserved for himself adequate reward in the scheme. He was already extremely wealthy but was avaricious and wanted more. Also, he would dearly love a peerage.

In 1747, however, another influence entered the life of the Prince in the figure of John Stuart, Third Earl of Bute, and he was much more important than the fat, stodgy Bubb Dodington. In contrast he was an extremely polished and handsome man of about thirty-five, with an imperious air and sweeping, graceful manners. He was said to have the most elegant legs in London.

The royal pair met him at Egham Races and in no time they were both captivated by the very personable Earl. He became a favourite at their Court and Frederick even encouraged him to have a flirtation with the Princess. Apparently he succeeded in his endeavours for the Princess became enamoured with the handsome Earl. The fact that he was married (in 1736 he had married the daughter of Lady Mary Wortley Montagu) had, of course, no bearing on the situation.

Three or four years later Frederick lost interest in Bute but the Princess still found him fascinating.

Suddenly on the 20th of March 1751 the Prince of Wales died. He was forty-four. It is said that a game of cricket was the cause of Frederick's death. He was playing on the lawn of his country house when he was struck on the body by the ball. Doctors diagnosed this accident as the reason an abscess formed in his side from which his fatal illness developed.

His body was cut open and his heart and intestines were placed in a box, wrapped in red velvet, and buried with due ceremony in Henry the Eighth's Chapel.

The funeral took place at Westminster Abbey on the 13th of May, but the King did not trouble to attend. The chief mourner was the Duke of Somerset and the ceremony was very ill-attended.

Frederick had been disliked and his death was followed by a spate of cynical, obituary verses. His unofficial epitaph taken from one of these lampoons was ironically appropriate:

> *Here lies Fred,*
> *Who was alive and is dead.*
> *But since 'tis only Fred*
> *Who was alive and is dead.*
> *There's no more to be said.*

George II was sixty-eight when his despised son died and he said quite openly and vehemently that " he was glad to be rid of him." This also appeared to be the general opinion.

Frederick, if he had done nothing else of importance, had amply provided for the continued succession of the House of Hanover. He left eight children and at the time of his death the Princess was expecting another one. This last child was born in July 1751 and was christened Caroline Matilda. The other eight were : Augusta, George William Frederick (the new Prince of Wales), Edward Augustus (Duke of York), Elizabeth Caroline, William Henry (Duke of Gloucester), Henry Frederick (Duke of Cumberland), Louisa Anne, and Frederick William. His widow was thirty-two, and the new heir to the throne, George William Frederick, was thirteen.

The Princess Dowager had been left a settlement of £50,000 a year and was living with her children at Leicester House. Now that his son was no longer around to annoy him the King felt more tolerant towards his daughter-in-law, although he did say : " I oblige her, but she wants to reign before her time."

Leicester House was again the meeting place of the Opposition and Bute, whom George II hated, was the major influence. Usually in attendance was the gross and ugly Bubb Dodington, who was still seeking his peerage. Together they advised the Princess in the instruction and preparation for kingship of the heir to the throne. They were mainly concerned with their own careers and in consequence his education was neglected in the cause of the faction.

Prince George certainly needed educating. He was stupid, slow, and indolent, and never showed the least desire to learn. At eleven he was unable to read and seemed contented with ignorance. His tutors quarrelled amongst themselves as they struggled to mould the dull and unresponsive clay. It is said that his mother urged him to " be a king ", and one can well imagine her exasperation with the almost hopeless material she had in hand. She was constantly summoning the Earl of Bute or Bubb Dodington to discuss her fears and worries. " His education," she admitted, " had given her much pain; his book-learning she was no judge of, though she supposed it small and useless; but she hoped he might have been instructed in the general understanding of things."

Already he evinced the signs of future imbecility. He was good-natured enough and obviously honest (which his mother in her anxiety took consolation in repeating), but he was diffident and at times silent and morose. He suffered with an inferiority complex and when crossed he did not show his anger by an outburst of temper (in this he was very unlike his grandfather who used to kick his hat and sometimes his wig up and down the room when he was annoyed); instead he became obstinate and sullen. In all, the young George was not an attractive personality.

In adolescence the Prince of Wales fell under the influence of the Earl of Bute and it was a spell that was to last for twenty years. Without a father and inculcated with a hatred of his grandfather, the impressionable youth turned to hero-worship Bute the elegant, man-of-the-world with a " theatrical air of the greatest importance."*

The handsome Earl, sophisticated and plausible, made a great impression on the young Prince. Indeed, Bute's influence with the heir to the throne was stronger than that of anyone else. Even the opinions of the mother were secondary to those of his " dearest friend ", as George generally referred to Bute, and on several occasions the Prince dropped a hint about the inadvisability of women interfering in politics.

He vowed " that he would never, never change, that he owed everything to his friend and would always be loyal; and if his friend ever deserted him then he would abjure the Crown and would retire to some distant region, there to meditate upon his own unforgivable sins."

And so the association between the Princess, her backward son, and the Earl of Bute, became even more intimate, until in 1757, it was common knowledge, or at least common belief, that the Princess and the Earl were lovers. Horace Walpole, the son of Sir Robert Walpole dared to say that he was " as convinced of amorous relations as if he had seen them together."

On the 25th of October 1760, the King died and the Earl of Bute was already firmly established as the most powerful influence in the land.

The clownish, rampaging George died from a stroke. His was not a royal deathbed: it was a water-closet at Kensington Palace.

The funeral took place at night, when with due pomp and ceremony he was buried in Westminster Abbey. In his will he decreed that his coffin should be laid alongside Caroline's, with a side removed from each so that their ashes could mingle together in eternity. It was a strange request from one who had

* Waldegrave.

lived his life in licentious selfishness. He had ruled for more than twenty years after his wife's death but the love they had shared so many years ago was always bright in his memory, and he kept his promise never to marry again.

There were few tears shed at his funeral and then by those who had misgivings for the future. George II had always felt indifferent to the people and affairs of England and, in turn, when he died little sorrow was felt at his passing.

His interests, after himself, were Hanover, the Army, and women. Apart from his brief role as " The Little Captain " at Dettingen, he was unpopular. That he was brave is unchallenged, but it is also as unanimously agreed that he was coarse, crude, uncultured, mean, and unfeeling towards others. He was a disappointing and ineffectual king, yet despite this, his reign ended in a blaze of glory and England was more prosperous than she had ever been before.

During the last few years of the King's reign Pitt had grown stronger as George became weaker and the death of Henry Pelham in 1754 gave him his opportunity.

In 1756 he launched Britain into the Seven Years War determined to follow his plan for increasing the country's wealth by winning an empire. Soon after the start of the war the King managed to oust him from office but was forced to recall the ambitious and daring Minister.

Pitt's policy was successful and 1758 and 1759 were years of victories. The French were defeated by Wolfe in Canada and the valuable trade gained was a rich bounty; Clive was successful in India; the French Navy was destroyed, and the French Army was routed by the Allies at Minden. Everywhere French possessions were being captured and England was growing rich. The dreams of William Pitt were coming true.

CHAPTER FOUR

GEORGE THE THIRD

I

GEORGE III was twenty-two when he came to the throne in
1760, following the death of his grandfather. Physically, he
resembled the pattern of his forebears, being heavy jowled, with
the same protruding eyes and receding chin. But he was young
and amiable, quite tall, and was considered to be good-looking.
His writing was that of a child and he read only haltingly.
Mentally and emotionally he was retarded.

The kingdom he inherited was one dominated by the patri-
cians. They were recognized as superior beings and they revelled
in their position. The King stood aloof as a powerful figure of
awe and reverence. Bribery was rife and titles and positions were
the dues of the fortunate. The nobles fell to their knees in the
presence of the Sovereign just as they had knelt to George II.

The reign of George III was to see momentous changes, not
least the tremendous growth of the middle-class. When the new
King came to the throne, the world of trade, the professions,
the church, literature and the arts were beneath the dignity of
" fine gentlemen " ! Theirs was a world of debauchery, pleasure,
gambling, drinking and idleness. It was all to change, for the
obsequiousness of the commoners was to be replaced by a
driving, compelling urge to progress.

By 1760 the population of Britain had steadily grown to more
than six and a half millions* but the ruling aristocracy repre-

* The official estimate from the records of christenings and burials in
1750 is 6,517,035. By 1851 the population had risen to 27,513,551, and
fifty years later to 41,609,091.

sented only the peak of the pyramid of the population, and two completely different ways of life were in juxtaposition; elegance and luxury, poverty and filth.

The rich lived in magnificent style and dressed in a profusion of bright colours and costly materials; ermine, silks, satins and brocades always exquisitely embroidered with gold or silver thread and with ornate buttons. The gentlemen vied with their ladies in the fantastic display of ostentatious fashion. The elegance of their silk-stockinged legs and long coats was set off by the floating gracefulness of the lavishly bejewelled ladies in their wide, billowing dresses, decorated in the most extravagant manner. It was embarrassing for a woman accidentally to show her legs, yet the intentional display of her breasts caused little notice. Manners were rigid and morals were lax.

The aristocracy by tradition were the political rulers and the sons of peers were automatically returned to Parliament, usually when in their early twenties: other representation was negligible. This was the accepted way of life and there was little hope of an improvement in the lot of the poor, whose conditions of existence were appalling.

They lived in foul stews of filth and wretchedness, resigned to their fate. As a result they were violent, savage and desperate. Murders, looting and all the crimes in the calender were commonplace. Their consolation was drink—and drunkenness at the cost of a few pence had greatly increased with a resulting increase in crime and lawlessness.

Gin was the cheapest and most popular drink and the consumption rose from 3,500,000 gallons in 1727, to 7,000,000 gallons in 1742, and it exceeded 11,000,000 gallons in 1751. Taverns exhibited signs: " Drunk for a penny. Dead drunk for twopence. Free straw." The gin-shops were frequently brothels and sometimes the brothels were even part of theatres.

To counteract the growth of lawlessness the law became more ferocious; a trivial theft was sufficient to send the wrongdoer to the gallows, whether it was man, woman or child. Women were often burned, even for theft, and this law in fact was not repealed until 1794.

Hangings were public and a popular form of entertainment. Every few weeks fêtes were held around the gibbets with their dangling corpses. The lash and the pillory were other diversions, often resulting in the death of the victim.

Life was cheap and savagery was everywhere, in the streets, in the Army and the Navy, and in the sports—bare-knuckle fighting, bull-baiting and cock-fighting; always there was a pleasant thrill in the sight of blood. Violence and disease made life a lottery and Hogarth has portrayed for ever the brawling, lusty, vicious scene. At any time only a spark was sufficient to inflame the citizens to become a wild, rioting mob with a lust for destruction.

Living always in the shadow of violent death, a gambling fever gripped everyone, rich and poor alike. Anything, whether important or inconsequent, could be the reason for a wager, and the stakes were sometimes ruinous. Life was a hectic affair to be lived to the full and the devil take the hindmost. This was the rule of existence for the rich and for the starving rabble herded in crowded tenements amidst the squalor and stench of filth and disease. It was generally accepted as the natural order of things, but a few enlightened minds were realizing that this was not the true destiny of mankind, and the spirit of agitation and reform was gathering impetus.

The expansion of Britain's foreign trade and increased prosperity made her one of the leading commercial nations in the world and with it came the growth of the middle-class. The merchants and new industrialists were becoming a power in the land, seeking their place in the social structure.

To the awakening masses the young King represented respectability and the new " trading class " looked to him to maintain national stability, whilst they furthered their commercial ambitions.

The new King had advantages over his predecessors. He had been born in England and spoke the language almost like an Englishman. He was sober and respectable with a leaning towards religion.

On the 31st of October, during the first week of his reign, he issued his first proclamation from Leicester House: " For the encouragement of Piety and Virtue, and for preventing the punishing of Vice, Profaneness and Immorality." He declared he was determined " to discountenance and punish all manner of vice, profaneness and immorality, in all persons of whatever degree or quality . . . and particularly in such as are employed near our royal person." Games of chance were to be forbidden on Sundays and during the times of divine services all chocolate-houses, coffee-houses and taverns were to be closed.

The coffee-houses and the chocolate-houses were the forums of the community and groups of men with the same profession or ideas used them as meeting places where they could exchange their views. There were coffee-houses for poets and writers, for merchants, for lawyers, for traders, for the clergy and the other various sections of the public. At this time there were more than five hundred of them in London, each with its separate group. Coffee-houses were not teetotal and they were ousting the taverns as the centres of discussion.

Coffee was first introduced into England about the middle of the seventeenth century when an English merchant named Edwards brought from Turkey a supply of coffee and a Turkish servant, Pasque Rosée, to prepare it. In his small circle the drink became popular and he decided to open a coffee-house in St. Michael's Alley in Cornhill. Pasque Rosée's Coffee-House as it was named was a tremendous success and the idea caught on. By the end of the century there were hundreds of them all over London and as they prospered some of them became the forerunners of the present-day clubs and other institutions.*

White's Chocolate-House, which was founded in 1693, became " White's " and others followed, Almacks, Brooks's and Boodle's. Naturally gambling played a big part in the activities for the Coffee-Houses were the social centres where one gossiped, listened to scandals, spread rumours, discussed politics and spouted one's convictions. In consequence they represented the opinions of the public. The new King was an improvement on the last, was the coffee-house decision.

At the time Lady Hervey summed up the general attitude when she wrote : " Everyone, I think, seems to be pleased with the whole behaviour of our young king; and indeed so much unaffected good nature and piety appears in all he does or says, that it cannot but endear him to all."

George was determined to comply with his mother's frequent

* " Lloyd's " was started by Edward Lloyd before 1688.

exhortations to " be a king ", but his first speech to Parliament on the 18th of November was not received with enthusiasm. Earl Bute, his mentor and " dear friend ", had drafted the speech and in it the policy of Pitt was spoken of as " the bloody and expensive war ". It was obvious that he intended to pursue a different policy—one of peace, and this attitude made him unpopular.

The Ministry of Pitt and Newcastle had been successful in capturing the bulk of the world's trade, although Pitt's policy had also been expensive.* But now England was more prosperous than she had ever been before.

No doubt George III was sincere in his beliefs for he had become convinced, by the propaganda of Bute and the Princess Dowager, that he had inherited from his grandfather a corrupt and unscrupulous set of Ministers. He lost no time in making changes. Within a few months George Grenville entered the Cabinet, Lord Holderness was dismissed, Bute became Secretary of State, and Pitt was defeated in the Cabinet. Bute was now in power " with the ear of the King ". Bubb Dodington also achieved his ambition for he became Lord Melcombe. It was apparent that the King intended to rule Parliament by appointing his chosen Ministers to the Cabinet. The visions of glory were fading.

The King was unused to power, for he had been kept in the background by his grandfather's hatred of his father. Strangely enough he himself was never known to mention his father's name.

Although George III inherited the sensuality of his grandfather and father, promiscuity did not influence his sense of duty as Sovereign. He had had love affairs before he came to the Throne, but immediately he was proclaimed King he determined to marry at all costs. The choice was a strange one, for the little Princess Charlotte of Mecklenburg-Strelitz was extremely ugly, so much so that even he, with an inherited gross taste in femininity, winced when he first saw her.

The Princess Dowager and Earl Bute were responsible for the choice. When the King expressed his intention of marrying as soon as possible, they had arranged for Colonel David Graeme,

---

* An unprecedented sum of £15,500,000 was voted in 1760, whilst there were 100,000 troops under arms.

an elderly Jacobite and the Earl's nominee, to visit Germany to consider the suitabilities of the Protestant princesses. He was given the list of Anhalt-Bernburg, Brandenburg-Schwedt, Brunswick, Darmstadt, Gotha, and Mecklenburg from which to select a suitable bride. His reasons for the choice of the seventeen-year-old Charlotte Sophia are not known.

2

The principality of Mecklenburg-Strelitz was a typical minor and impoverished German dukedom, about 120 miles long and 30 miles wide, with five small towns, the ducal town being Neu-Strelitz. The revenues were about £15,000 a year which in England was about the income of an unimportant peer.

Charlotte Sophia was the sister of the reigning duke, Adolphus Frederick, who had succeeded to the dukedom in 1751. His mother, the Dowager Duchess, was still the ruling influence although the Duke was married. Thus Charlotte had been brought up to respect both her mother and her brother, and the relationship perhaps offered to Colonel Graeme a similarity to the Princess Dowager and George III in England. The fact that she was small and ugly with a flat nose and a very large mouth did not enter into the reckoning.

Lord Harcourt of Nuneham was appointed Master of the Horse and was sent on a special mission to Strelitz to make the formal proposal. On the 17th of August, 1761, he sent back to England an account of his reception in which he said: " I reached this place on the 14th; on the 15th the treaty was concluded and despatched away to England. *L'affaire, en vérité, n'était pas bien pesée.* This little Court exerted its utmost abilities to make a figure suitable to the occasion, and I can assure you they have acquitted themselves, not only with magnificence and splendour, but with a great deal of good taste and propriety. Our queen that is to be has seen very little of the world, but her good sense, vivacity, and cheerfulness, I daresay, will recommend her to the King and make her the darling of the British nation. She is no regular beauty, but she is of a very pretty size, has a charming complexion, very pretty eyes, and finely made; in short, she is a fine girl."

To reimburse him for his trouble and expenses Earl Harcourt was given the handsome sum of £4,000 by royal warrant.

In the interval between the informal and formal proposals the future bride's mother died, but this event was not allowed to interfere with the marriage plans. An official ceremony took place immediately, Drummond, the British Ambassador, acting as the King's proxy.

He knelt with the Princess and they were symbolically married. The Princess was then laid upon a sofa upon which Drummond placed his foot to indicate the invasion of her bed. The betrothal was celebrated with a magnificent banquet, and Charlotte was addressed as " La Reine ". She was now the Queen of England.

After the banquet a long procession of thirty coaches left Strelitz for Stade, the port on the Elbe, where the royal yacht was waiting. The journey took three days and included a visit to her husband's territory of Hanover where another banquet was held in her honour.

At Stade the English reception committee was waiting for the first sight of their Queen. In the English suite were the beautiful Duchess of Ancaster and the even more beautiful Duchess of Hamilton, and Charlotte stared at them in surprise as she timidly asked—" Are all Englishwomen as beautiful as you are?"

The famous Admiral Anson was in command of the squadron which was to escort the royal yacht to England and to the firing of cannons and ringing of bells they set sail. The weather was stormy, but as the King had arranged his coronation date and was expecting his Queen to take part—they could not wait for the gale to end.

For ten days the ships were tossed about in stormy seas as they battled against the elements and it is recorded that Charlotte acquitted herself well whilst the others were in a constant state of sea-sickness. The two ladies she had brought along to attend to her needs, Schwellenberg and Hagedorn, and the English Duchesses, were unable even to look after themselves.

The ships reached Harwich at three in the afternoon of Monday the 7th of September and Admiral Anson decided it was wiser to land his royal charge at once, instead of continuing up the Thames to Greenwich where an official welcome awaited the

party. They staggered ashore on unsteady legs much the worse
for the stormy voyage.

Early the next day they travelled to London and in the
afternoon cheering crowds met the procession, for practically
every coach in London had been driven out to meet them on the
Essex road and to return with them.

As the carriages swept through cheering London the young
Charlotte was confused by the tumult, the booming of cannon,
the bells and the hectic speed of events. She was even more
confused when the Duchess of Hamilton said, " We shall hardly
have time to dress for the wedding." " The wedding?" queried
the Queen. " Yes, Madam; it is to be at twelve."

At the gate of St. James's she was met by the Duke of York
and escorted into the Palace to be the centre of a hubbub of
noise and strange faces; one of which was her husband's.

In the confusion Charlotte almost knelt to the Duke of Grafton,
who shook his head. She then turned to kneel to the King. He
raised her gently and kissed her hand. The friendly Duchess of
Hamilton smiled at her in sympathy.

" You may laugh," said Charlotte quite seriously, " you have
been married twice, but to me it is no joke !"

After this brief meeting Charlotte was taken to meet the
Princess Dowager and was shown her magnificent trousseau.
Then followed a hasty bustling as she was " fitted " by the dressmakers, for the wedding was to be at nine o'clock, not twelve,
and there was a State dinner before the ceremony.

There was some delay and the procession was not ready to
move towards the Royal Chapel until almost ten o'clock. The
service was performed by the Archbishop of Canterbury and the
Duke of Cumberland gave the bride away.

At eleven o'clock they returned to the drawing-room and sat
down to another banquet which lasted until three in the morning. The customary ceremony of the guests filing through the
royal bedroom to see the married couple in bed was not observed,
at Charlotte's request, and was not revived on future occasions.

An observer, Horace Walpole describes the new Queen as
" not tall, nor a beauty, pale and very thin; but looks sensible
and is genteel. Her hair is darkish and fine; her forehead low,
her nose very well, except the nostrils spreading too wide; her

mouth has the same fault, but her teeth are good. She talks a good deal and her French is tolerable; possesses herself well, is frank, but with great respect to the King." It had been a busy day.

The Coronation took place a fortnight later on the 22nd of September 1761 and it was a muddle of splendour and incompetence. The preparations had not been completed by the appointed time and the chairs of State for the banquet in Westminster Hall had been forgotten, so had the Sword of State. The ceremony was postponed until the afternoon but still no one seemed to be properly instructed in the procedure.

It was certainly a blaze of magnificence but everything seemed to go wrong; the Queen had toothache, the King was bad-tempered because of the muddle, and when the procession entered Westminster Hall after the ceremony the Hall was in darkness and was only lighted as the King entered.* The banquet revealed by the sudden illumination was meagre and disappointing, and a large number of important guests had not been invited including all the Knights of the Bath. To cap it all, Lord Talbot, the High Steward responsible for the banquet arrangements, entered the Hall on his horse as part of the opening ceremony, but he came in backwards. The horse had been trained to withdraw in this manner, but at the vital moment it wheeled round and backed up to the table despite the frantic efforts of Lord Talbot to pull its head round.

The critical eye of Horace Walpole noted it all : " The multitudes, balconies, guards and processions made Palace-Yard the liveliest spectacle in the world; the Hall was the most glorious. The blaze of lights, the richness and variety of habits, the ceremonial, the benches of peers and peeresses, frequent and full, was as awful as a pageant can be; and yet for the King's sake and my own I never wish to see another; nor am impatient to have my Lord Effingham's promise fulfilled.† The King complained that so few precedents were kept for their proceedings . . . Well it was all delightful, but not half so charming as being over. The gabble one heard about it for six weeks before, and

---

* Heidegger's system of lighting was used.
† Lord Effingham, the deputy Earl Marshall, admitted to the King that there had been great neglect but said he had taken care to ensure that the *next coronation* would be better.

the fatigue of the day, could not be well compensated by a mere puppet show; for puppet show it was, though it cost a million."

A notable absentee at the Westminster Hall banquet was William Pitt. His defeat had brought to a halt his brilliant political career. In October 1761 he resigned. He was then an ailing fifty-two.

3

In accordance with custom the King and Queen made a state visit to the City on Lord Mayor's Day and watched the procession from the usual vantage point—the house of Quaker Barclay in Cheapside opposite Bow Church. One of the daughters of the Barclay family left an account of the occasion:

"As the royal family came, they were conducted into one of the counting-houses which was transformed into a very pretty parlour for that purpose. A platform was raised in the street, on which, their Majesties alighted, my brothers spread a carpet; and as soon as they entered the procession began . . . After the royal pair had shown themselves to the populace for a few moments from the balcony, we were all introduced; and you may believe at that juncture we felt no small palpitations.

"His Majesty met us at the door, which was a condescension we did not expect; at which place he saluted us with great politeness; and advancing to the upper end of the room, we performed the ceremony of kissing the Queen's hand, at the sight of whom we were all in raptures, not only from the brilliancy of her appearance, which was pleasing beyond description; but being throughout her whole person possessed of that inexpressible something that is beyond a set of features, and equally claims our attention. To be sure, she has not a fine face, but a most agreeable countenance, and is vastly genteel, with an air, notwithstanding her being a little woman, truly majestic." She was apparently in two minds about her opinion of royalty for she said that the King's brother noticed her daughter: "her sweet face made such an impression on the Duke of York, that I rejoiced she was only five instead of fifteen."

The Lord Mayor's Day was on the 8th of December and Pitt's resignation was still rankling in the public mind. It was made evident to the King that his popularity was waning for he was treated with indifference and a few hisses, whilst Pitt, taking part in the procession, was cheered wildly as soon as he appeared and the crowd surged round his carriage. When the court favourite, Lord Bute, was sighted the mob pelted him with refuse and stones and only his bodyguard of pugilists prevented his being dragged from his coach.

Even in the Guildhall the attention paid to Pitt was most marked although it was noted that the royal pair behaved with commendable dignity and amiability. Despite her unattractive appearance Charlotte made a favourable impression on the people she met but the crowd were obviously disappointed and shouted jeering remarks about her face.

After the first few weeks of gaiety, attending dinners, balls, the theatre and the opera they settled down to a quiet life. They were a simple pair and their tastes and habits were mild ones. Their court was dull but it was certainly more virtuous than those of George's forefathers; and they were faithful to each other. Their lives followed a set pattern of punctuality. Day after day the routine was the same; at the same hours the King had his dinner, his evening concert, his backgammon; whilst the rest of the court yawned, bored by the prosaic time-table.

Charlotte spent her leisure time in reading, embroidering, learning music, and generally improving her education and English. Unfortunately her husband and his mother the Princess-Dowager treated her as a child and she was not allowed to mix freely with the ladies of the court. Madame Schwellenberg, who knew little of English ways, was her constant companion and acted almost like a governess to the seventeen-year-old Queen.

The young royal couple lived in a modest way. Their household was large and was burdened with sinecures inherited from George I and George II, when the Minsters had used the royal household as a means of rewarding their supporters. The Whig Ministers were against economies in this direction and the King was forced to reduce his own personal expenses. Fortunately his tastes were simple, and also he liked to be surrounded by paid " friends ". As time went on however he filled the vacancies with servants of the middle-class to which he always felt a leaning, for he disliked the nobility as a class.

George III was now becoming unpopular on all sides. It was well-known that he was completely under the domination of his mother and her influence was resented by rich and poor alike.

The Princess-Dowager and her favourite Bute were the subject of the ribald jokes of the day, bawdy ballads told of the relationship and the caricaturists postured them in suggestive cartoons. But the criticisms went beyond indecent jokes for Bute was openly insulted whenever the mob saw him. His chair was attacked and the symbols of the association, a jackboot and a petticoat, were burnt in public after being used as banners by the mob.

In January 1762 there was an outbreak of rioting when Newcastle resigned and Bute stepped into his place. He was a petticoat Prime Minister for the Princess-Dowager was responsible for his political elevation.

Bute was disliked because he was a Scot, because he was believed to be the Princess-Dowager's lover and because he was vain and incompetent. He was not a schemer and not a villain but he had clever and more unscrupulous men around him. The Paymaster, Henry Fox, and the Chancellor of the Exchequer, Sir Francis Dashwood, launched the Government into a policy of wholesale bribery and corruption. They threw out the honest men and replaced them with their own kind. The rest they blackmailed or threatened with dismissal into supporting the King and thus ensuring the safety of their own positions. The King was aware of their malpractices and sometimes expressed regret at the " necessity ", as he called it, " of having to employ such men."

Behind the political intrigues was the Princess-Dowager but her infatuation for Bute appears to have been the motive rather than personal ambition. She was in receipt of £64,000 a year and spent little, nor did she give it away; certainly very little was spent on her children. Bute on the other hand suddenly became wealthy and began to live in fantastic style, due gossip said, to the generosity of his mistress, " the wanton widow."

The Princess-Dowager wielded a power far greater than her abilities justified but, at least, she had one talent and that was in controlling her pious and backward son. She considered George to be stupid but well-intentioned, as indeed he was, and she ruled his life. He was her only amenable son, for his brothers were wild, unruly profligates.

The poor, undesirable Charlotte was as tractable as her husband and every evening the young pair visited his mother at Carlton House as in duty bound and the quiescent young Queen was " shut up in a room alone for hours " whilst the other three held their discussions. She was made to realize that she was but a cipher in the royal family of England.

The Princess-Dowager was not fond of Charlotte and it was said that she was responsible for an upset in the royal household. She told the King that reports had reached her of wranglings amongst the court staff which were due to the unfair distribution of favours by Madame Schwellenberg. George gave orders that she was to be dismissed and sent back to Germany.

Queen Charlotte was very distressed when she heard that she was to lose her friend and companion, and in the presence of the Princess-Dowager she asked her husband to change his decision. George agreed that she should remain but censured his wife about her familiarity with Schwellenbreg. It is said that the Princess-Dowager gloated over the incident and " continued cold and distant to her daughter-in-law."

The King's brothers, Edward, William, Henry and Frederick, were in 1762 aged respectively twenty-three, twenty, eighteen and twelve. They were an unruly, boisterous brood quite different in character to the dutiful George. Their aunt, Princess Emily, said of them that they were " the best natured young asses in the world." Princess Emily's opinion was certainly tempered with kindness for they were coarse, ignorant and selfish; traits in their characters that became more marked as they grew to manhood; apart from Frederick the youngest who died when he was fifteen.

The eldest of the family was Augusta, a year older than George, a meddlesome and ambitious young woman; whilst Caroline the youngest member of the family was a pretty child of eleven.

The most sensible member was the King's uncle the Duke of Cumberland (whom George II had so dearly wished to be his successor) but he was virtually ignored by the rest of the family and took no part in royal affairs. George III had been indoctrinated with dislike and suspicion of his uncle Cumberland by the Princess-Dowager and it was a barrier that had grown stronger with the years. When George was a boy his uncle had tried to amuse him by showing him his armoury at Windsor. When he took down a sword the boy had recoiled in fear and the Duke had said bitterly : " What can they have told the boy about me?" To her death the Princess-Dowager hated him, and she was the dominant force in the royal family.

George III and his Queen had little in common with his brothers and were suspicious of them. They were treated as subjects (the front rank of course) for the King would not allow any familiarity to affect the dignity of the crown.

They took their royal duties seriously, this young King and his Queen. He studied and persevered with his limited brain-power to learn the rudiments of geography, the Army List, and all the items of the many uniforms, the Court etiquette, and the details of the duties of every member of his court and household staff. His efforts were rewarded and he earned the reputation of being an authority on family histories, genealogies of the gentry, and military uniforms. For her part, Charlotte bore him fifteen children to ensure the succession.*

4

Prince George was born on August 12th 1762 and the young father fairly bubbled with delight. The christening ceremony of the heir to the throne was appropriately magnificent for it was the first since the days of Charles I.

When the baby was a fortnight old privileged visitors were given the honour of seeing him in his cradle which had a fence round it to prevent them from coming too near. Refreshments and wine were provided and the wine bill alone was £40 a day; which was an omen for the prodigious quantities the Prince was to consume in later life.

* George, Prince of Wales (1762-1830), Frederick, Duke of York (1763-1827), William, Duke of Clarence (1765-1837), Edward, Duke of Kent (1767-1820), Ernest, Duke of Cumberland (1771-1851), Augustus, Duke of Sussex (1773-1843), Adolphus, Duke of Cambridge (1774-1850), Octavius (1779-1783), Alfred (1780-1782), Charlotte (1766-1828), Augusta 1768-1840), Elizabeth (1770-1840), Mary (1776-1857), Sophia (1777-1848), Amelia (1783-1810).

The domestic life of the King and Queen was dull and un-eventful. Parties were given at St. James' Palace twice a week when music was the usual entertainment. The King's private band performed and the proceedings were very rigid and formal, in marked contrast to the previous reigns. Their country home was the old palace at Richmond.

George did not like the cramped quarters of St. James's and bought an old brick mansion which stood at the end of the Mall. It was the palace of the Dukes of Buckingham and was in the style of Marlborough House, linked by colonnades to two pavi-lions. He purchased it from Sir Charles Sheffield for £21,000 and made only a few alterations, the chief one being a new main staircase.

Buckingham House as it was called became known as the " Queen's House " and everything connected with it was known as " the Queen's ". This was to bring the running of the house under their personal control and to avoid the restrictions which would have been automatic if the costs had been taken from the Civil List.

About this time the King appealed to Parliament to make pro-vision for his wife, who he said was " eminently distinguished by every virtue and amiable consideration." The handsome jointure of £100,000 a year with two palaces was settled upon her. Somerset House was one being the ancient dower-house of Eng-lish Queens but it was in a dilapidated condition. The house at Kew with its 120 acres of beautiful gardens was bought from a Mr. G. Molyneux, who had been a secretary to George II, and in these residences for the next ten years the King and Queen with their children lived a life of quiet domesticity.

The State receptions were held in London and Society was not invited to their country homes. George was happiest when play-ing the part of the country squire, mixing freely and chatting with the countryfolk, apparently with more thought for pigs than politics. Nevertheless he was intensely interested in affairs of State, being obsessed with his royal duties and although politic-ally obtuse he persisted in interfering in government matters. He was not intelligent and often he exhibited the unwavering obstinacy of stupidity.

His method of interference in government affairs was by indirect influence, for the Cabinet system was now too firmly rooted to be disturbed by royal prerogative. He introduced into the House of Commons a group of his sycophants to vote as he decreed. They became known as " the King's Friends " and his policy was not only almost catastrophic to the nation's welfare but also greatly disturbing to his own mental equilibrium.

The rumblings of revolt were first heard in June 1762 when John Wilkes, the Member for Aylesbury, jumped into the political arena by launching a newspaper called *The North Briton* in which he criticized the policy of the Government.

Wilkes was a rumbustious fellow, ugly to a point of being grotesque, squinting, leering and demoniacal; a rake-hell who feared no one; a laughing, exhulting, devil-may-care villain, with principles and a savage turn of phrase to back them up.

The Peace of Paris had been concluded in February 1763 and Wilkes attacked the King and the Peace with : " It is indeed the Peace of God, for it passeth all understanding." His April issue of *The North Briton,* Number 45, shocked the King and could not be ignored.

On the 29th of April Wilkes was arrested on a charge of seditious libel and imprisoned in the Tower. But he was not to be subdued. He asserted that he had been wrongfully arrested and claimed damages from Halifax, the Secretary of State. By now he had captured the public imagination and when Chief Justice Pratt decided in his favour and awarded damages against Halifax, the slogan " Wilkes and Liberty " ran like a fire throughout the country.

In the face of mass hysteria Bute resigned and George Grenville was appointed in his place. George was nearly demented by the success of Wilkes and the mere mention of his name was sufficient to drive him into a blind rage. The " King's Friends " were set like hounds on a stag to bring Wilkes down.

The second prosecution was based on some papers which had been found during the search of Wilkes's house at the time of his arrest. Among them was a reprint of No. 45 and an obscene poem called *An Essay on Woman,* which was a parody based on Pope's *Essay on Man* and the hymn *Veni Creator Spiritus.* A copy of the poem and the No. 45 were handed to the Secretary of the Treasury at a time when Wilkes was in France visiting his daughter at school. When he returned to England he faced an attack in both Houses.

The charge of sedition was revived and No. 45 of *The North Briton* was declared to be indeed a seditious libel, despite a spirited defence by Wilkes. In the House of Lords the *Essay on Woman* was voted a blasphemous libel. The tide was turning against Wilkes. But there was worse to come, for Wilkes had been called " a cowardly, scandalous and malignant scoundrel " by Samuel Martin, the Member for Camelford and a duel with pistols resulted. Wilkes was wounded in the side but even when he believed he was dying he acted magnanimously. He urged Martin to escape and promised to keep the duel a secret to avoid his incrimination.

In December when he was well again he fled to France. Shortly afterwards in 1764 he was declared an outlaw and expelled from the House of Commons.

The King appeared to have won, but public opinion was still on the side of Wilkes and the symbol of liberty " 45 " was chalked everywhere stirring the mob to rioting while the petti-coat and jackboot were again being burnt in the streets.

The hostility of the mob to his mother, to Bute, and to him-self, the strain of battling with Wilkes and the over-taxing of his brain with matters of State all contributed to the King's bout of insanity in February 1765 when he was twenty-seven. The real nature of his illness was kept secret and as he was suffering from a cold at the time it was rumoured that he had consump-tion, the disease which had killed a brother and a sister. But in the palace the truth could not be hidden for his strange actions left no doubt but that his mind was affected. During a short period of sanity George himself brought up the question of a regency, and the feeling of the House of Lords was demonstrated when they omitted the name of the Princess-Dowager. The Queen was named as Regent although the question was raised as to whether she had been naturalized. However the King re-covered before the Bill was presented.

George now began to spend money lavishly for political pur-poses (one estimate of the amount involved was £200,000 in a year) and began to purge the Opposition element. There would not be another Wilkes. But a far greater problem than Wilkes was gradually taking shape: the unrest in the American colonies.

In March 1764 Grenville had attacked the liberty of the British colonies in America by proposing taxation. By February 1765 he had formulated his plan. It was to be the Stamp Act, which required a duty to be paid to the English revenues (it was calculated the revenue involved would be £60,000 a year) on all legal documents drawn up in America.

It was passed almost without comment, but in America it created a wave of bitter antagonism; it was an infringement of liberty and there was widespread rioting.

The Opposition pounced on the colonial uproar, linked it with the fresh Wilkes demonstrations and attacked Grenville, the Minister responsible for the mishandling of both problems. He was unable to stem the flood of criticism and in May he asked to be allowed to resign. George was not ready for this sudden turn of events and insisted that Grenville and his chief Ministers should remain in office.

In the meanwhile the King surreptitiously appealed to Pitt to return as the one man capable of sorting out the tangle. Pitt refused and after seven weeks of political wavering George called in another Whig, the Marquis of Rockingham, a handsome, egotistical man of thirty-five, to form a Ministry.

Almost immediately the new Ministry became involved in debates on the American question. Pitt, a sick man, returned to speak in the House when with biting, forceful eloquence he denounced the Stamp Act and stirred the members to cheers. The Stamp Act was repealed. In America the colonists were jubilant and a statue was erected to Pitt in New York. They also erected a statue of gilded lead to George III; which was pulled down in 1776 and ironically was later melted into bullets for use against his soldiers.

The Government was floundering in a sea of troubles and the King once again turned to Pitt for help. In July 1766, he at last persuaded the recalcitrant Pitt to become Lord Privy Seal as the Earl of Chatham and a Ministry was formed by the new Earl and the Duke of Grafton. But Chatham was no longer capable of holding office. His mind had crossed the border of reason and he was insane.

Grafton was spending most of his time with his mistress Nancy

Parsons and the strong man of the Ministry was now Charles Townshend,* the Chancellor of the Exchequer. He was a clever politician but he was also a sycophant, and realizing the bitter disappointment of the King at the repeal of the Stamp Act he curried favour by imposing fresh duties on the American colonies.

The new taxes on such things as paper, paint, glass and tea caused violent indignation and widespread riots in America. The customs officials were attacked and the collection of the duties was fraught with difficulties. Inevitably this latest injustice had repercussions in England where it was regarded by the Wilkites as another attack upon the liberty of the subjects.

The voice of Edmund Burke joined the tumult shouting in the cause of liberty : " The people of the colonies are descendants of Englishmen. England, Sir, which I still hope respects, and formerly adored, her freedom. The colonists emigrated from you when this part of your character was most predominant, and they took this bias and direction the moment they parted from your hands. They are therefore not only devoted to liberty, but liberty according to English ideas, and on English principles. The temper and character which prevail in our colonies are, I am afraid, unalterable by any human art. We cannot, I fear, falsify the pedigree of this fierce people and persuade them they are not sprung from a nation in whose veins the blood of freedom circulates."

Townshend did not live to see the full extent of his folly for he died in September 1767 and Grafton began to seek a successor from among his reluctant Ministers. Lord North was chosen but he was hesitant and although he was appointed to the Exchequer he did not in fact take office until twelve months later.

Suddenly, to add to the King's trouble and frustration his *bête noire* the squinting rebel Wilkes came back to London. " Wilkes and Liberty " was again the cry and the mob went wild at the return of their demigod. They did not have to wait long for action.

With audacious impudence Wilkes offered himself as a Parliamentary candidate in the City. He was defeated but almost immediately he became a candidate in the Middlesex Election at Brentford.

* A grandson of Walpole's colleague.

The mob were with him to a man and marched through London shouting their support. Soon they were out of control and were rioting in the streets, smashing windows, dragging people from coaches, overturning sedan-chairs and attacking everyone who did not declare for Wilkes.

Wilkes was elected and the jubilant mob again stormed through London. Then, there were constables only in the City of London and as they were but few they avoided the path of the mob. The King was furious and declared that he hoped the rioters would attack Buckingham House so that he himself with drawn sword could lead his troops to battle with them.

But Wilkes himself was not to be so easily removed. He had posed a problem. He had been expelled from the House by the King but now he had been made a Member of Parliament by the electorate.

On the 27th of April 1768 he was arrested but as he was being taken to the prison at Southwark the mob surrounded the coach, released the horses and began to drag it back to the City. But Wilkes intended to stand his trial. He dispersed the crowd and gave himself up at the prison. On the 7th of May he appeared before Lord Mansfield but his case was adjourned.

Three days later his restive supporters stormed the gates of the prison. The troops were called out to disperse the mob and in doing so they killed seven people, including two women. The King signified his appreciation of the vigorous manner in which order had been maintained and the Secretary of War guaranteed indemnity for the troops.

When the case came up again on the 8th of June Lord Mansfield decreed that the outlawry was illegal. Wilkes was not released however and on the 18th of June he was again tried. This time he was sentenced to one year's imprisonment on each of two charges, the Number 45 of *The North Briton* and the *Essay on Woman*, with a fine of £500 on each count. The sentences were to run consecutively and he was to find £2,000 as security for good behaviour for seven years. It seemed the end of Wilkes, but he was quite unperturbed by the sentence, picking his teeth in the dock and smiling to his friends as he was led away.

From his cell Wilkes continued his campaign by writing letters, instigating an action for wrongful imprisonment, and bombard-

ing the House of Lords and the House of Commons with mani-
festoes and petitions. His sentence was confirmed by the Lords
and his expulsion was voted on the 4th of February after four
days of debate.

Not to be outdone Wilkes again offered to stand for Middlesex
and again he was returned. The government substituted a man
named Dingley but he withdrew in face of the violent hostility
shown towards him. Yet àgain Wilkes offered himself and was
returned unopposed. This Election was declared void. But now
the Wilkes affair had spread far beyond London. It had become
one of national importance and his supporters were almost an
additional party; the party of the mob. Throughout the country
there were demonstrations, petitions and riots. The government
was in danger but still George persisted in his blind determination to liquidate Wilkes.

A Colonel Luttrell was nominated as a candidate for the
Middlesex vacancy but Wilkes again won the day by a sweeping
majority. The matter was now ludicrous since the House of
Commons on the instructions of the King declared Wilkes to be
ineligible and Luttrell was elected. Wilkes was now receiving as
much public attention as the American dispute.

The voters of Middlesex were staunchly behind Wilkes, their
freedom was in danger. They sent a petition accusing the Government of violating the Habeas Corpus Act, of murder, of the
squandering of public money in the fight against their candidate,
and wholesale corruption. Soon other counties were joining in the
fight and the Government was facing open national revolt. The
King was being attacked on all sides.

A new force had joined the campaign against the King and
the Government; an anonymous letter writer who signed himself " Junius ". The letters first appeared in the *Public Advertiser*
and were widely taken up by other journals. They form the
most brilliantly destructive attack on a Government in the literature of politics. They were elegantly written, acidly accurate, and
invariably irrefutable. From the date the first letter appeared
a tremendous interest was aroused in the identity of the unknown
critic. The writer obviously possessed an intimate and precise
knowledge of people, politics, and events. Only an outstanding
brain could have conceived letters containing such concise sum-

maries of the political situation; and the language in which they were couched restricted to a few the number of people capable of writing such effective prose.*

The audacious critic published a letter on the 19th of December 1769 in which he assembled a shattering attack on the King himself and it was the climax of the campaign in the Press. On the 27th of January 1770 Grafton resigned and the Government fell.

Three days later Lord North became Prime Minister, although nominally he was First Lord of the Treasury. He was rather an obvious choice for although only thirty-eight he was already obese and in features he might have been a Hanoverian. In fact malicious rumours had already suggested that he was the result of an association between Frederick, the late Prince of Wales, and a member of the Earl of Guilford's family. He had protruding eyes, a receding chin and a manner of speaking as though he had a plum in his mouth.

Despite his uninspiring appearance he was popular in the House because of his inoffensive mediocrity. He could be witty and had a certain skill in debate, but above all he was honest and staunchly loyal to the King. After a succession of turbulent Prime Ministers George found the easy-going, very compliant North quite a pleasant relief. Now he would be able to rule as he believed a king should rule; without hindrance or criticism. North was his ideal Minister. But had George known of the troubles that lay ahead he would not have been as optimistic.

5

During the few years prior to this time there had been a harvesting of death in the royal family and although his mother was the only member for whom George III felt any affection the succession of deaths added to the shadows already flitting across the twilight mind of the King.

In 1765, his uncle the Duke of Cumberland died aged forty-four and in the same year his youngest brother aged fifteen also

---

* Dr. Johnson guessed they were written by Edmund Burke but the identity of " Junius " was never revealed. Nowadays he is usually supposed to have been Sir Philip Francis, the opponent of Warren Hastings.

died. In 1767, another brother Edward Augustus the Duke of York died at the age of twenty-eight, and in 1768, his sister Louisa Anne aged nineteen also died.

Other family troubles added to the burden of the King. When the Duke of Cumberland died in 1765 the title had passed to Henry Frederick and now in 1770 the young twenty-five year old Duke became involved in a scandalous divorce case. He had been having a passionate love affair with Lady Grosvenor, a young and beautiful woman, until the irate husband learnt of the association and cited him as co-respondent.

The case was heard in March 1770 and the Duke's unrestrained and completely compromising letters to Lady Grosvenor caused great amusement in court.

Grosvenor had his divorce and Cumberland had £10,000 damages awarded against him. George III was furious that for the first time a prince of the blood had appeared in a divorce court. The scandal shocked the country, but a few months later Cumberland again enraged the King by marrying in secret a very attractive widow, Mrs. Anne Horton, who was a sister of Colonel Luttrell of the Wilkes's affair. She was vulgar in manner and liberal with her favours. The Duke drove to St. James's Palace with a notice of the wedding to show to his brother. The King ordered Cumberland abroad immediately and published in the *London Gazette* a notice " that such persons who wait upon the Duke and the new Duchess would no longer be received at Court."

As a result of this affair George decided on the introduction of the Royal Marriage Bill. On February 20th 1772 Lord North stated in the House of Commons that the King desired a new law to guard the descendants of his late Majesty King George II. In March 1772 the Bill became law and it stipulated that none of the Royal family might marry under the age of twenty-five without the consent of the Sovereign. Six months later the Duke of Gloucester in sympathy with his brother Cumberland, admitted that he also had been secretly married six years before to Lady Waldegrave, the illegitimate daughter of Sir Edward Walpole. Her mother was a milliner. Gloucester, like his brother Cumberland, was also banished from Court.

In the meanwhile fate had dealt the Royal family two further blows. The King's youngest sister Caroline Matilda had been married five years earlier when she was fifteen to King Christian of Denmark. His chief occupation was the pursuit of women and in retaliation Caroline began to have a love affair with Struensee the King's Prime Minister. Struensee had been a court physician until raised to power by the King. He was young and extremely handsome and there had even been rumours of an unnatural association between King Christian and his Prime Minister.

Caroline made no secret of her love affair with Struensee and scandalized the people of Copenhagen by her conduct. Soon there was a public outcry and Struensee and his friend Brandt, who had also been involved, were arrested in January 1772 and charged with high treason and adultery. Caroline was also charged.

In April the two men were executed in the terrible manner prescribed by the Danish courts whilst Caroline, who would have suffered a similar fate but for a strong request for mercy from England, was imprisoned in the fateful castle of Zell, where three years later she died, aged twenty-three.

The news of her youngest daughter's troubles in Copenhagen was given to the Princess-Dowager at the end of January. She was not in a fit state to receive bad news. She was dying. For a long time she had been suffering from a throat infection but had borne the pain with stoicism. It was a cancer and on the evening before her death on the 8th of February 1772 she exhorted her eldest son in her croaking voice, as she had done many times before, " George, be a king!" She was fifty-two. George was doing his best to obey his mother's instruction but he was finding the strain of his duties extremely disturbing.

The death of the Princess-Dowager was greeted with delight by the people and they cheered her funeral procession. At the Abbey the mob rioted and tore down the black drapings. It was an ignominious burial sadly in keeping with public opinion for almost since she arrived in England the Princess had been hated and insulted. She had never lived down the scandal of Bute. Indeed the tale had grown with the telling and there was a fresh outbreak of criticism when it was known that she had not made a will and had not left any money. Her income had been £64,000 a year and as she had lived in an unpretentious style it had been presumed that she would leave three or four hundred thousand pounds. The finger of gossip pointed at once to the richly furnished houses and extensive estates of the luxury-loving Bute. It was a likely conjecture.

She had been the major influence in the King's life, certainly until 1763 when her power waned as George, encouraged by marriage and fatherhood, began to assert himself. Her stupidity made her dangerous for once she was pointed in a certain direction she seemed unable to change her course and she never had the best advice. She did much that was malicious and very little that was good. Always she had lived in the shadow of hatred and a few months before her death, when she was already seriously ill, two carts containing effigies of the Princess-Dowager and Bute had been dragged by the mob to Tower Hill. Here with due ceremony they had been beheaded and the effigies thrown onto a bonfire.

Since 1770 the King had also been receiving his share of abuse and his Government was under fire. Burke with biting phrases was attacking the power of the Throne and criticizing the mismanagement of American affairs. " Junius " had resumed his campaign in the Press which in turn led to retaliation by the Government and the freedom of the Press was in danger.

A messenger was sent to the City to arrest one of the printers. The City of London was ready for him and the messenger himself was arrested.

The man who had inspired the City to resist the attack on the Press was the astonishing John Wilkes, the arch-propagandist of liberty. He was now a Sheriff of London. The messenger was taken to the Mansion House where the Lord Mayor, Wilkes, and Alderman Oliver were sitting on the Bench.

Resolutely they defied the King and his Government by refusing to release the messenger. Instead they released the printer and charged the messenger with assault.

This open defiance forced the King to take punitive action. He gave orders for the Lord Mayor and Oliver to be taken to the Tower. With Wilkes he was more wary and summoned him to appear at the Bar of the House; but the incorrigible Wilkes defied the King by refusing to attend.

117

Again Wilkes had captured the public imagination; and there was a general outcry of indignation. The King's carriage was followed by a jeering, shouting mob and Lord North's carriage was attacked and torn to pieces on his way to Parliament. North was only rescued by his friends after a battle with the mob. In the face of this bitter antagonism it was considered unwise to press the charges against the Lord Mayor and Oliver. A few days later they were released, and in a futile attempt to save the dignity of the Government Wilkes was summoned to appear at the Bar of the House at a time when there was no sitting. The prosecution was dropped and the mob celebrated. Their hero had won again. A few years later he crowned his success by becoming Lord Mayor of London, but much was to happen before then and much greater issues were to confront the King and his Prime Minister.

6

For years the thirteen American colonies had been a problem. George III with his despotic belief in the power of the Crown viewed the Americans patronizingly as insurgent rebels. He and his Ministers failed completely to understand the situation. They did not appreciate the potentialities of this far-away land, nor did they realize the growing spirit of independence among the colonists, separated by the Atlantic from the mother country. America was the land of the underprivileged and Hector St. John de Crèvecoeur wrote : " The rich stay in Europe; it is only the middling and poor that emigrate." That America was regarded in England as a place without hope is evident for during the eighteenth century about 40,000 British convicts were shipped there as punishment. But the spirit of survival in man urged the emigrants and the transplanted to build their own way of life with hopes for the future. They were ceasing to be British and were becoming American.

The population was widely dispersed since each man claimed his own land and when the French were driven from the American continent vast areas were opened up to the British colonists. But the wide dispersal hampered social and educational development; roads were almost non-existent and there were only four towns of consequence, Philadelphia, the " capital " city, Boston with 3,000 houses, New York with 16,000 inhabitants, and Charleston, the city of the South. In these cities the new merchant class of America had their being. The duties imposed by Townshend in London were having a detrimental effect on their commercial existence. Bankruptcies were increasing owing mainly to the post-war slump, but the colonists attributed the numerous business failures to the enforcement of the new Acts and the ruling that all American exports to Europe must first be cleared through British ports was adding to the costs. A typical example was the trade in wines with Portuguese Madeira. The colonists had paid for the wine imports by supplying barrel staves to make the casks. Under the new ruling they had to pay cash to the British merchants for the wines and in consequence lost the trade in barrel staves. The colonists were not concerned with the fact that the Seven Years War had left Britain with a National Debt of more than £125,000,000 and that the Ministers of George III were faced with the problem of how to wipe out this huge debt.

In England it was considered quite reasonable that as the colonies had benefitted by the defeat of the French they should be forced to contribute towards the cost. In addition there was a large force of British regular troops garrisoned in America to prevent the French from regaining their lost territories, and it seemed logical also that the colonists should help to pay for the upkeep of these British forces. The enforcement of duties on a growing list of items together with restrictions to benefit British trade seemed to be the answer. A storm of resentment against the restrictions was brewing and the individual colonies were joining together in common protest.

The repeal of the Stamp Act did little to quieten the growing unrest for the right to tax the colonies still remained and in March 1770 a mob of rioters attacked a British sentry in Boston. In the confusion a misunderstood order caused the troops to fire into the crowd killing four of the rioters and the incident was called " the Boston Massacre ".

In June 1772 a warship H.M.S. *Gaspee* ran aground whilst on preventive duty against smugglers. The ship was boarded by a mob of irate " Sons of Liberty ", set on fire and gutted to the water-line. A Commission of Enquiry was set up but owing to lack of evidence the attackers were never discovered.

A boycott was declared on British goods, and as the colonists bought virtually all their manufactured goods from England the welfare of British trade was threatened. The repercussions were felt in London and North, in an attempt to end the revolt, repealed all the duties except the insignificant duty on tea. The King had insisted that this one should remain as a symbol of his authority over the unruly Americans.

The East India Company was in danger of bankruptcy and in 1773 Parliament passed the Tea Act, which granted the Company the monopoly of the trade in tea to America. By trading direct with America the East India Company eliminated the merchants in England, and the tea could be sold at half the previous price, which was less than the price asked by the American smugglers. But the tax was still in force, a jibe which united the thirteen colonies in their hatred against British autocracy. On the 16th of December 1773 three of the Company's ships carrying cargoes of tea were waiting to be off-loaded in Boston harbour. Gangs of irate colonists, disguised as redskins with painted faces, went aboard the ships and threw 342 chests of the " hate-provoking STUFF " into the sea.*

This act of defiance, symbolic in character and carried out without bloodshed, was described in England as " the most wanton and unprovoked insult to the civil power that is recorded in history." The example set at Boston was followed by similar happenings at New York, Philadelphia and Charleston. A large section of the colonists did not side with the illegal action of the Bostonians and at this stage a more understanding attitude in London could easily have changed the whole course of events. As it was, George III highly indignant at the defiance of authority was in no mood for conciliation. He said he was determined to give the Americans " a few bloody noses to remind them of their duty ". First the rebels must be brought to heel; then, and only then, could the question of the taxes be discussed.

Lord North, normally passive by nature, was stirred by royal example to simulate indignation, for he and his Ministers believed that only a token disciplinary action would be necessary. On

* The Boston Tea Party.

the 23rd of March 1774 he announced the punishment; the port of Boston would be closed and instead Salem, twenty miles along the coast, would be used, with the Customs at the nearby port of Marblehead. This change would stay in force until the cost of the tea and the accrued duties had been paid by the Bostonians.

The plan was criticized in the House, notably by Burke, General Conway, and a young politician Charles James Fox, but in May the Boston Port Act became law. It was to be enforced by additional troops in Boston and the Royal Navy in the harbour. A protest from Americans in London against the sending of troops to Boston was ignored and the fatal step was taken. In addition a new Act was introduced which ruled that any Crown official charged with a capital offence whilst collecting revenues or quelling a riot must be sent to England for trial. This was to avoid conviction by the Colonial Bench, for the English Court would almost certainly grant an acquittal, and it was regarded by the colonists as a *carte blanche* for the officials to use violence.

In July 1774 yet another Act was passed, the Quebec Act, which was a bribe to obtain the support of Canada. The French Canadians had their rights restored and it also established the security of the Roman Catholic religion. To the inhabitants of the thirteen colonies it was another twist of the knife and posters appeared urging the assassination of George III.

The Boston Port Act was now no longer only the concern of Boston for the news was spreading to other centres, carried by men such as Paul Revere who rode to Philadelphia, and the word " Independence " was on everyone's lips. It was decided by the colonists that a Congress should be held to consolidate the views of the various colonies and to decide the common action to be taken. In September 1774 the First Continental Congress was held in Philadelphia. It was attended by delegates from all the colonies except Georgia and on the 17th of October the Declaration of Rights was adopted stipulating " free and exclusive power of legislation ". A week later a complete boycott was declared on British goods.

Although the gauntlet had been thrown down there was still time for reason to prevail, for in November the King received a petition from the Congress asking for the blockade on Boston to be lifted and for the Act concerning Crown officials charged with a capital offence to be rescinded. The petition ended with the words " the bare recital of these Acts must, we presume, justify the loyal subjects who fly to the foot of his throne and implore his clemency." But despite this conciliatory attitude the King refused to consider the petition until they had agreed to submit to his despotic authority. He believed he had triumphed for Boston was bulging with 4,000 British troops (nearly a quarter of the population) and the harbour was like a cornfield with the masts of the Royal Navy, all under the command of capable Admiral Samuel Graves. Boston would be starved into submission.

The plight of the Bostonians was desperate for there was no work to earn food and the troops were causing a strain on available food stocks by the Quartering Act which gave a billeting officer the right to demand food and lodging for the soldiery. But to combat the hardship the other colonies rallied to the cause and carts with provisions lumbered into the town after dark. In this atmosphere of " hide and seek " the tension mounted daily and Gage (as General Gage) became the civil as well as military governor of Boston.

To keep up the morale of his troops Gage sent them out on route marches when they were often amused to see local militia drilling in the fields. But Gage himself was not amused when he learnt of surprise raids and thefts of arms, field-pieces and ammunition from his gun-sheds. His anger would have turned to trepidation had he known that nearly forty thousand men up and down the country were in training to mobilize against the British Forces and every route march of his red-coated troops now stirred greater preparedness, for they were seeking the hidden caches of arms.

General Gage was in a difficult position. His orders were to enforce the Acts of Parliament but the situation in Boston presented a problem. He appeared to be unable to decide what steps to take to achieve his objective. It might well be that he had formulated a plan, for the news that he was assembling a task force was carried by Paul Revere to Lexington which was close to Concord, where a Congress was being held. Fighting broke out at Lexington on the 19th of April 1775 and the colonists were apparently aware of the impending attack.

A brigade of British troops numbering about seven hundred were sent out on a manœuvre under the command of Colonel Francis Smith of the Lincolnshires with Major John Pitcairn of the Royal Marines as Second-in-Command. As they drew near to Lexington an advance party reported a concentration of the militia. Major Pitcairn with the intention of disarming the militia without the use of force gave instructions to his men that they must not fire without orders. A shot was fired (Pitcairn reported that the shot came from an American) and the English troops fired a volley in reply, killing eight men. The column then marched on the Concord where they destroyed the storage dumps which were their original objective. On the way back to Lexington they were ambushed by marksmen firing from the cover of rocks and trees, losing seventy-three killed and twenty-six missing. The King's troops had been fired on by his subjects and the American Revolution had begun.

Six weeks later the news of the Lexington episode reached London. The King became almost apoplectic with indignation. If the rebels wanted a fight then they could have one. Three Major-Generals, Burgoyne, Clinton and Howe, were sent out to assist Gage as Commander-in-Chief. The American forces were led by George Washington with two ex-officers of the British Army as his generals.

In July Congress submitted a final petition to the King. It was known as the Olive Branch Petition and it was conciliatory in tone but George III refused to consider it. Instead he issued a Proclamation declaring the American Colonies to be in a state of armed rebellion. Irrevocably he had involved the country in the most ill-advised war in Britain's history.

The war caused little excitement in England. Only a few people had a realistic appreciation of the American situation and the war appeared to be more of a disciplinary measure than an actual military involvement. The vastness of the Atlantic, which took sailing ships an average time of six weeks to cross, made America seem a remote place and the interchange of ideas and opinions was relatively negligible. The mass of the people believed the King to be right in his attitude because the Church, the aristocracy, the Universities and the merchants supported his views. There was however a minority led by Burke, Fox, Chatham, Dunning and Thomas Paine who were in sympathy with the colonists and opposed the use of force as a means of solving the problem. Burke in the House of Commons said: " The temper and character which prevail in our colonies are, I am afraid, unalterable by any human art. We cannot falsify the pedigree of this fierce people and persuade them that they are not sprung from a nation in whose veins the blood of freedom circulates." But it was unanimously agreed by all that the Americans lacked the manpower and the resources to offer any serious opposition.

As the months passed, and instead of overwhelming victory there came news of increased resistance, a disquieting feeling of doubt crept in. Fox was openly approving the defence of liberty and was gaining supporters and Wilkes, now Lord Mayor of London, was as outspoken as ever.

The King, however, was even more determined to teach the rebels a lesson they would never forget. His officers and men were not so enthusiastic and there was a general reluctance to journey so far to fight for what appeared to be an obscure cause. George resolved to hire German troops and despite opposition in both Houses a force of Brunswick hirelings were shipped to America to reinforce His Majesty's Army in America. But the mercenaries, capable soldiers though they were, did not bring a decisive result and even the King began to feel concern although he still showed optimism by saying that " in my opinion the Americans will treat before winter." By the end of 1776 the British forces could claim only the uneasy and tenuous occupation of New York as the reward for their efforts.

General Howe had replaced General Gage, who resumed his duties of Admiral, but Howe was faced with an unenviable task. His urgent message for fifteen thousand additional troops had yielded a mere one thousand five hundred whilst it was estimated that the colonists had forty thousand men under arms, and ill-equipped though they were they represented a formidable force against his twelve thousand trained soldiers. The reinforcements were not forthcoming because following the Seven Years War the total British standing army had been allowed to dwindle to

GEORGE I
(From the portrait painted in the studio of Sir Godfrey Kneller)

2

SOPHIA DOROTHEA OF CELLE,
WIFE OF GEORGE I
(Artist unknown)

3   SIR ROBERT WALPOLE, 1ST EARL OF ORFORD
(From the portrait painted in the studio of Jean Baptiste Van Loo)

4   WILLIAM PITT, 1ST EARL OF CHATHAM
(From the portrait painted in the studio of Richard Brompton)

5 GEORGE II (*From a portrait by R. E. Pine, which is the property of the Hon. Robin Neville. Crown copyright reserved. Reproduction by permission of the Ministry of Works*)

6 CAROLINE OF ANSBACH, QUEEN OF GEORGE II

(From the bust by F. M. Rysbrack. Reproduced by permission of the Trustees of the Wallace Collection)

FREDERICK LOUIS, PRINCE OF WALES, SON OF GEORGE II

(From the painting by F. Amiconi at Buckingham Palace. Reproduced by gracious permission of Her Majesty The Queen)

8

THE PRINCESS DOWAGER

(Anonymous engraving dated 1751)

9

JOHN STUART, 3RD EARL OF BUTE

(From the painting by Sir Joshua Reynolds)

GEORGE III

(From the painting by Sir William Beechey at Buckingham Palace. Reproduced by gracious permission of Her Majesty The Queen)

11 CHARLOTTE SOPHIA, QUEEN OF GEORGE III   *(From the painting by Allan Ra*
at Buckingham Palace, c. 1762. Reproduced by gracious permission of Her Majesty The Qu

12

JOHN WILKES

(Etching by Hogarth)

13

FREDERICK NORTH, 2ND
EARL OF GUILFORD

*(From the painting by
Nathaniel Dance)*

14
CHARLES JAMES FOX
*(Engraving by Ridley
after Drummond)*

15
WILLIAM PITT
*(From the replica
by John Hoppner)*

16   GEORGE IV AS PRINCE OF WALES

*(From the portrait by Thomas Gainsborough. Reproduced by courtesy of the
National Trust. Crown copyright)*

17

MRS. FITZHERBERT

*(From the painting by
Thomas Gainsborough)*

18

LADY JERSEY

19 GEORGE IV   *(From the painting by Sir Thomas Lawrence at Buckingham Palace.*
Reproduced by gracious permission of Her Majesty The Queen)

20   CAROLINE AMELIA ELIZABETH OF BRUNSWICK, QUEEN OF GEORGE IV

(From a painting by James Lonsdale)

21   PRINCESS CHARLOTTE AUGUSTA OF WALES AND PRINCE LEOPOLD
AT THE OPERA IN 1817
(Printed and engraved from a drawing by George Dawe)

22

FREDERICK AUGUSTUS, DUKE
OF YORK, SON OF GEORGE III
*(From a panel by Sir David Wilkie
in 1823)*

23

ERNEST AUGUSTUS, DUKE OF
CUMBERLAND AND KING OF
HANOVER, SON OF GEORGE III
(From a painting by George Dawe)

one hundred thousand. Howe was also under the great disadvantage of having his bases in England with the consequent delay in supplies, which included even the oats for his horses.

On the 4th of July 1776 the Declaration of Independence was signed and the American colonies became the United States. The die was cast and now there was no hope of a settlement except by force of arms.

The initial strategy of the King's forces was that General Howe would take Philadelphia by an attack from the sea whilst General Burgoyne would advance from Canada with a force of English, Germans and Indians towards New York. Howe's army would advance to meet Burgoyne thus forming a line to split the American forces. The plan was doomed from the start by lack of troops for the line would be so attenuated as to be useless.

In September 1777 Howe defeated Washington at Brandywine Creek and occupied Philadelphia. Burgoyne with his thirty personal wagons, champagne and women, captured the fort of Ticonderoga and believed he had beaten the Americans. But by September he found his army facing a force of 20,000 colonists; at least three times his own strength. At Saratoga on the 17th of October he surrendered his entire forces. The news was received in London as a major disaster and indeed it was, for instead of splitting the American forces the British had lost a wing and Philadelphia had to be evacuated.

But worse was to come, for a few months later in March, 1778, the Americans signed an alliance with France and England was faced with another war, at sea as well as on land. Still George III was determined to crush the Americans whilst at the same time he began to organize his forces in England to resist invasion.

His Prime Minister Lord North, however, had lost heart and begged to be allowed to resign, but George would not hear of it : " I wish Lord North to continue," he said, brooking no discussion.

In June Spain joined France and their fleets sailed into the English Channel. Invasion seemed imminent and there was a wave of feeling against the King and his determination to continue the American War. North was now desperate in his anxiety to be relieved of office, but the King was adamant in his refusal to accept the fact of the obvious inadequacy of his amiable and completely useless Minister. North remained against his will to make more inevitable blunders.

The news from America was still disquieting and North's Government, in an ill-advised attempt to encourage Catholics to enlist in the army, passed a Bill for Catholic relief. Minor though the reliefs were they led to the Gordon* riots in June 1780, the worst in English history. For a week London was terrorized by a mob of fifty thousand, burning, looting, killing, destroying everything in their path on a scale never seen before. "No Popery" became the slogan of terror.

Holland entered the war against England in 1780 and to counteract the despondency created by the bad news from America false reports were spread in London to bolster public morale, but soon the truth could not be hidden. On the 15th of October 1781 Cornwallis surrendered at Yorktown and the fate of England seemed sealed.

In Parliament Fox was condemning Government policy and North now without the support of the King, who had partially retired, at last resigned. His place was taken by Lord Rockingham who advocated peace with America and a curtailing of royal power. The tenure of the new Ministry was short-lived, however, for three months later Rockingham died and was succeeded by Shelburne, paradoxically with Fox now in Opposition. A political free-for-all followed and in desperation the King threatened to abdicate. In the London Clubs wagers were struck on the duration of the King's reign but a compromise was reached with Burke's Economical Reform Bill in 1783 which reduced the royal sinecures. The tide had turned for the King and a treaty with America was ratified in Paris on the 3rd of September 1783.

The provisional treaty had been signed in November 1782, but in February 1783 Lord North had again appeared on the political scene by joining Fox in the Opposition to overthrow the Shelburne Ministry, and when the treaty was ratified a Fox-North coalition was in power. The King now found himself, by his former friend's volte-face, on the side of the Opposition. It was an untenable situation but George did not endure it for long. His opportunity came when Fox introduced his East India Bill

* After Lord George Gordon, the President of the Protestant Association.

which aimed at the transfer of power from the Company to a parliamentary commission. The Bill passed the Commons, but the King arranged its defeat in the Lords by having a note circulated in which he said that any peers who voted for the Bill would be looked upon as his personal enemies. When, as was inevitable, the Bill was thrown out the King instructed both North and Fox to resign. A new Government was formed under the leadership of the twenty-four years old son of the Earl of Chatham, William Pitt, and Fox, allied with his friend the Prince of Wales, was again in the Opposition. The King had achieved his object, but by this act of arbitrary cunning he forfeited the confidence of the House of Commons and virtually it marked the end of his political power.

7

The Prince of Wales had always been a trial to his father and even as a young child he had taken delight in tormenting the King. For example, during the time of the Wilkes troubles it is said he shouted through the keyhole of his father's dressing-room " Wilkes and Liberty ", sending his father into an apoplectic rage. The King was never on good terms with his other sons, except perhaps with the Duke of York whose behaviour does not appear to have justified partiality, but his eldest son was the one for whom he felt positive dislike. The Prince of Wales was twenty-one and with his newly-attained independence in a position to return the dislike he had always felt. Thus he was instinctively drawn to his father's enemy the brilliant, licentious, Charles James Fox, particularly after the able tuition in debauchery the young Prince had received from his uncle, the Duke of Cumberland, whom the King detested.

Charles Fox was then thirty-four, a brilliant politician—" the first great statesman of the modern school ",—a supreme individualist, an arch-gambler in the wildest gambling age and a man who lived life to the full. He was witty, intelligent, courageous and amoral and the young Prince was completely under the spell of his personality.

Fox first entered Parliament as the Member for Midhurst in 1769 and by his marvellous ability as an orator he immediately made his presence felt. But life was to be enjoyed and he ignored political ambition for the sake of his personal feelings and his conscience.

He began as a Tory and became a Whig, but his open-mindedness lifted him above partisanship. His conscience, however, never troubled him with women until he settled down with Mrs. Armistead later in life, for he caroused and drank from dusk till dawn and was known in every pleasure-haunt in London. By his vitality and exuberance he swept everyone along with him, although not many could stay the course, for after posting all night from Newmarket or a two day session of gambling he would be as prepared for a game of cricket or horse-riding as he would for a literary discussion. In every way he was the antithesis of the King and it is easy to understand why the King hated him, apart from the obvious political reasons.

In 1784 Fox was elected as Member for Westminster and the event was celebrated by the Prince of Wales and the Foxites with greater gusto and enthusiasm than the occasion warranted, for Fox was the leader of a party opposing a Government majority of 250. Pitt was at " the head of a majority which made him the most powerful Minister ever known in the parliamentary history of England ". The King had retired and the period of parliamentary corruption was ended. Pitt, the precise, political genius, was able to pursue his policy of peace and parliamentary stability and the road ahead seemed to lead to peaceful prosperity.

8

In 1788 George III was fifty. He was stout, gross and red-faced, and his rheumy eyes boggled wildly. His walk was unsteady and he moved his head, arms and legs with a strange lack of co-ordination. Words tumbled from his drooling lips inconsequently and about his whole person there was a strange, irrational air. Alternating between moods of wild uncontrollable hilarity and blank coma-like dejection his peculiar behaviour was causing people to stare at him apprehensively. The signs of a deranged mind were obvious.

The mental strain of his interference in political affairs and the constant worry to the conscientious monarch of his six large, dissolute sons and their scandals, had become too much for the always shaky equilibrium of his brain and his mind sought escape in a world of unreality. The truth could no longer be hidden for he presented a pitiful spectacle—the King was insane.

In November, George was moved from Windsor to Kew where the Prince of Wales taking, as he thought, control of the situation chalked on the doors the names of the future occupants. He believed a Regency was a foregone conclusion and his view was shared by the majority for early in February Regency Medals were issued. By the 19th the King was recovering. In April a Thanksgiving Service was held at St. Paul's and the Regency was forgotten. The royal position was again stabilized.

But the period of royal tranquillity was not to be a long one for the rumblings of the French Revolution began to be heard from across the Channel. George and his Minister Pitt were at first unperturbed, for George remembered the French part in the American Revolution and Pitt with his mind set on peace did not believe England would be affected.

Charles Fox on the other hand said : " How much the greatest event it is that ever happened in the world, and how much the best." Burke, who had recognized the American revolt as the struggle of an oppressed people for liberty, paradoxically saw the French outburst as the work of irresponsible anarchists and his work *Reflections on The Revolution in France* published in 1790 seemed to express public opinion. Paine's *Rights of Man* published in the following year and said to have sold a million copies put forward the opposite view and the English Royal Family came into his reactionary line of fire : " It has cost England almost seventy millions sterling to maintain a family imported from abroad, of very inferior capacity to thousands in the nation." The radical opinions were spreading and George began to feel the rocking of his throne as Radical Societies came into being up and down the country.

The terrible horrors of the French Revolution in 1792 had a sobering effect on public opinion, halting in their tracks all but the most fervent agitators, and the news of the execution of Louis XVI in January 1793 shocked the nation. War in the defence of national security began to be considered as a possibility for it was conjectured that a French attack upon Holland, the ally of Britain, was imminent. In February 1793 the French forestalled any British action by declaring war against Great Britain.

The Duke of York was given the command of the British Expeditionary Force by the King, who saw his favourite son as the saviour of Holland and, indeed, of world security. By the end of the year the British Forces were in retreat and Pitt began to consider a change of command. The position on the Continent was desperate for Saxe-Coburg in command of the Allies was also proving inept as a military leader. The next year saw a succession of British disasters and in 1795 the French Army occupied Holland. Fortunately the British Navy still maintained control of the Channel, but as the French successes continued across Europe the fear of invasion came into everyone's mind. The fleets of Holland and Spain were supporting the French Navy; and in England, the withdrawn remnants of the Expeditionary Force, battered and defeated, were proof of the might of France. There seemed no hope of victory and Fox with thundering eloquence was denouncing the futility of continuance.

Crowds were assembling, agitating for peace, and when the King's coach appeared in the streets he was met with jeers and shouts. On one occasion stones were thrown through the window of his coach but George with his customary courage was unperturbed.

9

In 1795 England was also facing troubles across the North Sea. Ireland was in a state of anarchy. The bigotted obsession of George III to suppress the Roman Catholics was the cause, for in his opinion to allow them any governing rights was tantamount to heresy. A large Roman Catholic majority was ruled by a Protestant minority which was in the hands of a few families.

Since the American Revolution there had been a growing revolt and now the opposing factions were burning, looting, and committing atrocities against each other. England's war with France gave the Catholics hope that with French help they might obtain complete independence. Towards the end of the following year the rebels were ready to launch their military offensive against the British troops with the aid of French support. The French transports carrying 15,000 men ran into a gale, however, and were unable to land.

The next year, 1798, saw scenes of mounting ferocity and horror. The Irish peasantry armed mainly with pikes began their massed rebellion on the 23rd of May, but without sufficient armaments they were fighting a losing battle. A force of 1,200 troops landed in August but were unable to halt the rout. Further attempts to land French reinforcements were driven off and the rebellion was crushed, but not before appalling atrocities in which thousands were butchered, including prisoners, had been committed by both the rebels and the British militia. In all it was estimated sixteen thousand men had died in the blood-bath of terror.

Years before, in 1785, Pitt had already decided that a Union, both parliamentary and commercial, was the only solution to the problem of unrest in Ireland and the terrible massacre of 1798 decided him in the following year to open the debates for an Act of Union as the first step to widespread Catholic relief. He had succeeded in persuading his bigoted sovereign to agree to the first stage without disclosing his plans for further Catholic emancipation. The Union came into effect in 1801, when Pitt also incautiously revealed his additional intentions.

The King was furious when he realized the purpose of the new measures and Pitt was confronted with the alternative of the abandonment of his plans or resignation. He chose to resign and in February George instructed Addington to form a new Ministry.

The political upset and the King's pathological hatred of the Roman Catholics undoubtedly upset his mental balance once again and he became deranged. His illness was diagnosed by his physician Dr. Willes as a " phrenzy fever ", but his condition was unmistakable and the Regency Bill, drafted in 1789, was again examined. After appearing to recover in March he again suffered a relapse from which he never recovered. During that brief spell of sanity he declared that his recovery was dependent upon the rescinding of any plans for Catholic relief.

Pitt's health, after the strain of eighteen years in office, also broke down under this last disturbance and although he returned for a brief tenure of office in 1804 he never fully recovered and died two years later. He was then only forty-six years old.

From 1801 the King lingered on in a strange half-world, until in 1811 he became completely insane, deaf, blind, and pitiful. The death in 1810 of his favourite child, the young Princess Amelia, upon whom he doted, was the final straw that broke his tottering reason. He was frenzied and uncontrollable with grief. Now he was completely insane and for his safety " watchers " were appointed.

In his madness he rushed about his palace, sending the servants scurrying away in terror—shouting and raving as he argued and ranted with the ghostly figures of his demented imagination. For the first time in his life the strange, mad king became suddenly popular with the masses. They sympathized with him in his hour of affliction and grief.

The Prince of Wales became even more unpopular and when he was seen in public he was greeted with shouts and taunts. In the streets his coach was hissed and stoned. His brothers were treated with the same open hostility.

It is perhaps strange that the madness of George III should have been viewed with sympathy, for lunatics were treated as being possessed of demons and therefore beyond the scope of medical attention. To overcome the evils of the devil within, various methods of torture were used, floggings, chains and iron cages, being the most common treatment. The harmless, non-violent lunatics were free to wander around the countryside to be the butts of the cruelty and sadism of the people. The violent ones were chained to walls in the damp darkness of cells where they were visited regularly by keepers who whipped them into whimpering, submissive terror. A common practice was to exhibit the half-naked lunatics in cages and to goad them into wild ravings, for the benefit of the spectators, by prodding them with sticks and swords. Another form of treatment was the revolving chair which spun at a great speed until the poor unfortunate occupant was in a state of bewilderment. Buckets of water were thrown over them and some were made to sit in wells with the water up to their chins, or subjected to ' baths of surprise' which were trap-doors in the floors which suddenly precipitated the unfortunate patient into wells of water. The treatment was the same for both men and women. By merely imprisoning the King in a strait-jacket it is apparent that he was being treated with the lenience due to his royal person, and his illness was diagnosed by the physicians as ' the flying gout '.

The Regency Bill was passed in February 1811 and the Prince of Wales became, in fact if not in name, the King of England. George III was a sad, pathetic being, deprived of his kingship, yet still wrestling with his relentless sense of duty—but a king cannot rule in a strait-jacket.

10

Three great happenings had taken place during the last quarter of the eighteenth century, marking a turning point in the history of civilization. Although completely different in character they have been grouped together as ' revolutions '—the French Revolution, the American Revolution and the Industrial Revolution, for they were all part of a common impetus which suddenly seemed to motivate the spirit of mankind to progress, so that with the advent of the nineteenth century a new way of life was coming into being throughout the Western World, marking the birth of democracy and the modern way of life as we know it.

The French Revolution brought about the destruction of the *ancien régime* in France when that country was the leading nation of Europe. Rallied by the republican watchwords of Liberty, Equality and Fraternity the over-taxed masses (their leaders inspired by Diderot's *Encyclopédie,* considered to be the greatest intellectual achievement of the eighteenth century, and the ideas of Voltaire, Rousseau and other great thinkers) rose against the autocratic and dissolute system of government and the results had a far-reaching influence on the rest of Europe, particularly in England.

The passion for freedom ignited a spark in the hearts of enlightened thinkers in England and encouraged the advocates of Parliamentary reform, but the Revolution, begun with the best of motives, ran unchecked until it engulfed the whole of France and in its flow swept away the rights and possessions of all who stood in its path. In England, the excesses of the Revolutionaries spread such panic and alarm that even the mildest measures of reform were feared as the beginning of a similar period of bloodshed and massacre. In 1795 French patriotism began to give way to the imperialism of Napoleon which plunged Europe into war.

In the American Colonies the revolt against the domination of the Old World brought into being the United States of America; and the Declaration of Independence, stating that " all men are created equal " and " are endowed by their Creator with certain inalienable rights " awakened people in England to the unrepresentative nature of Government in the Mother Country, where a large majority were excluded from voting under the existing franchise. The spirit of reform was taking shape and the vision was becoming manifest on the other side of the Atlantic, for the War in America, in turn encouraged Ireland to repeal the statutes which made the Parliament of Ireland responsible to the Government in London; although it was not until 1801, following the passing of the Union Act, that the Union of Ireland was born.

The third revolution was not violent in nature but it was even more far-reaching in its effect. It was an industrial and commercial revolution brought about by the inventions of industry which were to change England from an agricultural country to an industrial one.

These inventions mainly concerned the manufacture of textiles, the forging of metals and transport. First Arkwright's water-frame was invented in 1769, followed by Hargreaves' spinning jenny, both to be combined in 1779 by Crompton's mule. Cartwright's power-loom which followed was the foundation of machinery used in factories today. Factories were created in place of domestic industry and the great social changes began to show on the face of rural England. Manufacture came to mean not ' made by hand ' but ' made by machine '.

Other developments followed; Watt's improvements to the steam engine made it the greatest mechanical influence of the Industrial Revolution. In 1777 the first iron bridge was built,

and the first steamboat was launched in 1788, to be followed
in 1790 by the first ship of iron.

These were the first of many inventions that were to change
the social structure of the world. Inevitably the sudden plunge
forward of industrial development brought in its wake the
wretched slave conditions of labour in the next century, but the
giant of progress was stirring to begin his long march forward
to a better world. With the tremendous changes in attitudes,
ideas, and general way of life the new world was bursting through
the chrysalis of the old. Mankind was thinking differently and
a new appreciation of the feelings and rights of humanity was
coming into being.

The increased tempo brought changes in fashions and dress
as people adapted themselves to the new conditions. Women's
dress became more restrained and less outlandish, although still
voluminous, and the low neckline revealing the breasts was considered immodest. With the women the change was gradual but
with men's dress the development was more drastic as befitted
their more active role. Elegance gave way to utility; the tricorn
hat gave way to the top-hat; the stockings to the pantaloons
that were to become trousers. Coats were more serviceable and
austere and the brocade, the embroidery and the embellishments
became outmoded. Pitt's tax on hair-powder in 1795 brought
about the eclipse of the wig and men now wore their own hair.
But the most significant change of all was when the sword by
which a gentleman showed his right to defend himself gave way
to the walking-stick, silver-knobbed and ornate. It signified a
lessening of violence and a change in manners; the change in
morals was not at first apparent.

It was a period of continual scene-shifting whilst across the
stage tottered the wandering, aimless figure of the King, still
clinging to the old way of life with his three-cornered hat, wig,
and stockings; an atrophied being with an uncomprehending
mind. The active reign of George III had ended, and the
Regency was now merely a matter of time.

CHAPTER FIVE

THE PRINCE REGENT

I

O N THE 5th of February 1811 the Prince Regent was sworn
in. The ceremony took place at Carlton House, which had
been given to him in 1783 when he was twenty-one.

His first action when he took possession had been to put into
effect his plans for extensive alterations, and the sound of
hammer and chisel were to become a continuous echo throughout
his life, as he indulged his passion for building and rebuilding.

He had celebrated the opening of Carlton House by giving a
grand ball and a description appeared in the *European Magazine*
of March 1784 :—

The alterations at Carlton House being finished, we lay
before our readers a description of the state apartments as
they appeared on the 10th instant, when H.R.H. gave a
grand ball to the principal nobility and gentry . . . The entrance to the state room fills the mind with an inexpressible
idea of greatness and splendour.

The state chair is of a gold frame, covered with crimson
damask; on each corner of the feet is a lion's head, expressive
of fortitude and strength; the feet of the chair have serpents
twining round them, to denote wisdom. Facing the throne,
appears the helmet of Minerva; and over the windows, glory
is represented by Saint George with a superb gloria.

But the saloon may be styled the *chef d'oeuvre,* and in every
ornament discovers great invention. It is hung with a figured
lemon satin. The window-curtains, sofas, and chairs are of the

same colour. The ceiling is ornamented with emblematical paintings, representing the Graces and Muses, together with Jupiter, Mercury, Apollo and Paris. Two *ormulu* chandeliers are placed here. It is impossible by expression to do justice to the extra-ordinary workmanship, as well as design, of the ornaments. They each consist of a palm, branching out in five directions for the reception of lights. A beautiful figure of a rural nymph is represented entwining the stems of the tree with wreaths of flowers. In the centre of the room is a rich chandelier. To see this apartment *dans son plus beau jour,* it should be viewed in the glass over the chimney-piece. The range of the apartments from the saloon to the ball-room, when the doors are open, formed one of the grandest spectacles that ever was beheld.

Now the Prince was nearing his fiftieth birthday and he was no longer the handsome figure of his youth. His face, in middle-age, still showed signs of his earlier distinctive handsomeness but the intervening years of dissolute living had also left their mark and his gross, corpulent body bulged within restricting corsets.* He was a bottle-scarred veteran in the war of life.

On the 19th of June Carlton House was again the scene of a grand " fête ", which included a ball and supper, ostensibly in honour of Louis XVIII and other French royalties, but it was in fact to celebrate the Regency. The three women, his treatment of whom had largely contributed to his unpopularity, were not present. His wife Caroline, whom he hated, and Charlotte, his fifteen-year-old daughter, had not been invited; the third one, Maria Fitzherbert, now fifty-five years of age, although invited did not attend the fête for she could not bear the humiliation of viewing from a relegated place the antics of the Regent with his latest favourite, Lady Hertford. When she had asked the Regent which was to be her place at the table he had answered, " Madam, you know you have no place." How could she attend after such a reply ?

The Prince who had revelled in his popularity was hissed by

* Corsets and " stays " had been in fashion for men since the fifteenth century but they reached their peak of popularity during the eighteenth and nineteenth centuries.

a jeering mob as he entered Carlton House, and Lady Hertford suffered the indignity of almost having her chair overturned by the hostile crowd. It was indeed an inauspicious beginning to the Regency.

2

The Prince of Wales had been a great disappointment to his father, who on August 12th 1762 had signified his pleasure at receiving the good news that his first-born was a boy, by presenting the fortunate and astonished messenger with five hundred pounds. His mother, Queen Charlotte, was so delighted that she had an effigy modelled in wax, and it was displayed on a crimson cushion to the cooing court ladies.

The birthday celebration was a magnificent affair and was repeated with determined regularity as royal births followed in steady succession. The birthday celebrations became almost an annual event.

The following years, for instance, a temple and a bridge were built in the gardens of Buckingham House which were illuminated with more than 4,000 coloured lanterns, and an orchestra of fifty musicians played during the festivities. No doubt many uninvited guests mingled with the crowd, for in those days the official protection of the royal dwellings was of a most perfunctory nature; and there are on record many instances of intrusions by mad persons and others. On one occasion a woman found her way into the Queen's Room, and another time a woman caught hold of the King as he was getting out of his chair; a man walked into the bedroom of the young Princess Elizabeth; and a woman with her three children fell on her knees before the Queen, presenting her petition for clemency for her husband, a forger condemned to be executed. There were many others, but the vigilance was not made more strict and the familiarity between royal family and subjects was not considered unusual. Indeed, even at Court, the King was treated in a casual and at times jocular manner.

The royal children were brought up at Kew under strict supervision; the King dictated the education of his sons (who were brought up in pairs) whilst the Queen devoted her attentions to the daughters. The girls were happy, the boys were not; for the King was despotic and ruthless in doing what he believed to be his duty, and if their progress was not satisfactory or their spirits too ebullient the tutors were instructed to flog them, which was often. On occasions the King himself plied the whip to make sure the lesson went home. He obviously believed flogging to be the panacea for most things and the Duke of Sussex was flogged for asthma; the treatment in this case appears to have been efficacious for he lived to be seventy. It also appears to have imparted religious knowledge to the Duke of York for he was elevated to the Bishopric of Osnaburgh before leaving the nursery.

George was a handsome youth, full of high spirits and blessed with a sharp, quick-witted intelligence and he hated being hammered into pattern by his unreasonable father. The two elder brothers were drawn together by a common bond and their escapades and improprieties were many. The Prince of Wales, in particular, being possessed of good looks and great charm of manner, had a few preliminary affairs with ladies of the court whilst still in his 'teens, before his first real love affair with the beautiful Mary Robinson.

Predatory sex is latent in every virile man and this was an uninhibited age. The virile, young male is always susceptible to the attractions of the female, and picture the Prince of Wales in the year 1779; a mere youth, seventeen years of age, with all the inflation and confidence of his position, entering the Royal Box of the theatre in Drury Lane. He was of medium height, a good-looking lad of stocky build with a florid complexion and an arrogant and confident manner. Always a connoisseur of beauty, is it surprising that the Prince was attracted by the beautiful actress Mary Darby Robinson when he saw her on the stage, young, delightful and vital; the première Shakespearean actress of her generation? In her memoirs she says: "But just as the curtain was falling, my eyes met those of the Prince of Wales: and with a look that I shall never forget, he gently inclined his head a second time. I felt the compliment and blushed my gratitude." Leaving the theatre she records that she met the Royal Family: "I was again honoured with a very marked and low bow from the Prince of Wales."

In the box with him was the Duke of York, a year younger than the Prince, and the two striplings whispered together as they admired the beautiful young actress. A few days later Lord Malden called upon Mary Robinson to deliver a message. It was a brief love letter addressed to " Perdita " and signed " Florizel ". She had been playing the part of Perdita in Shakespeare's " The Winter's Tale " and knew full-well that in the play it is Florizel who wins Perdita. From then onwards the letters delivered by the accommodating Lord Malden became a daily occurrence and one letter asked her to attend the Oratorio at the Opera House. Strategically, she occupied a box directly opposite the Royal Box. Soon the Prince and the Duke entered their box and by signs the Prince indicated that he was the writer of the letters.

Inevitably they met, by secret assignment, and the lovers' trysts continued. Soon their meetings became open ones and he escorted her everywhere until at last the *Morning Post* made the affair public property and forever identified the Prince as " Florizel " to Mary's " Perdita ".

The fact that she was married seemed to have little bearing on the affair. The daughter of a Mr. and Mrs. John Darby of Bristol, she now lived in Grosvenor Square, was married at fifteen years of age to Thomas Robinson. He was a spendthrift and gambler and the young couple were in no time surrounded by overwhelming debts. His creditors had him sent to the debtor's prison and Mary voluntarily accompanied him. After fifteen months they regained their liberty by obtaining securities to cover their debts. The means by which these bonds were procured is not known, but earlier the husband had urged Mary to prostitute herself to earn the money and she had indignantly refused. The marriage, therefore, was not a happy one and the husband delightedly encouraged her romance with the Prince.

She became the protegée of the fifty-seven year old David Garrick and in 1776 she made her debut in a Sheridan production and was an immediate success. Three years later, when she was twenty-one, she was the rage of London and it was then she came to the notice of the Prince of Wales. She was certainly far more experienced in matters of love than was he.

He lavished presents and jewels upon her and generously gave her a bond for £20,000 to be payable on his coming of age.

Mary Robinson was enraptured, and the romance was a spicy topic for the newspapers. The whole of London was agog with the scandal.

Their affair lasted exactly twelve months, and the ending was a bitter one. She returned his jewels but retained the bond and his passionate love letters. In an attempt to win him back she announced in the *Morning Herald* that she was pregnant and asked the event to be brought to Royal notice. Her device was unsuccessful for the Prince had now fallen in love with the beautiful Mrs. Armistead, who had been Mary Robinson's maid.

The Robinsons were once again in debt for they had been using the Prince's bond and letters as credit, and their creditors were becoming restive. Mary's price for the return of the letters and the bond was £25,000 and as the Prince was quite unable to raise this amount the matter was referred to his father. Negotiations followed and settlement was agreed at £5,000.

The handling of the monetary bond was entrusted to the capable hands of Charles Fox who commuted it for an annuity of £500 a year, half of which was to continue to be paid to her daughter for life. Fox seems to have dealt with the affair judiciously for Walpole records that in 1782 " Charles Fox is languishing at the feet of Mrs. Robinson," whilst his current mistress, Mrs. Armistead, became involved with the Prince; a situation which might well have been engineered by Fox. Indeed the King hated Fox and blamed him for the corruption of his son.

Mary celebrated by sitting for a portrait by Gainsborough and thus unwittingly attained immortality, Florizel was soon busy transferring his amorous attentions to other eager participants in the game of love, for although his interview with his father had been unpleasant, it had also been unsalutary.

Fate was not kind to Mary Robinson and troubles and disasters crowded upon her. When, a few years later, she became partially paralysed she devoted her energies to writing and published a number of novels and poems. She wrote to the Prince and in his reply he said, " should it be within the compass of my means to rescue you from the abyss you apprehend that is before you, I need not say that the temptation of gratifying others, and by the same means making oneself happy is too alluring to be neglected for a single moment." He did not, however, add Mary to his list of mounting debts, but when she died she was buried, as she had wished, at Old Windsor and thus found a nearness to the Prince in eternity.

3

In 1781 the King allowed the Prince to have his own household and also part of Buckingham House, which in 1775 had been settled on the Queen as a dower-house (in lieu of Somerset House which had been originally settled on her). He had paid for it the moderate sum of £21,000. It had been built in 1703 by Sheffield, the Duke of Buckingham, and years later when the Regent came to the throne, growing tired of Carlton House, he rebuilt it to form the present Buckingham Palace.

Now in 1781 he began to give full rein to his brilliant, flamboyant personality; and he created a sensation. Floridly handsome, debauched, intelligent, witty, drunken, good-natured, and above all charming, he sparkled as the complete antithesis of his father. Released from the bondage of parental restraint and strict tuition he devoted himself to extorting from life the greatest possible pleasure at whatever the cost. The day of Dandyism had dawned. This was the age when man was the peacock, and silks, satins, fine velvets, and extravaganzas of fashion were the feathers. He was everywhere, the theatre, the Opera, the cardroom, the stag-hunt, the ballroom; always ready for rowdyism, bouts of drunkenness, or some secret amorous escapade, in short : the leader of the current fashion in dress and morals, the *arbiter elegantiarum*.

It would be unfair, however, to judge the character of the Prince by his tinsel mode of living. On many occasions he had tried to take part in serious matters but each time he had been baulked by his father. He had been refused a commission in the army. He had not been allowed to inspect the country's fortifications, or to visit the provinces, and every suggestion or request he made to extend his activities was blocked by the King's refusal.

In turn, he did everything in his power to annoy his father; he arrived late for royal appointments, he chose as friends the enemies of his father, and although he consorted with the rakes, blackguards, and lowest company, he also sought the company of the most intellectual, notably Fox in politics, Sheridan in letters, and Burke in philosophy. If he was unkind to his father he was often thoughtful for others. He was a dandy but not a milk-sop. On one occasion he was present at a prize-fight between Earl and Tyne. Earl was killed and the Prince settled an annuity on the widow and true to his vow was never present at a prize-fight again. Even in his most uproarious moments there were times when he wished for something better to do and he often said " I wish anybody would tell me what to do." Once when his father reprimanded him for not rising early, he said, " I find Sir, however late I rise that the day is long enough for doing nothing."

When in 1783 the Prince came of age and took possession of Carlton House he entertained in an even more spectacular manner. Splendour was the keynote of his existence, whether it was dress, women, horses, debauchery or intellectual company. His brother, the Duke of York, who had been his earlier boon companion had been sent abroad and it was now that Sheridan became one of his closest friends, together with Fox and Georgiana, Duchess of Devonshire, three brilliant minds, which is a tribute to the Prince's own considerable intelligence.

The following year Fox stood for Parliament and Carlton House became his headquarters. It is said that the drunken pandemonium that followed, and which was the custom on such occasions during the eighteenth century, was more unbridled than usual. Despite the opposition of the King, Fox was elected and the brilliant, debauched, political genius was in, and with him went the enthusiasm of the Prince. Lord North was out of office and later the *London Gazette* announced that " His Majesty was pleased to appoint Mr. Charles Fox as Foreign Secretary."

The Whig Ministry offered the Prince an allowance of a hundred thousand a year, and the King, in the cause of popularity, offered to pay half the amount himself. The Prince, in retaliation, said he would only accept fifty thousand. Eventually a compromise was reached by adding the revenues of the Duchy of

Cornwall, but even this income was insufficient to prevent the Princely debts mounting at an alarming rate.

It was at this time that the Prince first met Maria Fitzherbert. He was twenty-two and she was twenty-eight and had been twice-widowed before she was twenty-five. Born a Smythe, and a Catholic, she first married a man named Weld, and shortly after his death she married Fitzherbert who died in 1781. Both husbands were Catholics. She was attractive without being beautiful and her white bosom was famous. She was intelligent without being intellectual and she had character. To the Prince she was the most desirable woman in the world. Around her always was a ring of suitors, for as well as being well-born she had also been well-widowed. The Prince joined the ring and they dispersed. Maria accepted his suit, but not as a mistress, and on this point she was adamant.

But there were two apparently insurmountable barriers between the Prince and his marriage to Mrs. Fitzherbert. First, the Act of Settlement decreed that if he married a Catholic he would forfeit his succession to the Throne, and secondly the Royal Marriage Act of 1772 stipulated that his marriage without the King's consent would be illegal.

The Prince was thus now faced with an Act which clearly stated that no descendant of the second George was allowed to marry outside the Blood without the King's consent, and in this case he knew it was a consent that would never be given. He was frantic with frustrated passion and when his pleading with Maria was of no avail he had himself bled three times in succession by different surgeons so that his pale face should stir her sympathy. When this ruse did not work he sent her a message saying that he had stabbed himself and that she must come to him at once. Maria went, but with four companions, to find the Prince daubed with blood but apparently unharmed. He begged and pleaded with her, but this hysterical charade made up her mind. She went abroad.

True to the lachrymose tendencies of his forbears, the Prince wept and was inconsolable. He was torn apart with grief and wrote letter after letter to Maria; one of them was thirty-seven pages long. He was willing to give up everything and asked the King for permission to go abroad. His request was refused.

He was desperate and settling that the future children of the Duke of York should be the heirs to the throne he made Mrs. Fitzherbent promise to marry no one else. Still she stayed abroad. At last his pleadings touched her heart when he promised to marry her in the Catholic Faith. She relented and returned to London. A few days later they were married in her own house which was near where the Marble Arch now stands. The Reverend Robert Burt performed the ceremony and received £500 for doing it. The marriage was illegal but canonical and Mrs. Fitzherbert had her certificate.

They honeymooned in secret, and returned to face the difficulties of the situation with all the sublime optimism of lovers enraptured with each other. The Prince escorted Maria in public openly and proudly. By his chivalrous insistence she was accepted everywhere, except at Court.

The young pair enjoyed life to the full although burdened with heavy and rapidly increasing debts. She lived in Park Lane, a house which had been left to her by her last husband but her income of two thousand a year was inadequate for the expensive life of the Prince's circle. She found she had married a rollicking, boisterous youth, in love with her but in love with life also. It is recorded in Raikes's diary : " Mrs. Fitzherbert never retired to rest till her royal spouse came home. But I have heard the Duke of York say, that often when she heard the Prince and his drunken companions on the staircase, she would seek a refuge from their presence even under the sofa, when the Prince, finding the drawing-room deserted, would draw his sword in joke, and searching about the room, would at last draw forth the trembling victim from her place of concealment." But women of that period were quite used to such wild, untrammelled drunken conduct, and sword play, mad dogs released amongst the guests, torn dresses and worse, lent excitement to a party. Their life together was stormy but they loved each other and his wild conduct was the custom of his day.

Maria had pledged her word to the Prince that she would never reveal the secret of their marriage and she never broke her promise; but on one occasion at least the Prince admitted it. Rumour spread and on March 21 1786, a caricature with the caption *The Wedding Night* appeared. It depicted the Prince and Mrs. Fitzherbert dancing together; on the floor between was a torn marriage certificate. A riddle was the topical joke, it went, "What is the difference between Mrs. Fitzherbert and a demi-mondaine?" The answer was, "Mrs. Fitzherbert would break the seventh commandment for a sovereign but not for half-a-crown."

The Prince and Mrs. Fitzherbert were in love for all the world to see and the people in the street loved the romance. Unfortunately the Prince's debts were mounting in staggering fashion due to the smallness of his allowance; and the King refused to discuss the matter until the Prince agreed to give up Fox and Mrs. Fitzherbert. This the Prince refused to do. In consequence he became so short of money that sometimes he used the common postchaise to Brighton, which was the equivalent of travelling second-class today, and often Mrs. Fitzherbert had to pay his fare—a sorry plight for a Prince.

In 1786 he asked Pitt, the Prime Minister, to obtain for him the £250,000 needed to settle his debts, but Pitt playing on the side of the King did not press the matter. The Prince retaliated by closing down half the rooms of Carlton House and dismissing his household staff. He settled pensions on the older members; but a number of his staff offered to work for him without wages which was proof of his considerate attitude to his servants. He sold his racing stud which to him was indeed a sacrifice for he was genuinely fond of horses.

The result of this display of poverty yielded results, for in April 1787 his financial embarrassment was brought before the House, when Fox, unaware of the marriage, flatly denied the fact. Mrs. Fitzherbert was aghast and complained to the Prince that Fox's statement reduced her to the level of a street-walker. The Prince was torn between the two, for obviously the denial of the marriage supported his case, and he pressed Sheridan to defend the honour of Mrs. Fitzherbert by making a speech in the House. Sheridan obliged and did it so adroitly that he neither contradicted nor corroborated the statement made by Fox. The discussion in the House produced an increase of ten thousand pounds in the Prince's income, a hundred and sixty thousand towards the payment of his debts and twenty thousand for buildings costs at Carlton House, which sums also produced a reconciliation between father and son—a brief respite for the Prince.

4

In August 1787 the Duke of York returned from his military training in Hanover and the Prince and he resumed their drinking, carousing and gambling together. Gambling was a fever in London society and the stakes were high. In an evening's entertainment the Duke of Bedford lost £70,000 to the Prince, but this was not an unusual amount, for sometimes a faro bank was worth as much as four or five hundred thousand pounds, and wagers of five hundred pounds on the turn of a card, or a thousand guineas on a horse did not cause an eyebrow to be raised. The young Princes scattered their I.O.U.s around the London Clubs and they even set up their own rival Club at Dover House under Louis Weltjie, who was chief steward at Carlton House. But it was at the seaside resort of Brighton that the Prince enjoyed himself most for here he was King, and Mrs. Fitzherbert was his Queen.

The Prince first visited Brighton, or Brightelmstone as it was then called, in 1783, on the recommendation of a doctor, Richard Russel, who advocated the health-giving properties of the sleepy, salubrious fishing village. The Prince was enchanted with the place and decided to stay. He bought a farmhouse on the Steyne, which became in 1787, the Marine Pavilion. It was built by Henry Holland, the architect of Drury Lane Theatre, to a simple, harmonious design, and the interior was of Adamesque classicism. It was to become the architectural toy of the Prince who added touch after touch of his personality, in conjunction with John Nash, whose monument is Regent's Park; until in 1821 it became an oriental palace, part Indian, part Chinese and part Turkish. It was dubbed Florizel's Folly, and throughout the years it has been jeered at and sneered at,* but still, with its domes, spires, minarets, and marble pillars, it remains a thing of beauty adorning the centre of Brighton. Around it the town had spread in homage.

Under the princely patronage Brighton became fashionable,

---

* Sydney Smith said: " St. Paul's must have gone to Brighton for the day and pupped."

emulating London, but gayer, more daring than the capital with its stodgy King and Queen. These were the happiest days of the Prince and they coincided with the unhappy days of the French Revolution. In England, Brighton was to Paris as the Prince's carriage was to the tumbrils serving the guillotine.

Never again will Brighton see such picturesque Watteau-like groups as the Prince's court leaving the Pavilion to go to the Races or to parade on the promenade, a crowd of "tandems, beautiful women, and light hussars"; the wits and the beauties of England. All types were mingled to form a hectic, heady conglomeration of colourful life—a carnival of gaiety, brilliance and dissolute enjoyment.

In Raikes's Diary a word picture is given of a typical scene: "In those days, the Prince made Brighton and Lewes Races the gayest scene of the year in England. The Pavilion was full of guests, and the Steyne was crowded with all the rank and fashion from London . . . About half an hour before the departure for the hill, the Prince himself would make his appearance in the crowd. I think I see him now, in a green jacket, a white hat, and light nankeen pantaloons and shoes, distinguished by his high-bred manner and handsome person. He was generally accompanied by the Late Duke of Bedford, Lord Jersey, Charles Wyndham, Shelley, Brummell, M. Day, Churchill and oh! extraordinary anomaly! the little old Jew Travis, who, like the dwarf of old, followed in the train of royalty. The Downs were soon covered with every species of conveyance, and the Prince's German waggon and six bay horses (so were barouches called when first introduced at that time)—the coachman on the box being replaced by Sir John Wade—issued out of the gates of the Pavilion, and, gliding up the green ascent, was stationed close to the Grand Stand, where it remained the centre of attraction for the day. At dinner time the Pavilion was resplendent with lights, and a sumptuous banquet was furnished to a large party; while those who were not included in that invitation found a dinner, with every luxury, at the Club-house on the Steyne, kept by Raggett during the season, for the different members of White's and Brookes's who chose to frequent it, and where the cards and dice from St. James's Street were not forgotten."

Mrs. Fitzherbert reigned with dignity and tempered-down the

rowdy, profligate element. These were the golden days of Brighton and on one such day, in November 1788, the Prince received the news that the King was ill and acting strangely. The Prince immediately posted to Windsor to be near the King and to join his brother the Duke of York. As they were sitting at dinner the King suddenly clutched the Prince of Wales by the throat, convinced that he was his enemy and the Duke of York his friend. They quelled his wild ravings, but the madness remained. He used to shake hands with an oak tree in Windsor Park and his insanity could not be denied; there was now talk of the Prince being made Regent.

For the Prince the time was inopportune, for his political adviser, Charles Fox, was abroad with his mistress, Mrs. Armistead. Courier after courier was sent to find him and he was at last located in Bologna. He returned as quickly as possible; the journey by jolting coach taking him nine days.

The Queen was furious at the idea of the Prince taking precedence over herself and the struggle began between the Queen and Pitt on one side and the Prince and the Whigs on the other. Both factions began creating their intended shadow cabinets and the battle was joined in the Commons. Partisan feelings swept the country and when the turmoil was at its loudest, the King recovered. A drawing-room was held to mark his return to health and ambitions subsided.

In the Spring of the following year the Royal family patched up their quarrel and were united in a makeshift sort of peace. Unfortunately the debts of the Prince again disturbed the family serenity for the King was angry when he learnt of the many schemes promoted by the Prince and the Duke of York to raise money.

The Prince again adopted his previously successful manoeuvre with Carlton House. This time it failed and public sympathy, touched by the King's illness, was on the side of the father. The Queen's hatred of her two eldest sons became more bitter than ever.

The animosity created by the proposed Regency Bill sparked off a quarrel between Colonel Charles Lennox, the nephew of the Duke of Richmond, and previously a supporter of Pitt, and the Duke of York—a duel resulted. Lennox fired at the Duke and the ball singed a curl at the side of the Duke's head. The Duke did not fire and Lord Rawdon his spokesman said the Duke had no intention of firing. If Lennox was not satisfied he could fire again, and the Duke stood ready, completely without fear. He had come to give Lennox satisfaction and his honour was satisfied.

When the Queen met Lennox at a ball at St. James's Palace she kissed her fan to him, but the Prince of Wales coming opposite Lennox during a dance turned away with his partner and left the floor. Queen Charlotte gave the signal for the ball to end. The Prince, ignoring Lennox, apologized to the Colonel's partner, and the sisters of Lennox asked the Duke for the singed curl as a memento of his fortunate escape. When the King heard of the duel he threw his arms round his favourite son, crying, " My dear Frederick! Heaven has miraculously saved your life and mine."

In February 1793 France declared war against England and the Prince asked to be given a command. The King refused his request and the Duke of York was made Commander of the British Forces to go abroad. Unfortunately, the Duke, though not lacking in courage, was incompetent and the expedition was a failure. The Duke was recalled and made Commander-in-Chief of His Majesty's Land Forces.

5

The year 1794 also saw the break-up of Mrs. Fitzherbert's idyllic romance. The Prince was never noted for consistency and his feelings for Mrs. Fitzherbert had been undermined by a meteor of a man, who had soared into the social firmament. He was George Bryan Brummell, or Beau Brummell as he came to be called, so that when the Prince met Lady Jersey, a grandmother but still extremely beautiful, he was already prepared to break with Mrs. Fitzherbert.

Beau Brummell, although he took no part in history, has earned for himself a niche in the Hall of Immortality. He was unique. Born the son of a valet who had made money, he was sent to Eton. It is said that when they first met, the Prince, who was visiting Eton, was so enchanted by Brummell's confident charm of manner that he promised him a cornetcy in his own regiment, the 10th Hussars. When Brummell was sixteen, the Prince, true to his word, gave him his commission, and the young man set out to make of himself a work of art. He succeeded, and re-mirrored in the Regency pool the legend of Narcissus.

His opinion on matters of taste and dress became law, and his intense preoccupation with meticulous cleanliness taught English society the essentiality of soap and water, for until Brummell, whether one washed or did not wash was merely a question of personal inclination. By sheer dandyism he became the supreme aesthete, the leader of fashion for all to follow.

Brummell was not only an arbiter of dress and manners; he was a cult. His biting wit, supreme egotism, and intrepid insolence captured the Prince's imagination. Brummell delighted him and consequently all English society.

This was a time of rigid class distinctions and yet by sheer nerve Brummell, a social buccaneer, rose from obscurity to become the most-feared and respected man in the fashionable world.

He was a phase and the nature of his success made his life a tight-rope on which he walked precariously. Inevitably, one day he made a false step, and fell. An illustration of the manner in which he maintained his balance is given in the following incident; when he didn't fall.

Brummell was sitting next to the Prince of Wales at dinner, when the Prince in a drunken, pettish mood, flung the contents of his glass into Brummell's face. There was an immediate and terrible silence, until Brummell, with perfect aplomb and instinctive presence of mind, threw his glass of wine into the face of the man sitting next to him, with a loud request that he pass the Prince's toast along the table. The man duly complied and the situation was saved.

In elegance he outshone even the Prince, who accepted his opinion on matters of fashion, or *bon ton* as it was called, without question, and they spent hours together discussing materials, cravats, styles and cut. But undoubtedly, it was the quick-witted insolence, and lively intelligence of Brummell that appealed to the Prince, for in a world where birth and position mattered so much more than they do today, the Beau climbed the social ladder to become the close companion of the leader of society. The oft-quoted story of Brummel's saying to the Prince, "Wales, ring the bell," was always indignantly denied by Brummell but the mere fact that it came to be believed is an indication of the sheer nerve of the man. He had the ear of the Prince and he was the enemy of Mrs. Fitzherbert.

The Queen saw in Lady Jersey an opportunity to end the Prince's liaison with Mrs. Fitzherbert and she encouraged his new affair. The odds against Maria Fitzherbert were too great and her unpredictable lover ended their association without giving her an explanation or reason. All she received was a curt note saying that he would never enter her house again.

At this time the debts of the Prince had soared to more than £600,000 and he was forced to accept the only course open to him for settlement—a dynastic marriage; this being the King's unalterable condition. The Duke of York had married, mainly at his brother's behest, to continue the succession, but the Duchess of York was childless. The Prince was thus beset on all sides and he finally nerved himself to accept his father's stipulation. As abruptly as he had finished with Mrs. Fitzherbert, the Prince acquainted the King with his agreement by saying, "I wish to marry!"

The King and Queen were delighted and all that remained to be done was to choose the bride. The choice rested between the King's niece Caroline, and the Queen's niece Louise. The Prince rejected Louise saying, "One of that family is enough," and he was supported by the Duke of York who recommended Caroline. So in true Guelph fashion he was committed to a German bride, Caroline of Brunswick. Lady Jersey also urged him to marry Caroline, for she believed that an uncomely wife would not displace her own influence. As events proved they were an ill-omened pair. Louise fared well by not being chosen for her destiny was to become the beautiful and happy Queen of Prussia.

Lord Malmesbury was despatched to Brunswick to arrange the union and during the negotiations the nuptial-bound pair were introduced to each other by an exchange of diamond-framed miniatures, which were highly flattering and inevitably disillusioning. At the end of December 1794 Malmesbury left Bruns-

wick with the bird safely caged, but owing to the war against
France the journey was fraught with delays and it was not until
three months later that they sailed for England.

Beau Brummell was the young captain in charge of the escort
awaiting them at Greenwich, and Lady Jersey, who had been
appointed Lady-in-Waiting to the Princess, was also there to
welcome the bride-to-be with presents of a white satin gown
and a turban hat, both calculatingly unbecoming.

When Caroline first met the Prince she fell to her knees. He
raised her to her feet, embraced her, and then turned to Malmesbury, saying, " Harris, I am not well. Pray get me a glass of
brandy." He then left immediately, and as Caroline watched her
heavy-paunched Prince Charming stagger away the disillusion-
ment was complete.

That evening a dinner-party was given to mark the occasion of
their meeting, during which Caroline, who was already aware
of Lady Jersey's true position, chaffed them about their association. Unfortunately her remarks were vulgar and crude as she
prattled on, swept along by her own coarseness. The hate she
engendered, that night, in the mind of the Prince was never
to be forgotten. Three days later they were married.

The wedding took place at St. James's Chapel on April 8th
1795 and during the ceremony the Prince was drunk. He continued his drunken bout until their nuptial night and Caroline is
reputed to have said " she left him, where he fell, under the
grate."

It was an inauspicious beginning, but on the 7th of January
1796 the Princess of Wales gave birth to Princess Charlotte in
succession to the Throne. Although the Prince behaved ruthlessly, even abominably, on numerous occasions, there are also
recorded many acts of kindness and thoughtfulness to prove that
in his strange make-up there was also a sense of sympathetic
understanding.

On this occasion he was frantic with agitation and during the
latter part of the Princess's pregnancy he was kindness itself;
during the period of labour he resorted to prayer.

However, the Prince, having consumated the marriage felt
himself free to give more attention to his affair with Lady Jersey.
This situation pleased the Queen who hated Caroline and had in

fact disliked her since the moment her own niece had been rejected as a bride for the Prince. The dislike was mutual, whilst in turn the King always showed a warm regard for Caroline.

Public feeling, which had always been against Lady Jersey, became even more bitter and often her carriage and servants were pelted with mud to the accompaniment of jeers and boos.

The Queen and Lady Jersey now joined forces to make the life of Caroline as unhappy as possible, and she returned insult for insult; until on April 30th, 1796, she received a letter from the Prince, in reply to her request for a statement from him setting out the terms under which they should live. He wrote: "Our inclinations are not in our power, nor should either of us be held answerable to the other, because nature has not made us suitable to each other." He ended the letter by saying he hoped "that the rest of our lives will be passed in uninterrupted tranquillity," which as later events proved was a vainly optimistic desire.

If Caroline had accepted the situation and retired, the rest of her life would have been happier, as it was she fought to maintain her position and their life was tempered by constant battles and irritations. The cauldron boiled over when a letter, which Caroline had written home, containing an unpleasant account of the Queen's conduct, was intercepted and passed to Lady Jersey, who lost no time in making the contents of the letter known, and sent in her resignation as Lady-in-Waiting to the Princess. Caroline at last found the situation untenable and left Carlton House to take a villa at Charlton, near Blackheath. Princess Charlotte remained at Carlton House under the care of a governess.

At last Caroline was happy. She had her own staff, congenial companions, and plenty of money; she was allowed to visit Charlotte as often as she wished and on these occasions the Prince took care to avoid meeting his wife. They communicated with each other through the medium of the governess, Lady Elgin.

That they were unsuitable to each other was an understatement. It was blatantly obvious from their first meeting. The Prince was meticulous about his personal appearance, whereas Caroline was sluttish and even needed to be persuaded to wash;

he was a dandy, she was a sloven; the difference in their personalities and mental outlooks was just as marked. They should
never have met.

The machinations of Lady Jersey recoiled upon her own head,
for she became even more unpopular than ever and at a party
given by the Duchess of Gordon the ladies ignored her. Indeed,
throughout her life she seems to have engendered nothing but
hatred, for as early as 1776 the *Morning Post* awarded her
twelve marks for Expression, eleven for Beauty and no marks for
Principles. In contrast history has nothing but good to record of
Maria Fitzherbert and in 1798 the *Morning Post* recorded that
" Mrs. Fitzherbert looks more elegant than ever."

The Prince, amidst the turmoil and unhappiness, again longed
for the pleasant company of the placid Maria. He decided to
drop Lady Jersey, but she was obstinate and although displaced
from favour she clung to him, refusing to accept the inevitable;
which was that the Prince was again in love with Mrs. Fitzherbert. Then followed a period when the Prince juggled precariously with all three—his two wives and his mistress.

For her part Maria was still in love with the Prince but was
torn between her principles and the dictates of her heart. At last
he decided he could not exist without her and threatened that
unless she returned to him he would make their marriage public
and damn the consequences. The soft heart of Maria was touched
and she agreed, providing she had the consent of the Pope. Her
Confessor was despatched to Rome and duly returned with the
canonical confirmation that Maria was her third husband's first
and only wife. Mrs. Fitzherbert returned to the Prince and
Gainsborough painted a picture of the reconciliation showing the
Prince, aided by Sheridan, pleading with Mrs. Fitzherbert. Thus
in June 1800 Mrs. Fitzherbert gave her own wedding breakfast so that her friends could meet her bridegroom.

At one time Maria had offered to discuss with Caroline the
best means of effecting a reconciliation between Caroline and
the Prince, but Caroline had refused saying that the Prince
would be angry if he knew Mrs. Fitzherbert had suggested it.
Now, in turn, Caroline reciprocated by saying, " This is the
Prince's true wife; she is an excellent woman." When the Prince
heard of this remark he was struck by the good-natured attitude

of one whom he had not considered capable of such a thought.

It was the end of Lady Jersey, and it was the beginning of eight years of happiness for the Prince and Mrs. Fitzherbert. They withdrew to Brighton and under her influence he reduced his drinking and became more tractable. There was a genuine love between them and they were happy; she was sincere, tactful and good-natured and understood his vagaries of temperament, whilst the Prince when his better nature was uppermost was charm personified. Mrs. Fitzherbert sought nothing for herself but the influence which the devotion of the Prince bestowed upon her. She became the intermediary between the Prince and the rest of the royal family. Together the infatuated middle-aged lovers set sail upon a stormy sea of financial and political troubles.

The social and regal aspirations of the Prince were thwarted and his intense dislike of his father, his mother and his wife became even more bitter. Pitt was still against a Regency and the Prince chafed impatiently as the King's mind wavered between sanity and madness. The Prince was astride a political see-saw as he urged one party and then the other to press his claims.

The war between England and France was intermittent and the Prince petitioned the King with letters asking to be allowed to serve in any command. From Brighton he bombarded his father with frightening alarms that England was on the verge of invasion. In reply the King gave him permission to meet the invaders when they arrived—Brighton was suggested as a post of military observation. The King was as determined to prevent the Prince earning any military kudos as he was to ensure the prestige of the Duke of York as Commander-in-Chief.

A surprising fact of the war was that England's two greatest commanders, Nelson and Wellington met only once in their lives, and then Wellington only recognized Nelson because he was one-armed. On that occasion they exchanged but a few desultory words.

The Prince was at Brighton when he received the news of Trafalgar and the death of Nelson, and he wrote a letter to Lady Hamilton expressing the deepest sympathy of Mrs. Fitzherbert and himself. But it was his brother, William, the Duke of Clarence, who felt the loss of Nelson most deeply for Nelson had been his hero. The bullet which killed Nelson was given by the surgeon to the Duke of Clarence and it was a treasured possession.

Austerlitz followed Trafalgar and the Allies' defeat also marked the death of Pitt on January 24th, 1806. The King sent for Grenville and the turn of the Whigs had come. The Prince, Grenville and Fox discussed together the future policy of Whiggery but for Fox, the worn-out giant, Fortune smiled too late, for he died a few months afterwards. The King forbade the Prince to attend the funeral. The Prince was grief-stricken and even a year later he was still wearing black in mourning for his friend.

When the only two great statesmen had made their exits the stage was clear for the lesser lights and an era of political frustration followed. The old King was now tormented by the troubles and roguery of both his Parliament and his family. Even his favourite, Princess Amelia, had caused him unhappiness for she was having a love affair with a Mr. Fitzroy, and it was said that she had confessed to her father that she had married her lover. But greater grief was in store for the King. In November 2nd 1810 Princess Amelia died suddenly. The blow was too much for his tottering reason and he relapsed into a state of complete and final insanity. The Regency was inevitable.

6

A few years previously the Prince had shown an interest in Lady Hertford, who was in her forties but still attractive, with the reputation of being the best-dressed woman in London. At that time, as she was married to an extremely wealthy peer, a liaison with the Prince who had little power and immense debts, offered but slight advancement in her social position. Now that the Regency was at hand he became a much more attractive proposition. Whereas before she had rejected his overtures, which had been a source of embarrassment to Mrs. Fitzherbert, now she encouraged them. The Prince visited her at Hertford House in Manchester Square, which now holds the magnificent Wallace Collection, owned by the nation and inspired by the Regent; for

Lord Hertford was like the Prince a collector of *objets d'art* and they shared artistic feeling as well as Lady Hertford.

The Prince first met Lady Hertford through a *cause célèbre* known as the Seymour Case. The sister-in-law of the Hertfords, Lady Horatio Seymour, left her daughter Minnie to the adoption of Mrs. Fitzherbert. When the parents of Minnie Seymour died the executors objected on religious and moral grounds, to the child being in Mrs. Fitzherbert's keeping. Lady Horatio Seymour had been friendly with the Prince and the executors also did not wish any misconstruction to be placed on the paternity of the child. Minnie, who was devoted to Mrs. Fitzherbert and the Prince, did not wish to be parted from them. She threw her arms round the Prince imploring: "You will fight for me Prinney?"

The Prince, always susceptible to children, offered to give the child a dowry of ten thousand pounds provided she was allowed to stay with Mrs. Fitzherbert. The case went before the House but Eldon, the Tory Lord Chancellor, adjudicated in favour of the executors. An appeal against the decision was made and it fortuitously coincided with a change of Government. Erskine, the Whig Lord Chancellor, gave the child to the care of Lord Hertford, who was head of the Seymour family, and he in turn, influenced by his wife, placed the child with Mrs. Fitzherbert. Thus Maria gained a daughter and lost a husband, for the Prince formed an attachment to Lady Hertford.

The Prince always regarded Minnie Seymour as his own child and when he parted from Maria Fitzherbert his feelings for Minnie remained the same. Letters survive showing the great fondness between them, and years later when she married a George Dawson Damen the Prince gave her a handsome dowry.

It is possible that the Prince, as the prospect of his becoming Defender of the Faith came nearer, was influenced by the fact that Lady Hertford was a strong Protestant, but undoubtedly he also realized that Mrs. Fitzherbert had lost her physical attractions and justifiably had also become an embittered woman. He always leaned towards women advisers and this time he weighed in the balance the opinion of Mrs. Fitzherbert, which was that he should stand by the Whigs, against the physical attractions and opinion of his new favourite, Lady Hertford, that he should retain the Tories.

He accepted Lady Hertford's counsel and it was the beginning of the end for Maria. Lady Hertford was invited to the Pavilion at Brighton and the situation became untenable for Mrs. Fitzherbert. She wrote the Prince a letter in which she said : " Whatever may be thought of me by some individuals, it is well known Your Royal Highness four and twenty years ago placed me in a situation so nearly connected with your own that I have a claim upon you for protection. I feel I owe it to myself not to be insulted under your roof with impunity. The influence you are now under and the conduct of one of your servants,* I am sorry to say, has the appearance of your sanction and support, and renders my situation in your house, situated as I am, impossible any longer to submit to."

The rebuff given to her by the Prince when she asked to be told her place at the Regency Gala was the final blow. She again wrote to him : " You, Sir, are not aware, in your anxiety to fill your table with persons only of the highest rank, that, by excluding her who now addresses you merely for want of those titles that others possess, you are excluding the person, who is not unjustly suspected by the world of possessing in silence unassumed and unsustained a rank given her by yourself above that of any other person present. Having never forfeited my title to Your Royal Highness' public as well as private consideration by any act of my life, to what could this etiquette be for the first time imputed? No one, my dear Sir, has proved themselves less solicitous than myself. But I cannot be indifferent to the fair, honourable appearance of consideration from you, which I have hitherto possessed, and which I feel I deserve and for which reason I can never submit to appear in your house in any place or situation but in that where you first placed me many years ago."

Mrs. Fitzherbert retired gracefully and took a small house at Parson's Green. The Prince, perhaps with a twinge of conscience, visited Brighton now only occasionally and on the rare occasions in London when they met they ignored each other. Mrs. Fitzherbert's withdrawal however was eased by the Regent when he settled her outstanding debts, which were considerable,

* The Prince's Secretary, Blomfield, an artillery officer promoted for his musical accomplishments.

and she was already in receipt of an annuity of £6,000 a year, secured by a mortgage on the Pavilion. From the letters preserved in the British Museum Mrs. Fitzherbert's future correspondence was always of a pecuniary nature. The worst ending to a love affair. She died at Brighton in 1837.

7

When Caroline left Carlton House for her villa at Blackheath in 1796, the Prince allowed her to see their daughter, Charlotte, without hindrance, and she used to drive up to London constantly to play with her child. On these occasions the Prince avoided meeting her, but the Princess had accepted the situation for she was happy in being her own mistress. Then in December 1798 the Prince made an attempt at reconciliation by sending Caroline a letter, inviting her to dinner at Carlton House and also to spend the winter there. Unfortunately Caroline enjoying herself at Blackheath did not relish a return to Carlton House and she refused the invitation. The lost opportunity was a turning point in her life, for the Prince began to restrict her visits to Charlotte.

The declined overture was not necessarily the only reason for the attitude of the Prince. One of her Ladies-in-Waiting, Lady Charlotte Bury, reveals in her Diary that Caroline was eccentric, boring and vulgar, and that often she was guilty of strange and even scandalous behaviour. She burdened her guests continually with her tales of woe and recriminations against her husband and everything she said or did was reported back to the Prince; accounts which were probably vitriolically embellished on the way.

Caroline began to adopt children as a reprisal for the adoption of Minnie Seymour by the Prince and soon collected nine of them. They were not brought up as her own children but whenever she entertained they were trotted out as Caroline's party-piece. Later she adopted another child, William Austin, the son of a sail-maker, and this baby claimed a special place in her affections for he was treated as her own child. She called him " Willikins " and all her frustrated mother love was lavished upon her latest acquisition; she doted on him. She liked to think he was really her own child, and indeed gossips agreed with her. Caroline's reply when she heard of these rumours was, " Prove it and he shall be your King." The rumours, however, were not to be dismissed so lightly, for the Prince saw in them the grounds for divorce from a wife he believed to be unfaithful.

It came to Caroline's ears that a friend of hers, Lady Douglas, who lived with her husband Sir John Douglas at Blackheath, had been impugning her character. Caroline terminated the friendship and made a bitter enemy. Sir John Douglas was in the service of the Duke of Sussex, and in 1805 the Douglases signed a statement, before the Duke, in which they alleged that Caroline had said that Willikins was her own child. They also alleged that she had committed misconduct with a number of men including Sir Sydney Smith, Captain Manby, George Canning, and Sir Thomas Lawrence the painter.

In 1806 Caroline, who was now living at Montague House, was visited by the Duke of Kent who reported officially that the King had appointed a commission to investigate the allegations. The report of the Delicate Investigation cleared the Princess of having an illegitimate child but added a rider finding her guilty of indiscretions.

To clear her name the Princess had the whole affair made into a book by Spencer Perceval who supported her case. Five thousand copies were printed but were never issued, for the Grenville Ministry was replaced and in the succeeding Government Perceval was appointed Chancellor of the Exchequer, and for him the time was inopportune. Caroline cynically remarked that she had only committed adultery once—and that was with the husband of Mrs. Fitzherbert.

In April 1807 a Minute of Council cleared the character of the Princess, and she was again received at Court and given rooms at Kensington Palace. The whole nation applauded the vindication and Caroline was cheered wherever she went, in the drawing-rooms and in the streets. In June, the Prince and the Princess met at the court celebration of the King's birthday. They came face-to-face, he bowed, she acknowledged the bow and they exchanged brief remarks which were to be their last words, for they never spoke to each other again.

Among the guests who witnessed the venom-charged meeting of the Prince of Wales and his Princess, at the King's birthday celebration in June 1807 was Charlotte, their daughter; a lively, talkative eleven-year-old hoyden. She was accustomed to being in the centre of controversy for from birth she had been torn between father and mother and grandfather.

The King had always felt concern about her upbringing for he did not regard his son as a suitable father. In turn the Prince was determined to keep her himself and even more determined to keep Charlotte away from her mother, whom he was sure would turn his daughter against him. To obtain the military command which he so anxiously sought the Prince offered to allow the King to take charge of Charlotte's upbringing. When the command was not forthcoming he withdrew his offer to the intense annoyance of his father, who had already planned and discussed at great length his schemes for her education. They compromised with a joint control which resulted in constant friction, for the King also wished Caroline to have her say.

Charlotte lived first in the hectic atmosphere of Carlton House, through which a caravanserai of art dealers, architects, furniture dealers, artists, jewellers, tailors, and shopmen constantly passed ministering to the whims of the Prince. In one year he spent a hundred thousand pounds on furniture, twelve thousand on china, three thousand on ormulu, and thousands more on jewellery and silverware. At night it was the place of drunken orgies and wild, strange happenings, often involving middle-class girls introduced for the occasion. Later, Charlotte lived at Lower Lodge, Windsor and at Warwick House, a building in Carlton House yard. In the summer she went to Weymouth, the King's favourite resort, and sometimes to Bognor. Her instructors, preceptors and governesses changed with the vagaries of her father and grandfather, for they were the pieces on the chess board in the battle for control.

It was at this time that the Prince demonstrated his acute perceptivity of recognizing ability in others by inviting a young lawyer, Henry Brougham, to meet him. Brougham was a man of exceptional intelligence and forcefulness and the Prince admired his astuteness and brilliant conversation. He became a frequent guest at the Pavilion but Brougham was a careerist and, as later events proved, his road did not lead to Carlton House.

Charlotte was a boisterous, mischievous and yet shrewd child, capable of striking a servant and yet never incapable of finding an excuse or of writing a honeyed apology for a wrong-doing. She was incorrigible and full of pranks. She referred to her grandmother as "the Merry Wife of Windsor", and of her grandfather she said: "I understand he is as mad as a puss!" She was lively and intelligent, with a will of her own, and of this strange family she was probably the most popular member.

In 1809 and 1810 the royal family was the centre of two unsavoury incidents that had the whole country talking. In the first episode the King's favourite son, the Duke of York, was involved. A demi-mondaine, Mary Anne Clarke, had been his mistress, with a house in Gloucester Place and twenty servants to attend to her needs. The affair had ended in 1806. The Duke of York, who was Commander-in-Chief of the Army, was accused in the House of Commons of conniving with her in selling commissions in the Army.

Mary Anne Clarke was examined before the House in support of the charges, and from her portrait it is evident she made a very attractive witness. The investigation lasted seven weeks and meanwhile the Duke resigned his post as Commander-in-Chief. The result of the proceedings was that he was exonerated; with his reputation somewhat tarnished. In 1810 Mary Anne published in book form her version of the affair which she titled *The Rival Princes*. In it she attacked Colonel Wardle, the Member of Parliament who made the accusations against the Duke of York, and Major Dodd, Secretary to the Duke of Kent. She alleged that they were acting on behalf of the Duke of Kent who wanted to remove his royal brother from the command of the army so that he might occupy the position himself. The Duke of Kent, she asserted, through Dodd promised to give her "five thousand pounds, besides four hundred a year secured to me—my debts all discharged—and a house furnished in any style of elegance I pleased," if she lent her support to the charges.

The other scandalous episode concerned the Duke of Cumberland. One of his valets, an Italian named Sellis, had attempted to kill the Duke in his bedroom at St. James's Palace, and it was said he then committed suicide. The Duke was wounded undoubtedly, and the valet was dead, but the circumstances were suspicious and in the evidence were many discrepancies that were never explained. It was rumoured that the Duke had murdered his valet. The Prince of Wales took his brother into Carlton House whilst the London mob were allowed into the Duke's bedroom to view the bloodstains. After due investigation the Duke was exonerated.

In the following year, 1811, Charlotte was fifteen. She was precocious, tall, and well-developed for her age, both mentally and physically, with a white skin and rounded body, and was already interested in the opposite sex. When she heard the news that her father was giving a fête at Carlton House on the 5th of June she was desperate to attend what promised to be the most magnificent ball that London had ever seen.

It was indeed a splendid, breath-taking affair but Charlotte was not there : instead she had been sent to Windsor to be out of the way. Caroline had not expected an invitation and had not received one, but she allowed her Ladies-in-Waiting to attend and even gave them new dresses for the occasion; whilst she sat it out at Kensington Palace with three friends to keep her company.

The date was June 19th and not the 5th as first planned, for the arrangements had taken longer than anticipated, and indeed the affair was truly staggering in its conception.

At eight o'clock in the evening St. James's Street, and the adjoining streets, were jammed with the carriages and sedan chairs of the arriving guests as they made their way in a long, colourful procession to Carlton House, which was ablaze with lights and decorations.

Inside the house there was a long table, two hundred yards long, with two table-sprigs, each a hundred yards in length, branching through the house into marquees and then into the gardens. Strategically the guests were seated so that from every position the Regent could be seen sitting at the crossroads of the tables, resplendent in his scarlet uniform against a background of blue silk hangings with the fleur-de-lis design in gold.

He was surrounded by the glitter of silver plate, with a huge crown and the letters " G.R." above his head. In front of him a silver fountain played and the water ran down a flower-decked channel the entire length of the table, in which small fishes swam. The whole scene was brightly and glitteringly illuminated by masses of magnificent chandeliers and candelabras. Bands played in flower-decked tents in the gardens as innumerable courses (for the entrée there was a choice of one hundred dishes) and magnificent wines followed one after another, and gaiety, laughter and debauchery swept the many hundreds of guests gaily far into the night.

A large crowd gathered in front of Carlton House, and for a few days after the fête pandemonium broke loose. Many people were injured in the rush when the gates were opened to allow the populace to view the scene of the bacchanalian banquet with which the Prince Regent made his bow.

9

Lady Hertford was the new guiding force in the Regent's life. His tastes had outgrown young and frivolous women for he realized that their immaturity was inclined to make him appear grotesque. From this time he loved only middle-aged women and Lady Hertford was a prime example of her kind, combining beauty, brains and sophistication.

Her son, Lord Yarmouth entered the Royal Household, where his father already had a post. He had bright red whiskers and was known as the " Yarmouth Bloater ", or sometimes " Red Herrings ". A caricaturist depicted Lady Hertford as Delilah, snipping the locks of the Prince, as Samson, sprawling between her knees. Standing by, giving advice, was Lord Yarmouth.

Isabella Seymour, Lady Hertford, was a vain, conniving woman and cautiously she refused to live under the same roof as the Prince, except when he visited her at Ragley Hall. When in London he called on her at Hertford House and every afternoon his yellow carriage with drawn purple blinds could be seen in Manchester Square. Hertford House was the " Gaunt House " in Thackeray's *Vanity Fair*; although it was an anachronism on the part of Thackeray when he said, " the Prince and Perdita have been in and out of that door," for Perdita had died in 1800 and never visited Hertford House.

Lady Hertford was a Tory and a staunch Protestant and she influenced the politics of the Regent accordingly. The Prince already had his list of possible new Whig Ministers but when Grey advocated the exclusion of two of the Regent's friends, Sheridan and Lord Moira, he abandoned the Whigs and retained the Tory, Perceval. The Whigs had also opposed the re-appointment of the Duke of York to the Army, but the Prince, on assuming the Regency, immediately arranged for his brother's return to the Horse Guards as though the Mary Anne Clarke affair had never happened.

Unfortunately Perceval did not prove to be so accommodating in matters of finance as the Regent had hoped, and he found a more compliant member of the Cabinet in Wellesley, the brother of the famous General (on whom the Prince had bestowed an Earldom as one of his first acts on becoming Regent). The Wellesley family were to be a great political influence in the Regent's life.

The powers of the Regent during the first year were curtailed, but in 1812 these restrictions were lifted. Lord Grey and Lord Grenville, the leaders of the Whig party, expected to be given office. The Prince was torn between his Whig friends and the Hertfords. He suggested a coalition, which was rejected by Grey and Grenville. On May 11th, 1812, the problem was resolved, for the Prime Minister Spencer Perceval was assassinated in the lobby of the House of Commons* and the Government fell.

The Regent dallied with his decisions concerning the appointment of Ministers. He was again desperately short of money and hoped to find a combination which would ease his financial difficulties, and also be capable of advancing the country's military affairs abroad; Wellesley was deputed to arrange a fusion of the two sides, but when the Hertfords opposed him he was relieved of his duties. Lord Moira also failed to form a Government and eventually the Regent entrusted the task temporarily

* By a man named Bellingham.

to Lord Liverpool; but as events turned out he was to remain in office for fifteen years.

Sheridan stayed with the Regent and said that the Prince was acting according to his conscience. This was the advice given by the Prince to Sheridan when he told him how to vote on the Catholic Question. Erskine, the Whig Lord Chancellor, when asked by Lady Hertford why, as the Prince's friend, he had not voted for the Government said the Regent had told him to vote as he felt. The explanation that the Regent once gave for not supporting the Whigs was that he "withdrew himself from his early friends for the good of the country." Of these friends, Fox was dead and Sheridan was drunk. Time was to test his decision for he had come to power at a critical time; the country was at a low ebb with an insane King and only a retreat to show for its military endeavours.

It was about this time that another friend also suffered an eclipse. The friend was Beau Brummell. The details of the quarrel are not clear, but the most quoted incident is that the Regent spoke to Lord Alvanley at a ball but ignored Brummell who was standing near. Brummell retaliated by saying in a loud voice, "Alvanley, who is your fat friend?" These few deadly words spread around London and spelt the end of their friendship.

Brummell was still friendly with the Duke and Duchess of York, however, and often stayed with them at Oatlands, near Weybridge, but he made the fatal step on the tight-rope along which he had always balanced. The man who made of himself an incomparable masterpiece of individuality, the supreme egotist, ended his days at Caen, poverty-stricken and insane; a man sneered at and jeered at : yet when Byron had been asked to place in order the three greatest living men he had replied : " 1 Brummell, 2 Napoleon and 3 myself."

That Byron should say this, even half-jestingly, establishes the tremendous effect that Brummell made upon the people of his period : surely the only possible period in which he could have existed. He was unique.

The Prince Regent was an egocentric and very sensitive to any criticism of his appearance, but undeniably, on many occasions beneath a selfish exterior he revealed a kindly and thoughtful nature. At the time of the Brummell insult his health had deteriorated; he suffered from violent headaches and his sight was bad. His mode of living and the tremendous amount of alcohol he consumed were bound to exact a toll and it is surprising that the effects had not become evident earlier.

He became even more unpredictable. His drinking increased and as Charlotte, now old enough to be critical, used to say, " too much oil has been put into the lamp." He became more reckless and was careless about being seen drunk in public and was often violent and abusive. Yet despite his sometimes detestable attitudes he still could be charming and likeable when in the mood. One trivial incident is an example of his forbearance. A boy, the son of the Comptroller to the Regent's Household, bragged to his friends that the next time he dined at Carlton House he would ask the Prince to ring the bell. When the time came, the boy courageous with champagne duly made his request. The Regent rang the bell, and when the servant appeared, said in a tolerant voice, " Put that drunken boy to bed!" On another occasion he chaffed with a servant and when the servant overstepped the mark in repartee, he said good-naturedly, " This is all right between us, Sam, but be careful with Norfolk."

The panacea for his ailments in accordance with the custom of his day was to be bled profusely for it was thought that to withdraw the polluted blood was to remove the cause. Only an extremely strong constitution could have withstood for so long the Prince's gruelling treatment.

With the old King safely out of the way the Regent was now free to arrange the upbringing of his daughter, Charlotte, as he wished. He decided that she should spend more time at Windsor with the Queen, although the old lady, burdened with her grief, prim and severe, was hardly a suitable mentor for a dogmatic and precocious hoyden. Charlotte hated the situation.

She talked and chattered jumping from one topic to another in her exuberance. Life was an adventure to the coltish Charlotte and the restrictions at Windsor were irksome; she longed for freedom. Probably she was happiest when she visited her aunt, the Duchess of York, at Oatlands, for this strange menagerie of a household, where fifty dogs ran about the house and where ostriches, kangaroos and other animals roamed the grounds, was a complete contrast to life at Windsor, or anywhere else for that matter.

When she drove around London in her carriage with Lady de Clifford, her head Governess, she was delighted by the attention she received. She returned the encouraging shouts of the mob by bowing, waving and smiling, and the crowd loved her for it. In those days it was customary for the people to express their likes and dislikes of the Royal Family as they felt fit. They shouted advice and opinions and often threw refuse at the carriages if the particular member was in disfavour.

It was all very exciting to Charlotte and very disquieting to the Regent, who was jealous of the popularity of Charlotte and annoyed by the expressions of sympathy for Caroline. Inevitably when they met there was a clash of wills and they bickered childishly; for she was too much like her father to submit easily and she took her mother's side.

The meetings of mother and daughter were now restricted to once a fortnight and when the Regent heard that Caroline had visited Charlotte at Windsor he sent her a message that she was not to go there again. Caroline's reply was that if she could see her daughter weekly she would obey. To make matters worse, Lady de Clifford, who had been appointed by the Regent, quarrelled with him and gave up her post. It is said that she revealed to the Regent in confidence that Charlotte was encouraging the attentions of Captain Hesse of the 10th Hussars, who was the natural son of the Duke of York. The Regent saw a potential scandal in Charlotte's affair with the devil-may-care young officer and forbade her to see him again. The Regent lost an ally and Charlotte gained a friend in her ex-governess, for Charlotte kept Lady de Clifford informed of events by letter. When the Regent heard of this he had Charlotte's letters intercepted. The indignant Charlotte challenged her father on this point and the fissure between father and daughter widened.

The appointment of a new governess caused another family storm. Charlotte's seventeenth birthday was very near and she wrote to her father requesting that instead of a new governess she be allowed to have her own establishment with Ladies-in-Waiting. The Regent, having in mind her recent affair with

Captain Hesse,* believed that strict surveillance was the best safeguard and replied that as long as she lived she should not have an establishment unless she married. Not to be deterred Charlotte wrote to Lord Liverpool seeking his support. The Regent was furious at Charlotte's subterfuge and visited her at Windsor. For support he took along Lord Eldon, the Lord Chancellor, and the persistent Princess was arraigned before the old Queen, the Regent, Lord Eldon and Lady de Clifford. She was the only calm one in the resulting scene of abuse and invective, but afterwards with one of her aunts she sobbed out her feelings of frustration and humiliation. It is said that this clash with her father was the cause of the slight stammer she developed whenever they met.

As a compromise the Regent decided that the two assistants to the Duchess of Leeds, the new head governess, were to be called not governesses but Lady-companions. Unfortunately the Regent decided that one of the Lady-companions should be a Miss Cornelia Knight, who had been in the Queen's service for seven years, which annoyed the Queen. After a great deal of wrangling, letter-writing and heart-burnings the Regent had his way and Miss Knight was given the post. But what was more important to Charlotte was the news that in future she herself was to be installed at Warwick House and would live at Windsor on alternate weeks.

Warwick House is situated in a corner of what was the courtyard of Carlton House and here, the Prince decided, his daughter would be under his watchful eye. He supervised and arranged her life and entertainments down to the last detail, and she was surrounded by his rules and regulations. The most rigid of these rules was that Charlotte was never to be left alone with her mother for one single instant, but this rule served to draw the two females together in a fellow feeling of conspiracy and evasion. Thus, the estrangement of father and daughter grew, and as Charlotte's popularity increased as a result of her presence in London so the Regent's jealousy became almost insane in its intensity.

* Captain Hesse went abroad and continued his philanderings. He became the lover of the Queen of Naples until the liaison caused a scandal. After a series of similar affairs he was killed in a duel of honour by Count Leon, a natural son of Napoleon.

The sympathy of the people was with Charlotte and Caroline, and as their popularity grew so the antagonism towards the Regent became more marked. Throughout his life the Regent was the subject of lampoons, squibs, caricatures, notably by Gillray, Rowlandson and Cruikshank, and as he drove down St. James's Street and saw the crowd outside the shop where these cartoons were exhibited he must have boiled with indignation.

This was the age of " privilege " and the privilege extended to the Press; provided the owners of the journals were on the side of authority. On the rare occasions when the publishers of these libels were prosecuted they were given heavy fines and long terms of imprisonment, but apparently the risk was worth the sensation the libels caused. There was even " privilege " in prison, for if one had the money, prison was not such a bad place : friends could be entertained and food and wine sent in.

In February 1813 readers of the *Morning Chronicle* were entertained by a long letter from Caroline to the Regent. The letter which took up nearly two whole columns outlined her grievances in some detail.

Apparently the instigator of the letter was Henry Brougham who was very much in sympathy with Caroline. He had written her a twelve-page letter stating her case and advising Caroline to send a letter in similar terms to the Regent and also to the Lord Chancellor.

Caroline sent her letter to the Regent on the 14th of January. It was returned unopened. Accompanying the letter was a short note from the Prime Minister, Lord Liverpool, saying that he had been ordered by the Regent to say that " having some years ago declared he never would receive any letter or paper from the Princess, His Royal Highness intended to adhere to that determination."

Brougham told the Princess to return the letter to Lord Liverpool with a command that he should present her petition to the Regent. Again it was returned to Caroline, and again she sent it to Lord Liverpool; this time asking Lord Liverpool and the

Lord Chancellor to read the letter to the Regent. Lord Liverpool replied stating that he had acquainted the Regent with the contents of the letter.

On the 19th of January she asked for a reply, and as she did not receive one she wrote again on the 26th. The reply to this letter was a brief one and ended by saying: " His Royal Highness was not pleased to signify any commands upon it." Caroline sent a copy of her letter to the *Morning Chronicle*.

The immediate effect of the letter appearing in the Press was first felt by Charlotte. She was ordered not to see her mother and three days later the Regent and Lord Liverpool arrived at Warwick House. The outcome was a very wretched interview. Finally the Regent said " that an investigation was being made with respect to the conduct of her mother, on the result of which depended her ever being allowed to visit her again." Charlotte was grief-stricken. The Regent said he would come back in a day or so and acquaint her with the result of the investigation.

The days went by and Charlotte did not receive the promised visit. She was wretched and in a state of trepidation, for she had heard that Sir John and Lady Douglas, the authors of the previous Caroline scandal, had been visiting Carlton House. At last she could not stand the suspense any longer and sent her father an affectionate note asking to see him. He replied that the time was not opportune but when this unpleasant affair was settled they would, of course, meet with pleasure.

So, in suspended misery Charlotte spent her days. She refused to leave the house and became silent and morose. Sir Henry Halford, the court physician visited her, anxious about her health, and tried to persuade her to take some exercise. She refused as she also refused the invitations to dinners and the theatre.

Eventually Charlotte was told by her friends that her refusal to appear in public was lending credence to a rumour concerning herself and her cousin, the son of the Duke of Clarence and Mrs. Jordan. To dispel the rumour she agreed to be seen taking a drive in the park every day.

The affair of Caroline and the war with Napoleon vied with each other as the topics of the day.

The final result of the former was an anti-climax for when the report of the investigation arrived at Warwick House it turned out to be nothing more than a raking over of all the ashes of the previous " Delicate Investigation ". The report gave all the evidence detrimental to Caroline but did not include the judgment of acquittal. For three days it filled the front pages of the newspapers but it had the opposite effect to the one the Regent had planned. It disgusted everyone and the Regent was in " universal contempt ". The sentimentality of the masses was stirred by the picture of a mother being kept away from her daughter by a domineering husband, and Samuel Whitbread brought tears to the eyes of the Members in the House by his poignant portrayal of the situation. Caroline was deluged by letters of sympathy, and when she visited the Opera or the Theatre the audience rose to her with a storm of applause both as she entered and when she left. Caroline was jubilant and her parties became more hectic and the music round the piano became more noisy and squally. She is reported to have said : " Oh my Gott! let out the poor dear old King and shut up my husband."

The Regent had been having second thoughts about the affair, and on the 25th of February he visited Warwick House and gave Charlotte permission to visit her mother the following day. A few days later Caroline's carriage passed Charlotte's and the daughter ordered her coachman to follow her mother's carriage. From their carriage windows they enjoyed a few minutes' conversation near the Serpentine, surrounded by a sympathetic crowd of onlookers. The Regent heard of the meeting and was furious, so obviously the reprieve was only a momentary one.

Charlotte's life at Warwick House continued its dull, monotonous way, punctuated by the occasional visits of her father and, of course, the resultant bickerings. In the wings, watching the satirical comedy being played by father, mother and daughter was Henry Brougham and he nicknamed them " The Prinnies "—Old P., Mrs. P., and Little P. As an aggrieved Whig he prompted Caroline and Charlotte to enjoy the annoyance of the Regent. He even gloated over the physical infirmities and ill-health of the Regent, whose gouty leg was always good for a laugh.

On August the 12th the Regent celebrated his birthday by giving a party at Sandhurst and all the royal family were present. He ignored the Warwick House contingent, however, and in retaliation Charlotte turned away from the Queen. It was a dismal affair for Charlotte, but apparently the Regent enjoyed it after his fashion, for at the end of the evening he was seen with the Duke of York amongst a heap of other inert figures beneath the table.

The Regent and his daughter differed almost automatically but on one thing they were agreed. It was that she should marry and the sooner the better. To Charlotte it meant freedom and to the Regent it represented the means by which he could get his too-popular daughter out of England. To this end he had chosen as the intended husband the hereditary Prince of Orange, who was " a very thin ill-looking man in a plain suit with the star of the Black Eagle of Prussia." He had been two years at Oxford and had served on the Duke of Wellington's staff in the Peninsular. His ineffectual manner, his plain face, and his ingratiating flaccid trick of shaking hands almost continually, were not likely to appeal to the ebullient, outspoken Charlotte. She found him nauseating. If she had to marry she decided it had better be her thirty-seven-years-old cousin, the Duke of Gloucester. The Regent objected to her choice and so there was a stalemate.

The 7th of January 1814 was Charlotte's eighteenth birthday and as a celebration she was allowed to visit her mother. In February the icy fingers of a relentless winter gripped England. In London it was bitterly cold, so cold indeed, that the Thames froze; tents, booths and sideshows were erected and for weeks a fair was held on the ice. Charlotte was confined to Warwick House and in the meantime the Prince of Orange returned home.

During the following spring letters were received from the Netherlands formally asking her to marry the Prince of Orange, accompanied by his portrait and a present of jewellery. Charlotte was told she was now engaged. She was panic-stricken at the thought of leaving England and sent a letter to the Regent begging to be shown the marriage contract and asking for a clause to be inserted which would prevent her being kept out of

England against her will. The Regent refused her request, saying that the contract was the business of the fathers.

Although the Regent advocated his daughter's marriage to the Prince of Orange he himself did not find the young man's company entertaining for he did not invite him to stay at Carlton House. Instead, the effusive suitor lodged with his tailor from whose house he sallied forth daily to woo the future Queen of England.

II

April of this year saw the drama of Napoleon reaching its finale. The Russian campaign and the Peninsular war had forced the Emperor to abdicate. He was given a pension and a retreat on the Isle of Elba.

England was interested in the creation of the United Netherlands as a military bulwark against France, and thus the marriage was of political importance. The Grand Duchess of Oldenburg, sister to the Emperor of Russia, was in London and left her name at Warwick House. She was staying at the Pulteney Hotel in Piccadilly and here Charlotte visited her, chaperoned by the Duchess of Leeds. It was believed that the Grand Duchess during the ensuing private conversation expressed strong views against the forthcoming marriage, as the bond between England and Holland was not in Russia's interest. News of the meeting reached the ears of the Regent and he gave instructions that Charlotte was to see as little as possible of the Grand Duchess, for he did not wish his plans to be disturbed.

Arrangements for the wedding were now under way and the Regent sent to Charlotte the list of guests he had prepared. Charlotte scanned the list and saw that her mother's name had been omitted. Thereupon she struck out the name of the Prince of Orange and returned the list to her father.

King Louis XVIII was restored, making a triumphant state entry into London and investing the Regent with the Order of the Holy Ghost. Charlotte was not given a place to watch the procession and with Miss Knight, one of her Lady Companions, she drove into Piccadilly to view the celebrations. The crowd was so great in Piccadilly that their carriage was held up outside the Pulteney Hotel. As usual, whenever she was seen, her carriage was surrounded by a cheering and delighted mob. The Grand Duchess sent word inviting Charlotte and Miss Knight into the hotel. As they left the cheering was resumed.

The defeat of Napoleon had turned London into a carnival of excitement. Foreign Kings, Emperors, Dukes, Princes and Generals poured into the capital, and the Regent exercised his ingenuity and vivid imagination to the full in devising a round of continuous entertainment. The London scene, with pagodas and temples in the parks, had an Oriental air, alive with the sound of laughter and the popping of harmless guns, for the war was now a game and on the Serpentine miniature battleships fought mock battles.

Outstanding amongst the foreign visitors was Alexander I, Emperor of All the Russians, an imperious, awe-inspiring figure. Included in his retinue was Prince Leopold, the third son of the Duke of Saxe-Coburg-Saalfield, a young man destined to play an important role in the drama of England's history. He was twenty-three, a serious pale-faced young man, studious and ambitious, and already he was experienced in the ways of the world.

12

The Russian Ambassador lived in Harley Street and Leopold found accommodation at a greengrocer's in the nearby Marylebone High Street. Thus two princes, on a romantic mission for the hand of Princess Charlotte, were conducting their suits from prosaic lodging. The Prince of Orange believed that the marriage was virtually settled, and that apart from his visits to Warwick House he was free to enjoy himself as he wished; whilst Leopold, much shrewder, was playing a more cunning game. He had already been introduced to Charlotte by the Grand Duchess at the Pulteney Hotel, and had heard of Charlotte's objections to going abroad; he would be happy to stay in England.

Charlotte's engagement was now in its final stages. The Regent visited her at Warwick House in order to persuade her not to insist on the inclusion of the clause in the marriage contract concerning her residence out of England, " as a mark of civility to the House of Orange." Charlotte was adamant on this point, but in the meanwhile the preparations for her marriage were progressing. The Queen had already ordered her trousseau, and, according to Creevey, Brougham reported, " that he has had direct intercourse with the young one and that he has impressed upon her this fact that, if her mother goes away from England, as she is always threatening to do from ill-usage in the country, that then a divorce will inevitably take place, a second marriage follow, and then the young Princess's title to the throne be gone."

This news was extremely disquieting to Charlotte, for like her mother, she already had eyes on the Queenship of England. It was an added reason for remaining in England. She wrote a letter to the Prince of Orange ending the engagement, and threw herself tearfully into the comforting arms of Miss Mercer, her new governess. The news spread in ever-widening circles, as royal affairs are wont to do, until it became public gossip.

To Leopold it was the signal for him to begin a campaign of insinuation. Discreetly, he positioned himself so that " his dark handsomeness " should be noticed by Charlotte whenever possible. William of Orange, tearful and resigned, returned home and the field was clear. The nation's sympathy was with Charlotte and the Regent became even more unpopular as a domineering father.

Caroline wrote at this time that her daughter " has resumed her former character of intrepidity and fortitude, as her father frightens her in every way." The Regent was furious at the baulking of his plans; he dismissed Charlotte's household and ordered her to go to Windsor. " Depend upon it, as long as I live, you shall never have an establishment unless you marry," was his final remark. The furious Charlotte flounced from the room, determined to run away. Dressed in her bonnet and shawl she ran out into the narrow lane that led past the royal mews, in the centre of what is now Trafalgar Square, to Charing Cross, where there was a hackney-carriage rank. She jumped into the first coach and giving the driver a guinea told him to take her to Connaught Place, at the end of Oxford Street, where her mother lived.

Caroline was not at home, having gone to Blackheath for the

day, but Charlotte was not alone for long. Soon after her arrival a string of hackneys began to arrive. The Regent, immediately he heard that Charlotte had run into the open streets, ordered everyone in sight to bring her back, and soon a host of persuaders were on their way, among them the Duke of York, the Duke of Sussex, Lord Eldon, Lord Ellenborough, Brougham, the Bishop of Salisbury, Ladies-in-Waiting and eventually Caroline, who was returning home when a messenger gave her the news that Charlotte had " run away ". The assembly developed into a dinner party and from what she thought was her stronghold Charlotte sent a letter to her father in the form of an ultimatum. His reply was that she must " submit unconditionally ". The escapade developed into a long argument with everyone surrounding Charlotte, and it was not until dawn that Brougham persuaded her to return to Carlton House. As Charlotte left there was a tearful scene between mother and daughter, which ended with Caroline in hysterics.

The Regent ordered Charlotte into quarantine at Cranbourne Lodge, Windsor, where she was only allowed occasional visitors. An order, in the Regent's handwriting permitting Charlotte's governess, Miss Mercer, to pay a visit to Cranbourne Lodge still survives. Charlotte had a great affection for Miss Mercer and during their separation she wrote a daily, and almost illegible, letter to her governess. Ironically, Miss Mercer herself came near to the throne of England, for the Duke of Clarence, later William IV, proposed to her. She married the son of Talleyrand, however, and thus became an ancestor of the Lansdowne family, in whose archives the letters from the Princess are preserved.

During her stay at Windsor Charlotte received a shock; it was a letter from her mother saying that she was going abroad. At the beginning of August Charlotte was allowed to visit Connaught Place once again. This time to say ' goodbye ' to her mother and, though neither of them suspected it, this was a last goodbye, for they were never to meet again.

In September Charlotte, accompanied by her Lady-attendants, was taken to Weymouth for a holiday. She was back again at Cranbourne Lodge in November, but in the following Spring she was permitted to return to Warwick House; still jealously guarded. The monotony of her existence was relieved only by occasional visits to the Theatre and the Opera, but she had gained her way by dismissing the unwanted suitor, the Prince of Orange. The handsome figure of Prince Leopold was not to be seen for he had left London for Coburg at the end of July.

Meanwhile, across the channel the Continent was in a state of turmoil. Napoleon had escaped and the Hundred Days had begun. The fate of Europe was in the balance and the ominous sounds of rolling wheels, deadly drum-beats and marching feet were everywhere; filling the air with dread.

CHAPTER SIX

THE SAXE-COBURGS

I

THE FAMILY of Saxe-Coburg to which Prince Leopold belonged was an amazing one, for although their duchy was small and relatively unimportant the members exerted a great influence in the affairs of Europe and, as events transpired, particularly in the history of England.

In 1806 a Franco-Prussian war broke out and Francis Frederick-Antoine, the reigning Duke of Saxe-Coburg-Saalfield, occupied as he was with his rebellious, tax-burdened people, was unable to take part. Instead, his eldest son and heir, Ernst, fought against France. When the French victory came, Napoleon did not vent his anger against the father and allowed the Duke to send a plenipotentiary to sign the pact of allegiance to the Rheinbund. Before the pact was signed Frances Frederick died.

Napoleon who had been magnanimous to the father vengefully turned upon the son, the new Duke Ernst I. The duchy of Coburg was confiscated and the Duke's private fortune was declared forfeit. Ernst was desperate and approached the Czar of Russia to intercede on his behalf.

Ernst had first met the Czar in 1795 when he had accompanied his mother and three sisters to Petersburg. Empress Catherine had commanded her relative the Duchess of Coburg to bring her daughters for appraisal, as she wished to select a wife for her grandson, the brutal Constantine. The choice had fallen on the unfortunate Juliane, the youngest and prettiest of the trio. Catherine then sent the Duchess back to Coburg, but

Juliane stayed; and also Ernst for the Empress had taken a fancy to the good-looking eleven-year-old boy and made him a Colonel in her Grenadiers.

The three children played together whilst Juliane was groomed for marriage and the bride-elect became the butt of the two boys. Ernst diplomatically did not object to Constantine's cruelties and together they enjoyed brutal amusements; " firing live rats from cannon in the Marble Palace, kicking hussars to death," and generally entering into the vice of Petersburg. He was more astute than Constantine and kept in favour with Catherine, the Grand-Duke Alexander and the Grand-Duchess Elizabeth.

He now took advantage of his previous diplomacy and the Czar duly exerted his influence with Napoleon. Duke Ernst was permitted to enter the Confederation of the Rhine, but not content with this concession he made a claim for compensation for the damage that had been caused by the French troops as they swept through the neutral state of Coburg.

At this time, Duke Ernst is described as : " A tall young man, with the head rather stooping and covered with a profusion of black, curly hair, his physiognomy handsome, his stature elegant, his demeanour cold and haughty." He was nearly twenty-four. With his youngest brother, Leopold, he ventured to Paris to press his claim in person.

Duke Ernst and Prince Leopold were impressed with Paris. The Paris that fourteen years before had been the dreadful scene of bloodshed, anarchy and terror, was now in 1807, a triumphant and glorious city—vast sums of money from the subjugated states had swelled the coffers of the Treasury and the fruits of victory were sweet. Napoleon commenced a tremendous programme of public development to embellish his Capital. Bridges, arches, monuments and thoroughfares were built, including the Rue Napoleon (now Rue de la Paix) and the Temple of Glory (now known as the " Madeleine "). The city was rigorously cleansed, the stinking gutters which ran down the centre of the streets and flooded in wet weather were abolished. He instituted the first numbering of houses and by this simple method created order out of confusion.

Paris and Napoleon were at their zenith. The Court was magnificent, unequalled in Europe, and was graced by a collection of beautiful women, amongst whom Napoleon's sisters, the voluptuous Pauline and the pretty Caroline, were not outshone. These were the days of luxury, debauchery, and an imperial splendour, surpassing even the magnificence of ancient Rome. The Royal Courts of Europe vied with each other in their hedonism and brilliance, whilst on four of the thrones sat maniacs. In Portugal, the mad Maria I dressed in a child's clothes. In Denmark, Christian VII was an imbecile with loathsome habits. The King of Sweden was already showing signs of lunacy, whilst in England, George III had been hovering for almost ten years on the brink of complete insanity; but in Paris the brilliance of Napoleon shone like a star.

It was the age of youth; Napoleon himself was only thirty-eight and life was a continuous round of imperial functions, masked balls and theatrical entertainments, whilst for the populace there was a succession of fêtes. The rulers and princes of Europe were drawn to Paris like a Mecca and were entertained at the Royal Court and at Fontainebleau. The Emperor was surrounded by sycophants awed by the magnificence. Amongst these were a crowd of German princelings, once arrogant but now subservient. They received scant notice from Napoleon for he considered them to be a burden to their country, these "hungry flies who feasted on the wounds of their Fatherland," as Treitschke calls them; and a menace to France. Their petty principalities were innumerable and Baron Stein, for example, from his castle at Lahn alone, could view eight of them. Napoleon reduced the number to thirty-eight amongst which fortunately for Ernst and Leopold was Coburg.

The two young men found themselves unpretentious accommodation to suit their purses and settled down to enjoy themselves, whilst they waited an opportunity to approach the Emperor. In November Napoleon left Paris for Milan and the two brothers decided to await his return. In this very enjoyable city of Paris the brilliance of the social season was undiminished by the Emperor's absence for the programme he had planned was faithfully carried out.

Unfortunately Duke Ernst discovered that despite his youth and good-looks he did not have so much success with the Parisian ladies as he had expected. They found him abrupt, conceited and his French atrocious. He contemplated returning to Coburg : then he met for the first time Pauline Panam, a beautiful goddess of a girl, slender and yet voluptuous. " Her features were of the purest Greek type, her magnificent dark hair waved back, in rich masses from the white brow, and over the tiny ears; at the neck it was braided with a ribbon of gold. Her eyes were black, velvet soft, and had the long curling lashes for which the maids of Chio and Smyrna are famous, her complexion glowed with the bloom of tenderest youth. With her simple, classical white robe, a golden fillet her only adornment, she was, where all were fair, supremely beautiful." He found her delightful, vivacious, witty and yet naïve. Suddenly Pauline left with her chaperone.

Ernst discovered that she lived in the Rue Chantereine (later renamed Des Victoires) the street in which Bonaparte had wooed Madame de Beauharnais and where he had lived for a short time after his marriage.

Pauline Panam lived with her widowed mother and her widowed sister Madame Lingis, and when Ernst visited Rue Chantereine he found her playing with her sister's child Josephine, who was two years younger than Pauline. With her voluptuous, well-developed figure, the aunt seemed much older than the niece.

Her father had been a prosperous Greek merchant, living in Smyrna until forced to flee from the Turkish massacre of the Christians in 1780. Penniless, the family arrived in Marseilles but in a few years, with industry and business acumen, Alexandre Panam amassed another fortune. Again disaster overtook them. During the French Revolution his factory was destroyed and his business ruined. Soon afterwards he died, and his widow was left to fend for herself and her two children. Then followed years of trouble as the widow and her eldest daughter struggled to rebuild the business. They succeeded to some extent and were able to sell the concern for enough money to enable them to live modestly without working. They moved to Paris.

From the start Duke Ernst dazzled the Panam household. He was handsome, brilliant and full of promises, one of which was that he would arrange for Pauline to become one of the ladies-of-honour of his sister, the Grand Duchess Constantine; but he did not consider it worth-while mentioning the fact that his sister had already left her brutal husband. He became a constant and welcome visitor to the house. Ernst was a libertine and had seduced many girls in Coburg, now he was to add another name to his list. In her memoirs Pauline Panam describes the incident.

" He came that morning; I had been for some days indisposed, and continued in bed; my sister had just left the house.

" ' My dear little one,' he said, ' I am very unhappy; my affairs demand my presence in Germany; I must begone, I must quit you.'

" I immediately wept bitterly; he took his seat at the foot of my bed, and dried my tears with kisses. The sudden news completely overcame me; suffering and ill as I was I had no power left but to sign, and had no thought of resisting his caresses. The more he talked to me, respecting this unfortunate separation, the more copiously my tears flowed. He redoubled his ardour to alleviate my sorrow, whilst I became more incapable of extricating myself from his arms. He took advantage of this situation, he profited by my sorrow, my ignorance, my weakness; I became culpable, without feeling conscious of my faults. Never did a woman fall more blindly into the abyss. I was but fourteen."

2

In the following January Napoleon was back in Paris and the entertainments became even more splendid to celebrate his return. The Emperor was in great demand and there were too many claims on his time for Ernst to approach him. The Duke was receiving constant messages from Coburg urging him to return home. His mother, Duchess Augusta, was impatient and believed Ernst was wasting time and money in Paris on a hopeless cause. But now Ernst had an additional reason for staying.

At last a direct command came from the Duchess. He determined to make a final attempt to speak to the Emperor and then return to Coburg; and with him he intended to take his delightful plaything.

His long delayed audience with the Emperor yielded absolutely nothing and now there was nothing to keep him in Paris. He discussed with Madame Panam his plans for Pauline, and the widow was delighted at the prospect of her daughter becoming a Lady-in-Waiting to a Grand Duchess. She herself would accompany her daughter to hand her over to the royal patroness.

This was an unexpected setback to Ernst's plans and he set out to convince the mother that the long tiresome journey would be too much for her. Reluctantly she agreed, but instead she insisted that her other daughter, Madam Lingis, should go with Pauline. Fortune favoured Ernst for Madam Panam became ill and Madam Lingis was unable to leave her. The Duke now suggested that Pauline could travel to Coburg with little Josephine. The idea delighted Madam Lingis, who was pleased that her own daughter would share in the good fortune.

The two girls would wear men's clothing, which was not unusual, for since the time of the French Revolution it had become a habit for ladies to seek protection in masculine disguise. The Duke was to leave immediately and they were to follow. After a desperate, terrifying journey, in which their sex was revealed, the two girls at last arrived at Coburg.

Ernst was faced with a dilemma as he waited the arrival of the two girls. The Grand Duchess, who had never forgiven him for his friendship with Constantine, refused to entertain the suggestion of Pauline's becoming a Lady-in-Waiting. She had been indignant at the story of Pauline. She did not mind how many village girls he seduced for she could always dispose of them, but a *maîtresse en titre* was unthinkable. Augusta had other plans for her son.

The Duchess of Coburg was a domineering woman. Her four daughters had married in accordance with her wishes and she intended that her three sons should do so also.

Juliane's marriage had established an alliance with the imperial family of Russia. The second daughter, the beautiful Antoinette, had married Prince Alexander of Würtemburg, and from a contemporary description of him it was not for love: "Prince Alexander was shockingly ugly, a huge tumour disfigured his forehead, and there was something brutish about his face." He also suffered from gluttony, and when Antoinette awoke after their wedding night, she saw him in bed beside her gnawing at a ham-bone like a hungry, ferocious dog. He was the brother of Empress Maria and in consequence was appointed Imperial Russian General-in-Chief. They moved to Petersburg and the beautiful Princess Antoinette died shortly afterwards.

The eldest daughter, Sophie, because she was very plain was allowed to marry for love, or at least, to accept the first suitor that came along. He was the Austrian Count Emmanuel Pouilly Mensdorf.

Her other daughter, the little Princess Victoria, was married in 1803 to the elderly, decrepit, hereditary Prince of Leiningen, and after his death she was to make a second marriage in 1818 to Edward, Duke of Kent, and became the mother of Victoria, the future Queen of England.

The marriage plan for Ernst was an ambitious one. After careful and deep thought the Duchess had decided that the best bride for her eldest son would be the Grand Duchess Anna Paulowna, Czar Paul's daughter, who was at the time a mere child. The Dowager Empress Paul, who was the sole guardian of her daughters, was not opposed to the idea. She did not consider it a brilliant match for a Russian Grand Duchess, but she liked Ernst and was prepared to acquiesce. She said that in due course, Ernst might pay court to the Grand Duchess Anne. The Duchess of Coburg was determined therefore that this girl from Paris should not be allowed to interfere with her grandiose scheme.

Ernst was desperate and gave orders that when the girls arrived they were to be taken to an inn. Here he met the two girls after their long and arduous journey. Pauline describes the meeting.

" Scarcely had we alighted at the inn when the Prince came to visit us. Some embarrassment was depicted on his countenance, notwithstanding which he gave a forced smile. 'O Ernst!' I cried, and precipitated myself into his arms. He embraced me and questioned us respecting the dangers attending our journey, our fears, our health, *and what had we expended!*"

Hardly the propitious moment for an ardent lover to bring up the matter of accounts but the Duke had a frugal mind when money was involved. Suddenly as he saw her, young, beautiful and attractive, his ardour revived. He determined more than ever that she should stay in Coburg; the town he lauded when he was away from it, and found dull when he lived in it, would be bright with Pauline.

Coburg was in the pattern of the usual petty German Court, narrow, bigoted and formal; whose Dukes " aped Louis XIV, built huge palaces, cherished a blighting etiquette, and led lives as dull as those of the aged and torpid carp in their own stew-ponds, whilst, still in imitation of their model, they held as a necessary feature, in the dreary drama of their existence, ponder-ous dalliances with unattractive mistresses, in whom they fondly tried to discover the charms of a Montespan or a La Vallière."

The revenues of the Duchy were barely sufficient to maintain the marshals, chamberlains, ladies-in-waiting, grooms, lackeys, and servants, all in faded uniforms and liveries; the balls and entertainments were correspondingly dull. The Duke was the nominal head but the Duchess governed as during her husband's lifetime. The ladies of the Court were plain, shabby and stodgy.

The Duke had a difficult choice to make. He dared not defy his mother and yet he could not bear to lose Pauline. Taking a middle course he decided that Pauline must stay incognito in Coburg. French refugees in Germany were commonplace and two such foreign youths would be barely noticed, but the Duke of Coburg visiting them at the inn would certainly excite com-ment; a secluded retreat must be found. The first place that came to his mind was a trusted gardener's cottage in the palace grounds and it was here that the two girls, still disguised as boys, were installed behind lowered blinds.

For a few weeks they endured this life of seclusion and Pauline's days were brightened only by the visits of her ducal lover. Ernst decided that making love under the very nose of his formidable mother was tempting fate too much. He arranged for the girls to be escorted to a farm at Essau, about three miles away from the palace. In her memoirs Pauline describes their room as " being five feet in width and fifteen in length. Eight lofty win-dows lighted this chamber, while a large green German stove served to heat and encumber it. At one end was suspended a small canopy of brown calico, simple and ragged; in the centre a little farm-house table; the sides being decorated by three chairs, in the construction of which nothing but timber had been employed; and to these were added a chest of drawers of white wood. On the same floor, and divested of any portal, was my destined bed-chamber, where by way of compensating for the numerous openings which dispensed the light of day in torrents through the rest of the mansion, this damp apartment had only to boast one little window. Here were two beds and a small table bereft of one of its legs, but which stood firm, having the wall as a supporter." This wretched dwelling was far from being the magnificent palace that Ernst had pictured to her in Paris.

It was not long before it was noticed in Court circles that the Duke had formed the habit of taking rides into the country, and always he was alone and stayed away for hours. His sister, Countess Mensdorf, scented an amorous escapade and had her brother followed. She was prompted not only by curiosity but also by the desire of preventing her brother incurring their mother's anger, for the Countess was an amiable, good-natured person and liked Ernst. With her husband she visited the farm and immediately she saw Pauline, guessed her identity. Here, she realized, was not a calculating French adventuress but a simple, naïve girl, sweet, innocent, and beautiful.

To confirm her first impressions she challenged Ernst with her discovery and invited him to bring Pauline to her home which was a few miles from the palace. They spent a pleasant morning together and as they parted the Countess said, " My poor child, from the first moment I beheld you I guessed your secret, and pitied you. Believe me; you shall find a friend in me!" She was as good as her word and a few days later Pauline was escorted to the home of another sister, the Grand Duchess Constantine, where she spent two happy days. She began to be optimistic about her future, and wrote :

" The kindness manifested towards me by the Duke's two sisters was calculated to inspire a hope of more propitious days in future, and I returned to Essau with a contented mind, full of confidence respecting the destiny that awaited me.

" I was not, however, to enjoy this state of tranquillity for any lengthened period. In my excursions to Coburg and its environs, Prince Leopold, brother of the Duke, had seen me; perhaps he had formed part of the cavalcade which I had so unfortunately encountered near the farm of Eberhard. Be this as it may, he was not satisfied with a casual glance but resolved to pay me a visit.

" For this purpose a very singular and incommodious time was selected; seven in the morning being the hour when he rang at the door of my house. I was still in bed, fatigued with the walks I had taken during the week, when he announced himself by whistling a French air, in one of the compartments leading to my bed-room. Astonished beyond expression, I jumped from my couch, and had covered myself with my dressing-gown, just as he entered.

" He is a tall young man, with a deceitful expression in his countenance, having an ungracious, sentimental smile. After excusing himself, in bad French, for the mode of his introduction to my presence, he began to commiserate my situation, and blame his brother, intimating how strongly he was interested in my welfare, deprecating the badness of my lodging, and expressing fears as to the state of my health in so wretched a habitation. I made no reply, but no sooner had I found an opportunity of approaching the door than I fled from his presence, proceeding with celerity from one chamber to another. I mounted the staircases, traversed I know not how many desolate apartments, and at length took refuge in an old loft, which served as a granary for flour. I immediately closed and secured the door, and secreted myself behind the sacks, when five hours passed before I summoned sufficient courage to quit my place of concealment.

" On descending I found the Prince was gone; but the Duke speedily after made his appearance. It became necessary to detail to him all that had transpired, when a scene took place of the most terrible jealousy, fury, passion, and irritated pride, which I used every effort to appease in the best way possible."

The story of Pauline reached the ears of the Duchess of Coburg and persuaded by her two daughters she consented to receive the young girl. Like her two daughters she succumbed to the attractive naïveté and glowing beauty of the little Parisienne and soon Pauline became a court favourite. Neither the Duchess nor the Grand Duchess Constantine would have ever considered giving the little bourgeoise the position of Lady-in-Waiting but they were quite happy to have the child around them as an unpaid companion.

Unfortunately this happy state of affairs was not to continue for long. Pauline found she was pregnant. She was panic-stricken and in a welter of tears told Ernst of her condition. He received the news with dismay and his one thought was to hide the fact from his mother, who by now had lost her enthusiasm for the gay little creature from Paris. The Duchess had received two letters which had caused her some annoyance. They both concerned Pauline.

The first letter was from Pauline's sister, Madame Lingis, who thanked the Duchess for her kindness to her sister and asked when she was to commence in the household of the Grand Duchess as maid-of-honour, as promised by the Duke. The second letter, which had been addressed to the Duke and opened by the Duchess, was from Pauline's brother, Auguste. He was indignant about the whole affair and demanded to be told Pauline's exact position at the Ducal Court. Failing receipt of this information he also demanded that the two girls should be escorted back to Paris without delay. The brother's disregard of Princely privilege irked Augusta, as much as her son's refusal to be satisfied with the *droit du seigneur* he held over his subjects in Coburg. She showed the two letters to Ernst and said the girls must be sent home immediately.

The Duke would probably have accepted this solution with alacrity if Pauline had not been pregnant, for although he still loved his young mistress the price of pleasure was becoming too high. Now he had responsibilities and an even higher price to pay. The resourceful Duke had a plan. The younger girl, Josephine, had been sent to a school at Amorbach, to be out of the way; now Pauline could join her niece, to await her confinement and still be within reach.

He therefore told his mother that Pauline was to join her niece at Amorbach, to await the arrival of Auguste Panam, who would escort his two young relatives back to Paris. The Duchess was surprised at her son's ready acquiescence but she was satisfied. She sent a letter to her son-in-law, the Prince of Leiningen, who lived at Amorbach, asking him to take care of Pauline until the arrival of her brother.

In the charge of a Counsellor Titel, Pauline duly arrived at Amorbach and was handed over to the school authorities. She was unhappy for the rules were strict, and she was lonely; being allowed to see Josephine only on Sundays. The Prince of Leiningen was considerate, but his bitter opinions of the Coburg family disquieted her. He said the Duke's callous conduct was typical of the whole family, and that he, himself, had been deceived by them.

The unhappy girl became restless and even more wretched. She persuaded the Prince, against his wishes, to arrange her return to Coburg, where she was again installed at the inn. The Duke was furious and ordered her to remain in her room, but instead the desperate girl marched to the palace to throw herself on the mercy of the Duchess. The mercy was not forthcoming for the Duchess was furious. She regarded the influence of the girl as being responsible for the Duke's reluctance to travel to Russia to pay his suit to the Grand Duchess Anna. In the stormy battle that followed when the three of them were together, the Duchess was the victor. Pauline promised to retire to some quiet place to have her child and Ernst agreed to go to Russia. Madame Lingis was to be asked to join her sister at Coburg.

When Madame Lingis arrived she was taken to the inn and not to the palace as she had expected. Here she found her daughter, who had been brought from the convent at Amorbach, and the very unhappy Pauline. Now she saw things in their true light and she was in a quandary. One thing was certain; she could not take Pauline back to Paris until her brother Auguste rejoined his regiment. Herr Titel provided the answer, for he promised that the Duke would be generous, and suggested that in the interests of peace she should write reassuring letters to her brother and her mother. So, allowing her imagination full rein she painted a glowing picture of life at the Coburg Court, and said that the girls were too young at present to be given official positions but that their future was assured.

Frankfort, it was decided, was the most suitable place of seclusion and Madame Lingis and her two charges were established in comfortable accommodation in the town. Here they would have been content had the remittances arrived from Coburg. Letters arrived regularly from Ernst in Petersburg but they contained only promises. Then even these ceased, and in desperation Pauline wrote to Prince Leopold for help.

He replied : " Mademoiselle—I remit you by M. Titel a hundred florins, to supply your exigencies, and let me advise you to be economical, as it is not convenient to send money at all times; live, therefore, in such a way as to regulate your expenses to your finances.

" (Signed) Leopold, Prince of Saxe-Coburg."

It was an ignoble revenge for the wound his vanity had suffered when Pauline rejected his advances. Pauline continued to plead for monetary assistance but her letters were unanswered. On the 4th of March 1809 Pauline's child was born. He was christened Ernst, after his father, the Duke of Coburg.

In the meantime, Ernst's affairs in Russia were not progressing satisfactorily. The scandal of the Duke's liaison with Pauline had been reported to the Empress, who had decided that he was not a suitable match for her daughter. Her own unhappy experiences with an insane husband and his offensive mistresses made her determined that her daughter Anna should not suffer a similar fate.

Earlier, Napoleon, hoping for an alliance, had shown an interest in her daughter, Catherine, and the Empress had been precipitated into marrying her to the Duke of Oldenburg. Now, with an imperial divorce imminent Napoleon might turn his attentions to Anna. To forestall him she decided to allow the Duke of Coburg to stay in Russia so that when the time came she could declare that he was affianced to Anna.

Ernst now regarded himself as being officially engaged to the uniformed young girl, and therefore felt free to enjoy himself in other directions. Petersburg offered a multitude of opportunities and the Duke took care to be discreet; completely unaware that he was being watched by the spies of the astute Czarina. He remained in Russia until the Spring of 1809, when war broke out between Austria and France and he was recalled to Coburg. In accordance with the terms of the Rheinbund the Duke was allied to France, which he found disconcerting as his brother, Ferdinand, held a command in the Austrian Army. He sent his small force of Coburgers to join the French Army but excused himself from military duty, on the grounds of ill-health following a fall from his horse.

In July, he visited Frankfort and called to see Pauline and his four-months-old son. Their distress disturbed him but he returned home without donating anything except promises to alleviate the sordid conditions of their existence. The occasional remittances that arrived from Coburg were soon swallowed up, for to add to the burden, Madame Panam, lonely and ill in Paris, had now joined her two daughters and her grandchild.

Frankfort was some distance from the scene of military operations, but the whole country was in a state of ferment. Prices were high, conduct was wild and lonely women needed protection. Pauline became friendly with a retired French general, who was a wealthy landowner in neighbouring Wilhelmsbad, and through his influence Madame Lingis obtained a position at Dresden as *dame de compagnie*. On the way to Dresden Pauline visited the Coburg Court to make her plea for assistance in person. Her long interview with the old Duchess was a stormy one. Pauline was determined not to leave Coburg until she received assurances for the future welfare of her child. After a month of misery she was visited by a Major Szymborski, representing the Duke, and after some persuasion he obtained her signature to a contract. The terms were:

Article 1—An allowance will be made to Madame A. P. Alexandre (the name which Pauline had assumed) *of 3,000 francs, as an annual pension.*

Article 2—This sum will be paid by a banker resident in the city she shall inhabit, so that every two months one sixth of the amount may be drawn.

Article 3—The debts of Madame A. P. Alexandre contracted at Wilhelmsbad, and the amounts which have been given in by her, shall be liquidated.

Article 4—Money shall be found to defray her expenses as far as Dresden.

Article 5—Twelve hundred francs shall be paid to procure the furniture necessary for her apartments.

Article 6—All the debts she shall in future contract are not to be liquidated.

Article 7—Madame A. P. Alexandre shall as speedily as possible quit the estates of His Serene Highness the Duke of Saxe-Coburg, and never return; without which the 1st, 2nd, 3rd, 4th and 5th articles are invalid.

It was a piece of paper that was to prove as valueless as his promises.

3

Pauline, or the widow Madame Alexandre as she called herself, was soon established at Dresden with her mother, and for a time she found a certain happiness in the gay city on the banks of the Elbe. Then one day the Duke of Coburg visited her. She was now seventeen and had grown more beautiful than ever. Ernst was enchanted and was furious when his advances were rejected. He came several times to pay her court but without success. Finally he accepted Pauline's refusal and returned to Petersburg for a final attempt to win the Grand Duchess Anna. Now he was no longer needed by the Dowager Empress as a pawn in her political game and was rejected outright. In Coburg he met his mother's reproaches and bewailings of poverty in silence. During the war he had smuggled arms to the enemies of France and had amassed a small fortune in consequence, and for this information to have reached the ears of Napoleon would have spelt disaster, for Napoleon already hated the Coburgs; Ferdinand, who was on the side of Austria against France, and Leopold, who held rank in the Russian Army, had prompted the Corsican to say : " Wherever I go, I find a Coburg in the ranks of my enemies."

The Spring of 1812 again saw Ernst in Dresden; this time as a Prince of the Rheinbund to meet Napoleon, for war with Russia had broken out and the Russian Army was on the banks of the Niemen.

" Napoleon's excuse for engaging in this war was that Russia by permitting trade with England, was destroying his system of Continental blockade. Germany was ruined by the passage of innumerable masses of troops, which were gradually pushed towards Poland. In May Napoleon invited the German Sovereigns to Dresden. The Empress of Austria, and the Empress, the King of Prussia, the King of Bavaria, the King of Würtenburg, the Queen of Westphalia, and all the minor German Princes, went there. All the Ministers of these various Princes went there also. The Duke of Coburg and his brother Ferdinand went also to

Dresden. The younger brother, Leopold, did not think it safe to appear, as the Emperor Napoleon had, in 1811, expressed a wish to employ him. He went to Vienna and then to Italy, to be quite out of the way.

" Germany was, at the beginning of 1812, in the lowest and most humiliating position; Austria and Prussia sunk to be auxilliaries; everybody frightened and submissive, except Spain, supported by England.

" The two elder brothers were chiefly at Coburg. The Mensdorffs came also; as well as Victoire, the Princess of Leiningen."*

On the 29th of May, the forces of the Emperor were ready to do battle and Napoleon left Dresden to lead them. " All the news that reached Germany were favourable to the Emperor Napoleon."*

In November, vague rumours brought the news of Napoleon's disatrous campaign in the snows of Russia, and the Coburg Princes were delighted. Ferdinand left for Vienna to take command of some Austrian troops. Leopold left for Kalesch in Poland, where the Emperor Alexander had his headquarters, and became the first German Prince to serve in the Russian Army. He was attached to the staff of his brother-in-law, the Grand Duke Constantine who commanded the Guards. Ernst returned to Coburg to bide his time before committing himself.

In the early hours of the morning of the 14th of December a lone sledge swept into the streets of Dresden. It was Napoleon's return. Four days later he was in Paris.

When the news arrived confirming the destruction of the French army, Austria and Prussia, former allies of Napoleon, declared war on France. The allies signed a decree stipulating that all the German Princes must unite against Napoleon. The Duke of Coburg's time had come to join the side of the victorious. The King of Saxony alone refused to turn against his former ally and was forced to flee his capital.

In the meantime, Pauline's plight had worsened, for she was a Frenchwoman in a town surrounded by the enemies of France, and Saxony was soon to become the cockpit of Europe. Napoleon marched to Germany at the head of a new army of 300,000,

* Reminiscences of King Leopold—Letters and Reports to Queen Victoria —Volume for Private Circulation 1862.

young and old. Nothing could halt them and on the 7th of May the allies retreated through Dresden, half their ten thousand vehicles carrying wounded and dead. Five days later Napoleon arrived, and riding with him was the King of Saxony. He stayed in Dresden for a week and then left to win another victory at nearby Bantzen. Then he received news of a defeat at Vittoria, spelling the end of his power in Spain.

The allies, 200,000 strong, attacked the Saxon capital and Napoleon brought in reinforcements of 60,000. The battle raged, a pall of smoke blotted out the sun, bullets and cannon balls filled the air and the streets became a carnival of horror and devastation.

Amidst the tumult Pauline huddled with her child and her sick mother, expecting death at any moment. Nightfall brought respite but the next day the fearful carnage was resumed; until in the evening the allies retreated. Pauline sought the aid of some French generals and was given a pass for Frankfort.

In November, the three princes of Coburg, Ernst, Leopold, and Ferdinand, arrived in Frankfort. Ernst was engaged on another marriage project. He sought the hand of the Princess Hermanie of Anhalt-Schaumberg.

When Pauline heard of his arrival in the city she tried to speak with him but he refused to meet her. The Prince Primate, who had befriended Pauline when she had lived in Frankfort before, spoke on her behalf to the Duke but to no avail. Another friend, Count Trogoff, also recited at length the whole pitiful story to the Grand Duke Constantine when he visited Frankfort, who since his wife had left him, hated the Coburgs. He visited Pauline and was shocked by the poverty-stricken conditions in which she lived. He promised to help her. Pauline must have looked askance at the husband of the beautiful Juliane of Coburg. He was hated and feared and his appearance did not belie his reputation, for he had inherited his father's repulsive looks. Fortunately he was not so sensitive about his ugliness as his father had been. The Emperor Paul had once ordered a soldier to be knouted to death for having alluded to him as " baldhead ", and had issued a proclamation threatening a simi-lar punishment for anyone in his domain who used the term " bald " referring to the head or " snub " applying to the nose.

Constantine was both bald-headed and snub-nosed. His ferociousness and vicious nature made him detested by the army. Eventually this general hatred compelled him to waive his rights of succession to Alexander in favour of his brother Nicholas.

Whatever his motives, he was very kind to Pauline and her young son, Ernst. He listened sympathetically to Pauline and Madame Panam as they recounted their dismal story. They answered his questions with sincerity and obviously he believed them for he ordered a considerable sum of money to be made available for their needs. As he left them he embraced little Ernst commenting on his likeness to the Duke of Coburg, adding, " No one can say he is not of the family."

The Duke of Coburg was furious when he heard of the interference of his brother-in-law, but he realized that the Grand Duke was too powerful a person to be antagonized. In addition he also knew that a scandal at this time would jeopardize his chances of marrying the rich Princess Hermaine, whose great wealth was under her own control. He therefore adopted a policy of repentance.

" As if by a magic metamorphosis, the most consummate cruelty gave place to an immediate and apparently profound repentance.

" No sooner had Prince Coburg ascertained that His Imperial Highness had paid us a visit than he came to me. What a change ! The Duke was no longer the same being; caresses, promises, he was prodigal, in short, of every kindness !

" The Duke presented himself daily to weep over the injuries I had experienced; I was provided with some money, and my debts were discharged, and I beheld Ernst in the arms of his father.

" I was anxious to let the Duke know, that, during the recent visit, His Imperial Highness had deigned to promise my mother that the welfare of my boy should be attended to, and that he would not fail to repeat his call."*

Ernst tried to persuade Pauline that the Grand Duke had evil intentions but her confidence was not to be shaken. He tried, therefore to discredit her with Constantine through other people, one of whom was Prince Leopold. Constantine was not deceived

* Memoirs of Madame Pauline Panam.

and insisted upon Leopold accompanying him to Pauline's house. Here confronted with the girl and her mother Leopold was forced to admit the truth of her assertions.

Constantine became more determined than ever that Pauline should be given fair treatment. He even presumed to insist that the Duke of Coburg should deposit a large sum with a reputable banker, the capital to be in the boy's name, the interest to be paid to the mother.

This was a bitter pill but the Duke swallowed it and pretended to agree. The following day a document was delivered to Pauline and in the afternoon she received a visit from the two brothers-in-law. The document contained all the terms stipulated by the Grand Duke and in consequence he advised her to sign it. According to the terms the Duke was to pay the capital to a certain banker within one month, her outstanding debts were to be settled and she was to be given money for her immediate needs. In consideration of these payments Pauline and her child were to leave Frankfort immediately. The Duke suggested Augsburg as her destination but agreed that she be allowed to go to Vienna instead.

Baron Fichler, an emissary of the Duke, was to conduct Pauline and her son to Vienna and, if they wished, Madame Panam could join them later.

The next day they set out for Vienna in an old Berlin, and as darkness came Pauline and her son fell asleep to the jolting rhythm of the carriage. Suddenly they were in a revolving world of shaking blows and splintering wood. They found themselves, almost insensible, at the bottom of a stony ravine amidst the wreckage of the carriage. As she returned to consciousness Pauline saw the Baron and the postillion looking down with apparent composure from the edge of the gorge. She realized that the Berlin had been overturned into the ravine, not by accident, but with the deliberate intention of killing her son and herself, and at the last moment the two men had thrown themselves clear.

Pauline struggled to her feet, and displaying great courage and presence of mind she adopted a dictatorial attitude, commanding Baron Fichler to give her assistance. The Baron was astonished that his victims were still alive and he dared not refuse her commands. He conducted Pauline and her son, both suffering from lacerations and minor injuries, to a nearby village inn where they received medical attention.

Then, weak and shaken as they were, he had them taken in a coach to his home, which was an old convent three hours journey away from the inn. They remained here for eight days, virtually prisoners of the Fichler family. Pauline, in a state of fear and suspicion, refused to eat, or allow her son to eat any dishes of which the family did not also partake.

Her suspicions were justified for on one occasion she noted that wine given to her was poured from a different bottle. She pretended to drink some of the wine and then offered her glass to the Fichler's eleven-year-old son. The boy took the wine from her and was about to drink when his mother suddenly struck the glass from his hand, saying, " Do not drink! do not drink!" She then hurried her son from the room.

Baron Fichler was unable to meet Pauline's accusing stare, and after a few minutes of acute embarrassment and guilty silence, he was forced to admit that the wine had been poisoned. Pauline then adopted the offensive and conjured up a whole family armed against him. Her brother, she said, was waiting to receive her in Vienna, where her sister also lived being married to an important official. By this subterfuge she made the intimidated Baron agree to her immediate departure. He even gave her a hundred florins and arranged the conveyance for their journey.

In Vienna Pauline found rooms at the " Royal Emperor " and lost no time in presenting the letter, given to her by the Duke of Coburg, to the banker Stamitz, Then came the most disillusioning blow of all, the letter purpoting to be a guarantee for a large sum of money was a letter of no consequence whatsoever. It was, in fact, never intended to be delivered.

With very little money left her plight was becoming desperate, until one day she was fortunate to meet in the Prater, the delightful Viennese Park, the retired General who had befriended her in Wilhelmsbad. He introduced his companion, who was the celebrated and distinguished Prince de Ligne. The venerable Prince was captivated by her beauty and when he heard her dismal tale of misfortunes he became her protector. Through his influence the doors of the aristocracy were opened to her.

4

Charles Joseph, Prince de Ligne, was born in Brussels in 1735, and was now one of the most distinguished men in Europe. It had been said of the Prince de Ligne that "he was the last *gentilhomme* in Europe capable of travelling across the country with a lady, and never permitting himself to lean back in the carriage."

He had had a remarkable career. At seventeen he was an ensign in his father's regiment and five years later Marie Thérèse made him Colonel. When he was twenty he had dutifully married, on his father's orders, the Princess Lichtenstein, who was fifteen. He had only seen her once before the ceremony and they had never spoken. Marriage was not a hindrance to his amatory adventures and they always remained on excellent terms with each other.

In 1759 he was sent by Marie Thérèse to Versailles, where his gay and witty charm made him an immediate success at the court of Louis XV. He was tall and handsome, a sparkling conversationalist and an excellent dancer of the minuet; but after a short time when he became bored with the aged King and the arrogant Pompadour he moved to Paris.

Then came more campaigns and in 1763 when peace was signed he was a Major-General. He was the friend of Voltaire, Marie Antoinette, Frederick the Great, and Emperor Joseph II of Austria. Everything he did was in the "grand manner", and when he visited Catherine II of Russia, to ask for the 400,000 roubles which were owed to him, he was received with such gracious hospitality that he did not bring up the question of the debt. Instead, he said afterwards: "*Il me paraissait peu délicat de profiter de la grâce avec laquelle on me recevait, pour obtenir des grâces.*"

He became an intimate friend of Catherine II and he accompanied her on her triumphant tour of the Crimea which had been won from the Turks. Prince de Ligne describes this fantastic journey: "Accompanied by a large suite, and of course the reigning favourite (who was aged 20), the Empress started from Petersburg in an immense sleigh, fitted up like a luxurious room, large enough for eight persons to move about in comfort, drawn by 30 horses, of which there were frequent relays. The weather was, as usual at that time of year, intensely cold, and huge fires were lighted along the road, to make the temperature more agreeable. At Kief a fleet of 80 ships awaited H.I.M. The decks had been transformed into sumptuous saloons, hung with rare silks; each ship had its own band, and to the sound of music the imperial party sailed slowly down the River Dnieper through the country of the Cossacks to that of the Tartars, witnessing enchanting scenes. For they saw, not the dreary wastes they had expected, but plains covered with sheep and goats, shepherds playing on pipes, whilst, from picturesque villages, issued youths and maidens, gaily dressed, and hastened to the shores acclaiming their sovereign. These loyal subjects certainly resembled each other strangely, and, had the Empress alighted and visited one of these pleasing hamlets, she would have been disillusioned, for the whole thing was but a wonderfully devised stage-effect, arranged by Potiomkin, and the villages were sham villages, consisting only of flimsy façades, deceptive in the distance. It is a pity that the supposed habitants were real creatures of flesh and blood . . . for these wretched peasants of Little Russia, forced by Potiomkin to rush by cross-roads from one of the Empress's stopping-places to the other, there to welcome her with songs and acclamations, in her voyage along the Dnieper, when they had played their parts, were left to get home as best they could, and many died of fatigue and hunger. Over a thousand villages in Little Russia lost the greater number of their inhabitants, as well as their flocks and herds, but they served Potiomkin's purpose . . . the Empress was delighted."

The Prince de Ligne was an ardent traveller, and when one considers the terrible conditions of travel in those days, his journeys are amazing. In one year, he made the journey from Brussels to Paris eighteen times, and from Brussels to Vienna fourteen times.

When he was not travelling and his military duties permitted, he lived at his ancestral home, Beloeil, near Brussels. He spent his time there gardening and writing, and on his own printing-press forty volumes of his works were produced.

The death of the Emperor of Austria, Joseph II, marked the

beginning of a disastrous period for the Prince de Ligne. The new Emperor did not favour him; his country was invaded by the French, and in the revolution that followed he lost Beloeil and all his great wealth. Then came the most grievous blow of all; his son whom he idolized was killed in battle. Never again did he allow his son's name to be mentioned in his presence. "*Il y a,*" he said, "*une manière terrible d'être supérior aux événements; cela s' achète par un grand malheur. Si l'âme a été emue par la perte de ce qu'elle a de plus cher, je défie les chagrins d'arriver, fortune perdue, persecutions, injustice, tout semble insignifiant!*"

The Prince moved into a small, modest house in Vienna, alone with his sorrow; but one cannot live with the dead and slowly he began to emerge from the shell of his grief. He gave small supper-parties and soon his simple home became the meeting place of the aristocratic and intellectual society in Vienna. He was dignified and charming, truly a " Grand Seigneur " although Baron de Meneval writes of the Prince de Ligne who was a frequent guest at the Schonbrunn of the French Empress Marie-Louise : "*Il avait une forêt de cheveux gris, dont les hôtes parasites s'egâraient sur les fauteuils, où le Prince s'assuyait.*"

The fare he offered at his table was plain but it was spiced with the sparkle and wit of his conversation. Pauline was a regular visitor at the " Hôtel de Ligne ", which was the name given to his modest dwelling by Viennese society, and here she also met the French colony of Vienna who made it their rendezvous. The sound of French voices was music in her ears for now, embittered by her experiences, she hated everything German.

5

In the meantime the Coburg Princes, who were the cause of Pauline's hatred, were busying themselves in the affairs of Europe.

Leopold in his *Memoirs,* written years later when he was the King of the Belgians, pinpointed their movements during the few months prior to the Congress of Vienna in 1814, and with customary primness he refers to himself in the third person :

" In December a great part of the allied army took the direction of Switzerland. The Grand Duke Constantine and Prince Leopold paid a second and longer visit at Amorbach. The Duke remained at Frankfort to take command of a German corps d'observation, which was to blockade, and, if possible, to take Mayence,* where a considerable French force had remained. The Prince Ferdinand, after some demonstrations against Mayence, went with the Austrian Army to Switzerland, and afterwards to Franche Comté, in Eastern France, where he remained. The great headquarters of the Emperor of Russia and the King of Prussia occupied Bâle on the 12th of January 1814. The Grand Duke Constantine went with Prince Leopold to Elfenau, near Berne, the residence of the Grand Duchess Anna Feodorowna. His ardent wish was a reconciliation. Unfortunately it did not take place. The great army struggled on in France; political difficulties preventing it going on after the battle of Brienne, on the 2nd of February, to Paris, which might easily have been done. Only on the 30th March the attack of Paris took place. On the 31st the allied army entered Paris. Prince Leopold entered it at the head of the cavalry he commanded, and remained at Paris : the Duke, after an armistice with Mayence, settled its evacuation by the French, and came to Paris. Prince Ferdinand came there also. In the middle of June the Duke went to Germany—Prince Ferdinand also. Prince Leopold accompanied the Emperor Alexander to England. The events which took place then are known. The Duke and Duchess of York were most friendly, so was the Duke of Kent. The Regent was much irritated, first, by Princess Charlotte refusing the Prince of Orange; afterwards by her flight to her mother. The majority of the public were favourable to Prince Leopold—even Ministers— particularly the Wellesley family, Lord Castlereagh, etc.

At the end of July, Prince Leopold left London. Before that he was graciously received by the Regent, who had verified that no unfair intrigue had taken place. He assisted at a splendid ball at Carlton House, which closed the season, and where he received demonstrations of kindness from the whole family. The Prince opened the ball with Princess Mary, not yet Duchess of Gloucester.

* Now known as Mainz.

The Duke of Sussex and the young Duke of Gloucester were not at that time received by the Regent or his Ministers. Prince Leopold went through Holland to Amorbach, where the Prince of Leiningen had died unexpectedly. He assisted the Princess to settle her guardianship. The three brothers met at Amorbach, and afterwards at Coburg.

At the end of August the Duke and Prince Ferdinand went to Vienna, where the Congress had begun its sittings. Prince Leopold, who had remained with his beloved mother, joined them towards the end of September. The Duke entrusted a good deal of the management of what he hoped to obtain to Prince Leopold."*

It had been announced that the Congress, at which the destinies of the countries of Europe were to be decided, would be held in Vienna. The official opening of the Congress was to be on the 1st of October and in September the capital was invaded by thousands of visitors; the city was in the throes of excitement as monarchs, princes, generals, diplomats and representatives of all the European nations except Turkey, arrived with their retinues. The Imperial Palace was the centre of the activities and here Francis II was host to the visiting royalties. The cost of his table was 350,000 florins per week, whilst the extraordinary expenses during the Congress amounted to 40,000,000 marks. Equipages were provided from the royal stables and three hundred magnificent carriages, specially built for the occasion, were provided for the important guests.

The streets were ablaze with brilliant uniforms and splendid liveries. It was indeed a royal fête and the Austrian capital was in the throes of excitement celebrating the peace.

The Prince de Ligne was *persona grata* everywhere and Pauline, under the wing of his sponsorship, was caught up in the wild whirl of gaiety and social festivities. The Prince wrote of the Congress: "The whole of Europe is in Vienna. The tissue of politics is embroidered with fêtes. It is a royal mob. From all sides come cries of 'Peace, justice, equilibrium, indemnity! Heaven knows who will reduce this chaos to a semblence of order. Everyone wants something. I, alone, am but a spectator

* Reminiscences of King Leopold.

of the show! I shall claim nothing, unless it be a hat to replace the one I am wearing out, saluting sovereigns at every street corner."

One afternoon Pauline was sitting with the Prince de Ligne in the Prater, watching the fashionable parade pass to and fro. The Emperor Francis with the Empress Marie-Louise went by in their carriage, accompanied by a group of horsemen. Outstanding amongst the group was a handsome young man on a mettlesome black Ukranian charger. He was wearing the magnificent uniform of the Austrian Hussars. For a moment his eyes met Pauline's, he hesitated and then passed on. It was Duke Ernst of Coburg.

A few days later Pauline received a visit from Ernst. His object was to silence the gossip concerning his relations with Pauline and the attempted assassination. Mute with horror, she listened to him as he calmly explained away the attempt on her life as an unfortunate accident. When he left she sighed with relief.

The Duke with his violent nature, unpredictable temper and constant machinations had made many enemies. His evil reputation was proving an embarrassment to his two more placid brothers and was jeopardizing the success of their plans. Ferdinand was hoping to marry the wealthy Princess Kohary, whilst Leopold had an even greater ambition, the matrimonial first prize of Europe; the hand of Charlotte, future Queen of England. The sauve Leopold now persuaded Ernst to allow him to control the Coburg affairs.

Whilst the ambassadors schemed and plotted their way through the labyrinth of the Congress deliberations, the royal personages gave themselves to a round of pleasure that went on through the day and night, and the " Committee of Entertainments " set up by Francis II was kept busy devising new forms of entertainment. When the snow came sleigh parties were organized on the frozen lake at Schonbrunn, and an eye-witness was surprised to find that " an English attaché, Sir Edward W . . ., a member of the English Skating Club, accustomed to astonish promenaders in Hyde Park, on the Serpentine, was the most expert performer. He executed wonderful feats, pirouettes, and figures; and traced the monograms of the Empress, the

Queens, and other personages so beautifully on the ice, that they left their sleighs to admire his skill."

Another Englishman, the Ambassador Lord Stewart, who became the Marquis of Londonderry, was one of the would-be comforters of Pauline. She rejected his advances more gracefully than the beautiful Countess C., who slapped his face when he took liberties with her.

The winter ended on a tragic note for Pauline. The Prince de Ligne was taken dangerously ill, and within two days was dead. His funeral did justice to the high regard in which he had been held and the Monarchs and Princes paid him homage when he was buried at Kalenburg; a great and noble spirit had left Vienna, but the gaiety was not affected. Two of the Coburg Princes, at least, were taking advantage of the general air of festivity to further their plans, as can be noted from the following report :

" During the Congress Prince Ferdinand gained the heart of the blooming heiress of Kohary. The Duke of Wellington and Lord Castlereagh, and all the English, showed a marked kindness to Prince Leopold. The Duke of Kent was so kind as to favour some communication with Princess Charlotte, who expressed her determination to remain firm in her plans. I forgot to mention a subject which has since been told as a proof of the great poverty of Prince Leopold when he was in England in 1814. He came with the Emperor Alexander, and as long as the Emperor remained himself in England, the lodgings of the persons who had come with him were paid by him. The Russian Ambassador, Count Lieven, had the charge of locating the suite, and as they lived in Harley Street, they lodged the people near it, and had taken a rather indifferent lodging for Prince Leopold in High Street, Marylebone. The Prince had nothing to do with the choice of that lodging, and as soon as the Emperor had left, he lodged himself in Stratford Place, in a house where General Count Beroldingen, the Würtembourg Minister, lodged, and where he remained till he left London. He might have explained these things before, but he had not thought it worth while."*

On March the 1st, however, news arrived that threw Vienna

* Reminiscences of King Leopold.

into a state of trepidation. The message was handed to Talleyrand, and it was a simple one, delivered dramatically.

Talleyrand who often said: "The tongue was given one to conceal one's thought," possessed the grand manner; although the Duke of Argyll wrote of him in his diary: " Monsieur Talleyrand is the most disgusting looking individual I ever saw. His complexion is that of a corpse advanced in corruption. His feet are distorted in every possible direction.* His having learned to walk steadily with such wretched materials is proof that he is a man of considerable abilities "—a cruel judgment.

The account of the delivery of the message is interesting.

" Talleyrand," says Count de la Garde, who was an intimate of the Prince, " always kept up the custom of the Petit Lever; and his, in coquetry, resembled Mazarin's or Pompadour's.

" A certain number of intimates would be admitted into the Prince's room; and there wait silently, until the heavy bed-hangings were drawn back revealing Talleyrand's recumbent form. His valets now proceeded to wrap him in a white, frilled muslin dressing-gown, and propped up on pillows, the diplomat breakfasted, discoursing the while to his friends. He was a master of the lost art of conversation.

" He (Talleyrand) never told anything one could possibly know, nor anything others had already said or written. He talked very little about himself, and a great deal about the distinguished people with whom he had relations.

" Then he arose; and two hairdressers commenced operations on his abundant hair; producing, after an hour's work, that elaborate arrangement of powdered curls noticeable in Talleyrand's portrait.

" *Lo toilette de la tête et des mains achevée, on passait a celle des pieds,*" writes de la Garde; " *détail moins récréatif, à cause de l'odeur nausé abonde de l'eau de Barège dont on se servait pour fortifier sa jambe boiteuse.*"

" Finally, the first valet de chambre, whose task, hitherto, had been merely to superintend, advanced; put on the Prince's cravat, and tied it with a perfection of which he alone held the secret."

On the morning of the message, Talleyrand lay abed sipping

* He was crippled as the result of an accident in childhood.

chocolate, whilst he held his usual reception. Seated beside his bed was beautiful Madame Edmond de Périgord, his niece by marriage, discoursing on the Court theatricals in which she was to play a leading part; they were to be rehearsed that afternoon at Princess Metternich's.

A letter was brought in from Prince Metternich.

" Doubtless to inform me at what hour, today he will be at the Congress," said the Prince. But Madame Edmond had opened the note. She gave a cry of dismay saying :

" Napoleon has left Elba ! "

At this portentous announcement, a thrill of horror ran through the Prince's visitors, even his servants in their excitement forgot for a moment to look impassive. The destinies of empires were affected !

" My dear Uncle, what about my rehearsal?" she asked.

" It shall take place," replied Talleyrand with perfect composure.

The rehearsal duly took place in the afternoon, for the evening performance of " The Barber of Seville ", but the audience were not interested : they were shocked by the news.

For five days the ominous portent clouded everyone's thoughts, and then on the 6th of March came the frightening news that Napoleon had landed in France. The reports of the Emperor's triumphs struck fear into the hearts of the Coburg Princes and they left Vienna. Louis XVIII had fled to Ghent and by the middle of June the Austrian capital was deserted. The thousands who had come to the Congress had scurried homewards.

CHAPTER SEVEN

BIRTHS, DEATHS AND MARRIAGES

I

THE NEWS of the great victory at Waterloo was delivered to
the Regent in as histrionic a fashion as even he could have
wished. The Regent and the Duke of York were among the
guests at a dinner and ball, in the house of a Mrs. Boehm in St.
James's Square. As the guests were sitting at the table they heard
the sounds of cheering in the Square. The uproar grew louder
and suddenly the doors of the dining-room were flung open;
framed in the doorway stood the dust-begrimed figure of an
army officer, his uniform blood-stained. He was holding the
poles of three flags bearing the eagles of France. Dramatically
he saluted and threw the colours at the feet of the Regent. Lord
Liverpool then read out the despatches delivered by Major
Percy; and when he had finished, the Regent, greatly moved,
said: " I congratulate you, *Colonel* Percy."

The era of Napoleon was ended and his sun was setting forever behind the stark outline of St. Helena. The Czar of Russia
was anxious to form a Holy Alliance but the Regent replied
that the British Constitution would not permit him to accept
the suggestion; nevertheless he agreed with the principle of the
Alliance—that the Sovereigns of Europe should " take the divine
precepts of the Christian religion as the unalterable rule of their
conduct." Having said this, he passed affairs into the relentless
hands of Castlereagh, a relative of the Hertfords and the most
rigid Tory in the land. It was the eclipse of the Whigs.

In the following year, Leopold who was now in Berlin,

received a letter from the Regent inviting him to return to England; with the invitation was an accompanying letter from Lord Castlereagh, whom Leopold had met at the Congress in Vienna. On the 21st of February he landed at Dover and two days later drove down from London with Castlereagh in a post-chaise to the Pavilion at Brighton. Four days later Charlotte also arrived at the Pavilion with the Queen and two of the Princesses.

Charlotte and Leopold represented to each other a means of salvation. They were both young and attractive and inevitably they fell in love. Leopold found the wayward Princess abrupt and gauche but *le Marquis Peu à Peu,* as the Regent nicknamed him, had overcome more difficult obstacles and was undeterred. The Regent, although suffering from gout and in a wheelchair, was at his charming best, in his favourite surroundings with the solicitous Lady Hertford in attendance, and he agreed to the engagement of the young couple. Charlotte returned to Cranbourne Lodge, but now she was happy at the prospect of an early marriage and freedom.

The date of the wedding was to be the 2nd of May and in the meanwhile Leopold was a guest at Clarence House, where he made almost continuous appearances on the balcony for the appraisal of the London crowds that assembled in the stable-yard. They were not disappointed in what they saw, for he was a handsome young man of good physique and they approved his grave dignified manner and noble bearing; their dear Charlotte, their future Queen, had found her Prince Charming.

They were married at Carlton House and when they left for their honeymoon at Oatlands near Weybridge, London was wild with delight as the Tower guns thundered out the news of the royal marriage.

After the honeymoon Charlotte and Leopold went to live at Camelford House in Park Lane and in the summer of 1816 they took up residence at Claremont, near Esher. The house had been built by Lord Clive but had seen many changes of occupancy; now it had been prepared as a royal residence and for weeks there had been a bustle of activity in the house. " Well, thank Heaven I am here at last!" said Charlotte as she stood in the oval, black and white marble hall, and as the weeks went by Claremont was indeed heaven to the happy young lovers.

Leopold, who prided himself on being a man of the world, decided to educate in manners the abrupt, tempestuous Charlotte; and he succeeded. In his doing so there was friction, but always the impetuous girl yielded to his wishes. " If you wish it I will do it," she used to say and gradually she began to enjoy his domination. To Charlotte, Claremont was a new, happy world, away from the browbeating of her father and the machinations of the royal family in London. She was in love with love, and her adored Leopold with his calm solicitous manner was all she needed from life.

Around them they had their attendants, but the patient, formal Leopold was also a determined, calculating young man and he would allow no intrusion from outside; no interference whatsoever was permitted, not even from the Queen or the Regent. Charlotte floated on a cloud of contentment and every day was a day of idyllic happiness; to be censured for her inevitable gaucheries was all part of the delightful game. They entertained and gave parties but they were happier when the doors had closed on the last guest.

Leopold had introduced into the household at Claremont a German doctor, Christian Fredrich Stockmar, three years older than Leopold; a young man destined to play an important part in royal affairs. He had met Prince Leopold in Coburg, where his father was a magistrate, and Leopold, impressed by his manner and ability, had brought him to England as his personal physician. Stockmar writes of his first meeting with Charlotte : " She was handsomer than I had expected, with most peculiar manners, her hands generally folded behind her, her body always pushed forward, never standing quiet, from time to time stamping her foot, laughing a great deal, and talking still more. I was examined from head to foot, without losing my countenance. My first impression was not favourable. In the evening she pleased me more. Her dress was simple and in good taste." The calculating Stockmar, so like his master in many ways, soon revised his first impressions, for Charlotte and he became good friends and she used to confide in him. " Stocky ", as they called him, fitted perfectly into the Claremont ménage. " In this house," he wrote, " reign harmony, peace, and love—in short, everything that can promote happiness. My master is the best of all husbands in all the four quarters of the globe; and his wife bears him an amount of love, the greatness of which can only be compared with the English national debt."

In this rural retreat the happy days turned into months and the following year brought promise of even greater happiness, for Charlotte was expecting a child. The news was received with great jubilation and soon in the London Clubs enormous wagers were being made on the sex of the embryonic heir.

Stockmar was offered the post of one of the physicians-in-ordinary but judiciously refused the honour, for he realized that as a foreign doctor he would receive little credit, and if things went wrong he would certainly have to take the blame. His sagacity was proved right by later events.

The honour of Chief Physician was given to Sir Richard Croft and, as was the custom of the day in England, he prescribed a course of bleeding and a bread-and-water diet. Stockmar was against the treatment and for three months he watched in trepidation, until he could keep quiet no longer. He begged Leopold to interfere, but Croft was adamant and the treatment continued.

On November the 3rd Charlotte's time had come and she commenced labour. It was a cross-birth and the incompetent Croft was unable to cope with this complication. Fifty agonizing hours passed, until on Wednesday evening the child was born. It was a boy, and it was dead.

After her prolonged labour this was an anti-climax, but Charlotte was brave and bore her disappointment with stoicism; she was young and there would be another time. The waiting Ministers were dismissed and the attendant doctors went to bed. Leopold's long vigil, for he had remained with Charlotte since she had taken to her bed, was ended. He was exhausted and returned to his room.

At midnight Charlotte was in great pain, she complained of a strange feeling in the head and was numb with cold. Within minutes the three doctors were at her bedside. In desperation hot water bottles were brought and she was plied constantly with brandy. "They have made me tipsy," she groaned to Stockmar. It is said that at this stage Stockmar warned the doctors that she was sinking and offered advice, but Croft, the jealous and incompetent, turned upon him, saying : " Are you or I, sir, in authority here ?" Stockmar left the room.

A few minutes later from the next room he heard Charlotte calling, " Stocky ! Stocky !" He returned and saw her last agonizing contortions; then it was all over. Charlotte was dead. The time was 2 a.m. on November 6, 1817. She had paid dearly for her brief happiness.

The dread task of telling Leopold that his wife was dead fell to Stockmar for Croft could not face his awful duty. At first the Prince, awakened from his sleep of exhaustion, refused to believe it, and together they went into Charlotte's room. Grief overcame him as he knelt by her bedside and kissed her cold, dead hands. His world had come to an end.

2

The Regent was staying with the Hertfords in Suffolk when the news reached him that Charlotte's condition was giving cause for concern. He posted through the night on Wednesday, but he was too late, for the news of the tragedy at Claremont awaited him at Carlton House. He was distraught with grief and shattered by the emotional shock. To calm his devastation he was subjected to copious bleeding but he was inconsolate.

The Queen was taking the waters at Bath and had only been there two days when she received a message saying that the Princess had got safely through her accouchement. The same evening at dinner another letter arrived. It contained the fatal news, and the Queen fell back in a seizure. Two days later she recovered sufficiently to travel back to London to console her son.

The death of Princess Charlotte was a national calamity and the grief was sincere. Byron wrote :

> " *Of sackcloth was thy wedding garment made;*
> *Thy bridal's fruit is ashes: in the dust*
> *The fair-haired daughter of the Isles is laid;*
> *The love of millions! how we did entrust*
> *Futurity to her!*"

Sir Richard Croft paid for his inefficiency. He shot himself.

By a lamentable though probably intentional oversight the death of Princess Charlotte was not officially notified to her mother. Caroline was in Italy when the news reached her and she erected a small, somewhat pathetic monument in the garden of her villa.

She had sailed from England in the frigate *Jason* on the 16th of August 1814 and the Government as well as the Regent had sighed with relief when she left. On the eve of her departure the Regent had given a toast: " To the Princess's of Wales damn and may she never return to England." The politicians who were using her cause as a political lever were annoyed at " her desertion ", as Brougham and Whitbread* jointly described it, but their attempts to dissuade her from leaving had failed, for Caroline preferred the delights of the Continent to the torments of England where she would never be happy. For privacy she embarked at Lancing but her outlandish appearance and crowds of attendants caused quite a stir on Lancing beach. In particular she showed great concern about a long, tin case on which was painted in bold, white letters, " Her Royal Highness the Princess of Wales, to be always with her ". What was in the case is not known, but she certainly had no intention of travelling incognito.

With her went the boy William Austin and a suite: Ladies Charlotte Lindsay and Elizabeth Forbes, Sir William Gell, Colonel St. Leger, Keppel Craven, Captain Hesse, and Dr. Holland. In addition there was Siccard a steward, six German servants and an English coachman.

Caroline bought an old London and Dover mail coach for the transportation of her servants and baggage, and it created a sensation in every foreign town they visited. The bizarre party's wanderings in Europe were more like the movements of a circus than a royal tour. Caroline visited Brunswick, and was received by her brother. Immediately she plunged into a wild, hectic round of gaiety; theatres, suppers, dances, masquerades. She turned night into day and often roused musicians and guests in the small hours of the morning to hold a ball. Her conduct was

---

* Not long afterwards Whitbread committed suicide by cutting his throat.

wild and unpredictable. She decided the appearance of her male attendants was too drab and devised for them a costume which was not very popular. It consisted of gaily decorated coats and waistcoats, plumed hats and moustaches; which was too much for Colonel St. Leger who resigned his post and returned to England with Lady Charlotte Lindsay.

The strange party wandered on to Frankfort, Strassburg, Bern, and Lausanne to Geneva. Here Caroline was entertained by the ex-Empress Marie Louise of France and the Saxe-Coburg Princess Juliane, who was separated from her husband, the vicious Grand Duke Constantine. Caroline shocked everyone by appearing at a masked ball as Venus, naked from the waist upwards, when she sang a duet with the ex-Empress.

The next call was Milan, and her suite were finding it hard to keep up with her relentless round of pleasure. Lady Elizabeth Forbes, Sir William Gell and Keppel Craven left her service, exhausted and disgusted. She decided to replace them with Italians. An outstandingly handsome ex-soldier named Bartolomeo Bergami was recommended for the position of courier by the Marquis Gheslieri. He was of magnificent appearance, over six feet in height, topped by a mane of black hair and he bore an excellent character. Caroline engaged him and very soon he was dining with her and acting as her personal attendant. He wore the uniform of a Hussar and was always at her side.

The winter and spring were spent at Naples where they enjoyed the hospitality of King Joachim Murat. The climax of their stay was a ball held in honour of King Joachim, at which Caroline and some of the ladies appeared as symbolical figures. Caroline as the " Genius of History " again wore an all too-revealing costume.

The Regent's spies followed the wavering path of the ridiculous party as it wandered across Europe and every move and action of the pathetic, gambolling Caroline was reported back to London. The remainder of the year was spent at Rome, where Caroline had an audience with the Pope and the English newspapers reported that she had adopted the Roman Catholic faith; then on to Genoa, Milan, Venice and the beautiful Italian Lakes. Dr. Holland had left her and Captain Hesse had rejoined his regiment when the War of the Hundred Days broke out, so that more Italians joined her party, including Countess Oldi, Bergami's sister. Bergami was now her equerry and had been given by King Joachim, at Caroline's request, the rank of Captain in the Army. At her summons a Lieutenant Hownham (also spelt Hownam, or Hannam) had travelled from England to join her party. He was one of the boys she had adopted years before and he remained with the party. Bergami was promoted to Chamberlain. They settled for a time in the Villa d'Este, a large house which Caroline bought, and here at Lake Como the party led a wild and expensive existence, large sums being lavished on the Bergami family (his daughter Victorine and his brother had now joined them).

The next move was to Elbe and Sicily and from there they sailed to Tunis, where Caroline was delighted with the graciousness of the Bey; until a British Naval squadron under Lord Exmouth arrived to bombard her host and his pirates. Exmouth judiciously persuaded Caroline to leave before the bombardment commenced to prevent her being seized as a hostage.

In April, 1816, they moved eastwards through Greece, Constantinople, Ephesus, and reached Jerusalem, where she founded the new Order of Saint Caroline. It was dedicated to Sancta Carolina and the lilac ribbon, the red cross and the motto chosen by Caroline (*Honi soit qui mal y pense*) of a Knight of St. Caroline, were conferred upon " Willikins ". The Grand Mastership was made hereditary in the Bergami family. When this news reached the ears of the Regent he was furious for he realized that the fantastic farce was parodying his name throughout Europe.

During the autumn Caroline and her party shuttled between the Villa d'Este and Bergami's villa near Milan, creating scandals by their uninhibited behaviour.

Every country in Europe now echoed with Caroline's mad prattle and the Government tried in vain through diplomatic channels to curtail her antics. The spring of 1817 saw her at Innsbrück and Carlsruhe; whilst at Baden, Lord Redesdale reported that she made any official reception difficult by insisting on wearing half a pumpkin to keep her head cool, and her appearances in Turkish costume earned her the title of " The

216

Mad Princess ". The presence, however, of the critical English and Hanoverian officials dampened her half-demented enthusiasm and she returned to Italy with her circus.

In London the scandalous truths and untruths were being built up into a formidable dossier of evidence and the Regent saw in Bergami the means of divorcing his detested wife. His chief supporter in the Cabinet was Lord Castlereagh, who had first seen the possibility of a divorce in 1815 when an account of Caroline's behaviour in Genoa reached London. She had appeared in the streets of this town dressed like a pantomime fairy, with a pink bodice cut almost to the waist, a skirt revealing her plump knees, and wearing a ludicrous hat with swaying feathers. She was driven in a shell-like carriage drawn by little circus ponies, with outriders similarly mounted and in front, also on a pony, rode Bergami dressed exactly like King Joachim of Naples. In the carriage with her was " Willikins ".

In January 1816, when further reports had arrived, Castlereagh wrote to his brother Sir Charles Stewart, then Ambassador in Vienna, instructing him to collect evidence against the Princess of Wales. As most of Italy was then under Austrian rule this was the most influential means of securing witnesses. Hanoverians were sent to Italy to organize spies to keep Caroline under observation, to bribe servants, and to produce proof " as would for ever deliver the Prince Regent of having a woman so lost to decency in the relation of a wife ". By the end of 1817 a mass of evidence had been collected and Vice-Chancellor Leach, who was the Regent's personal legal adviser, considered the information and reported that the proof was not in sufficient detail. This opinion was put before the Cabinet but the " Milan Commission " that followed was not a Cabinet measure—although it was instituted by Leach with the consent of the Prime Minister, Lord Liverpool, and the Lord Chancellor Eldon, whilst Castlereagh provided the facilities for the investigations through the Embassies at Vienna and Munich. The expenses were more than £33,000 and were paid by the Government.

Three Commissioners and Sir Charles Stewart visted Milan in September 1818 and remained there for several months diligently collecting evidence which was returned to Leach for examination. In turn it was passed on to Lord Liverpool who presented a report to the Cabinet. The Regent wanted the divorce to be obtained by some parliamentary procedure but the Cabinet objected on the grounds that his own record would not support his case. They realized that Caroline's tongue would be a dangerous weapon when it came to open recriminations. Three times the Regent insisted and each time the Cabinet demurred; the affair had reached an impasse.

3

The death of Princess Charlotte threw the whole country into mourning and gave rise to bewildered speculations as to the future succession. The dissolute conduct of the royal brothers had been viewed by the nation with a certain tolerance, for it was thought that the elderly sons of George III were only an interlude until Charlotte became Queen. Her marriage to the handsome, popular Prince Leopold was regarded with delight; they would begin a new line which would by-pass the immediate progeny of the old mad King, who were all elderly; the married sons were without legitimate children and the daughters were childless or unmarried. In any event they were all over forty. After the tragedy at Claremont there loomed the prospect of a rapid succession of old and decrepit sovereigns and in Parliament there were dismal visions of a possible foreign succession should the line become extinct, when one of the young Dukes of Brunswick would become the sovereign. This it was thought might well lead to a revolt and a republic.

The outlook was one of conjecture. The Prince Regent was now a debauched, obese figure and even if he succeeded in divorcing Caroline and remarried, it was doubtful if he would succeed in producing another child. The next-in-succession, the Duke of York, had been the first of the sons to marry. In November 1791 he became the husband of the good-looking Frederica of Prussia, the daughter of Frederick William II. The old King had been delighted, for the Duke of York was his favourite son and he had been anxious to see him suitably married. George III made no secret of his favouritism towards Frederick, and once, when the Prince of Wales and the Duke of York were enjoying one of their drunken bouts Frederick toppled from his chair in a stupor and fell to the floor. George rose unsteadily to his feet and pointing to his prostrate brother, with mock solemnity said: "And there according to our royal father lies the hope of our family."

Unfortunately the Duke and Duchess had not produced an heir and they were unlikely to do so now. They had parted after six years of marriage on fairly amicable terms, the Duke setting up his own establishment, but he often joined the famous weekend parties at Oatlands, Weybridge, where the Duchess had taken up residence. Parliament therefore requested the Dukes of Clarence, Kent, Sussex, and Cambridge to marry, and promised them an adequate marriage settlement for the purpose.

The other son, the Duke of Cumberland was probably the most hated man in England. He was ugly, vindictive, vicious, and surrounded by dark, evil rumours of murder and horrifying debaucheries. Lady Jersey said he had caused the death of four men; he had been exonerated from guilt in the case of his valet's death, but he had certainly been the cause of one man's death and this probably gave rise to the rumour of his terrible malpractices. Lord Graves, the Duke's Comptroller, had committed suicide on seeing a caricature of his wife in the arms of the Duke. In the caricature the lady's face was hidden but the face of Cumberland was unmistakable. The legend to the drawing was "A violator of graves" which probably instigated the evil rumour. However, he was certainly vindictive with an uncontrollable temper and of sinister appearance, which was made more malevolent by the loss of an eye. He had lost it at Tournay, where he had lifted a French Dragoon from his horse by brute strength. No one wanted the hated Cumberland as King at any price.

The Duke of Sussex, Augustus, had followed his eldest brother's example and in 1793 had made a clandestine marriage to Lady Augusta Murray, who was created Lady d'Armeland in 1806. There were two children of the marriage Sir Frederick d'Este and Ellen, afterwards Lady Truro, but the King by virtue of the Royal Marriage Act declared the marriage void. Prince Augustus refused to part from his wife for several years, but not until he did so, in 1801, would the King create him a peer—as

Duke of Sussex, and allow him his full income. He refused to re-marry whilst Lady d'Armeland was living.*

The other three brothers were more amenable. In May 1818 there was the English ceremony for the marriage of the Duke of Cambridge and Princess Augusta of Hesse-Cassel and on the 11th of July the double wedding of the Duke of Clarence to the Princess Adelaide of Saxe Meiningen and the Duke of Kent to Prince Leopold's sister the widowed Princess Victoria of Leiningen, took place in the old Kew Palace. The Duke of Kent had already married Princess Victoria on the 29th of May at the ducal Palace of Coburg and this was the English ceremony.

The double wedding was a private affair. A drawing-room in the old palace was fitted with an altar and the Archbishop of Canterbury and the Bishop of London conducted the service. The newly-weds received the blessing of the old Queen, who then retired, whilst the other members of the royal family dined together. For their wedding night the Duke of Clarence and his bride drove to his apartments in the stable-court of St. James's, whilst Kent and his Duchess went to Claremont, which had been given to her brother Prince Leopold for life and where he was still living.

At first Leopold had been stunned by the loss of his young wife for, without Charlotte, life for him was empty. His nights were sleepless; he had no appetite for food and he rarely spoke, enduring his grief silently. Charlotte's death had also brought to an end his carefully calculated plans for the future: fate had taken from him in one fell stroke his happiness and his ambition. " He is convinced," wrote Stockmar at the time, " that no feeling of happiness can ever again enter his life."

Leopold was fortunate in having Stockmar as a friend, for he alone enabled him to overcome the numbing despair of his grief. He never left the Prince but was with him night and day. With his intelligent, sympathetic mind he fully realized the magnitude of Leopold's sorrow and by his tender understanding

---

* After her death he married Lady Cecilia Buggins (she changed her name to Underwood) in 1831. She was created Duchess of Inverness in 1840.

he guided Leopold along the road back to normality. His sister's marriage again brought some happiness into his life.

4

The old Queen was present at the double wedding, but at the beginning of July she had been taken ill whilst out for a drive. The carriage immediately returned and the doctors were summoned. It was with difficulty that she struggled through the wedding ceremonies of the Dukes of Clarence and Kent.

In the previous year, 1817, she had had the first warning that her health was failing. A few months earlier her brother, the reigning Duke of Mecklenberg-Strelitz, had died from a stroke of apoplexy. This news and an attack on the Prince Regent in January, as he was returning from the House of Lords, had caused her grave concern. The death of her namesake Princess Charlotte was also a great shock to the old infirm Queen. It is true they had not been on the happiest of terms with each other, but her visit to Bath at the time when the birth of the Princess's child was due was hardly improper. Nevertheless her absence was bitterly resented by the people, who linked her name with the neglect which many believed to have been the cause of the death of the much beloved Charlotte. When the Queen returned to London there was a demonstration of hatred against her. The mob, devoted to Princess Charlotte and in sympathy with the Princess of Wales, believed that the old Queen had in some way plotted the tragedy.

The Queen was on her way to the Mansion House when an infuriated yelling mob surrounded her coach. Heads were thrust into the carriage, reviling her and demanding to know what she had done to Charlotte. The sick and aged Queen was not intimidated, but had not her footmen fought their way through the dense crowd, aided by the High Constable of Westminster, she would undoubtedly have come to grievous harm. This was not the first time she had to face the threat of violence in unpoliced London. In 1815 she had been on her way to hold a State Drawing-Room at St. James's, when her chair was surrounded and stopped by a hissing, shouting crowd, hurling insults and crying out to be told what she had done with

Princess Charlotte, who they believed had been imprisoned.

The Queen pulled down the glass of her chair and said imperiously: " I am above seventy years of age. I have been more than fifty years Queen of England, and I was never hissed by a mob before." Cowed by her spirit the crowd dispersed and she proceeded to the Drawing-Room. When she was due to return to the Queen's House the Prince of Wales sent some gentlemen to escort her. The intrepid Queen resented this slight upon her courage and ordered them to return to Carlton House saying: " You have left Carlton House by his royal highness's orders. Return there by mine—or I will leave my chair and go home on foot." But now she was a sick woman and was terribly disturbed. In the evening she again suffered an excruciating spasm.

In April, she had attended the wedding of Princess Elizabeth to the Prince of Hesse-Homburg and had borne herself with great dignity although obviously in pain; but these ceremonials were a great strain upon an old and ailing woman driven only by her determination and spirit.

She had wished to be near her husband at Windsor in what she realized were the closing months of her life, and the first stage of the journey was to be the old palace at Kew. Here, where she had spent so many happy days she halted: and was destined not to leave. She lingered on in her illness for a few tortured months until November when her condition became grave. Messengers were sent to summon the Regent, the Duke of York and other members of the family. Finding that the condition of their mother was not worsening they returned to London, with the exception of the Princesses Mary and Augusta who sat with her during the night. The next morning the family were again summoned. The Queen was in a coma but as they entered her room she regained consciousness, holding out her hand to her eldest son and smiling in recognition. In a few moments she was dead.

An account of the Queen's last moments was given by the Duke of York to Mr. Croker who describes the scene in a letter to Mr. Peel: " The Queen died about five minutes to one. The Prince, the Duke of York, the Duchess of Gloucester, and Princess Sophia were in the room; she had been breathing hard and

loud for half an hour as she sat in her chair; suddenly she
stopped and, drawing a long sigh, expired. Her hand fell over
the arm of her chair, and her head and body fell towards that
side on which she had not been able to lean during her illness.
The Prince was extremely affected, and they were obliged to give
him some cordials to prevent his fainting."

Queen Charlotte's life had been a long and difficult one.
Saddled as she was with an insane husband and a dissolute
brood of sons, it is not surprising that her life became a series
of trying situations; one incident following closely on the heels
of another. Inevitably, in such an unpopular household, she
was given her share of the abuse and the most common accusations against her were German narrow-mindedness and avarice.
In every lampoon and cartoon directed against her these themes
appeared.

Many years after her death a particularly virulent attack was
made upon her memory in an article in the *Edinburgh Review,*
1838. Her secretary, Sir Herbert Taylor, replied in her defence
and his reply appears to be a fair analysis of her character:

" Queen Charlotte," he says, " was a woman of excellent
sense, and though her qualities were not brilliant, and had not
been improved by early education, she had since acquired a
general knowledge of most subjects which form the ordinary
topics of general conversation. Her intercourse with many persons
of information and talents enabled her to take a fair share in
general conversation. Nor did she ever commit herself by what
she said. She came to England with many German prejudices,
which do not seem to have been entirely shaken off. I admit that
she was plain in person, and that age, frequent childbirth and
infirmities had destroyed the symmetry of a figure which those
who had seen her Majesty on her arrival in England described to
me in favourable terms. I deny that her manners and disposition
rendered her unamiable. On the contrary, those who approached
her found her courteous and obliging, and surprise was often
expressed that her manners were so good as to cause one to forget that her figure was other than graceful. She was kind and
considerate towards her attendants and servants, most of whom
had passed many years in her service. She was ever disposed to

encourage amusement and cheerful conversation, but, on the other hand, she adhered strictly to etiquette, and she knew how to check the approach of anything like familiarity of manners or too great freedom of conversation. Her court was most respectable. I grant that it was not a gay court, and if blame attached to the queen, it was not sufficiently considering that her daughters had arrived at a time of life when greater indulgence and some relaxation of uniform routine would have been agreeable and reasonable; but that uniformity of routine had become habitually imperative, a sort of second nature, and allowance must be made for the circumstances in which she was placed by the recurrence of the King's lamentable illness."

On examining the two accusations against Queen Charlotte's character one finds that during her long life she had virtually no influence upon society or manners. In fact she appeared to avoid making herself and her court the centre of social life and fashion.

The astute Whig families obtained for themselves the important posts around the monarch and during the reign of George III when political party distinctions became pronounced it was almost impossible for Tory members to appear at court. The term, the " King's Friends ", was used openly by the King and " the Prince of Wales's Opposition " were excluded. During North's ministry from 1770 to 1782 the same dull set formed the courtiers around the King, and it was not until Fox's party came into office that brighter faces appeared; " a new company, comprehending all the young and splendid part of the nobility ", made the King's Birthday Court in 1782 more magnificent than it had been for years. An observer reported that there was " a novelty which gave it a peculiar charm; not a face was to be seen of the circle which had been seen there before." This implied that the court had never seen the élite of London society; the Duchesses of Devonshire, Grafton and Gordon, the Rockinghams, Cavendishes, Foxes and others. The Queen feared the brilliance of the " Opposition ", the like of Fox, Burke and Sheridan, and preferred the " King's Friends ". She therefore withdrew from any kind of intimacy with the political group and concerned herself only with those who took no part in the intrigue of politics, but even with these Charlotte maintained an atmosphere of cold formality.

The Drawing-Rooms were treated as a formal occasion with a rigid ceremonial. It was the custom for the assembled guests to stand in three or four rows on both sides of the ante-room forming a passageway. The King then walked portentously between the ranks, noting the faces but addressing not a word to anyone. Behind him came the Queen accompanied by her Ladies-in-Waiting and occasionally she inclined her head to a peeress she knew personally. The princesses followed, each accompanied by an officer of the Household and a Lady-in-Waiting. When their Majesties reached the entrance to the drawing-room they stood still and waited gravely whilst the guests slowly filed past them, each receiving a brief word of greeting, passing out by the opposite door.

As the years went by the royal receptions became fewer and the conduct more rigid. Society in turn became more malicious. It was known, for instance, that Queen Charlotte hated high feathers yet every women attended the Drawing-Rooms wearing the tallest feathers she could find; hoops spread wider and plumes became taller against her wishes, so that the Queen was always " out-of-fashion " when compared with the other great ladies.

Taste and fashion during the era that included the French Revolution, the secession of the American colonies, Napoleon, and Waterloo, were more grandiose than ever before; vast fortunes were spent on buildings and pleasure, palaces and entertainments. Gambling, bribery, drunkenness and immorality were rife, and the same tolerance applied equally to men and woman. In a world such as this Queen Charlotte, the German provincial at heart, was a stranger.

It was the rule of German courts that there was one standard for a man and another for a woman; a man could not be injured by his reputation but a woman could lose hers very easily. This was Charlotte's standard, for to her the husband was the supreme being, and this attitude was borne out by the Queen's encouragement of Lady Jersey's affair with the Prince of Wales and her harsh treatment of his wife the Princess.

When the itinerant Princess Caroline received the sporadic news that the old Queen " was on her last legs," she was charitably indifferent, writing ironically: "There was a time when such intelligence would have gladdened me." Time and distance had softened her feelings which they could never have done for Queen Charlotte, who was relentless as far as women were concerned, but paradoxically by her own standards she could overlook the most scandalous conduct in a wife providing the husband condoned it; preserving appearances was the criterion of conduct—so much for Charlotte's narrow-mindedness.

Their Majesties did not enjoy entertaining and in fact avoided it; when they did so the parties were small and the fare meagre. This deprived the London tradesmen of a custom to which they felt they were entitled. When the royal couple took up residence at Kew the beautiful gardens were famous, but they were allowed to deteriorate owing to the King's disinclination to spend money on their maintenance. It was probably foolhardy courage and not economy which prevented him from allowing himself or any of his family to be guarded, even during the worst period of rioting, and of course this attitude was slavishly followed by the Queen. When they came up to town they were almost like ordinary citizens and the mob often surged round them.

In 1783 Burke's Bill for greater royal economy, which had as its aim the reduction of the expenditure by George III in connection with secret political purposes, failed in its object. The King's reaction was unexpected; he did not curtail his political spending but instead he reduced his personal expenses. Queen Charlotte also introduced economies into her household. The pages, half of them German and as concerned about their official standing as the Queen was about her own, had at this time attempted to resign. The reason was that they felt they had been insulted by the Prince of Wales who, having designs on the wife of a groom, had promoted the husband to be a nominal valet and introduced him into the house to take his meals with the pages. The Queen refused their request, but took the opportunity of adding that in view of the necessity for economies it had been decided that certain changes in the household would have to be made. In future, persons of a lower class would be employed, as they would be satisfied with a lower standard of living.

The number of staff was also reduced and a man named

Grosley relates that he one day wandered into the palace without being halted. Inside he met a footman and asked : " Whether the King was living there—' He is there in the next room ', remarked the man dryly, and passed on without troubling himself about me. I slipped quietly downstairs again, and outside was asked by the guard for money to get brandy with."

This was the period of the King's greatest unpopularity. Historians have often written that the people were solidly in agreement with the King's attitude to the American colonies and that his ignorant and obstinate opinion was the national view. This is not borne out by contemporary records; the aristocracy, the gentry, the merchants in the City, the tradespeople and the lower classes, all hated him. The long duration of the American war incurred the hatred of the manufacturing, shipping and trading communities throughout the country. Wesley recorded : " They heartily despise the King and hate him with a perfect hatred."

The unpopularity came to a head at the time of the Wilkes riots when the Queen tried to strike a note of public sentiment by giving a ball for the young Prince of Wales, but Alderman Beckford retaliated by giving a banquet to Wilkes. The mob were again incited to riot and during the Queen's ball a hearse, lit by blazing torches, was dragged by a jeering hostile crowd into the courtyard of St. James's Palace. The implication terrified the Queen for the King's safety.

Every detail of their court and domestic life was bandied around London through the gossip of their servants; as many of them were boarded out they widened the field of tittle-tattle. Gillray portrayed the King as obese and stupid; the Queen was depicted as a small mulatto creature, avariciously collecting gold coins in her apron, or starving her children, and in many other variations of stinginess.

Parsimony was forced upon her by the King although she was also thrifty by nature. At Weymouth, for instance, she saw that a draper was holding a sale of calico at sixpence a yard for ready money. She bought his entire stock and then made him wait for payment. The draper told his customers and the housewives were indignant at the loss of a bargain. She gave financial support to three schools, one for orphaned daughters of army and navy

227

officers, another for the daughters of poor clergymen and the third for the training of poor girls as servants. At the second school embroidery was taught but the entire work produced was reserved for the Queen and her daughters. Her charity in this case was certainly motivated by thrift.

Her insistence on the rigid observance of royal etiquette was relentless, particularly in regard to standing, and at the christening of Princess Charlotte she was asked if Lady Townshend, who was very delicate, might sit down. Her reply to this request was tart: "She may stand, she may stand."

Another side to her nature is shown in a letter she sent to Lord Harcourt directing him to dismiss a servant:

"My Lord, I want you to exert your authority in dismissing my footman Oby, as soon as possible, as his unquenchable thirst has now become so overpowering that neither our absence nor presence can subdue it any more." She goes on to describe how some important messages were found by the Duke of Cumberland in the man's pocket as he lay dead drunk in the street. She added: "As I write a tippling letter, I think it not amiss to mention that Stephenson had appeared twice a little *Bouzy,* the consequence of which was a fall from his horse. The surgeon declared him to be at least over dry, if not drunk; a reprimand to him will be necessary, for should it happen again he must go also."

Perhaps Fanny Burney, that intimate of the Queen, should have the last word, for she indicates Charlotte's remorseless love for her husband and her relentless sense of duty: "The Queen indeed is a charming woman. She appears to me full of sense and graciousness, mingled with delicacy of mind and liveliness of temper. She speaks English almost perfectly well, with great choice and copiousness of language, though now and then with foreign idiom and frequently with a foreign accent. Her manners have an easy dignity with a most engaging simplicity, and she has all that fine high breeding which the mind, not the station gives, of carefully avoiding to distress those who converse with her or studiously removing the embarrassment she cannot prevent . . . Their behaviour to each other speaks the most cordial confidence and happiness. The King seems to admire as much as he enjoys her conversation, and to covet her participation in everything he either sees or hears. The Queen appears to feel the most grateful regard for him and to make it her chief study to raise his consequence with others, by always marking that she considers herself, though Queen to the nation, only, to him, the first and most obedient of subjects."

5

Although they had fulfilled their obligations and were now legally married the royal brothers, the Dukes of Clarence and Kent, were both disappointed in their financial expectations. The Government introduced proposals to increase their allowances and also the Duke of Cumberland's but the motions were defeated in the House of Commons. The Duke of Wellington made a pungent comment on the situation : " By God! there is a great deal to be said about that. They are the damnedest mill-stones round the neck of any Government that can be imagined. They have insulted—*personally* insulted—two-thirds of the gentlemen of England, and how can it be wondered at that they take their revenge upon them in the House of Commons? It is their opportunity and I think, by God! they are quite right to use it."

Castlereagh had asked for £10,000 a year for the Duke of Clarence and £6,000 for the younger princes. A hectic scene was witnessed in the Commons which resulted in a vote of £6,000 to Clarence and nothing to the other two. Eventually, however, Kent was also granted £6,000 a year.

The Duke of Clarence's income at this time was £18,000 plus quite a large sum out of Admiralty profits which was granted to him by the King, but he was in debt to the tune of £60,000, with little prospect of repaying such an amount. He had always lived in the shadow of his elder brothers, in comparative obscurity; but as with them, money was a problem he could never solve.

When William was fourteen his father noticed that he was already beginning to follow in the steps of his brothers, George and Frederick, and to remove him from their bad influence the King decided to send him to sea. Thus on the 15th of June 1779 he joined the crew of the *Prince George,* Captain Robert Digby's flagship, and embarked at Spithead, welcomed by the jeers of his shipmates.

Life at sea in those days was brutal and violent, and the language of the tough-sinewed sailors was blasphemous and coarse; every sentence being larded with swear words. Here cooped up in the dark, evil-smelling bowels of the ship with three hundred others, William found life as a midshipman very different from the pleasures of London, but with spirit he settled down to the hard routine : " I am entered," he said to his shipmates," as Prince William Henry, but my father's name is Guelph, and therefore, if you please, you may call me William Guelph, for I am nothing more than a sailor like yourselves." He was accepted as one of themselves, and indeed, was willing to brawl and drink with the best of them. He saw action in two naval battles, when under the indomitable command of Admiral Rodney the fleet captured a Spanish convoy of sixteen vessels and the escorting seven men-o'-war off Sandwich, and when later off Cape St. Vincent they defeated another Spanish fleet.

He returned to England in a blaze of glory, and immediately rejoined his brothers in their escapades and dissipations, but now with even greater enthusiasm, for his rollickings in foreign ports had gained him experience and whetted his appetite. Again his father intervened; his leave was cut short and he was sent back to sea. This time he took part in the relief of Gibraltar, and then his ship crossed the Atlantic; which made him at sixteen the first Prince of the Blood to land on American soil. In New York he wandered about the town without any guard, which prompted a plan by Colonel Ogden of Washington's army to capture this valuable prize. General Washington thought the plan was a good one and replied to Ogden in a letter dated March 28th 1782 :

Sir,

The spirit of enterprise, so conspicuous in your plan for surprising in their quarters and bringing off the Prince William Henry and Admiral Digby merits applause; and you have my authority to make the attempt, in any manner and at such a time, as your own judgment shall direct. I am fully persuaded that it is unnecessary to caution you against offering insult or indignity to the persons of the Prince and Admiral, should you be so fortunate as to capture them; but it may not be amiss to press the propriety of a proper line of conduct upon the party you command. In case of success you will, as soon as you get them to a place of safety, treat them with all possible respect, but you are to delay no time in conveying them to Congress, and reporting your proceedings with a copy of these orders. Take care not to touch upon the ground which is agreed to be neutral—viz. from Rayway to Newark, and four miles back.

G. Washington.*

This bold plan apparently did not materialize but it certainly gives rise to interesting speculations.

During his service he met Nelson and years later said : " I was a midshipman on board the *Barfleur,* lying in the Narrows off Staten Island, and had the watch on deck, when Captain Nelson, of the *Albermarle,* came in his barge alongside. He appeared to be the merest boy of a captain I ever beheld, and his dress was worthy of attention. He had on a full-laced uniform, his lank unpowdered hair was tied in a stiff Hessian tail of an extraordinary length; the old-fashioned flaps of his waistcoat, added to the general quaintness of his figure, produced an appearance which particularly attracted my notice, for I had never seen anything like it before, nor could I imagine who he was, nor what he came about. My doubts were, however, removed when Lord Hood introduced him to me. There was something irresistibly pleasing in his address and conversation, and an enthusiasm, when speaking on professional subjects, that showed he was no common being."†

His liking and admiration for Nelson was reciprocated for they became intimate friends and met on many occasions afterwards. Indeed, Nelson became his hero.

When William next returned to England, George III decided that his sailor son should now make the Grand Tour and in July 1783 William set out for the Continent. In Hanover he met his brother Frederick, and as always easily led, he amassed here a pile of gambling debts. Promptly he was moved on to Berlin.

<hr>

* Washington's Writings, edited by Jared Sparks.
† Life of Lord Nelson by Rev. J. S. Clarke and J. MacArthur.

Once again in London at the end of the tour, he was promoted to Lieutenant. Two months later he was again promoted and as Captain was given the frigate *Pegasus*. October 1786 saw him off Antigua, where he resumed his friendship with Nelson, who was the commander of the station, and it is probably here that he had his first lessons in reform; a word that was to become the symbol of his reign.

In Antigua on March 12 1787, Captain Nelson married Fanny Nisbet and Prince William stood in for the bride's father to give her away. Shortly after the wedding Nelson took his bride to England and William was dejected as their ship sailed from English Harbour.

After a few days of despondency he suddenly decided to leave Antigua and without instructions he sailed to Halifax. As a disciplinary measure he was ordered to Quebec where he would have been forced to remain for the winter. Instead, in defiance of orders he set sail for England. This was a strange lapse on the part of the young prince for he had, following Nelson's example, already, on several occasions shown himself to be a keen disciplinarian. His arrival in England was reported to the Admiralty and the King was furious with his son. William was ordered to Plymouth and forbidden to leave his ship during her refitting preparatory to the return voyage to the port from which he had sailed.

The arrival in Plymouth of his two elder brothers, who had posted down to see him, however, encouraged William again to disobey orders and he entered with them into a round of entertainments. Nelson arrived to discuss the situation with him and meanwhile the Admiralty maintained a discreet silence. The result of the visit was that William returned to Halifax without more ado, but the disgrace made him determined to be strict in impressing the lesson on others. This did not prevent him, however, from taking an active interest, as correspondence proves, in the welfare of his men.

He appears to have atoned for his misdemeanours, for when he again returned to England he was made Duke of Clarence and was given an apartment in St. James's Palace and £12,000 a year. Unfortunately he again came under the influence of his brothers George and Frederick and the amount proved insufficient for he was involved with them in attempts to raise loans. As a country residence he was given Clarence Lodge in the Old Deer Park at Richmond, but this was only for a short time for the house was damaged by fire, and he moved to Ivy Lodge, near the ferry. Here he settled down to a quiet bucolic existence, which was, however, enlivened by a young, vivacious girl, Polly Finch. She was of humble stock and had been brought down by his favourite brother, George, to keep William company. She did not entirely succeed for in a short time the twenty-five year old William was hankering for adventure and the sea again. But for reasons known only to himself the King had decided that his son's active service was finished and his future naval career was to be on land, which was a pity for William was a good sailor.

At the Admiralty he was treated with tolerant indifference and his frequent agitations were ignored. As the country was at war, he wrote an impassioned patriotic letter to the Lords of the Admiralty asking to be sent to sea on active service, but when this letter was also ignored he wrote to his father:

March 24th, 1794.

Sir,

On the 15th of this month I addressed a letter to the Lords of the Admiralty, of which I transmit you a copy, soliciting from them that employment in the service of my country to which my rank and character entitle me. To neglect they have added insult, inasmuch as they have withheld from me even that courtesy which is due to every individual who makes a respectful tender of his services at a momentous period like the present, when everything that is valuable to an Englishman is at stake, and the throne on which you sit is endangered by the machinations of regicides and revolutionists. As in this treatment of the Lords of the Admiralty my character as a naval officer becomes seriously implicated, I am emboldened to make this request to my royal father, soliciting from him that he will be pleased to issue his commands to the Lords of the Admiralty to grant me that employment which I desire, or publicly to state the grounds on which refusal is founded.

William.

The King was unrelenting and his reply was emphatic; it doomed William forever to be a dry-land sailor. His ten years' service had made him a real sailor and the results of the training stayed with him forever. Huish, that harsh critic of the Prince of Wales, said of William: "He had been bred up in a good school when serving in the Navy. He was accustomed to see things with his own eyes, call them by their plain names, submit to his superiors and self-denial, and judge by matter of fact, not prejudice. His Royal Highness was untutored in the chicanery of a Court, and saw nothing through that jaundiced medium; it was from this cause the Court had no sympathy with him and he lay so long in the background."

Undoubtedly he was a sailor at heart and his lower-deck language in which swear-words generally took the place of adjectives and verbs, was shocking. He was blunt in speech and manner, saying the first thing that came into his head and he delighted in the telling of coarse stories in mixed company without even noticing the resultant embarrassment. Boisterous and unpredictable, he good-humouredly swept aside etiquette and stiff behaviour; his weapon was the bludgeon not the rapier. Reunited with his brothers, he joined in their dissipations, gambling, drinking and everything else that London and Brighton had to offer to make up for the loss of his career.

He had many women but lost his heart to only one. She was Dorothy Jordan, an actress, and the bluff, hearty William had first seen her at Drury Lane Theatre when she appeared in a farce, "The Spoil'd Child." When she came to London in October 1785, farces were not yet popular; heavy drama was the vogue. Yet Dorothy Jordan changed the trend and comedy became popular. She swept from success to success and was the toast of the town.

Her reputation was not unblemished, for when still a child in Dublin she had been seduced by a notorious character named Daly, who saddled her with an illegitimate child. After that she had many affairs since she was a warm-hearted woman and virtue was not an asset in an actress. One of the affairs was with a Richard Ford and apparently she loved him for she bore him four children. From all accounts she was a good mother to her five children, whilst Ford hovered in the background playing the part of husband. The money she earned they spent as fast as it came.

Farcical comedy was just the entertainment likely to appeal to the jovial Duke's sense of humour and Mrs. Jordan, as she was called, was also just the good-natured, gay and uninhibited type of woman to appeal to his heart. He visited Drury Lane time and time again, but she managed to keep him safely at a distance, for she was reluctant to part from the father of four of her children. When she played at Richmond he was more successful although the romance had a sordid beginning—money. The three of them made a squalid bargain by which William bought her from Richard Ford, and William was probably the only one of the three who was not mercenary for he was genuinely in love. With Mrs. Jordan the change was probably made for the benefit of her children as she realized that Ford would not marry her. Ford was certainly satisfied with the bargain, for in due course he became Police Magistrate and Sir Richard Ford.

The *Morning Post* reported :

" The comic Syren of the Old Drury had abandoned her quondam mate for the superior attractions of a Royal Lodge, to which Little Pickle* was long invited. This movement the Gossip Fame had for some time anticipated, but it was not until Saturday last that she quitted the comforts of a private situation could af-FORD."

Despite the cynicism at the beginning of their association they settled down into a pleasant, domestic routine and made Petersham Lodge their home. Accommodation was found for Mrs. Jordan's children in the neighbourhood and there was no hindrance to her seeing them as often as she liked. Mrs. Jordan continued her stage career and it is said that often the Duke, who was always in debt, collected her salary himself; sometimes even asking for an advance against the next amount due.

They continued to live together in happy obscurity for twenty years and the fashionable world saw William only occasionally, whilst the Court ignored his existence. Their first few years together were spent at Petersham Lodge, but in 1797 the Duke was made Ranger of Bushey Park and they moved to Bushey House. They had ten children; most of them born at Bushey. The other

* She played the part of " Little Pickle " in " The Spoil'd Child ".

children were lodged nearby and they intermingled freely with the Fitzclarences.

In the intervals between births Mrs. Jordan still made appearances on the stage although the fire which destroyed Drury Lane in 1809 deprived her of her main revenue. It was on this occasion that Sheridan, called to see the end of his theatre and the beginning of his ruin, bravely made his famous quip whilst sipping wine on the scene of the disaster: " May not a man drink at his own fireside?"

William still maintained his great interest in the Navy, keeping up a regular correspondence with his hero Nelson. When Nelson lost his arm William insisted that he should stay at Bushey until he had fully recovered, and when he was killed the Duke received from the surgeon the fatal bullet, which he always treasured. Nelson's body, pickled in rum and upright in a barrel, was brought back to England in the *Victory*. From the ship it was taken to Greenwich to lie in state.

The establishment of the Regency changed the Duke's viewpoint. His heavy indebtedness and Mrs. Jordan's loss of income, due to the theatre fire, made life extremely difficult and he began to consider making a wealthy marriage as a solution. He had been abroad at the time of the Regency Debates but he had always been devoted to his brother and presumed that as Regent he would not object to his finding a wealthy wife outside the bounds imposed by the Royal Marriage Act.

As a first step in his plans he decided to break with Mrs. Jordan. The exact terms of the settlement made between them are not known but it does seem established that he gave her an adequate pension.* The disillusioned Dorothy Jordan went abroad.

The caricaturists and lampoonists were delighted by the return of the forgotten prince to the fold of ridicule; the desertion and his unavailing efforts to find an heiress were pounced upon with glee. Here are some samples:

* According to contemporary records he did maintain the payments and was not responsible for her subsequent financial troubles in France, where she died in dire distress, being buried by public subscription; but this does not absolve him from guilt and his cruel act of rejecting her after she had borne him ten children stands as a stigma on his character.

" What! leave a woman to her tears?
Your faithful friend for twenty years;
One who has wasted half her charms,
The fond companion of your arms?"

and:

" Qoth Cl—ce, heav'n inspir'd, ' I'll wed;
I'll live no more in fornication,
But take a virgin to my bed
And serve and gratify the nation.'
One at this moment I would wed
With sixteen thousand pounds per annum
For such a prize as that I'd bed,
For aught I care, the devil's grannum."

and another, following the rejection of his proposal to a Princess
of Denmark:

" She read it through with great attention
And praised the R—l swain's invention.
Then straightway beckoned to a page,
From a court guide to learn his age.

That once found out was quite enough.
The courier brought back this rebuff:
' I am fifteen, you're fifty-three,
They're ages that can ne'er agree '."

For the next few years the Duke of Clarence remained a
bachelor despite his determined efforts to find a rich heiress,
and he was often made to realize that even as a Prince of the
Blood he was not by any means the irresistible suitor that he
had imagined himself to be. He found some consolation in the
fact that the Regent's whirligig of pleasure was revolving even
faster than before, and gratefully he clambered onto it.

The death of Princess Charlotte in 1817 changed the position
of the Duke of Clarence suddenly; now he was next in line to
the throne after the Duke of York. That he should marry was

imperative and the old Queen and the Prince Regent took a hand in his affairs. Queen Charlotte selected his bride and brother George talked him into it.

The bride-to-be was Princess Adelaide and the negotiations were soon concluded with her mother, the Dowager Duchess of Saxe-Meiningen, who was more concerned with the importance of the match than the qualities of the husband. In the eyes of the Princess marriage with an elderly man, more than twice her age, with a reputation for hard-living and ten illegitimate children, could not have appeared quite the same attractive proposition. Nevertheless there was a prospect, if not a strong one, of wearing the English crown.

Amelia Adelaide Louisa Theresa Caroline, to give her name in full, was born in 1792 and was the eldest child of the reigning Duke of Saxe-Coburg-Meiningen. When his son and heir was born eight years later he showed his liberalism by inviting the People to be the god-parents. He was an enlightened sovereign, if eccentric, and ruled his tiny state, which was only about the size of Hertfordshire, with dignity and moderation. He died in 1803, when Adelaide was eleven, and his Duchess became Regent.

Europe was in a turmoil and rigid economy was necessary but the Duchess played her part well. There was a younger daughter, Ida, and the two girls received a strict and moral upbringing. Ida married Duke Bernard of Saxe-Weimar but there appeared to be little prospect of Adelaide marrying until the arrival of the proposal from England.

At this time Adelaide was twenty-five, and although not a beauty she had a pleasant and amiable disposition and was gentle and reserved in manner. She arrived in London accompanied by her mother in the July of 1818, and they stayed at Grillon's Hotel in Albemarle Street. There was no one to greet them, the Duke of Clarence being out of town, but the Regent arrived after dinner to pay his respects and to finalize the date of the wedding.

A few days after the ceremony the Duke and his bride travelled to Hanover for the honeymoon. Here they joined the Duke and Duchess of Cambridge, month-old newly-weds, and the two Duchesses became friendly. In March of the following year they became mothers on successive days, but Adelaide's joy was shortlived for her baby died after only a few hours.

They stayed in Germany until October when they returned to England. The travelling conditions were dreadful and Adelaide, not in the best of health, was ill at Walmer Castle for several weeks. When she was well again they took up residence in the Duke's dirty and dilapidated apartments in the Stable-Yard, St. James's. Belatedly William agitated for these uncomfortable premises to be put in good order, as they had not been repaired for fifty years, but without success. In the Spring they moved to Bushey House, which was to become for Adelaide, as it already was for William, their real home. They lived here for ten years, interspersed with regular visits to Germany.

Adelaide was an admirable manager and her early lessons in economy stood her in good stead. She personally supervized the household arrangements and persuaded her husband to exercise more care in the handling of financial matters. Very soon the Duke found himself enjoying a much more comfortable and ordered existence than he had ever known and his moderation in food and drink greatly improved his state of health. He began to regard Adelaide in a new light, for he was honest enough to recognize her sterling qualities. Gradually she tempered down his abrupt, boisterous manner and he became a tractable man and an exemplary husband.

They both enjoyed a simple life and were friendly and hospitable to their neighbours. Fresh air and plenty of exercise gradually eradicated the marks of William's earlier dissipations and gave him promise of longevity. On the occasions when they ventured into the fashionable scenes, at Brighton and in London, the Duchess showed herself to be just as capable as she was at home and she became quite popular; a popularity marred only by the fact that she spoke English with a pronounced foreign accent and her voice was harsh.

The Duke must have missed the sound of children's voices around him, but this was not to be, for they were childless. In December 1820 Adelaide gave birth to her second and last child, a girl christened hopefully Elizabeth Georgina Adelaide, but she died when only three months old.

The other bridegroom of the double wedding, Edward, Duke of Kent, was even more disappointed than his brother William by the financial settlement on his marriage; his sacrifice he felt had been greater. He had been living with the woman he loved, Madame St. Laurent.

A few weeks after Princess Charlotte's death he was in Brussels and discussed the situation with the gossip Creevey, who was a Whig supporter with a voice in the right quarters, pointing out the Regent's difficulties in obtaining a divorce; the childlessness of the Duke of York; and the Duke of Clarence's position. He then spoke about himself : " Should the Duke of Clarence not marry, the next prince in succession is myself, and although I trust I shall be at all times ready to obey any call my country may make upon me, God only knows the sacrifice it will be to make, whenever I shall think it my duty to become a married man. It is now seven-and-twenty years that Madame St. Laurent and I have lived together : we are of the same age, and have been in all climates, and in all difficulties together, and you may well imagine, Mr. Creevey, the pang it will occasion me to part with her. I put it to your own feelings—in the event of any separation between you and Mrs. Creevey . . . As for Madame St. Laurent herself, I protest I don't know what is to become of her if a marriage is to be forced upon me; her feelings are already so agitated upon the subject." He then described how he had been sitting at breakfast a morning or two after the death of Princess Charlotte and he had been handed with his letters the *Morning Chronicle,* in which an article appeared mentioning the possibility of his marriage. " I did as is my constant practice, I threw the newspaper across the table to Madame St. Laurent, and began to open and read my letters. I had not done so but a very short time, when my attention was called to an extraordinary noise and a strong convulsive movement in Madame St. Laurent's throat. For a short time I entertained serious apprehensions for her safety; and when, upon her recovery, I enquired into the occasion of this attack, she pointed to the article in the *Morning Chronicle.*"

The Duke then spoke again of the Duke of Clarence: " My brother the Duke of Clarence is the elder brother, and has certainly the right to marry if he chooses, and I would not interfere with him on any account. If he wishes to be king—to be married and have children, poor man—God help him! let him do so. For myself—I am a man of no ambition, and wish only to remain as I am . . . Easter, you know, falls very early this year —the 22nd of March. If the Duke of Clarence does not take any step before that time, I must find some pretext to reconcile Madame St. Laurent to my going to England for a short time. When once there, it will be easy for me to consult my friends as to the proper steps to be taken. Should the Duke of Clarence do nothing before that time as to marrying it will become my duty, no doubt, to take some measures upon the subject myself." Two names, the Duke said, had been mentioned in this connection—those of the Princess of Baden and the Princess of Saxe-Coburg. The later, he thought, would perhaps be the better of the two, from the circumstances of Prince Leopold being so popular with the nation; but before any other steps were taken, he hoped and expected to see justice done to Madame St. Laurent. " She is," he explained, " of very good family, and has never been an actress, and I am the first and only person who ever lived with her. Her disinterestedness, too, has been equal to her fidelity. When she first came to me it was upon £100 a year. That sum was afterwards raised to £400, and finally to £1,000; but when my debts made it necessary for me to sacrifice a great part of my income, Madame St. Laurent insisted upon again returning to her income of £400 a year. If Madame St. Laurent is to return to live amongst her friends, it must be in such a state of independence as to command their respect. I shall not require very much, but a certain number of servants and a carriage are essentials." As to his own settlement, the Duke observed that he would expect the Duke of York's marriage to be considered the precedent. " That," he said, " was a marriage for the succession, and £25,000 for income was settled, in addition to all his other income, purely on that account. I shall be contented with the same arrangement, without making any demands grounded on the difference of the value of money in 1792 and at present. As for the payment of my debts," the Duke concluded, " I don't call them great. The nation, on the contrary, is greatly my debtor."

At this time Edward, Duke of Kent, was fifty years of age, a tall, bulky, florid-complexioned man, with the little hair he possessed dyed black. He held himself erect in true military fashion for he was proud of his military service, when he had earned for himself the reputation of being an unmitigated martinet.

He had been born in 1767 and when he was twenty-one his father sent him to Geneva for military training. Here he met Madame Alphonsine Therese Bernadine Julie de Montgenêt de St. Laurent, Baronne de Fortisson. Her husband was a colonel in the French Army. They had one daughter about twelve months old.

When he was twenty-three, Edward was posted to Gibraltar where Colonel de Fortisson and his wife fleeing from the French Revolution joined him and their friendship developed.

The colonel suddenly decided to leave Gibraltar and the French pair sailed for Canada, but by force of circumstance or design the young Prince followed and they were reunited in Quebec. At Kent House, in Quebec, the Duke was a generous host and it was here that the intimacy between Edward and the colonel's wife appears to have developed. Later when the colonel was killed at Fort Royal she flew to Edward's arms for sympathy. She is described as being: " charming, amiable, gentle and kindly. What charmed in her most was a certain infectious warmth, simple, natural, and well-bred." The same source also records: " The mistress of the Prince's house was the beautiful Julie de St. Laurent, widow of a Baron de Fortisson."[*] A few months afterwards Madame St. Laurent gave birth to a son, and by then she was living with the Duke of Kent.

After this she accompanied him abroad on his military tours of duty, including his service in the West Indies where he distinguished himself as a first-rate commander. In 1802 he was appointed Governor of Gibraltar, a mutinous garrison, but his ruthless severity caused his recall and ended his active military service. He now settled down with Madame St. Laurent, in the

* *Le Bulletin des Recherchés Historiques.*

only way the Royal Marriage Act permitted, to a life of unmarried domesticity applying the same military precision to their
household affairs; but despite his income of £24,000 a year, his
efficiency did not prevent him from being heavily in debt. He
was at cross-purposes with his brothers, having quarrelled with
most of them, his altercation with the Prince Regent being a
particularly violent one. In consequence, as a means of retaliation, he became a strong supporter of the Whigs, the Political
Opposition. It is obvious therefore that the Regent's influence
did not persuade this brother to seek himself a wife.

Whether money or duty prompted the Duke of Kent's decision
to dismiss his mistress and marry is not known, nor is the exact
fate of Madame St. Laurent. One reasonable report says that
she retired to a convent in Paris. At the beginning she was in
distressed circumstances for Louis Philippe sent an appeal to
help her through Mrs. Fitzherbert. She remained there until the
Duke's death in 1820, after which she spent the rest of her life
in Canada and the United States of America. The son of whom
the Duke of Kent was supposed to be the father, was adopted
by Robert Wood, who had been a body-servant to the Duke of
Clarence, and later the boy took the name of his adoptive father.

Great grief must have clouded the separation, and supposition
is inadequate in describing the sorrow, tears and perhaps hysteria
which attended the simple, but final act, that determined the
divergence of paths in the lives of these two people, who had
lived and experienced so much together for nearly twenty-eight
years.

7

The new Duchess of Kent was Victoria Mary Louisa, Princess
of Saxe-Leiningen, born Princess of Saxe-Coburg, the daughter
of Francis, Duke of Saxe-Coburg-Saalfield. Her three brothers
were, therefore, Duke Ernst, Prince Leopold and Prince
Ferdinand.

In 1803, when she was seventeen, she became the second wife
of the elderly Prince of Leiningen, but in 1814 the Prince died,
leaving her with two children and the regency of the principality.
When her brother Leopold married Princess Charlotte it had

been suggested that she should marry the Duke of Kent, but at that time her responsibilities and her two children decided her refusal.

The death of Princess Charlotte in 1817, however, changed her mind and when the Duke of Kent again proposed she accepted him. She had seen him only once before.

Princess Victoria was then thirty-two, a short, plump and nondescript person with brown hair and brown eyes. She was cheerful but garrulous and given to gesticulation. What Edward's first impressions were are not recorded, but she was favourably impressed with his tall and military bearing and thought his conversation " very agreeable ". Stockmar had a different view. Through his shrewd eyes the Duke's face " betrayed calculation."

They were married by Lutheran rites and then travelled to London for the Church of England ceremony at Kew. After the honeymoon the prosaic couple began their married life in rooms at Kensington Palace burdened by debts; their only servant was a cook.

The lack of money weighed heavily on their happiness. His brothers and sisters refused to help them in any way and the new Duchess was treated with marked discourtesy. The Duke decided they were too poor to live in England and in October 1818 they left for the Continent, moving restlessly between Belgium and Germany until at last they settled in his wife's dower-house at Amorbach. Here their life was quiet and uneventful until, just when the Duke was becoming bored with his hobby of tinkering with clocks and watches, the Duchess announced that she was pregnant. To the Duke this was a spur to uproot themselves once again for he was determined that his child should be born in England.

Almost immediately they hired a carriage and loaded with their paraphernalia set off for the Channel coast, undaunted by the inclement weather and bad roads. The Duchess and her fourteen-year-old daughter, Feodora, the servants, the dogs and canaries were crowded inside the coach, whilst the hardy Duke mounted the box.

At 4.15 on the morning of Monday, May 24th, 1819, at Kensington Palace* their daughter was born, with the Arch-

* A gilt plate above the mantelpiece of the room attests the fact.

bishop of Canterbury, Wellington and Canning acting as official witnesses; but as the child only held fifth place in the succession it was a birth that received little public attention. Two months earlier the Duchess of Clarence had lost her child a few hours after the birth, but it seemed likely that she would again become a mother, and in any case, there was a good chance that the Duchess of Kent would also have another child, perhaps a boy, to take his position before this daughter in the line of succession.

The Prince Regent attended the christening ceremony on June 24th, apparently with the intention of pleasing the Emperor Alexander of Russia, the most powerful monarch on the continent of Europe, who was to be a godfather, and at the same time of annoying his brother. He had learnt that Kent had chosen Elizabeth as the name for his daughter and when the Archbishop of Canterbury asked for the name by which the child was to be baptized the Regent quickly replied, "Alexandrina." The father diffidently requested the addition of another name. "Certainly," said his brother, "Georgina." The Duke demurred, suggesting "Elizabeth", but the Regent swept this aside, saying conceedingly: "Very well, then, call her after her mother. But Alexandrina must come first." So, to the great annoyance and chagrin of the father, the child was christened Alexandrina Victoria.*

8

Three months later, Madame Siebold, the German midwife who had assisted at the birth of Princess Victoria, was in attendance at the birth of the Duke of Coburg's second child. On the 26th of August 1819 a boy was born at Rosenau, the ducal summer palace, about four miles from the town of Coburg. He was christened on the 19th of September in the Marble Hall at Rosenau, when he was given the names, Francis Charles Augustus Albert Emmanuel; but Albert was the name by which he became known.

Duke Ernst had been the last of the three Coburg Princes to

* In August, 1819, Princess Victoria was vaccinated. This was the first time that royal sanction had been given to this operation, and consequently its popularity was accelerated.

find himself a wife. In 1816 his brother Ferdinand had married the Princess Kohary of Hungary* and the old Dowager Duchess Augusta had been delighted. She was even more delighted when her favourite son, Leopold, became the husband of Princess Charlotte and England settled upon him the sum of £50,000 per annum.

In the meanwhile the handsome Ernst was still searching for an heiress. He blamed his lack of success on the girl Pauline Panam. Everywhere she was pointed out as his victim. Her beauty and charm aroused sympathy in the hearts of her listeners, and the attempts on her life made an exciting story in which his role of the villain doomed him as a suitor. The presence of his little son, Ernst, the innocent victim of his affair with Pauline Panam, gave undeniable credence to her story.

The Duke of Coburg decided to kidnap the child so that he could then hold the boy as a hostage to force Pauline to enter a convent, where she would be forgotten. His plan failed, so as an alternative measure he demanded the formal custody of his son. When she refused he stopped her income. The desperate young mother appealed to Constantine, who gave her money and added another to the list of the Duke's infamies.

The continuous tirade against the Duke of Coburg reflected adversely on the family name and Ferdinand took a hand in the affair. At his request Prince Metternich intervened. He sent for Pauline and offered to take care of her son. He said: " Resign him over to me. I will conduct myself towards him as if he were my own child; I will answer for his safety. I will place him in a college, and you shall have an ample allowance. What the Duke pays you is not sufficient for your support; you require at least six times as much. Ernst must have an income of fifteen thousand francs, a title, and bear his father's name; for I will legitimatize him, and take him under my protection. When he grows up to manhood I will pave the way for him through life; and the title of Comte, that shall be conferred upon him, will assist, and not prove detrimental to his fortunes."

Pauline said she still feared that the Duke would harm the

* Ferdinand's son, also named Ferdinand, became King Consort of Portugal by his second marriage in 1836 with Maria da Gloria, Queen of Portugal; he was father by her of two successive Kings of Portugal, Pedro V and Luis.

boy but Metternich reassured her and promised her regular access
to her son. He then said: " Such are my offers. Will you accept
them? Refuse and the Prince will wholly abandon you. I do
not wish to press you; reflect well: you certainly cannot entertain an idea that I am leagued with the Duke to cause your
son's assassination?"

She returned home frightened and undecided. " Notwithstanding all these boasted advantages, I found it difficult to
make up my mind and yield my darling boy. A secret instinct
whispered the perfidiousness of diplomacy."

The next day she wrote to Prince Metternich accepting his
proposals and delivered the letter in person. He was pleased with
the success of his intervention and said, " I am very glad you
acquiesce with my proposals. All will terminate much better than
you suppose. But now that I am on the point of entering into
this negotiation, pledge me your word of honour that you will
give no further publicity to your tale; I extract this from you.
In all the elevated societies nothing is talked of but your history;
the Duke incessantly reproaches our police; and you have forwarded a Memoir to Archduke Regnier, wherein there are very
strong passages."

Pauline gave her word: " Prince, I suffer in silence." Soon
afterwards an event took place that halted the negotiations—
Duke Ernst found himself a wife.

On the 1st of July 1817 he married Princess Louise, the only
child and heiress of Duke Augustus of Saxe-Gotha and Alten-
burg.*

Princess Louise was a pretty, petite child of sixteen, shy, emotional and inclined to be tearful, but now on her wedding day
she was animated and happy. Her father, the old Duke, gave
away one thousand loaves of bread to the poor, and there were
loud cheers as Louise drove away with her husband across the
border into Coburg.

Here the newly-weds were welcomed by the Dowager Duchess
Augusta, who threw her arms round her son's shoulders, saying
to Louise in a loud voice: " *Ich wünsche dass der kleine Ernst,
dir so gut ein werden moge wie du mir einer geworden bist.*" (I

---

* On the death of Duke Augustus, Ernst became Duke of Saxe-Coburg-
Gotha, and later, ceded Saalfield.

hope that little Ernst will become as dear to you as you have become to me.) She then embraced Louise, who was flushed with the excitement of the wedding, and recorded her first impressions of her daughter-in-law in her diary: "She is a charming tiny being, not beautiful but very pretty, through grace and vivacity. Every feature of her face has expression; her big blue eyes often look sad from under her black lashes, and then again, she is a happy wild child . . . I hope she will grow as she is very short . . . I had half the town for tea because everybody wished to congratulate me."

Also there amongst the family gathering to welcome the young bride was Ernst's widowed sister, Princess Victoria of Saxe-Leiningen, with her little daughter Feodora. Destiny had brought them together, in readiness for the time when the names of their future children, Victoria and Albert, were to be imperishably linked.

9

However highly the stern and forbidding Duchess Augusta may have thought of her son Ernst, he was certainly not a good husband and marriage did not sate his appetite for sexual adventures. Louise, a spoilt child, also began to seek love in the arms of others and very soon "in Coburg, the very sparrows on the roof twittered of the amours of the Duke and Duchess." The name of a Chamberlain at the Court, Baron von Meyern, came to be closely linked with hers. He was a charming, handsome, cultivated man, many years older than Louise and of Jewish extraction. This affair has caused the appearance, in many books and documents, of the allegation that Baron von Meyern was the father of Albert, her second child; and that Louise by her infidelity introduced Semitic blood into the veins of the Royal Family of England.

Inevitably with two such waywards spirits there was a separation, followed by a divorce in March 1826. The marriage was not a happy one, and a separation took place in 1824, when the young Duchess finally left Coburg and never saw her children again. She died at St. Wendel in 1831, after a long and painful illness, in her 32nd year.

The Dowager Duchess of Gotha, her stepmother, writes to the Duke the following account of her on 27th July 1831 :

" 'The sad state of my poor Louise bows me to the earth . . . The thought that her children had quite forgotten her distressed her very much. She wished to know if they ever spoke of her. I answered her that they were far too good to forget her; that they did not know of her sufferings, as it would grieve the good children too much.' "*

In the autumn of 1832, six months after his wife's death, Ernst married his own niece, Princess Mary of Würtemburg, the daughter of his sister Antoinette, who was the wife of Duke Alexander of Würtemberg.

In the meantime Pauline Panam remained in Vienna hoping that Prince Metternich would conclude the negotiations concerning her son's welfare. Nothing happened and her requests for information were ignored. She gave up hope and returned to Paris with the intention of pressing her claims from the safety of her own country.

She sent a letter to the Duke of Coburg, in which she threatened to publish her Memoirs, which were in the safe-keeping of the King's Notary at Paris, together with the Duke's incriminating letters, unless he made adequate arrangements for their son's future.

As a result of this letter prolonged negotiations began, first with M. Javon, Agent of the Court of Coburg in Paris, and when he failed, the Duke persuaded the Duc de Richelieu to act on his behalf; but still they were unable to reach an agreement. In desperation, Pauline sold her Memoirs and they were duly published in 1823. They aroused tremendous interest in France, but the publication was suppressed in Germany.

From this date no further mention appears of Pauline or her son in any works of the period. Thus at the zenith of her beauty she vanished from the scene and her fate is one of conjecture.

10

In December 1819 Caroline was in Italy when she received the news that the old King George III was dying. She immedi-

---

* From a Memorandum, written in 1864, by Queen Victoria.

ately sent word to Brougham signifying that she would return if the *country* would protect her. (She was certainly aware of the Milan Commission and of the Regent's malicious intentions, since she had on several occasions sent her steward Siccard to England for the purpose of bringing back all the information and gossip he could collect concerning her position and the Regent's attitude towards her.) Otherwise, she would prefer to live abroad for " the few years I am to remain upon this wild globe." The Ministers were disconcerted and discussed with Brougham the best means of bribing her to stay away from England.

In January 1820, whilst they were deciding on the precise offers to be made to Caroline,* the Duke of Kent died unexpectedly. The robust Edward was spending the winter at Sidmouth and had returned from a walk in the rain, soaked to the skin. Inflammation of the lungs set in, and five days later on the 23rd of January, this tough, hardy soldier of many campaigns was dead. As he was dying he had spoken of the Regent, saying, " If I could shake hands with him now I should die in peace." His Duchess, who had faithfully sat beside his bed for the entire five days of his illness, was once again a widow.

By a coincidence the young Dr. Stockmar was also at Sidmouth and staying at the same house " Woolbrook Glen ". Two years before he had stood at the deathbed of Princess Charlotte and now, with his curious *penchant* for being present when he was needed, he watched the Duke of Kent fighting his last battle. Shrewdly he advised that a will be prepared immediately, for he realized that although the Duke's material possessions were negligible, the guardianship of his eight-months-old daughter was of vital importance and must be assured to the Duchess. The wisdom of his advice was proved by later events.

The finances of the Duke were in a parlous state and his Duchess was stranded at Sidmouth without the money to pay for her return to London. Fortunately her brother Prince Leopold came to her rescue and himself conducted the Duchess and the little Victoria back to Kensington. She was in a quandary. Her own £6,000 a year was dwarfed by her hus-

---

* The offer eventually made, in February 1820, was a revenue of £50,000 on condition of her remaining abroad.

band's immense debts, and she must have pondered whether to return to Amorbach and obscurity or to remain in England, amongst strangers in an alien country, to establish her daughter as an English princess. Prince Leopold offered to contribute an additional £3,000 a year, so she stayed with the child she adored and of whom she said " *C'est mon bonheur, mes délices, mon existence.*"

Six days later, at midnight on the 29th of January, the hand of death added to the Royal Scroll the name of George the Third of England, and the great bell of St. Paul's tolled the end of the longest reign as yet in English history. So the blind, imbecile father, whose life had been full of tribulations, followed his harsh, bigoted, virtuous son into the Royal Mausoleum at Windsor. The Duke of Kent's coffin had entered with difficulty, for it was so large that it became wedged in the entrance.

The Prince Regent was not present at the King's death for he himself was seriously ill; indeed he almost joined his father.

CHAPTER EIGHT

GEORGE THE FOURTH

I

THE DEATH of George III decided Caroline to return to England, for according to the reports she had received the time was now opportune. The distress caused by the increased taxes following the war had given stimulus to the resentment felt towards the new King's lavish spending and there was a corresponding wave of sympathy towards the injured Caroline. Ricks were burning in the country and orators were stirring riots in the towns.

Caroline was in Rome and requested a sovereign's escort from Pope Pius VII. Diplomatically Cardinal Consalvi refused to supply one saying that " the Papal Government does not know that the Queen of England is in Rome." Her position was an ambiguous one for she was no longer Princess of Wales and had not been announced as Queen. In consequence she was refused a courier's passport by the French Minister, but not to be outdone she obtained one as a private traveller from the English Consul. Her journey across France was not an easy one.

At Calais she was met by Brougham, who wasted no time in telling her of the Ministers' offer, which she rejected after a short discussion with Alderman Wood, an ex-Lord Mayor of London, who was now an Opposition M.P. He had taken it upon himself to meet the Queen at Calais as the spokesman of her supporters. Obviously he impressed Caroline for she replaced Bergami with the talkative Wood. They crossed the Channel by ordinary packet-ship and landed at Dover, where without orders the guns from Dover Castle saluted her arrival.

24   EDWARD AUGUSTUS, DUKE OF KENT, FOURTH SON OF GEORGE III

(From a painting by Sir William Beechey in 1818)

25 THE DUCHESS OF KENT, 1841
(From the portrait by John Lucas at Windsor Castle. Reproduced by gracious permission of Her Majesty The Queen)

WILLIAM IV

(From a miniature by Charles Muss at Windsor Castle. Reproduced by gracious permission of Her Majesty The Queen)

27
ADELAIDE AMELIA, QUEEN OF WILLIAM IV
(From the painting by Sir Martin Archer Shee at Buckingham Palace. Reproduced by gracious permission of Her Majesty The Queen)

28

BARON STOCKMAR

(From the portrait by John Partridge at Buckingham Palace. Reproduced by gracious permission of Her Majesty The Queen)

29

BARONESS LEHZEN

(From a miniature by O. Koepke at Windsor Castle. Reproduced by gracious permission of Her Majesty The Queen)

30   QUEEN VICTORIA, 1843

(From the painting by F. Winterhalter at Windsor Castle. Reproduced by gracious permission of Her Majesty The Queen)

31　WILLIAM LAMB, 2ND VISCOUNT MELBOURNE

(From a painting by John Partridge)

32   **LEOPOLD, KING OF THE BELGIANS**

(From the portrait by F. Winterhalter at Windsor Castle. Reproduced by gracious permission of Her Majesty The Queen)

33

SIR ROBERT PEEL, 1826

(From the portrait by Sir Thomas Lawrence. Reproduced by kind permission of the Earl Peel)

34

HENRY JOHN TEMPLE, 3RD VISCOUNT PALMERSTON

(From a painting by F. Cruikshank)

35   QUEEN VICTORIA, 1843

(From the painting by F. Winterhalter at Windsor Castle. Reproduced by gracious permission of Her Majesty The Queen)

36　　　　THE PRINCE CONSORT, 1840

*(From a portrait by John Partridge at Buckingham Palace. Reproduced by gracious
permission of Her Majesty the Queen)*

37   EDWARD VII AS PRINCE OF WALES, 1859
*(From the oil sketch by F. Winterhalter at Buckingham Palace. Reproduced by
gracious permission of Her Majesty The Queen)*

THE PRINCE CONSORT, 1861

(From the picture by Smith after Corbould at Buckingham Palace. Reproduced by gracious permission of Her Majesty The Queen)

39   BENJAMIN DISRAELI, EARL OF BEACONSFIELD
(From the painting by G. E. Millais)

WILLIAM EWART GLADSTONE
(From the painting by S. P. Hall)

41

QUEEN VICTORIA, 1899
(From the painting by Bertha Muller after Henrich von Angeli)

The new King, who had been proclaimed at Carlton House, was furious when he heard that his wife had landed in England. He told the Cabinet that unless they gave him a divorce he would find Ministers who would. Castlereagh voiced the feelings of the Cabinet by saying judiciously that Parliament " might stamp upon her conduct the stain which the voice of Europe affixes to it," and Prime Minister Lord Liverpool, to keep his job, proposed a Bill of Pains and Penalties; in truth it was to be " The Trial of the Queen ". It is to the credit of Canning, who had been on friendly terms with Caroline, that he gallantly offered his resignation, but it was refused.*

Elated by the warmth of her welcome Caroline swept into London. The dilapidated old carriage she used was greeted by cheering crowds everywhere and when she arrived at Alderman Wood's house in South Audley Street Caroline was surrounded by a dense mob shouting their support. For the two days she stayed there crowds never left the street, whilst Caroline made continuous bowing appearances like a prima donna, if a rather uncomely one; being " very stout, wearing a black wig with long curls hanging on both sides of her face, her eyebrows painted black, her cheeks horribly rouged, she had given to the naturally good-humoured-looking countenance an unpleasantly bold and stern expression, enhanced by wearing a large hat with a huge bow and a plume of immense ostrich feathers." On the advice of Wood, who realized she was causing too much of a disturbance, she moved to Portman Place and later to Brandenburgh House, a mansion in the country at Hammersmith.

The somewhat mollified George now withdrew to Windsor, leaving the divorce to his Ministers, whilst he made his plans for the Coronation, which had been postponed because of Caroline's arrival. This was a subject to which he gave very grave attention and it was an absorbing topic between him and his new favourite, Lady Conyngham.

The Trial of Caroline of Bunswick began in the House of Lords, where the Government were certain of support; after four weeks of secret examination of the evidence the Bill of Pains and Penalties was introduced by the Prime Minister. On

* During the trial he retired to France and resigned afterwards.

the 17th of August 1820 he brought in " An Act to deprive Her Majesty Queen Caroline Amelia Elizabeth of the title, prerogatives, rights, and privileges of Queen Consort of this realm and to dissolve the marriage between His Majesty and the said Caroline Amelia Elizabeth ".

The comical Caroline was undaunted despite the fact that if found guilty she could be executed, as Anne Boleyn had been.* She bobbed into the House of Lords, her ringlets shaking, ducked to the throne, ducked to the Peers, and jumped into her chair. The roll was called of the Peers of the Realm and the Trial began. As a Bill it was given the usual three readings, but between the first two readings witnesses were called whom the Peers were allowed to question. The Queen's Attorney-General Brougham and her Solicitor-General Denman were in turn permitted to question witnesses and the Crown lawyers in her defence. The first reading was passed by a large majority.

Imagine the anticipation of the prurient Peers as they prepared themselves to examine the scandals and immoralities of this strange comical figure that was their Queen; the malicious sharpening of wits; the hypocritical moralizing: the general assumption being, of course, that Caroline was guilty.

The Bill was supported by the Cabinet, the Bishops and the Irish Union Peers and some of the royal Dukes, the royal family being divided on this delicate subject; Gloucester and Sussex were for Caroline whilst York and Clarence supported the King.

The questioning was a "free-for-all" and Denman introduced Clarence with "come forth thou slanderer and let me see thy face," whilst Brougham described the King as "this shape if shape it could be called, what seemed its head the likeness of a kingly crown had on." Sir Thomas Tyrwhitt as Black Rod was the recipient of a riposte from Caroline when she said: " Well, Sir Thomas, what is your master trying me for? Is it for intermarrying with a man whose first wife I knew to be alive?"

So the verbal battle raged. The Villa d'Este was countered with the Brighton Pavilion. Caroline's familiarity with the servants brought forth the King's remark to a waiter: " This is all very well between you and me, Sam, but beware of being equally familiar with Norfolk." Whilst in the folds of his gown Brougham

* In English Law a Queen's adultery is treason.

254

kept his ace, the marriage with Maria Fitzherbert—the Queen had attended Mass and might even be termed a Catholic; but the King had married one.

The main charge against Caroline was that she had slept on the deck of a polacca (a small boat which carried cargo and cattle below deck) under an awning (a " tent " the Prosecution called it) with Bergami. The Italian interpreter, voluble and gesticulative, was ridiculed by the adroit Brougham and Denman as he spoke for the hired crew of servants and waiters. The evidence of disgusting details, given without hesitation was riddled with " *non mi ricordo* " (I don't remember) and the House began to doubt her guilt, but Caroline's impulsive outburst created a bad impression and swung some of the sympathy the other way.

The case for the prosecution lasted from the 17th of August to the 7th of September, followed by an adjournment. The case for the defence occupied from the 3rd to the 30th of October, after which the second reading of the Bill took place on the 6th of November. It was passed by a majority of twenty-eight. Four days later the majority was reduced to nine for the third reading. Liverpool then announced that the Ministers would not proceed and the Bill was withdrawn.

This was a moral victory for Caroline but an astute move by the Ministry. The Lords had found her guilty but had prevented an acquittal, which was very likely, by the Commons. This point was lost on the public who considered it to be a proof of the Queen's innocence.

The whole country had watched the progress of the Trial with tremendous interest and it was the over-riding topic of the day. Now the verdict was known the national reaction was amazing. London, where every ship had bunting, and the big towns Manchester, Glasgow, Dublin, Liverpool, Edinburgh and others were the scenes of wild rejoicing; everywhere being illuminated for three nights whilst a gigantic fête took place. On the 29th of November Caroline, still seeking the limelight, caused a wild and noisy demonstration in the City when she went to St. Paul's to offer thanksgiving for her deliverance.

The King's retaliation was in the form of a message: " His Majesty having determined that the Queen shall form no part of the ceremony of his coronation, it is therefore the royal pleasure that the Queen shall not attend the said ceremony." Her triumph was therefore short-lived.

The Coronation took place on July 19th 1821, at Westminster Abbey, and Caroline, ignoring the rejection of her petitions to be invited which she sent to everyone who might have influence, was determined to be present. She arrived at the Abbey at 5.30 in the morning accompanied by Lord and Lady Hood, Lady Anne Hamilton and Keppel Craven. Their two carriages reached the great door of Westminster Hall without hindrance, but when they arrived, the doors which had been opened just before to allow the King's procession to enter, were hurried closed. The door-keepers barring the way asked for the tickets of admission. " This is your Queen," said Lord Hood, " she is entitled to admission without such a form." " Yes," shouted Caroline, " I am your Queen : will you not admit me ?" The men, obeying orders, ignored her. Three entrances were tried with the same negative result.

At last after an angry altercation between Lord Hood and the guards, the small party dejectedly drove away and returned to Brandenburgh House. They were followed by mixed groans and cheers from the crowd gathered outside the entrance.

Meanwhile the King, dressed in heavy robes of crimson velvet, emblazoned with gold stars, and " wearing a hat with a monstrous plume of ostrich feathers, out of the midst of which rose a black heron's plume," was directing operations within the Hall. At ten o'clock on this hot July day the coronation procession passed into the Abbey and it was noticed that the King, protected from the sun by the royal canopy of embroidered yellow silk, mopped his brow many times. Henry Brougham, as a Baron of the Cinque Ports, helped to hold the canopy over the King whom he had described so disparagingly during the Queen's Trial.

The Coronation was carried out with strict observance of tradition and it was not until five and a half hours later that the King returned to Westminster Hall for the banquet, tired but happy; delighted as he had been by the pomp and ceremony and the cheers of the crowd. In Westminster Hall, the magnificent setting, the ornate ceiling, the pillars and the flashing glitter of silver and glass as he looked down the table had given a happy sparkle to the eye of the King. That night London celebrated with fireworks, drink, revelry and abandon, and the noise of gaiety must have added to Caroline's unhappiness.

Her dejection did not last long apparently for a few days later she is reported as attending a dance and enjoying herself. She also attended Kean's performance of *Othello* at Drury Lane and her presence caused a demonstration in the Theatre.

On Monday the 30th of July she again visited the Theatre to see Kean's *Richard III* but during the performance she was taken ill. It is said she had drunk a glass of lemonade and was in great pain soon afterwards, when she cried " I have been poisoned!" The next day her doctor diagnosed internal in-flammation. She was bled with leeches and given enough " castor oil that would have turned the stomach of a horse ". A week later, on the 7th of August she was dead.

On the 3rd of August she had made her will leaving all her property to William Austin, the child she had called " Willikins ". She left £500 to the Hoods and her old carriage to Stephen Lushington, her doctor, who had been present when she died; coincidentally it was also his wedding day. Her body she be-queathed to Brunswick directing that on the coffin should be engraved the words—" Here lies Caroline the injured Queen of England ". The plate was duly set on the coffin but was subse-quently removed. The word " injured " was probably substituted on the plate, for Brougham records that the word " murdered " was the one actually used by Caroline.

Ironically, even in death she continued to cause trouble. To avoid a demonstration the King had ordered that the funeral *cortège*, on the way to Harwich, should not pass through the City of London. The route from Brandenburgh House was to be Kensington, along Church Street into Bayswater Road and then north up Edgware Road. The news leaked out, however, and when the procession reached Church Street they found the entrance barricaded. Troops arrived to escort the *cortège* through the Park, but the gates near Knightsbridge Barracks had been closed by the mob and could not be opened. The funeral moved to the gates near Park Lane, where the soldiers fought their way through the crowd and the funeral entered the Park. At the

Cumberland Gate, which is now Marble Arch, another mob awaited them. The crowd had torn down the park railings and they used the bars as weapons against the escorting soldiery, who were forced to open fire, killing two people and wounding many others; but the *cortège* was again on the route.

At Tottenham Court Road, however, the procession met another barricade and this time the weight of the mob forced the funeral into Drury Lane. The troops were powerless for the following crowd had joined the demonstrators and the funeral was swept towards the City, along the main road under Temple Bar. Caroline had gained her last victory and the demonstration which the King had tried to avoid duly took place. The shops were closed, black bunting was draped everywhere, the windows were crowded with faces, and crowds dressed in mourning lined the route in pouring rain.

At Brunswick on the 24th of August the coffin was laid in the ducal tomb beside the coffins of her father and brother, who had both been killed in the Napoleonic war. The ceremony took place at dead of night in accordance with the custom of their house. She was fifty-three.

Caroline was a strange unpredictable creature, unloving and unloved. She was indiscreet, tactless, wearisome and rude. Life with her was described in the diary of one of her Ladies-in-Waiting, Lady Charlotte Bury, as being " life in a madhouse ".

Thwarted mother love was undoubtedly one of the reasons for her strange behaviour but thwarted ambition was very likely the main cause. An obsession for revenge ruled her life and this pre-occupation with spite probably unhinged a mind already weak, for madness was hereditary in her family; two of her brothers were feeble-minded and were excluded from the succession. Another brother, Frederick William, was a melancholic and his elder son was indisputably insane. Thus when Caroline landed in a strange land she was all too ill-equipped both mentally and by nature to deal with, what was doomed from the start to be, an impossible marriage. Whether she was innocent or guilty of adultery is still an enigma and from her Trial no one emerged with credit.

2

George IV had waited long and impatiently for the crown to be placed on his head and when the time came he was exhausted. There had been some difficulty about the Crown itself, which was apparently supplemented with hired jewels and in the British Museum there is a letter dated April 22, 1823, from the King to the Prime Minister on the subject: " The retention of this was certainly a question of great feeling with me, but I would yield that up by making it a question of judgment and expediency. Let me therefore not embarrass you, but do what you think best. I am sadly fatigued with yesterday and often feel as if other coronations would soon follow mine. Such alas! is the history of all classes."

At the other end of the social scale there was also unhappiness, indeed abject misery. Before the end of the war Brougham had prophesied that: " The dismissal of officers and other war functionaries will throw thousands out of employ, who will sooner or later ferment and turn to vinegar." It had been a true forecast, for on the day that peace was signed the Government demobilized half a million men and there was a great reduction in the Government requirements of food and clothing. As Robert Owen said: " When peace was signed the best customer went out of the market." Victory instead of bringing plenty brought penalties. Works and factories were closed down and in consequence the coal miners also suffered.

In 1815, to prevent the same thing happening in agriculture the Government passed the Corn Law, but as it did not control price fluctuations it did not achieve its object. Wheat was 52s. 6d. in 1816 and rose to 111s. 6d. in 1817, and then dropped to 45s. very soon afterwards The Corn Laws prevented the consumer from taking full advantage of the drop in price; farmers went out of business and the agricultural workers were thrown out of work. The shortage of bread caused food riots and the wrecking of machinery in the factories, where the workers blamed the new machines for the lack of work.

The exigencies of war had also caused a great increase in the employment of child labour, without providing the regulations to govern the conditions and hours of work. At the same time the use of water-power increased the rate of production in industry and in the textile industry, for example, the employment of orphans and pauper children was permitted on a large scale. Their normal working day was fifteen hours and during their meal breaks they were expected to clean their machines. Cruel methods were devised to keep them awake but there were still many accidents caused by exhausted children falling into the machinery. In 1819 an Act was passed which forbade the employment of children under nine, with a limit of twelve hours up to the age of sixteen. The Act only applied however to the cotton mills and it was not rigidly enforced.

In the coal-mines the conditions were even worse, and children of both sexes often worked in complete darkness. Sometimes they were as young as only five years of age and the normal daily work period was sixteen hours.

These were common examples of the deplorable labour conditions of the times that led to widespread rioting. Noteworthy amongst the riots were the Spa Fields Riots which followed a turbulent meeting at Bermondsey. The mob broke into gunsmiths' shops and were only dispersed after great difficulty and bloodshed. In 1819 there was the famous march of the Blanketeers when ten thousand workmen, each with his own blanket, marched from the North to present a petition to the Regent and as a result caused mass meetings to be held up and down the country.

In Manchester a crowd of some sixty thousand people gathered in St. Peter's Fields. The yeomanry used excessive violence in dispersing them and there were many hundreds of casualities. Derisively the affair came to be called the Peterloo Massacre in odious comparison with the Battle of Waterloo and Shelley found inspiration in the riot for his " Masque of Anarchy ". To preserve order a series of laws called the Six Acts, which limited the right of public meeting and penalized political pamphlets, was passed in 1820 but they only temporarily restored peace and the new reign began when the country was in a state of seething unrest. Work was scarce and wages were at starvation level. Bands of workers tramped from town to town in search of employment and dire necessity brought in its train an increase in crime. The

Law was barbarous and there were 223 offences to which the death penalty applied, whilst in 1820 there were more than 100,000 persons in gaols. At the Spa Fields riots the French tricolour had been displayed and demands made for parliamentary reform. The governing class had been thrown into a panic by this symbolic portent; safety lay in the severity of the Law.

The King was appalled by the brutality of the savage sentences and when the Recorder of London submitted his list of persons under sentence of death he often commuted the penalty or pardoned some of the prisoners. Even Greville who was usually scathing in his references to George observed: " The heaviest Recorder's report that was ever known, I believe; seven people left for execution. The King cannot bear this and is always leaning to the side of mercy. It not infrequently happens that a culprit escapes owing to the scruples of the King."

The majority of the people, like Greville, thought the King's clemency was misplaced for the mob dearly loved a hanging; the terror of the condemned; the pantomiming of the hangman; and the wild, spasmodic convulsions of the victim afforded the crowd a thrill of sadistic pleasure, particularly when it was a woman at the end of the rope. To obtain the full measure of their enjoyment they gathered round the gallows hours before the event in the same way as the people of Paris had collected round the guillotine.

The impetus given to the cause of humanism by the French Revolution, exemplified by Rousseau's famous dictum : " Man is born free and everywhere he is in chains," had been halted by the Napoleonic wars. France, in defeat, returned to the *ancien régime* but the French civilization nevertheless had advanced a further stage beyond England's. Her legislative and administrative systems had been reorganized and the sale of Church lands had increased peasant holdings so that the soil was able to support a larger number of people. A strong national spirit had been created by the abolition of feudal privilege and the ambitious were given more opportunities.

In Britain the reaction had been slower but the spirit of reform was materializing and the democratic movement, which was gathering momentum on the Continent, was becoming active. England had grown rich as a nation of shop-keepers and expanding trade abroad had confirmed the policy of isolation, but on the other side of the balance sheet there was a huge national debt as a result of the war, bringing increased poverty and degradation for the manual workers. Politically the scene was the same, for George IV, who had been the hope of the Whigs and the Reformers was now quite content to leave the *status quo* unchanged. He was too intelligent not to be aware of the trend of events but too indolent and selfish to do anything about it: " Things will last my time," he said.

But from the ranks of the new middle-class, voices of the enlightened were making themselves heard, those of Adam Smith, Jeremy Bentham, Robert Owen, Dugold Stewart, Mrs. Fry; and perhaps loudest of all, the voice of Francis Place. The last named is of particular interest for he played a leading part in all the progressive movements of the period. He had had a humble beginning as a journeyman tailor and his early married life was spent in a single room with his wife and the first two or three of his fourteen children. His wages barely supported them at starvation level, but in a few years he had built for himself a prosperous tailoring business in Charing Cross Road. In the meantime apart from his business he waged his campaigns for freedom and the rights of man. Soon the reformers were joined by others, but it was to be a long struggle and success was still many years away.

3

Immediately after his coronation George IV began to make plans to show himself in his Empire. First he decided to visit Ireland, a country in which he had long ago expressed interest. In a letter to Lord Keith dated February 20, 1797, he had said " that he wished to go to Ireland to cement a reunion between the two countries. I am ready to go to Ireland not only now but at any future period to endeavour to restore tranquillity, if it is not too late for my hopes of success, but I am confident that no measure could tend so much to the restoring general tranquillity to that disturbed and much injured country as my going Lord Deputy there."

He sailed for Ireland in the royal yacht at the beginning of

August and when they were off Holyhead he was given the news that Caroline was ill. On the 7th of August he received a message that she had died. A few days before he left England he had learnt of Napoleon's death but there is no evidence to prove the story that when he was told his greatest enemy was dead, he had replied naïvely: " Is she?"

Ireland was delighted with the large, florid, witty, hard-drinking George and his entry into Dublin on the 17th of August was his greatest personal triumph. He was accompanied by a hundred carriages and a thousand horsemen and was greeted with wild cheers, which swelled even louder as he continuously pointed to the huge bunch of shamrock in his hat. Never a hypocrite he thought the Court mourning was too drab for the occasion and " he wore a bright blue coat with brass buttons."

Dublin was a gay city and he entered wholeheartedly into the spirit of gaiety. His speeches warmed the Irish hearts for when he spoke he expressed his true feelings: " This is one of the happiest moments of my life. I feel pleased being the first of my family that set foot on Irish ground. Early in my life I loved Ireland. My heart was always with them."

As Prince of Wales he had expressed strong sympathy with Irish and Catholic claims and in 1797 had " made serious communications to Pitt with a view to the Viceroyalty and pacification of Ireland." He had disagreed with force as a method of dealing with the Irish problem, stating in a letter: " That system was fully and fatally tried in America and failed. The Irish are a brave and high-spirited people and more numerous than the Americans were at the commencement of hostilities."

After his visit in 1821 he said " that my presence in Ireland has been productive of very beneficial results." Certainly he effected a truce, and after a banquet at which he had been bold enough to say to the Irish gentry: " You all made a great mistake; you should have made terms as the Scottish did," O'Connell presented him with a laurel crown.

Having been crowned in England, and now symbolically crowned in Ireland, George decided to have another coronation in Hanover; furthermore after his splendid reception in Ireland the hostility of the London mob was not an inviting prospect. He embarked at Gravesend on the 22nd of September for Calais, where occurred the famous meeting with the exiled Beau Brummell. The King caught a glimpse of the pale face of Brummell in the crowd; it was the last sight they had of each other for George did not send for the fallen Beau and Brummell was too proud to request an interview.

On the way to Hanover George dined with the King and Queen of the Netherlands and was a tremendous success, throwing the King and Queen into gales of laughter with his wit and mimicry. The Duke of Wellington who was present at the dinner told a friend : " He had a most extraordinary talent for imitating the manner, gestures, and even voice of the people. So much so, that he could give you the exact idea of any one, however unlike they were to himself." The Duke in describing this dinner said that " to the great astonishment of the company, both the King and Queen, without any apparent cause, were at every moment breaking out in violent convulsions of laughter. There appeared to be no particular joke, but every remark our King made to his neighbours threw them into fits."

In Hanover he again received an enthusiastic welcome and his coronation delighted his Hanoverian subjects, for whilst he was here he abolished torture from the law of Hanover which was a popular move. In addition, as the King of England was also King of Hanover, a bulwark was created against French or Prussian aggression, for it introduced the power of England into continental politics. On this occasion Castlereagh and Metternich were brought together and George sent for Princess Lieven to ensure Metternich's enjoyment and complaisance. The object was to unite Europe against Russia's designs on Turkey and Castlereagh gave the King credit for this subsequent happy result.

The next year the King intended to be present at the Conference at Verona but Lady Conyngham refused to travel with Lady Castlereagh whom she disliked, so George planned a visit to Scotland instead. Again he was rapturously received for by a deft touch he sported the Stuart tartan and followed it up by knighting Scotland's greatest painter, Henry Raeburn. During this visit he celebrated his sixtieth birthday and on the same day, Lord Castlereagh, distraught with the strain of British foreign policy and perhaps the victim of blackmail, committed suicide by cutting his throat. This was a catastrophe for England, for Castlereagh had understood Europe better than anyone except Metternich.

The obvious successor was Canning, whom the King had hated since the time of the " Delicate Investigation ", but after a futile attempt to have Canning sent to India as Governor-General or " Grand Mogul " George yielded to the weight of opinion and sent for Canning. He described it at the time as " the greatest sacrifice of my opinions and feelings in my life ", whilst to Canning he said " that the brightest ornament of his crown is the power of extending grace and favour to a subject who may have incurred his displeasure." Thus did he bow to the inevitable.

The Under-Secretary at the Foreign Office, one of the few against Canning's appointment, resigned and Canning with a masterly diplomatic stroke appointed the twenty-five years old son of the Conynghams to fill the vacancy. Lady Conyngham was delighted and her pleasure spread to the King, although George, astute as he was, already recognized the merit of Canning and it is recorded that " the King's unfriendly feelings ceased as soon as he became persuaded that Mr. Canning's policy was really advantageous to the nation which he ruled."*

4

Lady Conyngham was in effect the Queen of England. She had decisively eliminated Lady Jersey (who removed herself forever by dying a few days before the Coronation) and her other rival, Lady Hertford. The quarrel between Lady Conyngham and Lady Castlereagh had arisen because Lady Castlereagh had remonstrated with the King when he had rejected her relative Lady Hertford from his favour. She was, in fact, quite capable of speaking up for herself for at the time of the advent of Lady Conyngham somebody asked her if she was aware of the King's admiration for Lady Conyngham and whether he had spoken to her about the lady? She replied " that intimately as she had known the King and openly as he had always talked to her upon every subject, he had never ventured to speak to her upon that of his mistresses."

* George Canning and his Time (Stapleton).

It is perhaps doubtful whether Lady Conyngham ever was his mistress. She was elderly, and so was he. In addition he was suffering from ill-health. At the time Princess Lieven described Lady Conyngham by saying " she had no political ideas nor opinions, no intimate relation to society, dominated by the strongest leaning towards diamonds and money, after this towards love and fashion. She pleased and suited the King." George still talked of marrying again and Lady Conyngham's daughter had even been suggested as a possible bride.

The caricaturists were vitriolic in their portrayals of Lady Conyngham; she was depicted as a bird of paradise beside an eagle; a juggler balancing the crown and sceptre; a mare between the royal shafts; using the crown as a pincushion; as a doll; and in many other, much worse, allegorical guises. Their attitude must have wounded her deeply for apart from the annoyance of the public condemnation she found the job was not the sinecure that it was generally believed to be. She found she had become a royal nurse-maid pandering to his whims and tempers, for his health now demanded full-time attention. Revealingly Greville noted that " she looks bored to death and she never speaks, never appears to have one word to say to the King, who however talks without ceasing."

That she did exert considerable influence, however, is apparent, since many dismissals and promotions were traced to her and she succeeded in bringing her family to Court; her husband was made a Marquis and one of her sons became Master of the Robes. However she appears generally to have had a good influence and it is fair to record that she spent a great deal of her time co-operating with the King in drawing up some of the legislation, forbidding, for instance, the whipping of women, cruelty to horses and cattle, the use of mantraps in game preserves and in saving condemned criminals from the gallows.*

The King was suffering from gout brought on by dietetic abuse and he had also become grossly overweight; his legs, of which he had always been so proud, failed him now for they could barely carry his huge body and he usually moved about in a

---

* After the Lancaster Assizes of 1827, the King commuted 28 death sentences and at the City Assizes in August of the same year he commuted every death sentence except one for highway robbery.

wheel-chair. His love of horses never deserted him and he invented a platform with an incline which enabled him to be lifted into the saddle, but eventually he found riding to be too strenuous and discontinued it entirely.

He was at times irascible and Lady Conyngham, who was always amiable and good-natured, was often called upon to soothe him into a good temper again. It is apparent she chose the opportune moments to ask him for favours for he always acquiesced. She was seeking a husband for her daughter, Lady Elizabeth, who was also at the Court, and the King responded genially by promising a peerage as a bait. Her serenity and pleasant disposition pleased the King immensely and he once said to her : " Thank you, thank you, my dear; you always do what is right; you cannot please me so much as by doing everything you please, everything to show you are mistress here." He showed his gratitude in a practical way by loading her with jewels and expensive *objets d'art,* by paying the wages of her servants and, when the Conynghams gave a dinner at their own house by having the food cooked at St. James's and taken in special containers to Hamilton Gardens by hackney coaches.

Under the influence of his great Ministers the King's influence on politics became one of compromise and he became a constitutional monarch. Princess Lieven left a description of the King at this time in her Diary : " George IV had some amiable qualities. Unquestionably he had some wit and great penetration; he quickly summed up persons and things. He was educated and had much tact, easy, animated and varied conversation, not at all pedantic. He adorned the subjects he touched, he knew how to listen, he was very polished. For my part I had never known a person like him, who was also affectionate, sympathetic and gallant. But he was full of vanity and could be flattered at will. Weary of all the joys of life, having only taste, not one true sentiment, he was hardly susceptible to attachment, and never I believe sincerely inspired anyone with it. He was not a bad man, but was capable of bad actions. No one trusted him, none of his ministers had confidence in him nor could they much respect his wishes, for it was easy to make him change them."

It is easy to understand how his astute Ministers handled him, but there are many instances on record of his diplomatic acumen that are at variance with the Duke of Wellington's remark: " He never speaks of business nor even gives a thought to the state of England."

The Duke also said: " He never thinks of anything but building," and it is true that at this time he was never happier than when in conference with his architects, notably John Nash, Sir John Soane and Henry Holland, discussing his grandiose schemes. Work was in progress to finish the Pavilion (one addition was a bath with pipes to the sea); Buckingham House was to be altered at a cost of £719,000; Carlton House was to be demolished, the street widened and a carriage road constructed to Regent's Park; the City was to be replanned; Windsor Castle was to be altered. These schemes and many others were crowded upon his architects and they were given unequalled opportunities to exert their skill, for money was no object. The *Quarterly Review* published a pungent comment:

> " Augustus at Rome was for building renowned,
> And of marble he left what of brick he had found
> But is not our Nash, too, a very great master?
> He finds us all brick and leaves us all plaster."

This was a period of beautiful design and the inferior building construction was perhaps due to the impatience and sense of urgency that pervaded all the projects of George IV, as Regent and King; sadly the crumbling plaster has not withstood the ravages of time, but the buildings that remain are still pleasing in their balconied simplicity, with their Corinthian porticoes and predilection for light.

Windsor Castle was transformed from a dilapidated structure to the fine edifice it is today, and a guide to the castle issued during the reign of Edward VII states: " The restoration of the building in its present form is due to George IV, who employed Sir Jeffrey Wyatville as his architect ". Buckingham Palace is perhaps his greatest monument for it was rebuilt rather than restored. There are many others; the Zoo, Regent's Park, Waterloo Bridge, the stonework at Hyde Park Corner, Regent Street (although unfortunately the beautiful arcades on both sides of the street are no longer there) and it is striking just how much of London bears the stamp of George IV.

His interest was not confined to building however for he was a keen and knowledgable collector of paintings, furniture and silverware. He founded the National Gallery by recommending to his Government that they should buy, as the nucleus of a National Collection, Angerstein's thirty-eight pictures. The price paid was £300,000. He advocated to Benjamin West, the President of the Royal Academy that there should be a gallery and appropriately the colonnades of the demolished Carlton House form the portico of the National Gallery's impressive façade. As a patron of the Arts he encouraged Lawrence, Romney, Hoppner, Reynolds, Gainsborough and other painters, and an admirable musician himself he also was a patron of Beethoven. In literature he particularly admired Jane Austen and kept a set of her books in each royal residence. *Emma* was dedicated to him " by His Royal Highness's dutiful and obedient humble servant the author ".

As a patron of the Arts he was generous, but not always ethical in his methods of obtaining the money to pay for his appreciation of aesthetics. The Duke of Clarence had been left a legacy by his father but George decided that he himself was the heir to the late King's property and so he appropriated the legacy. In a similar manner he acquired from Prince Leopold the silver plate which had been a wedding present, on the grounds that it had been given to Princess Charlotte. This last act was probably motivated by feelings other than acquisitiveness for he disliked the Coburgs intensely and often had disputes with Leopold and the Duchess of Kent, whom he scathingly called " The Swiss Governess." Leopold had infuriated George by visiting Caroline during the Trial but with his customary caution he had delayed his visit until all the evidence had been given against Caroline, so that he could not be accused of " lobbying ", but nevertheless George had been so annoyed that he had vowed never to speak to his son-in-law again. The Duke of York, however, arranged a meeting and the King's curiosity concerning Caroline's reactions to the Trial so overcame his prejudice that he was soon engaged in an animated conversation with Leopold, bombarding him with questions.

Prince Leopold was still living at Claremont and was naturally reluctant to give up the income of £50,000 which he was receiving from the English Government. In addition he also supported his sister the Duchess of Kent in her determination to remain in England to guard the interests of her daughter Victoria.

George IV was fond of children and it is to his credit that he did not extend his dislike of the Coburgs to the little princess. She was taken by her mother to visit him at the Royal Lodge at Windsor and later she recorded what she remembered of the visit: " When we arrived at the Royal Lodge the King took me by the hand, saying: ' Give me your little paw!' He was large and gouty but with a wonderful dignity and charm of manner. He wore the wig which was so much worn in those days. Then he said he would give me something for me to wear, and that was his picture set in diamonds, which was worn by the Princesses as an order to a blue ribbon on the left shoulder. I was very proud of this—and Lady Conyngham pinned it on my shoulder . . . Then we went (I think the next day) to Virginia Water, and met the King in his phaeton in which he was driving with the Duchess of Gloucester—and he said ' Pop her in,' and I was lifted in and placed between him and Aunt Gloucester, who held me round the waist. (Mama was much frightened.) I was greatly pleased, and remember that I looked with great respect at the scarlet liveries . . . We drove round the nicest part of Virginia Water and stopped at the Fishing Temple. Here there was a large barge, and everyone went on board and fished, while a band played in another! There were numbers of great people there . . . I afterwards went with Baroness Lehzen and Lady Maria C. to the Page Whiting's cottage and here I had some fruit and amused myself by cramming one of Whiting's children, a little girl, with peaches. I came after dinner to hear the band play in the Conservatory, which is still standing, and which was lit by coloured lamps—the King, Royal Family, etc., sitting in a corner of the large saloon."

The Duke of Wellington, who was also present on this occasion, said: " In spite of the King's dislike of both her father and her mother, he cannot help being pleased with the little Princess." The King apparently was not as pleased with the Duke as a Cabinet Minister for he complained that he " always acted and spoke as though he were at the head of the army." This was true for since Waterloo he had been the nation's hero and he well-fitted the part. He was good-looking, charming, chival-rous, and a sparkling conversationalist. The fact that he was attractive and attracted to women increased his popularity.

Inevitably he became involved in affairs with his admirers and on one occasion, when he was being blackmailed, he gave the classic answer to blackmailers: "Publish and be damned." His wife adored him as did his mistress Mrs. Arbuthnot, who was always at his side together with her compliant aged husband. They made a happy trio and the Arbuthnots were as interested as the Duke himself in the advancement of his political ambi-tions.

The King had other ideas. He had been prejudiced against Canning at the beginning but now he was ready to admit that by his adroit handling of foreign affairs he had made England the most important political power in Europe. He said of Can-ning, "we fight and sometimes I beat him," but he was proud that in three years Canning had established English influence in the place of the French.

By nature the King loved to dissemble and with a wry sense of humour he enjoyed playing one Minister off against another. Canning and Wellington were often the dupes and after Lord Liverpool collapsed with a stroke, as they were both eager to occupy the vacant Premiership, the King was able to dangle the prize teasingly in front of one and then the other. Their respective supporters who tried to influence the King were also fair game, but his mind was already decided and when Peel spoke too forcibly in favour of Wellington the King revealed his hand by saying: "I did not want Canning upon Castle-reagh's death, but they forced him upon me. Now they want to force Wellington but I will not be bullied." Canning became Premier to the Tory disgust of Peel and Eldon who both resigned.

Canning achieved his ambition with the support of Lady Conyngham whose influence was now at its peak; her brother-in-law was the Governor of Canada and her former tutor had been made a Bishop. Wellington was furious and to show his disagreement with the appointment he resigned from the Army, believing that this step would make the King realize his error. One can therefore imagine his chagrin when by letter he received the jocular reply that "the King assures the Duke of Wellington that he feels the same regret in accepting his resignation which the Duke of Wellington professes to experience in offering it." The King was now treating Wellington with amused tolerance and he left the command of the army open "until his friend Arthur recovered his temper." This time was not far distant for in three months the brilliant Canning was dead, worn out by his own fanatical enthusiasm. His widow received a Peerage.

Canning's illness was the result of a visit to a funeral. The Duke of York had died a few months previously in January 1827, and on the day of the funeral the weather was bleak and cold with a biting wind. The ceremony was a prolonged affair and here Canning caught the chill that made the crack in his already weakened constitution. The King was overcome by the loss of his favourite brother and carousing companion but it was reported that the Duke of Clarence was apparently little affected and that at the funeral he chatted in an unconcerned, irreverent manner to all and sundry. William's unfeeling attitude was not because he did not care for Frederick, for although he never felt towards him as he did towards George, he had been the younger brother " hanger-on " in many of their escapades and the three of them were very close. But his own and his family's prospects had certainly improved, and he was the type of man to whom the lives of his wife and children, revolving round himself, were the only affairs that touched him deeply. He had been the sailor of the Royal Family and Frederick the soldier, but they had both been forced to resign. The Duke of York now stands in stone on his column in Waterloo Place, sharing the lofty eminence with Nelson in nearby Trafalgar Square, an exalted position which his military record does not warrant, and his career in the field ended the medieval custom of placing armies under the strategical command of Princes of the Blood.

Frederick was perhaps the most liked member of the Royal family, except by his creditors, for he left a mountain of debts, including the costs of the rebuilding of York House which was unfinished when he died.*

* York House was built on the site of Godolphin House and the architect was Benjamin Wyatt. It was renamed Stafford House which it remained until 1912; when the lease was bought by the first Viscount Leverhulme and the name was changed to the present Lancaster House.

Canning with an eye on the future had recently increased the salary of the Duke of Clarence by £9,000 a year and from his behaviour at the funeral it appears that William also believed the crown was near.

The Duke of Wellington, who was also looking to the future had expected to be appointed Premier on Canning's death but he was again disappointed for instead the ineffectual Lord Goderick was given the Premiership. " Goody ", as he was nick-named, was weak and inefficient and was ridiculed by his Ministers. On one occasion when he left London for the country an advertisement was published in *The Times* to find him. After a few months of bungling, " Goody " was driven to desperation by his own incompetence and resigned, bursting into tears as he spoke to the King. Wellington's turn had come and the King sent for him saying : " Arthur, the Cabinet is defunct."

There had been some heavy betting in the London clubs as to whether George would survive the Duke of York but apparently Canning had decided that Clarence, despite his asthma and hay fever, would survive them both for as well as the £9,000 increase in salary he also revived the office of Lord High Admiral for his benefit. Nothing could have pleased William more than this reunion with the Navy. Unfortunately he did not appreciate that the post was a decorative and not an active one, for when he became the head of the Navy he sailed away to sea in the yacht *Royal Sovereign,* whilst his Duchess followed his course round the coast on land, being entertained at the great houses at the various ports. With the feel of the deck beneath his feet Clarence was enjoying himself and reluctantly interrupted his voyage to attend Canning's funeral.

The Admiralty however viewed the affair with indignation and the President of the Admiralty Council, Sir George Cockburn, who had not been consulted, objected strongly to the Duke setting out on cruises as and when he wished, without authority. An acrimonious correspondence ensued between Clarence and Sir George Cockburn until the latter, realizing the futility of this method, appealed to the Duke of Wellington in person. The Prime Minister remonstrated with Clarence but without success and the Lord High Admiral continued to sail the seas. In retaliation he asked Wellington to replace Sir George with Rear-

Admiral the Honourable Sir Charles Paget, and as soon as possible.

Wellington decided to report the affair to the King, who wrote to his brother, saying in effect, " I am your brother, your best friend and your King so for my sake stop playing about with the boats!"

My dear William,

My friend the Duke of Wellington, as my first Minister has considered it his duty to lay before me the whole of the correspondence that has taken place with you upon the subject relating to yourself and Sir George Cockburn. It is with feelings of the deepest regret that I observe the embarrassing position in which you have placed yourself. You are in error from the beginning to the end. This is not a matter of opinion but of positive fact; and when the Duke of Wellington so properly call your attention to the words of your patent, let me ask how Sir George Cockburn could have acted otherwise?

You must not forget, my dear William, that Sir George Cockburn is the King's Privy Councillor, and so made by the King to advise the Lord High Admiral. What becomes of Sir George Cockburn's oath, his duty towards me, his sovereign, if he fails to offer such advice as he may think necessary to the Lord High Admiral? Am I, then, to be called upon to dismiss the most useful and perhaps the most important naval officer in my service for conscientiously acting up to the letter and spirit of his oath and duty? The thing is impossible. I love you most truly, as you know, and no one would do more or go further to protect and meet your feelings; but on the present occasion I have no alternative; you must give way, and listen to the affection of your best friend and most attached brother.

G. R.

This letter should have settled the matter but William did not regard it as conclusive and continued to bicker with Sir George. A week later Wellington intervened and after a discussion with William and Sir George the affair appeared to be settled.

Two weeks later he received a message from the Admiralty informing him that William had again sailed from Plymouth with " the squadron of ships and vessels." By now Wellington was becoming as angry as Sir George and he sent William a sharp reprimand. The reply he received angered him even more and he passed the letters to the King.

The King was also becoming irritated with the affair and wrote to Wellington :

August 11, 1828

My dear friend,

I have read with the most careful attention your further correspondence with the Lord High Admiral.

I will repeat to your Grace the words that I used to my brother when I had occasion to write to him on this painful subject, namely, " That he was in error from beginning to end."

I now desire distinctly to state, once for all, that I most entirely approve of all that you, in the exercise of your bounden duty towards me as my first Minister, have communicated to the Lord High Admiral on the subject now before me. When I appointed my brother to the station of Lord High Admiral I had reasonably hoped that I should have derived comfort, peace, and tranquillity from such an appointment; but from what has hitherto taken place, it would seem as if the very reverse were to happen.

Can the Lord High Admiral suppose that the laws are to be infringed, the rules of true discipline (which he knows so well how to uphold) are to be broken in upon? and that these things are to pass without notice or remonstrance by the responsible advisers of the Crown? Can the Lord High Admiral suppose that his best friend and his sovereign is to have no feeling under the circumstances? I am quite aware that I am drawing fast to the close of my life; it may be the will of the Almighty that a month, a week, a day, may call the Lord High Admiral to be my successor. I love my brother William; I have always done so to my heart's core! and I will leave him the example of what the inherent duty of a King of this country really is. The Lord High Admiral shall strictly obey the laws enacted by Parliament, as attached to his present

station, or I desire immediately to receive his resignation.
Such are my commands to your Grace,
Ever your sincere friend,

G.R.

The Prime Minister sent this letter to William and received a
reply the same day:

Bushey House,
August 11, 1828

My dear Duke,

Your Grace's letter of this day, enclosing a letter from His
Majesty, also of this day, accepting in its contents my resignation of the office of Lord High Admiral, together with copies
of your Grace's letters to the King of the 8th and 10th instant
have just reached me.

I have very little, under the present circumstances to observe
to your Grace, except that I trust in God, from the bottom of
my heart, that our justly beloved and gracious sovereign may
be spared to govern us all for many and many a day. However others might feel at the resignation of so high an office,
I can with equal truth and satisfaction declare that I retire
from this situation with the most perfect satisfaction to my
mind, as conceiving that, with the impediments thrown and
intended to have been thrown, in the way of the execution
of my office, I could not have done justice either to the King
or to my country.

I remain, yours sincerely,

William.

William also wrote to the King:

August 11, 1828

Dearest Brother,

I have just received from the Duke of Wellington your most
kind acceptance of my resignation of the office of Lord High
Admiral, for which I thank you from the bottom of my heart.
As the sovereign you could not have done otherwise, because
the King must support his Ministers. I have my story and

facts to relate, whenever you can give me an hour's interview . . .

Dearest Brother,

Yours most affectionately and unalterably,

William.

Even this was not the end of the matter for there were many
further discussions and more correspondence followed, but on
the 29th of August the Duke of Clarence finally left the Admiralty. Now that he realized his departure was inevitable
William left in very good spirits, shaking hands with everyone,
even Sir George Cockburn. As ex-Lord High Admiral he
resumed his quiet life at Bushey with his Duchess, who had not
enjoyed the round of " entertaining " at the Admiralty and the
intrigues of London. Life for them in the country was pleasant
and much healthier.

5

The King's health was deteriorating rapidly and there was
truth in his prophecy that his life was drawing to a close. He
was given to hysterical outbursts and was constantly quoting his
dead father's views, which was regarded by his Ministers as a
portent of approaching madness. He had an abhorrence of
business and the only man who could persuade him to do any
was Sir William Knighton, who had been his doctor and was
now the Keeper of the Privy Purse. Knighton had some undis-
covered hold over the King, for George loathed him and one day
said, " I wish to God somebody would assassinate Knighton."
Yet he was the only person who could handle the King and
even overrule Lady Conyngham's influence. Knighton's word
was law and no one knew why.

In 1829, English policy was mainly occupied with the Dar-
danelles and Dublin; Russia was at war with Turkey and the
armies of the Czar were advancing on Constantinople whilst in
Ireland the people were demanding religious freedom. Wellington's solution was Greek liberation abroad and Roman Catholic
emancipation at home.

The King who had been so much in sympathy with Ireland

now seemed to be haunted by his father's rigid Protestantism and during any discussion on the subject of Catholic emancipation he invariably worked himself up into a paroxysm of rage. The Duke of Cumberland was strongly anti-Papal and the Catholic Problem became a duel between Cumberland and Wellington. They posted to Windsor in turn to press their points of view and Greville wrote that " The Duke of Cumberland has worked him into a state of frenzy and he talks of nothing else in the most violent strain." Wellington often found the King in a blustering temper after his brother's visits and his only course of action was to wait until the royal rage had expended itself. The Prime Minister said after one of these visits : " Nobody knows the difficulties I have in dealing with my royal master . . . I am in a field of battle . . . Between the King and his brother it is next to impossible to govern this country." Whilst George in one of his lucid moments said waggishly : " Arthur is King of England, O'Connell King of Ireland, and myself Canon of Windsor."

At last the King gave in. He was tired to death of the whole affair and Wellington with the support of Peel introduced the Catholic Relief Bill in the House of Lords. The debate stirred up controversy throughout the country and as usual the Royal brothers were divided; Cumberland invoked his " sainted father " but the Whiggish-minded Dukes, Clarence and Sussex completely nullified his speech. There were, of course, many more important speeches and when the Bill was passed it marked the end of George IV's interest in politics and public affairs.

The King had virtually retired and he now showed a renewed interest in horse-racing, although he still remembered the " Escape " affair* and kept his vow, made in 1791, that he would never visit Newmarket Heath again. He spent his time gossiping, idling, admiring his treasures, whilst the dissolute life he had led remorselessly extorted its toll.

In Ireland Roman Catholicism had gained its freedom, whilst in Greece there was civil emancipation and at the end of her war of independence Greece needed a king. There were several

---

* Members of the Jockey Club blamed Chiffney, the Prince's jockey for the in-and-out running of Escape and refused to enter their horses in any race in which Chiffney was engaged. The Prince loyally supported his jockey.

candidates for the honour; France offered a Prince of Saxe, England a Protestant Prince of Hesse or alternatively the Duke of Sussex. But there was another candidate, Prince Leopold, who strongly favoured his chances.

The King's Ministers had avoided telling George IV of Leopold's ambitions and when he found himself the last to know, he was furious that a Prince of his family should have been offered as a candidate without his knowledge; particularly this one whom he hated.

6

Since the death of Princess Charlotte Leopold had remained in residence at Claremont attended by the faithful Stockmar. Here he lived detached from the outside world apart from periodic visits abroad.

During one of these sojourns he met Karoline Bauer, a beautiful twenty-one-year-old cousin of Stockmar. She was the carefully brought-up daughter of an officer in the Grand-ducal army at Potsdam and was one of the select few of chosen actresses permitted to appear in private performances before the King, Frederick William III. Leopold first saw Karoline in a play at the royal private theatre and was immediately enchanted by her beauty. He resolved there and then to possess her. Through his friend and adviser Stockmar he arranged a meeting and immediately made the offer to marry her—morganatically of course.

At this time Leopold was thirty-eight and the years had not dealt kindly with him. He was a bored, listless fellow; his pale handsome face was already lined, for grief had taken its toll, and he wore a black wig to hide his thinning, grey hair. Nevertheless, Karoline, buoyed by her cousin's glowing praise of Leopold, fell in love with him, for he was still able, when he exerted himself, to produce his old charm. They met on many occasions and their intimacy grew.

A few weeks later Leopold returned to Claremont after visiting Italy and as his ardour had not lessened, in May 1829 he sent his valet to Potsdam with a message begging Karoline and her mother to come to England. They were very undecided for Karoline had a brother, Karl, a cavalry officer but also a waster, who relied on a share of his mother's widow's pension to pay his debts, consequently he attempted to dissuade them. The promise of security in England, however, backed by Stockmar's advice, decided mother and daughter to make the journey.

They duly arrived in London and went to the villa in Regent's Park which Leopold had arranged for their accommodation. Unfortunately the ardent lover was not there to receive them. The following morning Karoline waited expectantly for his visit but he did not come and the disappointed girl burst into tears when her cousin arrived instead. His explanation of Leopold's non-oppearance was that he was staying at Marlborough House where political affairs made it difficult for him to get away, but the excuse did little to dispel the disappointment of Karoline.

When Leopold did eventually arrive at seven o'clock in the evening his visit was something of an anti-climax for he had now deserted the role of ardent lover and was once again the bored, listless widower. Again she burst into tears and threatened to return home. Stockmar, however, managed to persuade her to stay, promising better things for the future.

During the next few weeks Leopold made regular visits to this very convenient villa in Regent's Park but marriage was a subject he did not mention. Naturally the wedding was uppermost in the minds of both Karoline and her mother and they asked Stockmar, somewhat agitatedly, to press Leopold into naming the date. His advice was that they should wait a little longer, but at the end of June the matter was brought to a head when a letter was received from King Frederick William III of Prussia, who was fond of Karoline, demanding to know what was happening about her marriage. This was in effect an ultimatum and the unwilling Leopold was forced to make a decision between losing Karoline or marrying her. His reluctance suddenly vanished and once more he became the ardent suitor. They were married a few weeks later at the villa on the 2nd of July. The tension between them also disappeared and they enjoyed the blissful happiness of newly-weds.

Their idyll did not last long for at the end of the month Leopold had to visit Karlsbad and he left Karoline and her mother in Paris on the way. They were lonely and bored and short of money.

In the meanwhile Leopold's enthusiasm had again waned and

when he joined them in Paris he stayed at a different hotel. He appeared to be very busy and spent only an hour a day with the two unhappy women. Karoline remonstrated with him and in desperation asked to be given her freedom. This did not appear to suit his plans and he placated her by promising that when they returned to England he would arrange for a proper home for them, near to Claremont.

In December he returned to England and just after Christmas mother and daughter also returned. The promised " home-like residence " was a sad disappointment; the house was dilapidated and the rooms were dismal and dingy. For the first few days he did not visit them and when he did call he was morose and preoccupied. It was New Year's Day. Even Stockmar offered little consolation, for he also was ill-humoured and excused the Prince's and his own behaviour by saying that momentous things were happening and that they were both very busy.

So the weeks dragged by until early in February a jubilant Stockmar called to tell them that Leopold had been offered the crown of Greece. Hopefully Karoline expected that this would mean a change in her own fortunes and when Leopold himself arrived she cursteyed to the " King of Greece ". He ignored her little pleasantry, however, and her feelings suffered a further rude shock when he reviewed in detail the various European princesses as possible Queens of Greece. The poor girl was dumbfounded but the next day she told her cousin that she was determined to go back to Berlin where she intended to resume her stage career. But Stockmar was also having difficulties with the edgy Leopold, and he realized that Karoline's departure would increase his own discomfiture by making Leopold even more morose. Consequently he exercised all his wiles to persuade her to remain in England, at least until the Greek question was settled one way or the other. So she remained.

The calculating Leopold took a long time to reach a decision for he was reluctant to leave England, where he still had ambitions, and in this connection the King's health was an important factor to be watched closely. From his point of view his caution was justified, for in April the King became ill and in May Leopold, accurately assessing the seriousness of the illness, refused the crown of Greece. He believed that the Whigs who had supported his candidature for the crown of Greece would back him in the event of a Regency in England; and he also realized that George IV was dying.

Karoline and her mother had now moved back to the villa in Regent's Park and one day in June they were astounded to receive a visit from Karl Bauer; he was desperately in need of money. After a dreadful scene, during which he threatened to commit suicide, Karoline promised to give him some help from the small capital invested on her behalf by Leopold. Unfortunately when she asked Stockmar for the money he was furious, believing Karl's visit to be part of a plot to blackmail Leopold. When Leopold also became involved he too lost his temper and so in a screaming tirade of offensive epithets the love affair of Leopold and Karoline Bauer ended.

7

The King's illness had now entered its final stages and Greville described the last few weeks of his life, which the King spent in bed or in his dressing-gown, ringing the bell at all hours of the night and struggling during the day to keep insanity at bay. He had swelled with dropsy and had become a pathetic grotesque figure, hiding himself from sight, whilst a cataract clouded his own view of others. An operation was performed to remove the cataract and Wellington records that he was " always perfectly cool and neither feared operations or their possible consequences."

As he lay in his last bed delusions crowded upon him. He was in command at Waterloo winning glory in battles he never fought and riding winners at Ascot when he was ten stone too heavy; for unlike his father's last lunacies his hallucinations were happy ones. His only unhappiness was when his mind conjured up memories of Leopold and then he became incoherent with rage. Meanwhile the patient Leopold waited.

At three o'clock in the morning of June 26th George IV died. Knighton and Lady Conyngham were with him but round his neck was a miniature of the woman he loved best. Carr, a doctor who was present, was asked afterwards whether the miniature was a portrait of Mrs. Fitzherbert. He replied : " Yes, it is true what you have heard. I remained by the body of the King, when they wrapped it in cerecloth; but before that was done I saw a portrait suspended round his neck—it was attached to a little silver chain."

Lady Conyngham was forced to give up many of the jewels which she had received as presents from George and this must have been a bitter blow for she had well earned them. For ten years she had ruled as a queen, but she had also suffered martyrdom in health and happiness during the latter part of their association and did not deserve the condemnations which were heaped upon her; the last ignominy being a cartoon depicting the Conyngham family wheeling home a barrow filled with Windsor chattels.

"Thus ended the life of George the Fourth, one of the cleverest and most accomplished men in Europe, full of benevolence," wrote Sir William Knighton.

The death of George IV was a turning-point in European history for his passing marked the transition from the old feudal way of life to the new bourgeois democratic way. During his regency and reign England had attained new heights of power and glory, and there was greater national prosperity than ever before. The Georgian era had been a momentous one and the sovereigns do not deserve Byron's bitter dismissal of the parts they played in its achievements :

> " Justice and death have mixed their dust in vain,
> Each royal vampire wakes to life again.
> Ah, what can tombs avail ! since these disgorge
> The blood and dust of both to mould a George !"*

The period covered by their reigns saw the development of the monarchy from autocratic rule to constitutional government. In their days the sovereigns wielded a tremendous influence in deciding the political policy of the country and consequently their personalities, likes and dislikes, were of great importance both at home and in the country's dealings with other nations. They were not shadows, but real men and they were not afraid of power; indeed they were determined to play their allotted parts as Kings of England to the utmost of their ability.

* Windsor Poetics.

The British Parliamentary institutions have been described " as incomparably the greatest gift of the English people to the civilized world ", and from the accession of the House of Hanover began the elimination of the personal king from political life. The Georges were rulers in an epoch of transition and as such were merely men of their times.

Of the Georges, indeed of the Kings of England, George the Fourth as a personality, good or bad, is unique, and the wealth of material in biographies, memoirs, and letters, in assessment of his character as Regent and King is tremendous.

The standard has been set by the Victorian writers, who judged George IV by their own canons of pious hypocrisy, damning him for ever. They allow him very few virtues but all the vices. To judge him without taking into due account the conditions and conduct of his period is to take a phrase out of context.

Of his detractors Thackeray is in the van with his brilliant yet devastatingly malicious satire, written thirty years after the death of the Regent, in which he literally tears his character to shreds. The following is a sample :

" To make a portrait of him at first seemed a matter of small difficulty. There is his coat, his star, his wig, his countenance simpering under it : with a slate and a piece of chalk, I could at this desk perform a recognizable likeness of him. And yet after reading of him in scores of volumes, hunting through old magazines and newspapers, having him here at a ball, there at a public dinner, there at races and so forth, you find you have nothing—nothing but a coat and a wig and a mask smiling below it—nothing but a great simulacrum. His sire and grandsires were men. One knows what they were like : what they would do in given circumstances : that on occasion they fought and demeaned themselves like tough good soldiers. They had friends whom they liked according to their natures; enemies whom they hated fiercely; passions, and actions, and individualities of their own. The sailor King who came after George was a man : the Duke of York was a man, big, burly, loud, jolly, cursing, courageous. But this George, what was he? I look through all his life, and recognize but a bow and a grin. I try and take him to pieces, and find silk stockings, padding, stays, a coat with frogs and a fur collar, a star and blue ribbon, a pocket-handkerchief prodigiously scented, one of Truefitts best nutty brown wigs reeking wth oil, a set of teeth and a huge black stock, underwaistcoats, more underwaistcoats, and then nothing. I know of no sentiment that he ever distinctly uttered. Documents are published under his name but people wrote them—private letters but people spelt them. He put a great George P. or George R. at the bottom of the page and fancied he had written the paper: some bookseller's clerk, some poor author, some *man* did the work; saw to the spelling, cleaned up the slovenly sentences, and gave the lax maudlin slipslop a sort of consistency. He must have had an individuality: the dancing master whom he emulated, nay, surpassed—the wig-maker who curled his toupee for him—the tailor who cut his coats, had that. But, about George, one can get at nothing actual. That outside, I am certain, is pad and tailors work: there may be something behind but what? We cannot get at the character; no doubt never shall. Will men of the future have nothing better to do than to unswathe and interpret that royal old mummy? I own I once used to think it would be good sport to pursue him, fasten on him, and pull him down. But now I am ashamed to mount and lay good dogs on, to summon a full field, and then to hunt the poor game."

It is said that Thackeray gathered his information from the writings of Huish, a contemporary biographer of the Prince Regent, who specialized in the scandals of the period, and as Thackeray wrote his book as material for a lecture tour of America he was obviously writing with this audience in view, as well as the public in England. The contradictions of Thackeray's dissections are many but in an essay Max Beerbohm states: "So far as I know no attempt has been made to judge this [King] fairly. Thackeray judges him as he judged Barnes Newcomb and all the scoundrels he created."

Since then biographers have been more circumspect in their judgment and his virtues and achievements have been allowed to ameliorate the assessments of a character so darkly coloured with vice, indulgence and debauchery. George the Fourth had within him a broad streak of humanity, a virtue rare in an age of brutality. He was intelligent, a dandy, an aesthete and a supreme egoist. His faults were the product of his period and his own self-indulgence. Money was the keynote of existence in the Georgian epoch and he was the greatest squanderer of them all. After his death £10,000 in notes and coins was found in the pockets of his many suits. There were occasions when from the window of his coach he gave away gold coins, yet we read: " He had one peculiarity as regards money—that he was most liberal with it *as long as he did not see it*; but when he had a fifty-pound note in his pocket it was a bitter pang to him to spend five pounds of it. If he had paid the bill every Saturday night, those Carlton House banquets, which saddened the heart of Romilly as he sat and thought of the haggard and iron-bound fact of distress from Land's End to John O'Groats would very soon have been discontinued."*

His character was a compound of contradiction, a strange mixture of conceit, consideration, astuteness, naïveté, generosity, and cupidity so that his biographers have been confused in judging his many facets by their own standards. George himself was a discerning judge of character, quick to recognize ability in his friends and Ministers, although his sense of humour sometimes ran away with him for he teased them unmercifully and mimicked them in their absence. He was an actor with a sense of the ridiculous in private and a sense of dignity in public. He died without fear and without regret, saying rather pathetically when he was nearing his end: " I am very nervous, but very brave." During his reign much had been achieved and he took the first step towards constitutionalizing the monarchy. There have been many worse kings than George the Fourth—the self-styled " First Gentleman of Europe ".

* The Druid: The Post and the Paddock.

CHAPTER NINE

WILLIAM THE FOURTH

I

THE NEW King was at Bushey when the news of his accession was brought to him. It was six o'clock in the morning and even at that early hour he was already pottering about in the gardens, dressed " in his old green coat and white beaver hat ". Sir Henry Halford, George's physician, was the first with the news, followed soon afterwards by the Duke of Wellington and attendant Ministers with the official announcement.

William received the Duke quite calmly and solemnly, but after the necessary commiserations and platitudinous remarks he was unable to conceal his delight and he began to bounce and jog with excitement as the realization of his new position dawned on him. He had always been fond of his brother George but to use one of his favourite expressions, " this was quite a different thing." After years of unimportance he had suddenly become the most important man in the kingdom.

Speaking of the new sovereign Greville recorded the situation succinctly :

" His life has been passed hitherto in obscurity and neglect, in miserable poverty, surrounded by a numerous progeny of bastards, without consideration or friends and he was ridiculous from his grotesque ways and little meddling curiosity. Nobody ever invited him into their house, or thought it necessary to honour him with any mark of attention or respect; and so he went on for above forty years till Canning brought him into notice by making him Lord High Admiral at the time of his grand ministerial schism. In that post he distinguished himself by making absurd speeches, by a morbid official activity, and by a general wildness which was thought to indicate incipient insanity, till shortly after Canning's death, and the Duke's accession, as is well known, the latter dismissed him."

It was therefore with some trepidation that the Duke of of Wellington viewed his own future for he well remembered William's disappointment at the time of the commotion. But the hearty, friendly manner in which William greeted him set his mind at rest, and he realized thankfully that there was no vindictiveness in William's nature.

The new King went from one to the other, peering into their faces in his short-sighted manner, nodding his head and shaking hands vigorously.

After a few rounds of handshaking the new King hurried away half-trotting in his jogging way to tell his Queen the good news.

Adelaide burst into tears despite her husband's obvious delight, for apart from the expected feminine reaction she viewed the situation more dispassionately. During William's short term of office as Lord High Admiral she had experienced the " high life " in London and she saw in this new move the end of the happy domestic life which she so much preferred. In addition she must have had a few qualms about her husband's ability to handle the new situation.

She need not have worried, for William sailed into kingship like a frigate into battle, which pleased his Prime Minister immensely and Wellington said : " I have done more business with him in ten minutes than with the other in as many days."

Enthusiasm radiated from the new King and he was eager to be co-operative, but there were times when his exuberance, boisterousness, swearing and unpredictability spread alarm amongst his tenterhooked Ministers. He needed very careful handling. Characteristically, as he was about to sign the declaration he paused to make a sententious speech about his dead brother. He appeared to be moved and his voice was suitably mournful; then suddenly in an irascible tone he said : " This is a damned bad pen you've given me."

Now that the inheritance was his, William was somewhat awed by his new possessions. Almost immediately he inspected the Pavilion at Brighton and the still unfinished Buckingham Palace; then the Royal Lodge at Windsor. He had simple tastes and the gorgeous extravagance of everything he saw offended his spartan spirit; Buckingham Palace he hated; the Pavilion was embarrassing in its magnificence: therefore Windsor it must be, and the domestically-minded pair chose it as their permanent home. George's large retinue of French chefs and servants was dismissed and replaced by a lesser number of plain English ones: for William was determined that simple fare should be the rule.

The same attitude of mind also governed his general conduct and he strolled about among his people like a private person. He was quite willing to talk to anyone and in London he was always followed by a noisy, staring mob. On several occasions gentlemen had to force a way through the crowd for him so that he could get back to St. James's and once as he walked along St. James's Street a woman rushed up to him and kissed him on the cheek.

William enjoyed this rubbing of shoulders with his people, but wisely the Queen persuaded him to discontinue the habit of taking strolls, or at least to do it only in the early morning when the streets were deserted.

Similarly at Windsor he ordered the grounds to be thrown open to the public, but the people used to crowd even up to the windows and keepers had to be detailed to confine them to certain paths.

Reluctantly the good-natured William accepted a curtailment of his free and easy habits to please his wife. But he was determined to have a crowd around him and every day he invited a large number of guests to dinner. Usually there were too many for comfort and always they were an ill-assorted batch. As he was an early riser William liked to go to bed early whenever he felt tired. The vigilant Greville notes that William used to say: " Now, ladies and gentlemen, I wish you a good night. I will not detain you any longer from your amusements and shall go to my own, which is to go to bed, so come along, my Queen."

The King took his responsibilities very seriously, and after a few weeks we no longer invited guests to dinner. Instead he sat down every evening before a mass of papers requiring his signature. George IV during the last few months of his life had neglected his signatory duties, with the result that the new King was faced with an arrears of some 48,000 documents to be signed. William was determined to bring affairs up to date and although he was suffering from rheumatism in the hands he signed doggedly on with a bowl of warm water by his side into which he used to dip his fingers to relieve the cramp.

His duties often caused him to become agitated and over-excited and his Queen, who was always by his side, was the only person able to soothe his jangled nerves at these times. Indeed these bouts of wild agitation, when he used to prattle on in a preposterous manner, gave rise to behind-the-hand forecasts that he would end his days in a strait-jacket like his father. Perhaps if he had not had the counterbalancing influence of domesticity that might well have been his fate.

Queen Adelaide's primary concern was her husband's health and well-being, and once the initial burst of hospitality had died down she took control of the royal household arrangements so efficiently that in a short time they were operating as smoothly as they had done at Bushey.

At Windsor she installed a model dairy, built better cottages for the people employed on the estate and took a keen interest in everything that was happening there. Her kindly attitude and personal interest in the general welfare of the workers at Windsor made her very popular.

She was a woman with strong family ties and usually had some members of her family staying in the house. Children gave her great pleasure and she loved to be surrounded by them, in fact two or three of her sister Ida's six children were always living at Windsor. In 1831 the Duchess Ida brought all her children to England and they stayed for some months, whilst another nephew, Edward of Saxe-Weimar, visited the Queen so often that he came to be regarded almost as a son.

The Queen's affections also embraced her husband's children and grandchildren, in fact two of the King's daughters lived at the castle, whilst others of his numerous progeny often paid her long visits. The King's brother the Duke of Cambridge, who was the Viceroy of Hanover, sent his son to be educated in England and the boy also lived under the watchful eye of the Queen. Even the son of the hated Duke of Cumberland, Prince George,

who later became the blind King of Hanover, was often brought
to Windsor by his mother. Children bring out the best in human
nature and they one and all gravitated to the kindness and
tolerance of Queen Adelaide. One marked absentee from Windsor was the most important of them all, the heiress to the throne,
Princess Victoria; but this was not the fault of the Queen, but of
Victoria's mother.

The Duchess of Kent and William IV had never liked each
other and now that he was the King their dislike turned to
hatred. She regarded William with his illegitimate children, his
coarse language, sudden ejaculations, repetitive expressions and
habit of wiping his nose with the back of his forefinger* as a
disreputable old man who obviously failed to realize, or at least
to recognize, her importance as the mother of the heiress-presumptive to the throne. For his part William considered her to
be a meddlesome, tactless and waspish woman. They were both
right and it was inevitable that they should clash.

Queen Adelaide, when Duchess of Clarence, had been on
intimate terms with the Duchess of Kent and she now tried hard
to maintain the peace, but she was unsuccessful. Whenever the
King was forced by circumstances to meet the Duchess he found
it impossible even to be polite to her. Adelaide was informal by
nature, as was the King. Quite casually she once mentioned an
incident which illustrates her tolerant attitude; Lady Howe, the
Lord Chamberlain's wife, was travelling in a carriage with their
Majesties when her leg became cramped. " She suddenly popped
her foot on the King's knee, and next thrust it out of the window. She was very eccentric," recounted the Queen complacently. To admonish Lady Howe for this unseemly behaviour was
not in the Queen's nature. She merely laughed at the rudeness.

In contrast, the Duchess of Kent, with the crown in sight for
her daughter, became rigidly formal by design. She disliked the
rowdy Fitzclarences and their presence at Court made her determined not to allow her precious Victoria to mix with them.
Significantly she said that she did not wish her daughter to come
into contact with the company at Windsor because Victoria
might hear references to bastards which would encourage her to
ask awkward questions. On one occasion when she did unbend

* Hence the nautical term " snotty " for midshipman.

enough to visit Windsor she objected strongly to one of the King's illegitimate sons sitting at the breakfast table when Victoria was also present. Victoria was being brought up in a strict and pious fashion which was very different from the free-and-easy unbringing of the unruly Fitzclarences.

Since her husband's death in 1820 the Duchess of Kent had received no royal support whatsoever, either to pay her husband's debts or for the education of her child. George IV had shown his intense dislike of the Coburgs by practically ignoring her although he had never extended his dislike to the young Victoria. William had similar feelings, but as Princess Victoria became heiress-presumptive after the death of his second child in 1821, he agreed to the Duchess of Kent's being granted an allowance of £10,000 a year for the maintenance of the Princess.

The Duchess had an income of £6,000 a year of her own and from the early days of her widowhood her brother Leopold had allowed her an additional £3,000 a year. Otherwise it is almost certain she would have returned to her native Amorbach. As it was even with the additional income she had found it necessary to keep a watchful eye on expenditure. But any sacrifice was worthwhile to become the mother of a queen and at this time it was often remarked that the little Princess bore a remarkable resemblance to her grandfather George III.

2

In later life Queen Victoria described her childhood as "melancholy" and it was certainly strict and secluded. Her mother, obsessed with the self-imposed responsibility of preparing her daughter for queenhood smothered the child with attention. Every minute of her daughter's day was planned and the Duchess was always at her side, even during her lessons. Until she became Queen, Victoria never went upstairs or downstairs without someone holding her hand and at night vigilance was still maintained for her little white bed was in her mother's room.

Idolized by her nurses and spoilt by her teachers the plump, plain, waddling child began to realize her own importance and showed her feelings by flying into a tantrum whenever her wishes were thwarted.

But when she was five years old a stronger influence than her mother's, in the person of Louise Lehzen, began to take a hand in her upbringing. Fräulein Lehzen was the daughter of a Hanoverian clergyman and had first come to England from Amorbach as the governess to Princess Feodora, the Duchess of Kent's other daughter. Now she became the governess to Princess Victoria, or "Drina", as she was called in the family circle.

At first Fräulein Lehzen had been exasperated by her charge's outbursts of temper, but she soon realized that behind the waywardness there was a character of truthfulness and honesty that could be appealed to but could not be driven. She resolved to win the child's confidence and to her great satisfaction the plan worked; the obstinate little Princess became tractable, even eager to learn her lessons for she adored her dear, dear Lehzen.

Naturally German was Victoria's first language* and she next learnt English and French until she became virtually tri-lingual. She never completely mastered the English grammar, however, and her German accent was always quite marked. When she was eleven her mother arranged for her to be examined by the Bishops of London and Lincoln and the Archbishop of Canterbury, and her knowledge of Scripture, English history, Geography, Latin, Arithmetic, Drawing and Music was tested. The curriculum of education planned by the Duchess was found to be perfectly satisfactory and Princess Victoria was considered to be making excellent progress under the admirable supervision of Baroness Lehzen (George IV had elevated her to this Hanoverian rank in 1827).

For years the widowed Duchess had relied on the advice of her brother Leopold and the visits to Claremont had always delighted the young Princess, for in Victoria's heart her Uncle Leopold had taken the place of the father she had never known. But latterly these visits had become all too few, for Leopold was often travelling in Europe in the pursuit of his ambitions (this was the time of his affair with Karoline Bauer) and his advice had to be sought by letter. In consequence the Duchess turned more and more for advice to her Comptroller Sir John Conroy, who had been her husband's friend, and Baroness Lehzen.

* Since the arrival of George I in England, German was the language of the Royal Family.

Jealousy made enemies of these two confidants and their feud was to estrange mother and daughter.

Victoria was somewhat afraid of her mother, who was relentless in her dedication and was apt to resort to such methods as putting holly in the neck of her daughter's dress to make her keep her head up. The first place in Victoria's affections was given to her dear Lehzen. In turn, when Leopold left England to become the first King of the Belgians in July 1831 the Duchess had become even more attached to her major-domo Sir John Conroy and displayed her feelings to such an extent that Victoria noticed the familiarities, as did others, for the rumours of scandal began to circulate. Madame de Späth, one of the Princess's preceptors and the friend of Baroness Lehzen, allowed her indignation to overcome her prudence and unwisely remonstrated with the Duchess. She was instantly dismissed.

The Baroness who felt quite as strongly was, however, irreproachable in her behaviour and gave no hint of her disapproval. No doubt she similarly counselled Victoria, for she too said nothing, although she had been fond of Madame de Späth. But far more important than expressing her feelings was the awful prospect of losing her beloved Lehzen. But the criticism although unspoken could not be hidden and the Duchess bitterly resented the alienation of her child's affections. Her annoyance was apparent and her intimates played up to her bitterness by criticizing Baroness Lehzen whose stiff unbending manner, German middle-class habits, and inordinate liking for caraway seeds made her an easy target for caustic wit. The most bitter tongue was that of Lady Flora Hastings, a maid-of-honour to the Duchess, and the Baroness regarded her with malevolence from behind an unperturbed stare.

When Victoria was thirteen she began her journal and on every page there is proof of the great affection she felt for her dearest Lehzen. She was always a dutiful daughter, meticulously correct in her conduct towards her mother, but there is no doubt that the Baroness had won her heart as well as her mind. In her day-to-day comments she revealed her innermost thoughts, her sincerity and her pious resolutions. After her confirmation she wrote: " I felt that my confirmation was one of the most solemn and important acts in my life; and that I trusted in God

Almighty to strengthen my heart and mind; and to forsake all that is bad and follow all that is virtuous and right. I went with the firm determination to become a true Christian, to try and comfort my dear Mamma in all her griefs, trials, and anxieties, and to become a dutiful and affectionate daughter to her. Also to be obedient to dear Lehzen, who has done so much for me." Thus she set the pattern of her life.

3

The unhappy situation at the Duchess of Kent's lowly court was overshadowed by a much more important quarrel—the feud between the Duchess and William IV.

Queen Adelaide tried hard to maintain friendly relations but her letters to Princess Victoria reveal the growing estrangement. The King is mentioned frequently in the earlier letters as enquiring after the well-being of the Duchess, but gradually the references become less frequent, until they are omitted entirely and he merely addresses himself to Victoria. Throughout the correspondence the Queen revealed herself as a simple, ingenuous character, devoid of bitterness or rancour.

Soon after William's accession the Duchess of Kent began to show her antipathy and the Coronation on the 8th of September 1831, gave her the opportunity of demonstrating her antagonism, for pointedly neither the Duchess nor her daughter attended the ceremony. As it happened the Coronation was the most economical on record, for the unassuming William considered the affair a waste of money, and it was sneeringly dubbed the "Half-crown-ation". Nevertheless the slight administered by the Duchess did not go unnoticed. The King realized that the main reason for the Duchess's attitude was her dislike of the Fitz-clarences, which was hardly likely to improve his opinion of his sister-in-law. The rudeness with which the Duchess of Kent often treated the Queen annoyed him to such an extent that he was unable to conceal his disgust whenever they met.

Several times the sweet-tempered Adelaide tried to smooth the unhappy situation by notifying the Duchess that she would like to visit her niece at Kensington. On each occasion the Duchess made an excuse to avoid the meeting. That these rejections obviously hurt the feelings of the Queen added further bitterness to the King's attitude. Princess Victoria was only permitted by her mother to visit the King and Queen formally at their Birthday Drawing-Rooms and as these visits always entailed the presence of the Duchess the King did not enjoy even these rare occasions.

A change in the political situation caused the Duchess with " her talent for giving offence "' to become even more obnoxious, until the mere mention of her name made the King bluster and fume.

The prodigious extravagance of George IV had forced upon his successor strict economy. In Parliament there was a strong feeling against making a grant for the Queen's outfit and Adelaide provided everything from her own purse. The King gallantly stepped forward to say that he would bear the cost, and *pay by instalments*.

Queen Charlotte had been granted £54,000 for her outfit and naturally Adelaide had expected a similar amount. However she obviously did not reveal her true feelings, for the King's private secretary, Sir Herbert Taylor, recorded that : " No one could possibly express herself with greater good sense and good humour than the Queen on the subject of the outfit." The Cabinet were apparently shamed into action, for the House of Commons in arranging the Queen's dower settlement voted her an income of £100,000 and the properties of Marlborough House and Bushey. Magnanimously, the King, who confidently said the Queen's feelings were the same as his own, rejected the clause giving the Queen power to sell the palaces if she became a widow.

This was an opportune time to practise economy for the country was in the throes of unrest and political discontent.

4

Reform had been in the air for many years and now hard times, starvation and class injustices brought England to the verge of revolution. Riots and rick-burning were increasing and misery was forcing the oppressed working classes to take desperate measures to air their many grievances.

With the growth of industry the population had been reshuffled as new working areas developed. Iron and coal had both been known and used, but they had never been used together. The iron industry had traditionally been confined mainly to Surrey and Sussex, but the use of coal instead of wood in the smelting process moved the industry to the coal areas, the North and the Midlands. Watt's steam engine which had been first used in the cotton industry was now being adapted to other processes and Stephenson's first locomotive was in fact built to transport coal from the pit to the industrial centres.

Into the new areas came swarms of impoverished rural workers seeking a living wage; but as the supply always exceeded the demand, long hours and wretched working conditions resulted. To house the workers new towns sprang up, with narrow, mean streets of ugly " jerry-built " houses, box-like and insanitary.

The workers were slaves not citizens, for they had no say in the government of the country or in the control of their new local areas. Their lack of representation is illustrated for example by comparisons between areas such as Cornwall which had forty-four members and Scotland which had only forty-five; whereas Bolton, Bradford, Birmingham, Halifax, Leeds, Manchester and Sheffield were unrepresented. But it was the economic distress of the times, the starvation and misery, that were causing the unrest rather than the fact that political power was vested in a handful of great landowners controlling the majority of the seats. The Treasury controlled a hundred and sixty seats; whilst a hundred and fifty peers were responsible for the return of two hundred and fifty members to the House of Commons.

Mass meetings were being held in the towns; rural labourers were marching about the country, demanding a " living wage of half-a-crown a day "; and the effects were being felt in London where Peel's new police-force, formed in 1829, and alluded to as " Peel's Bloody Gang ", " Peelers ", and " Blue Devils " were keeping the agitators in check. Common hard times united the people and although there were differences of opinion as to the remedy for the national ailment they all agreed that the Government was to blame and Parliamentary reform was the first dose of medicine necessary to commence the cure.

The news in July of the second French Revolution had given

a great fillip to the cause of Reform. The revolution had centred round the Duke of Orleans, who became King Louis-Philippe and Lafayette, and achieved its object without bloodshed. The Reformers in England saw a parallel with their own case and realized that the overthrow of a Government need not be attended by the terrible scenes of the French Revolution of 1792.

The following month the lesson was driven home again by the news of a revolution in Belgium. Belgium had been united with Holland by the Treaties of Vienna, but the King of the House of Orange drove the Belgians to break away from their neighbours, following the example set in Paris by revolution. Prince Leopold of Coburg had received an invitation to be the new Belgian King.

Wellington was against the Belgian Revolution and had no intention of standing behind Belgium in her defiance of the Eastern powers of Europe, who were debating whether to challenge Belgium's right to independence in violation of the Treaty of Vienna. Only a change of British Government could save Belgium.

In England a General Election was pending, for as the law decreed at that time the death of George IV in June must be followed by an Election within six months. The news from the Continent certainly affected the result, for the Tory Administration was returned with only a slender majority, but the main reason for the diminished support of Wellington's Government was his declaration in the House of Lords that he was against any reform of Parliamentary representation.

The newly-elected Parliament met in November and in the King's speech there was no mention of reform; instead he spoke against the Belgian Revolution and ignored the vital issue at home. The Duke had forced his personal opinions upon the nation and the challenge was taken up. On a movement concerning the Civil List the Government was defeated and Wellington resigned. The King, who had always felt himself a Whig at heart, took pleasure in ignoring the aristocratic families who had ruled England for a century and a half by calling upon Earl Grey—" Lord Grey of the Reform Bill "—to form a Whig Cabinet. The day of Reform was dawning.

The Reform Bill, " the Bill to give everybody everything " as it was optimistically described, was introduced by Lord John Russell on the 1st of March 1831. It was hotly debated and passed its second reading by a single vote, amidst scenes in the House of Commons exceeding even the wild uproar at the trial of Queen Caroline in the Upper House. In Committee, however, the Bill was defeated and Parliament was dissolved on the 21st of April.

In June the second Reform Bill was introduced. On the 21st of September it passed the third reading only to be rejected by the House of Lords in October. Parliament then recessed and the momentous issue was in abeyance.

During this period of suspense riots broke out in Bristol, Derby and Nottingham and they were the most violent seen in many years.

At the third reading in December it was passed without a division. Grey now asked the King to create a number of new peerages to force the Bill through the House of Lords, but William refused. Grey had no option but to resign and Wellington was recalled. He was unable to form a Ministry and the King was forced to recall Grey and to agree to create the peers his Prime Minister needed.* The Bill was passed on the 4th of June 1832 and became law as the Reform Act on the 7th of June. The Reformers had won and the Middle Class had received recognition, for it effected a re-distribution of seats in accordance with the changed density of population. The House of Commons had asserted itself and for the first time in English history it no longer came under the autocratic domination of the House of Lords. The Reform Bill had formed the greatest political crisis since the Magna Carta and William IV, the politically obtuse, blunt and inexperienced, had weathered the storm well owing to his determination to act constitutionally.

The Act which had caused such a tremendous furore was generally regarded as a disappointment for it did not bring the spectacular results that had been expected. Power had not been transferred to the people but only to a section of about half of

---

* No peers were in fact created, as the Duke of Wellington and his friends abstained from voting. The device was first resorted to in the reign of Queen Anne when twelve new peers were created and on taking their seats were greeted by a sarcastic peer with: "Do you vote individually or through your foreman?"

the middle-class and it still excluded the working-man. But it was the first step in the cause of democracy, to be followed by others as a result, and five hundred thousand voters had been added to the lists.

The passing of the Bill had made the King popular, for the newspapers had reported that he was in favour of the Bill whereas he had been more concerned with letting his Ministers get on with the settlement of the worrying business rather than with active participation. The Queen was now unpopular for it was known that her Chamberlain, Lord Howe, was an opponent of any measures of reform. There had been agitation for William to dismiss Lord Howe but as he had for years been friendly with the Howe family, and knew Queen Adelaide was particularly attached to her Chamberlain, upon whom she relied for advice on points of etiquette, he staunchly refused to displace him. During the political crisis there had been a particularly violent campaign in the Press against the alleged interference of the Queen and her carriage had been attacked. No doubt Adelaide felt this was the beginning of a revolution and saw herself in the role of Marie Antoinette, but in view of her strong allegiance to her husband it is doubtful whether she ever attempted to alter the course of events. His health was always her first concern and it was obvious that the troubles of the Reform Bill had placed a heavy strain on his constitution for it was said that in one year he had aged ten. Kingship was not proving so pleasurable an experience as William had anticipated it would be. At dinner one evening shaking his head regretfully he said he wished he had been born a free and independent American, so much did he admire the country which was the birthplace of George Washington, the greatest man that ever lived. The sweet taste of sovereignty had indeed become bitter to induce such an abrupt about-turn of William's views. Now he was happier when he was away from the cares of State, at Brighton or at Windsor, but particularly at Brighton where the sea revived so many pleasant memories for the sailor-king.

His Queen, the gentle Adelaide, preferred Windsor and said she found it hard to leave Windsor for Brighton: " I had to leave so much I love behind me, the beautiful country, my bright cheerful rooms full of the busts and pictures I especially value, and above all the graves so sacred to me (of her baby and Princess Louise). To be near them does me good . . . to one who has lost so much even the remains which we only preserve in our memory are a precious possession which we would willingly forego."

In 1834, Adelaide's health gave William cause for concern for she had a persistent cough. He decided a holiday in her native country would be beneficial and knowing her reluctance to leave him he made all the arrangements without her knowledge. He arranged every detail even to the presents for her relatives, before he told her of his intentions.

Adelaide was shocked at the prospect of going away for six weeks, particularly as there were indications that he was heading for one of his bouts of excitability, during which she alone was able to soothe him. He was unusually talkative and seemed obsessed with a mania for military matters, visiting barracks and upsetting the routine with ridiculous orders that were giving concern to the Duke of Wellington. Before she would consent to go therefore she was determined to wait until his wild mood had passed.

In July he seemed quite settled and she left in the Royal Yacht with her brother, who had come from Meiningen, escorted by the entire fleet of the Yacht Club. But even now she sailed away with reluctance and she confided to one of her Ladies-in-Waiting that she was " more attached to the King than she was perhaps aware, more necessary to him than she had thought, and, in a word, that England was now her only true country."

In turn the King missed her grievously. Bachelor entertainments did not interest him. He was like a lost soul and plaintively said to Princess Lieven : " I could never explain to you, madame, the innumerable ways in which the Queen is of use to me."

When the Queen returned to London on the 20th of August the King was beside himself with delight and she was given a State welcome; cannons were fired and flags and bunting were displayed on the route to the Palace. Adelaide was in very good spirits and her health had undoubtedly improved. Her popularity seemed to have returned but the Ministerial changes the King made shortly afterwards revived the accusations against the Queen of meddling in State affairs.

5

The Reform Act that was the cause of the Queen's unpopularity also wrought a change in the public feelings towards the Duchess of Kent and her plump little daughter Victoria. They became popular and were no longer the representatives of a small opposition clique, but the symbols of the middle-classes and the new liberalism.*

The Duchess of Kent's liberalism was in fact superficial. She was surrounded by her husband's friends, mainly Whig leaders, and she was able to quote her husband's views and expressions, which gave the impression of a greater knowledge and enthusiasm than she actually possessed. Exclusively her thoughts and ambitions were devoted to the furtherance of her daughter's destiny as the Queen of England. Nothing else mattered.

The country realized that the little Princess alone stood between William IV and the awful prospect of the sinister, menacing spectre of Ernest, Duke of Cumberland, as the next sovereign. In everyone's imagination he figured as a frightful satyr whose ascendancy would bring about a national calamity. Shrouded as he was in evil and unspeakable rumours, the Duchess of Kent even feared for the safety of her child. The Radical newspapers fostered rumours of his evil machinations and Princess Victoria was guarded and watched by her nervous mother as though danger was imminent at all times.

Sir John Conroy who already saw himself as Prime Minister urged the Duchess to bring her charge from the seclusion of Kensington so that all the country could see her. With his help a succession of tours were arranged to show Victoria the extent of her kingdom, and the Duchess began to act as though her daughter was already the Queen and as though the King did not exist.

The journeys were so organized that they appeared to be a Royal Tour, with official receptions, speeches prepared by Conroy, and enthusiastic crowds everywhere. The Duchess with the cheers of the crowd ringing in her ears was already revelling in

---

* The Whigs began calling themselves " Liberals " and the Tories adopted the name " Conservatives," in 1828.

the role of Queen Mother and she dwarfed her plain and chubby daughter.

Naturally the newspapers pounced on the tours with glee and gave the events full prominence, with the result that every morning when the King opened his newspapers he was faced with the triumphs of the Duchess. He became almost apoplectic with rage.

But worse was to come, for one day he was told that the Duchess had given orders, whilst sailing in the Solent, that her yacht should be given royal salutes from warships and naval forts.

William always felt most strongly about anything connected with the Navy and this last act was something he just could not tolerate.

The Prime Minister and the First Lord of the Admiralty conferred agitatedly and a letter was immediately sent to the Duchess begging her to discontinue the practice. The Duchess bluntly refused to do anything of the kind and the King, now almost out of control, was forced to issue an Order in Council forbidding the firing of royal salutes to any ship except those having on board the King or his Queen.

To the long list of insults yet another incident was added on the occasion of Princess Victoria's fifteenth birthday. Queen Adelaide arranged a small birthday party but the Duchess of Kent, using as an excuse the death of a baby of the Belgian royal family, caused the celebration to be cancelled. Always she found an excuse to prevent Victoria meeting the King and Queen informally, and the various pretexts she used were calculatingly never quite plausible enough to veil her hostility. Once again the King was furious and the Queen was hurt.

The Duchess of Kent and her aggravations were becoming an obsession with William and he bitterly resented the fact that the Duchess would become the Regent if he died before Victoria attained her majority on her eighteenth birthday. He said with feeling : " I trust in God that my life may be spared nine months longer after which period, in the event of my death, no regency would take place."

The King would have liked his wife to have taken charge of the little Princess and to become Regent in the event of his death, but he knew it was a forlorn hope and there would be no point in even attempting to enforce this step, although he often threatened it.

William hated all the Coburgs and was fully aware of the voluminous correspondence between Victoria and her Uncle Leopold, in which the King of the Belgians guided the conduct of his niece and prepared her for her future *rôle* as Queen of England. Undoubtedly Leopold exerted a tremendous influence over the young Princess in her formative years and she turned to him, as a daughter to a father, for counsel. His letters to Victoria are preserved in their entirety and reveal how he instructed and advised her even to the minutest detail in foreign politics, constitutional procedure, the duties of sovereignty, family affairs; and to her he was a veritable fount of wisdom. The many hundreds of Victoria's letters to her uncle show that she wrote unreservedly about her innermost thoughts and impressions, and reveal her acute interest in everything that was happening at home and on the Continent. Consequently, when the King learnt that Leopold was putting into operation his plan for a Coburg marriage he was ready to take countering action.

In order to introduce Victoria to the Coburg princes two sets had already been sent to England by Leopold. When Victoria was fourteen the first pair of youths, the Princes Alexander and Ernst, sons of Leopold's sister the Duchess of Würtemberg, had arrived; to be followed two years later by the two sons of Leopold's other brother Ferdinand, the Princes Ferdinand and Augustus. Now in 1836, when Victoria was seventeen, the sons of the eldest brother, the reigning Duke of Saxe-Coburg, appeared on the scene. They were the Princes Ernest and Albert.

Ostensibly they came to visit their aunt, the Duchess of Kent, but the old Dowager Duchess of Saxe-Coburg who died in November 1831, had long cherished the dream of her grandson Albert marrying " the Mayflower ", her grand-daughter Victoria. She wrote many letters to her daughter the Duchess of Kent on this theme and in 1821 referring to her eldest son's children she said : " Leopold is very kind to the little boys. Bold Alberinchen drags him constantly about by the hand. The little fellow is the pendant to the pretty cousin." Her favourite son Leopold had taken up the plan from where his mother left off.

But William had other ideas and whilst Leopold and Stockmar were arranging the visit with the Duchess of Kent he was arranging the visit of the Prince of Orange and his two sons to Windsor. One of the sons, Alexander, was William's protégé and to give him a clear field William threatened to forbid the visit of the Coburg princes. The King is reputed to have said " that no other marriage would ever take place and that the Duke of Saxe-Coburg and his sons should never put foot in the country : they should not be allowed to land, and must go back whence they came," but his bark was always worse than his bite and Ernest and Albert duly arrived in England with their father the Duke of Saxe-Coburg. So did the Prince of Orange with his two sons.

The Prince of Orange himself had no love for Leopold for he had been a candidate for the hand of Princess Charlotte and used to say of him : " *Voilà un homme qui a pris ma femme et mon royaume.*" Perhaps he would have better luck with Alexander, he thought.

William's action in attempting to frustrate his plans was infuriating to Leopold and to assist his own cause he wrote an indignant, yet cunning, letter to his niece :

" I am really *astonished* at the conduct of your old Uncle the King; this invitation of the Prince of Orange and his sons, thus forcing him upon others, is very extraordinary. It is so, because persons in political stations and champions of great political passions cannot put aside their known character as you would lay your hat upon a table.

" Not later than yesterday I got a half-official communication from England, insinuating that it would be *highly* desirable that the visit of *your* relatives *should not take place this year*—qu'en dites-vous? The relations of the Queen and the King, therefore, to God-knows-what degree, are to come in shoals and rule the land, when *your relations* are to be *forbidden* the country, and that when, as you know, the whole of your relations have ever been very dutiful and kind to the King. Really and truly I never saw or heard anything like it, and I hope it will a *little rouse your spirit;* now that slavery is even abolished in the British

Colonies, I do not comprehend *why your lot alone should be to be kept, a white little slavey in England,* for the pleasure of the Court, who never bought you, as I am not aware of their having gone to any expense on that head, or the King's even having spent a sixpence for your existence."

The King, however, was determined to introduce a competitive spirit into the situation and arranged for Victoria to meet the four young men together at a function at St. James's Palace. He also threw in the young Duke William of Brunswick as an additional choice.

After a few days the Coburg princes returned home and Albert did not appear to have been particularly impressed with Victoria. He wrote to her that she was "very amiable and astonishingly self-possessed" (hardly the language of a suitor) and he added that the journey had given him "such a disgust for the sea."

On the other hand Uncle Leopold's approval of Albert was sufficient to convince Victoria of the young man's desirablility. She wrote to her uncle shortly after their arrival: "Albert is extremely handsome, which Ernest certainly is not, but he has a most good-natured, honest and intelligent countenance."

After the princes had returned to Coburg she wrote again: "I must thank you, my beloved Uncle, for the prospect of *great* happiness you have contributed to give me, in the person of dear Albert. Allow me then, my dearest Uncle, to tell you how delighted I am with him, and how much I like him in every way. He possesses every quality that could be desired to render me perfectly happy. He is so sensible, so kind, and so good, and so amiable too. He has besides, the most pleasing and delightful exterior and appearance you can possibly see. I have only now to beg you, my dearest Uncle, to take care of the health of one, now *so dear* to me, and to take him under *your special protection.*"

For years, already, Leopold had kept a watchful eye on Prince Albert and his brother, but particularly Albert, for Ernest's future was already settled as the next Duke of Saxe-Coburg, and for the next year the two princes lived in Brussels where Leopold could supervise their education before they entered the University at Bonn. He could also make sure that Albert did not

upset the family plans by forming an attachment for someone
else.

The Coburg scheme was all-important and had achieved great
success since the days when Napoleon had over-run the petty and
insignificant Duchy, and Ernst and Leopold had gone " cap-in-
hand " to Paris. Their power was spreading and they were infil-
trating into most of the powerful Courts of Europe. The old
Dowager Duchess of Saxe-Coburg had seen great achievements
by her children; her daughter Juliane had married the Grand-
Duke Constantine of Russia; Leopold had become the first King
of the Belgians four months before she died; Victoria had become
the mother of the heiress to the throne of England; Antoinette
married the Duke of Würtemberg, the brother to the Empress
Mother of Russia, and Ferdinand married the wealthy Hungarian
heiress the Princess of Kohary. If the Dowager Duchess could
have seen into the future she would have been gratified by even
greater developments; Leopold was to marry the daughter of
King Louis Philippe; the son of Ferdinand was to marry the
Queen of Portugal and father two kings, and her grand-daughter
was to become the most powerful Queen in the world with a
Coburg grandson as her Prince Consort—indeed an astounding
record of success for a relatively unimportant family—a record
in which calculating Leopold was destined to play a major part.

6

Shortly after the return of the Coburg princes King Leopold
himself paid a visit to his sister and her daughter in England and
now when Victoria was older she was even more impressed with
her uncle's character and ability: " To hear dear Uncle speak
on any subject," she recorded in her diary, " is like reading a
highly instructive book; his conversation is so enlightened, so
clear. He is universally admitted to be one of the first politicians
now extant. He speaks so mildly, yet firmly and impartially,
about politics. Uncle tells me that Belgium is quite a pattern for
its organization, its industry, and prosperity; the finances are in
the greatest perfection. Uncle is so beloved and revered by his
Belgian subjects, that it must be a great compensation for all his
extreme trouble."

William IV did not share his niece's high opinion of her Belgian uncle. He bitterly resented the fact that Leopold was busy tutoring Victoria for sovereignty and that they spent many hours together anticipating his early demise; an unsettling thought. He was forced to meet Leopold and found it difficult to hide his irritation. One day at dinner he watched Leopold, who did not take wine, drinking water. William suddenly burst out irritably with: " Dammit, sir! Why don't you drink wine? No one is allowed to drink water at my table!"

The King's intense dislike of Leopold was an offshoot of the bitter hatred he felt for the Duchess of Kent and it was obvious that this last outburst was a sign that the long-brewing storm was now overhead. Suddenly in August 1836 it broke.

The King invited the Duchess and Victoria to stay at Windsor for eleven or twelve days, which would include both the King's and the Queen's birthdays. The Duchess, however, annoyed William by declining to come before the 20th.

When mother and daughter arrived the King greeted Victoria affably enough, but suddenly turned upon the Duchess and stormily rebuked her in public for appropriating, against his orders, a suite of seventeen rooms at Kensington Palace. This was a bad enough start but worse was to come.

The next day was one of those hot days in August when tempers fray easily. It was the day of the birthday banquet and a hundred guests were present. At the end of the dinner the King rose to reply to the toast of his health and shocked everyone by launching into a tirade against the Duchess who was sitting next to him. Glowering down at her he said she was " a person surrounded by evil advisers and incompetent to act with propriety." Then continuing the attack he said: " I have no hesitation in saying that I have been grossly and continually insulted—by that person, but I am determined to endure no longer a course of behaviour so disrespectful to me. Amongst many other things I have particularly to complain of the manner in which that young lady (here he indicated the Princess Victoria who was sitting opposite) has been kept away from my Court; she has been repeatedly kept from my drawing-rooms, at which she ought always to have been present; but I am fully resolved that this shall not happen again. I would have her know that I am King, and I am determined to make my authority respected, and for the future I shall insist and command that the Princess do upon all occasions appear at my Court, as it is her duty to do."

The guests sat still with horror as the flood of vituperation burst forth and he said he hoped to God that he might be spared a few months longer so that the calamity of a regency might be avoided and the Crown would pass into the hands of the heiress-presumptive, instead of into the hands of the person now near him upon whom no reliance whatever could be placed.

Victoria burst into tears and the Duchess was white-faced and silent, her eyes glittering with hatred. Queen Adelaide flushed with embarrassment—Greville said : " The Queen looked in deep distress," and everyone was aghast.

The damage was irreparable and the break was final.

7

A few days before Victoria's eighteenth birthday on the 24th of May 1837 William was taken ill and it seemed as though his prayers were to go unanswered. He recovered, however, and a crisis was avoided.

The King did not feel well enough to attend the State ball he gave at St. James's Palace and Adelaide would not attend without him. He presented his niece with a grand piano but his real present followed a few days later. It was a letter in which he offered the Princess £10,000 a year to be at her disposal, independently of her mother.

The Lord Chamberlain, Lord Conyngham, was instructed to deliver the letter personally into the hands of Princess Victoria. At Kensington when he held out the letter to Victoria her mother reached out to take it. Lord Conyngham apologized and explained that he had explicit instructions to hand the letter to Princess Victoria personally. Without even looking at her mother the Princess then took the letter. Her mother was humiliated but could do nothing about it; except to complain that it was too much money to be in the control of a young girl and that she herself should be responsible for it.

Victoria acted resolutely and ignoring her mother's opinion

she wrote to her uncle accepting his kind offer. The arrangement however was never put into effect.

The King appeared to have recovered but the news of his illness had reached the ears of King Leopold and he sent several advisory letters to his niece. The attainment of his ambition was approaching and he was already choosing the members of her establishment.

Soon the Princess was being bombarded with letters from her uncle and they all contained words of advice. With daily regularity ideas, opinions and recommendations for this or that appointment flowed from his pen into the receptive mind of the young Princess :

" Two things seem necessary; not to be fettered by any establishment other than what *will be comfortable to you,* and then to avoid any breach with your mother."

" My idea, if it meets with your approbation, would be this : the Duchess of Northumberland would remain your first lady, Baroness Lehzen would fill a similar position to Mrs. Campbell and the Dean* would step into the position Dr. Short held . . . Resist mildly but *positively* any nomination of a Gentleman other than the Dean."

" They seem to think the King dying, which does not appear to be the case. Be steady my good child, and *not* put out by *anything;* as long as I live *you will not want a faithful friend and supporter."*

" The great thing would be to make no change, to keep Ministers and everything as it is, and to gain time; in this way *no one is hurt and no amour propre blessé.* For this reason I lean to your keeping Sir Herbert Taylor† for your official secretary, though I am not quite *decided* on the subject . . . Now I conclude and send this letter through Stockmar. My best regards to Lehzen."

* Dean of Chester, Princess Victoria's instructor.
† Private Secretary to the King.

" For the present the best plan is to continue to act as you have done hitherto; to avoid quarrels, but also to stick *firmly to your resolutions when once taken* . . . I mean to wait some more detailed accounts of what is going on in England before I give my opinion on what ought to be done in the case that the King's disease should take a more fatal turn."

" My winding up is, to keep your mind *cool and easy*, be *not alarmed* at the prospect of becoming perhaps sooner than you expected Queen; aid will not be wanting, and the great thing is that you should have some honest people about you who have your welfare *really at heart*. Stockmar will be in this respect all we can wish . . . *Speak sometimes with him;* it is necessary to accustom you to the thing."

" As I told you before, however, when we treated this subject verbally and in writing, I believe it to be your interest to act very mildly, *to begin by taking everything as the King leaves it.* By this system you avoid disappointing those whose hopes may remain unchanged, as your own choices, as it were are not yet made."

" In every letter I shall write to you I mean to repeat to you, *as a fundamental rule, to be courageous, firm and honest as you have been till now* . . . Should anything happen to the King before I can enter more fully into the necessary details, limit yourself to *taking kindly* and in a *friendly* manner the present administration into your service. *They are naturally friendly to your interests, as you are in fact the only possible Sovereign of the whole family,* with the exception of the Duke of Sussex, they can *serve* with *sincerity* and *attachment."*

" I shall today enter on the subject of what is to be done when the King ceases to live. The moment you get official communication of it, you will entrust Lord Melbourne with the office of retaining the present Administration as your Ministers . . . I have taken into consideration the advantage or disadvantage of my coming over to you *immediately.* I thing it is better to visit you later. If, however, you wanted me to come at any time, I should come in a moment. People might fancy I came to enslave you, while I glory in the contrary; and thirdly, that they might be jealous, or *affect* it at least, of my coming, as if I thought of ruling the realm *for purposes of my own* . . ."

This last letter was dated the 17th of June, 1837, and at this time King William was a dying man. He was too weak to walk but he attended to his duties from a wheel-chair, struggling to sign state papers with his crippled fingers. Although he was suffering great pain he complained very little. His Queen was stricken with grief for she knew his obituary notices were being prepared and she never left his side by day or night.

On the 19th of June, Princess Victoria wrote to her uncle: "Your *kind* and *dear* letter containing *most wholesome, prudent, sound and excellent advice,* was given to me by our *good* and *invaluable honest* friend, Stockmar, and I beg you to accept my thanks for it. Before I say anything else, let me tell you how happy and thankful I am to have Stockmar here: he has *been,* and *is,* of the *greatest possible* use, and be assured, dearest Uncle, that he possesses my most *entire confidence*!

"The King's state, I may fairly say, is *hopeless;* he may *perhaps* linger a few days, but he cannot recover *ultimately.* Yesterday, the physicians declared he could not live till the morning, but today he is a little better; the great fear is his *excessive* weakness and no *pulse* at all. Poor old man! I feel sorry for him; he was always personally kind to me, and I should be ungrateful and devoid of feeling if I did not remember this . . . "

Greville said that " in the disputes which took place between him and her mother, her secret sympathies were with the King; and in that celebrated scene at Windsor, when the King made so fierce an attack upon the Duchess's advisers, and expressed his earnest hope that he might live to see the majority of his niece, Victoria must have inwardly rejoiced at the expression of sentiments so accordant with her own."

8

The King was ending his reign to a chorus of laments. The blustering, simple, good-hearted William, cheerful to the last, was leaving the world more loved than any of his Hanoverian predecessors.

The 18th of June saw the sailor-king about to set sail on his last voyage. It was the anniversary of Waterloo and William remembered the date. " See if you cannot tinker me up to last over it," he said to his doctor.

The King did survive the day but he did not see the next one dawn. To the end his beloved Queen held his crippled hand and he tried to stem her tears with his usual jocular remarks. Theirs had been a happy marriage. He died at twelve minutes past two in the morning of the 20th of June 1837.

He had once said : " When I was a young man, as well as I can remember, I believed in nothing but pleasure and folly— nothing at all. But when I went to sea, got into a gale, and saw the wonders of the mighty deep, then I believed; and I have been a sincere Christian ever since." The last words of the Sailor King were : " The Church, the Church."

The Times was not eulogistic in its obituary notice of the King. " The events of his life afford no fit material for the biographer; they partake so much of the commonplace of history. The simplicity of William the Fourth's career before his accession to the Crown corresponds with that of his original mind and disposition. There was no involution or complexity in either. He met with no adventures on a wide scale; he displayed no gross, nor great, nor memorable attributes. There was little guile in his nature nor obliquity in his course."

William was a plain-speaker and once when a deputation of influential Freemasons waited on him expecting a ceremonious audience—he was a member of the Craft himself—they were astonished when the bluff King greeted them with : " Gentlemen, if my love for you equalled my ignorance of everything concerning you, it would be boundless !"*

Charles Greville, that caustic critic, summed up the King's defects and virtues surprisingly fairly :

" King William IV, if he had been born in a private station, would have passed through life like millions of other men, looked upon as possessing a good-natured and affectionate disposition, but without either elevation of mind or brightness of intellect . . .

* The Pocket History of Freemasonry (Pick and Knight).

King William was sometimes weak, sometimes obstinate, and miserably deficient in penetration and judgement, he was manly, sincere, honest, and straightforward. The most remarkable foible of the late King was his passion for speechifying. He has considerable facility in expressing himself, but what he said was generally useless or improper. He never received the homage of a Bishop without giving him a lecture; and the custom he introduced of giving toasts and making speeches at all his dinners was more suitable to a tavern than to a palace. He was totally deficient in dignity or refinement, and neither his elevation to the throne nor his association with people of the most distinguished manners could give him any tincture of one or the other. Though a good-natured and amiable man, he was passionate and hasty, and thus he was led into those bickerings and quarrels with the Duchess of Kent."

Lord Melbourne apparently had not varied his opinion for he said sincerely: "I am deprived of a most gracious master and the world of a man—I would say one of the best of men—a monarch of the strictest integrity that it has ever pleased Divine Providence to place over these Realms."

The King's funeral was on July 9th and from Greville's eye-witness account not many tears were shed despite the popularity of the King:

"Yesterday I went to the late King's funeral, who was buried with just the same ceremonial as his predecessor this time seven years. It is a wretched mockery after all, and if I were king, the first thing I would do should be to provide for being committed to the earth with more decency and less pomp. A host of persons of all ranks and stations were congregated, who loitered through the lofty halls, chattering and laughing, and with nothing of woe about them but the garb. I saw two men in an animated conversation, and one laughing heartily at the very foot of the coffin as it was lying in state. The chamber of death in which the body lay, all hung with black and adorned with scutcheons and every sort of funeral finery, was like a scene in a play, and as we passed through it and looked at the scaffolding and rough work behind, it was just like going behind the scenes at a theatre. A soldier's funeral, which I met in the morning—the plain coffin slowly borne along by his comrades, with the cap and helmet and sword of the dead placed upon it—was more impressive, more decent, more affecting than all this pomp with pasteboard crowns, and heralds scampering about, while idleness and indifference were gazing or gossiping round about the royal remains. The procession moving slowly through close ranks of Horse and Foot Guards holding tapers and torches in their hands, while at intervals the bands played a dead march, had, however, a very imposing affect. The service was intolerably long and tedious, and miserably read by the Dean of Windsor. The Queen Dowager with the King's daughters and her ladies were in the Royal Closet, and the FitzClarences in the one adjoining. At twelve o'clock she was to depart for Bushey, and a bitter moment it must have been when she quitted for ever the Castle where she had spent seven years of prosperous and happy splendour."

Queen Adelaide lost her main reason for living when William died. She broke down in a paroxysm of grief and became seriously ill for some time afterwards. She never really recovered from the blow and shut herself away from her friends and acquaintances. Even by the following Autumn her grief had not abated, and she devoted herself to her sister and her nephews. She was "for ever talking of the King and hoping she had thoroughly done her duty."

Adelaide had always been devoted to Princess Victoria and the new Queen asked her to choose from the furniture at Windsor whatever she would like to take with her. She lived the rest of her life in peaceful obscurity mainly at Hastings until she died at Bentley Priory, Middlesex, on the 2nd of December 1849. " I die in all humility, knowing well that we are all alike before the Throne of God," she wrote in her will.

" Poor dear Queen Adelaide" said a critic of the times " she never did anything that History is aware of save hold her tongue and help the poor."

9

The reign of William IV had seen the Whigs at their peak, the establishment of Parliamentary and Municipal Reform, the new Poor Law, and the Abolition of Slavery. Latterly the King had quarrelled with his Whig Ministers and the Tories began to regain lost ground. Lord Melbourne had succeeded Lord Grey as the leader of the Whigs but the Whigs still failed to recapture their former ascendancy.

William had commenced his reign with a leaning to Parliamentary Reform and he enjoyed the resultant personal popularity, but the unbridled nature of the national enthusiasm had made him fear that there would be a revolution and his own enthusiasm waned.

The Princess, however, had from a very early age been inculcated with Whig principles and she was suspicious of the Tory Politicians. It was obvious therefore that the Whigs were about to enjoy a resurgence of power.

Victoria understood to some extent the middle-class point of view although she still believed in the subordination of the classes. But as the young Disraeli said : "There were two nations in England between whom a gulf was fixed." In Manchester 50,000 were workless and there were similar numbers unemployed in the big towns of the Midlands. Britain was about to enter the terrible period of the "hungry forties" when low wages chased high prices; tea was 8/- a pound and bread was 1/2d. a loaf, whereas skilled workers were receiving less than fourpence an hour and labourers only ten shillings a week. It is estimated that one fifth of the population were paupers and in Leeds, for example, twenty-thousand workers earned less than one shilling a week.

Education for the masses was considered unnecessary and in 1837 £20,000 was all the Government voted towards the education of children throughout the entire country. A cynic observed that an item of £50,000 was voted for the rebuilding of the royal stables.

The Reform Act had not improved the dreadful economic conditions of the working-class, but now at least the middle-classes had a say in the government of the country. A new era was beginning and in the public mind the young Victoria was associated with the new set of ideas.

CHAPTER TEN

QUEEN VICTORIA

I

THE ARCHBISHOP of Canterbury and the Lord Chamberlain were in attendance at the bedside of William IV when he died. Immediately it was all over they left in a carriage post-haste for Kensington to break the news to the new Queen. They arrived at 5 a.m. but had difficulty in gaining admittance as the porter at first refused to disturb the household.

Eventually Baroness Lehzen was sent for and after some discussion she brought the Duchess of Kent. At six o'clock the Duchess wakened her daughter, trying hard to conceal her jubilation.

Princess Victoria came into the room with a shawl thrown over her dressing-gown. Lord Conyngham dropped on one knee and kissed the hand she held out to him immediately she heard the words, "Your Majesty". He then officially announced the death of the King and saluted the new Sovereign. Victoria first asked for news of her aunt and the Archbishop described the harrowing death-bed scene and Queen Adelaide's grief.

In her journal that day Victoria described the visit of the messengers and wrote: "I then went to my room and dressed. Since it has pleased Providence to place me in this station, I shall do my utmost to fulfil my duty towards my country; I am very young and perhaps in many, though not in all things, inexperienced, but I am sure that very few have more real goodwill and more real desire to do what is fit and right than I have.

"Breakfasted during which time good, faithful Stockmar came

and talked to me. Wrote a letter to dear Uncle Leopold and a few words to dear good Feodore. Received a letter from Lord Melbourne in which he said he would wait upon me at a little before 9. At 9 came Lord Melbourne, whom I saw in my room, and *of course quite alone,* as I shall *always* do all my Ministers . . . "

The doubts that the Prime Minister, Lord Melbourne, must have had about his future position were happily dispelled when the Queen said : " It has long been my intention to retain your Lordship and the rest of your present Ministry at the head of affairs." Thus she followed the advice so strongly advocated by her Uncle Leopold and no doubt repeated by the faithful Stockmar at breakfast.

The Prime Minister did not stay long, for the Privy Council was to meet at Kensington at eleven o'clock, and Victoria had begun her reign in a bustle of excitement and hurry.

At half past eleven the Queen entered the council-room. The assembled Dukes, Ministers, Bishops and others stared with excitement as their new Queen came into the room alone. Victoria was less than five feet tall and had lost some of her plumpness and they saw a plain, fair-haired, gently-rounded girl, in deep mourning (she was already wearing mourning for Queen Adelaide's mother Louise, Duchess of Saxe-Meiningen who had died on April 30) with a round clear-complexioned face, prominent blue eyes, a sharp, curved nose, above a small mouth which when she smiled revealed her gums and tiny teeth. In all she was not beautiful, not even pretty, yet she gave the impression of pleasing youthful dignity, calm and composed; a singular combination of innocence, gravity and confidence.

In a high, clear, careful voice she read the speech which had been prepared for her days before by Lord Melbourne. Then with the same confident dignity she rose from her chair and as the doors closed behind the small figure the stern, calculating councillors truly felt they had been in the presence of a Queen. Croker, a Tory Privy Councillor wrote : " I cannot describe to you with what a mixture of self-possession and feminine delicacy she read the paper. Her voice, which is naturally beautiful, was clear and untroubled, and her eye was bright and calm, neither bold nor downcast, but firm and soft." A few hours afterwards the great Duke himself said: " She not merely filled her chair, she filled the room."

When Queen Victoria left the council room she spoke to her mother: " Mamma, am I really and truly Queen?"

" Yes, my dear, that it is so," replied the Duchess.

" Then dear Mamma, I hope you will grant me the first request I make to you, as Queen. Let me be by myself for an hour."

When she returned from her solitude she gave the order that her bed was to be moved from her mother's room.

Within the next three weeks the entire royal household was moved from Kensington to Buckingham Palace and the Duchess of Kent was allotted a suite of apartments far away from the Queen's. Instead, Baroness Lehzen was given the bedroom adjoining the Queen's. Stockmar was also brought into the palace and given the adjoining rooms on the other side.

The new era had indeed begun. It meant the eclipse of the Duchess, who had struggled so determinedly and foolishly to establish her daughter on the Throne. Now she was relegated to the position of a subject and had to request the formal privilege of obtaining audience with the Queen. With the Duchess also fell her major-domo Sir John Conroy. He was dismissed from the royal service, although he still held office in the Duchess's household. To soften the blow of exile the Queen gave him a baronetcy and a pension of £3,000 a year. Baroness Lehzen had won. In her journal that day Victoria wrote: " My *dear* Lehzen will *always* remain with me as my friend, but will take no situation about me, and I think she is right."

King Leopold also believed that his hour had struck and almost immediately after the accession he wrote to his niece outlining four important rules:

" 1. I should advise you to say as often as possible that you are *born* in England. George III *gloried* in this, and as none of your cousins are born in England, it is your interest *de faire reporter cela fortement*.

" 2. You never can say too much in praise of your country and its inhabitants. Two nations in Europe are really almost ridiculous in their own exaggerated praises of themselves; these are the English and the French. Your being very national is highly important, and as you happen to be born in England and never to have left it a moment, it would be odd enough if people tried to make out the contrary.

" 3. The Established Church I also recommend strongly; you cannot, without *pledging* yourself to anything *particular, say too much on the subject.*

" 4. Before you decide on anything important I should be glad if you would consult me; this would also have the advantage of giving you time. In politics most measures will come in time within a certain number of days; to retrace or back out of a measure is on the contrary extremely *difficult,* and almost always *injurious* to the highest authority."

The young Queen was well supplied with advice and guidance by her three German counsellors. Baroness Lehzen and Baron Stockmar were always close at hand with their wisdom and diplomacy, whilst almost every day a letter arrived from her Uncle Leopold. The advice, and the manner in which it was presented by Lehzen and Stockmar could not be faulted, but at times the independent spirit of Victoria often made her wonder whether she was not being too well supplied by the constant stream of correspondence from her uncle.

Baroness Lehzen always insisted that she served the Queen in a purely personal capacity and never discussed public affairs or matters of state with the Queen. This may be so, if it is possible for a sovereign to separate completely the private and the official sides of life, but with Leopold and Stockmar it was quite different. They were intriguers of the first order.

King Leopold was ambitious for power, but far more did he crave the trappings and prestige of sovereignty. Stockmar was also ambitious for power, but for power in itself, like a miser for gold. He enjoyed the wielding, the string-pulling, the obscurity, the satisfaction of manipulating from an unseen position, and he was not motivated by personal gain. In every way they were perfectly complementary to each other.

Stockmar's skill had planned every step of Leopold's rise to eminence. From the tragic days of Princess Charlotte he had always been in the shadow of his master and it was his advice that had caused Leopold to refuse the crown of Greece and achieve the kingship of Belgium; and his diplomacy that had softened the refusal of Greece and negotiated the guarantee of Belgian neutrality by the great powers of Europe.

Leopold was a shrewd and clever man who from an early age in a chequered career had shown great diplomatic skill; but in Stockmar he had an aide whose cleverness even exceeded his own. It was as the emissary of Leopold that Stockmar had parted from his wife and children to come to England, for his was a relentless ambition that sacrificed anything for the satisfaction of achievement. He was a sick man, tormented by acute dyspepsia, with a look of pain behind his eyes, yet his speech was always calm and unhurried and his advice always astute and objective. He was a man of great caution and Leopold's letters from Brussels reveal the lack of Stockmar's influence. Or perhaps even Stockmar underestimated the determination and independent spirit behind the prominent blue eyes of Victoria, and failed to warn his master? But in any event another influence had entered the life of the young Queen in the person of the elegant, man-of-the-world, Lord Melbourne, the Prime Minister of England for the past three years.

2

Lord Melbourne was fifty-eight and Queen Victoria was eighteen. But despite the disparity in their ages they were enchanted with each other; or at least he set out to enchant and succeeded. In a strangely detached way they were in love; she felt the wide-eyed attraction of adolescence to experience, whilst he was enchanted by the inexperienced innocence of youth. Years and position prevented the bridging of the gap but in each other they found the happiness of association.

William Lamb, Lord Melbourne to be, was born on the 15th of March 1779, and only succeeded to the title in 1829. His father Sir Peniston had been a Gentleman-of-the-Bedchamber to George IV and as a reward received his viscounty. Sir Peniston was very wealthy and made a fruitful marriage with Elizabeth, the beautiful daughter of Sir Ralph Millbanke of Halnaby, Yorkshire.

They lived at Melbourne House, Piccadilly (now Albany) and it became a favourite meeting place of the Whigs, for Lady

Elizabeth was a fascinating and charming hostess. Here the Regent, Fox, Sheridan and the Regent's other witty, drunken, debauched intimates disported themselves, and with this background the path for William Lamb was an easy one. He had been to Eton and Cambridge and was called to the Bar in 1804, but when his elder brother died in 1805 he decided the legal profession was a boring occupation, particularly as at the time it interfered with his love affair with Lady Caroline Ponsonby, the only daughter of the Whig Earl of Bessborough. They were married in June 1805, and at the time it was considered to be a great match.

William's private income was only £2,000 a year, so his mother used her influence with Fox to get him into Parliament and he took his seat in January 1806. The young couple were living in an apartment at Melbourne House and they entered wholeheartedly into Whig society at its gayest. Their future happiness seemed assured but instead years of torment were ahead.

Lady Caroline was an incorrigible, roguish creature, attractive, tantalizing, irresponsible, and completely wayward. Her vivacity and immorality ruled her life, and her unfaithfulness, tempers, extravagances, and wild escapades caused her husband untold anguish and anxiety.

In the general election of 1812 William Lamb lost his seat as a result of his support of Catholic Emancipation and he returned to private life—a retirement that was to last four years. The year 1812 was an unhappy one for William Lamb. His wife Lady Caroline had met the handsome, insolent, brilliant Byron and they were in the midst of a frenzied love affair. For six months London society was titillated by the wild escapades of Caroline as she tried to stir in Byron a passionate hysteria to match her own. But Byron had had enough and there was a wild, emotional parting, followed by Caroline's attempted suicide.

For the husband who still loved his she-devil of a wife, with her beauty and her madness, it was a period of torment, stormy quarrels and make-believe reconciliations, whilst the rest of London looked on with cynical amusement. At last the storm in Caroline's mind appeared to be blowing itself out but Byron's death in 1824 revived her madness and she sought solace in laudanum and brandy. Four years later she died aged forty-two;

ironically leaving behind as a reminder of the unhappy marriage its only surviving child, a mentally-deficient son, who was a constant trial and a heart-breaking disappointment to his father. William Lamb returned to the House in 1816 as Member for Northampton, but the Byron scandal, which was exploited by his opponent, cost him his seat in the 1825 election. But two years later he was back again, this time under the wing of Canning, the Prime Minister.

Quietly and unobtrusively he climbed in the Whig Party esteem to become Home Secretary, and when Lord Grey retired from the premiership he slid gently into the vacant chair.

He wore his success lightly, but his nonchalant, carefree attitude to life and his whimsical smile hid a clever and cultured mind. Greville summed up the general opinion : " Everybody wonders how Melbourne will do it. He is certainly a queer fellow to be Prime Minister . . . I should not be surprised if Melbourne was to arouse his dormant energies and be excited by the greatness of his position to display the vigour and decision in which he is not deficient. Unfortunately his reputation is not particularly good; he is considered lax in morals, indifferent in religion, and very loose and pliant in politics."

Melbourne was now moving in the fashionable world of Politics, Clubland and Society with whimsical enjoyment. Handsome, elegant, wealthy and a brilliant talker, the dilettante politician was welcomed everywhere; particularly by women. This charm which he exercised on women landed him in trouble on several occasions. He had twice been a co-respondent in actions (now called divorce suits) and fortunately on each occasion first with Lady Brandon and then with Mrs. Norton the wife of the Hon. George Norton, he was on the winning side.

The opinion of his lackadaisical attitude to politics was due to his pose of unruffled indifference such as his habit of falling asleep in the Cabinet, or his idly occupying himself with blowing a feather whilst the delegates of the Society for the Abolition of Capital Punishment were heatedly pressing their point of view. Little did they know that the cynical poseur had already examined in detail during the previous night the pros and cons of their case and had reached a decision before they met. Nor did they realize that his closed eyes veiled a calculating activity or that his implacability had never prevented his condoning violent measures.

By birth an aristocrat and by belief a Conservative Melbourne, a Regency character, had risen to power through the party of reform although he himself disliked the Reform Bill. But he was an opportunist and the end always justified the means. One can therefore appreciate the unrest felt by this cynical man-of-the-world when he made his first obeisance to the new Queen, herself a daughter of Whiggism.

Calculatingly, from their first meeting he behaved impeccably, combining the precise air of deference with worldly courtesy; adding the assurance of a statesman to the benign solicitude of a father; the father Victoria had never known.

Adjusting himself to the situation, this association with a youthful yet powerful presence had for him all the elements of an autumn romance. The cynic who had revelled in the ribaldries of the Regency now exerted his fading charms on the young girl opening her eyes to a new and splendid world and her youthfulness was an elixir and a challenge to his charm. Relieved of the burden of his son, who had died in the previous year, he now devoted himself to the wide-eyed Victoria.

Greville was there to note the situation and records : " She is upon terms of the greatest cordiality with Lord Melbourne, and very naturally. Everything is new and delightful to her. She is surrounded with the most exciting and interesting enjoyments; her occupations, her pleasures, her business, her Court, all present an unceasing round of gratifications. With all her prudence and discretion she has great animal spirits and enters into the magnificent novelties of her position with the zest and curiosity of a child.

" No man is more formed to ingratiate himself with her than Melbourne. He treats her with unbounded consideration and respect, he consults her tastes and her wishes, and he puts her at her ease with his frank and natural manners, whilst he amuses her by the quaint, epigrammatic turn of his mind, and his varied knowledge upon all subjects."

No longer was the elegant figure of Melbourne seen sprawling in the Clubs of St. James's, nor was his droll wit now heard in the drawing-rooms; instead his evenings were spent sitting bolt upright, in the company of the Queen, discoursing politely on this and that, and deferentially explaining the intricacies of affairs of State.

For her part, Victoria was fascinated by the polished, mellifluous spell-binder. She hung on his every word, her blue eyes widening in expectation and occasionally " she laughed in real earnest, opening her mouth as wide as it can go, showing not very pretty gums." Everything was delightful, giving her " *the greatest pleasure* ", and she wrote to Leopold saying how happy she was with her Prime Minister : " Before I go further let me pause to tell you how fortunate I am to have at the head of the Government a man like Lord Melbourne. I have seen him every day with the exception of Friday, and the more I see him the more confidence I have in him; he is not only a clever statesman and an honest man, but a good and kind-hearted man, whose aim is to do his duty for his country and not for a *party*. He is the greatest use to me both politically and privately."

In her journal she wrote : " I really have immensely to do. I receive so many communications from my Ministers, but I like it very much." A few days later she wrote : " I repeat what I said before that I have *so many* communications from the Ministers, and from me to them, and I get so many papers to sign every day, that I have always *a very great deal* to do. I *delight* in this work."

Every day was a day of adventure, with riding in the afternoon after the pleasure of the morning's duties, then dinner and perhaps dancing, or the opera or the play; and always close at hand the reassuring, solicitous Lord Melbourne. Victoria revelled in the *rôle* she was playing and she loved her leading man the Prime Minister. The correspondence with her Uncle continued although he appears to have regarded the glowing references to Melbourne with some asperity because he began to stress the importance of having Stockmar " *constantly near* you . . . and to be useful to you he should be near you."

Soon he was able to examine the situation at first hand for Victoria invited her Aunt Louise and Uncle Leopold to pay a visit to England. In the middle of August they arrived and stayed with the Queen at Windsor. Lord Melbourne was also there and Victoria wrote in her journal : " The sound observations they make and the impartial advice they give me would make a most interesting book."

Apparently Leopold was reassured and more so when he received a short letter from his niece on his return to Brussels.

My dearest, most beloved Uncle,

One line to express to you, *imperfectly,* my thanks for all your *very* great kindness to me, and my *great, great* grief at your departure! God knows *how sad, how forlorn,* I feel. How I shall miss you, my dearest, dear Uncle! *every, every, where.* How I shall miss your conversation! How I shall miss your *protection* out riding! Oh! I feel *very, very* sad, and cannot speak of you both without crying!

Farewell, my beloved Uncle and *father*! May Heaven bless and protect you; and do not forget your most affectionate, devoted, and attached Niece and *Child*.

Victoria R.

He felt the time was opportune to make use of the family position for his own diplomatic purposes. His letters now began to deal at length with the foreign political situation and the personal content became less. Cautiously he increased the pressure. In his dealings with France and Holland it was greatly to his advantage to have the backing of England, and he began to urge Victoria, gently at first but with increasing force, to exert her influence to this end: "All I want from your kind Majesty is, that you will *occasionally* express to your Ministers and particularly to good Lord Melbourne, that, as far as it is *compatible* with the interests of *your own* dominions, you do *not* wish that your Government should take the lead in such measures as might in a short time bring on the *destruction* of this country, as well as that of your uncle and his family . . ."

There was a delay of eight days before Victoria replied to this letter and she was as affectionate as ever: "It would, indeed, my dearest Uncle, be *very wrong* of you, if you thought my feelings of warm and devoted attachment to you, and of great affection for you, could be changed. *Nothing* can ever change them!" The rest of the lengthy letter dealt platitudinously with political affairs but achieved nothing as far as he was concerned. Lord

Melbourne and Lord Palmerston had been consulted, she wrote, and were of the same opinion. The letter ended. " Allow me once more, dearest Uncle, to beseech you to use your powerful influence over your subjects, and to strive to moderate their excited feelings in these matters."

The king's reply was hollow. He said it had given him *great pleasure and satisfaction* but he thought he had been " put aside as one does with a piece of furniture which is no longer wanted."

Wisely he dropped the subject and reverted to family affairs with particular references to the Coronation on the 28th of June. For a few months the pattern was maintained and then with his own situation becoming desperate he decided to gain the support of England by sheer family authority: " You know from experience that *I never ask anything of you* ! I prefer remaining in the position of having rendered services without wanting any return for it . . . but *this* ought to be the object of our most anxious attention."

The Queen immediately sent the letter to Lord Melbourne, who composed a nebulous reply, which Victoria copied out almost word for word, adding a few affectionate phrases here and there.

Leopold had been treated with his own medicine, for he had previously advised Victoria that if people spoke to her on subjects concerning herself or her affairs without her desiring them to do so—" change the conversation, and make the individual feel that he has made a mistake."

Nevertheless he tried again but received from his niece another rebuff : " You must not think that it is from want of interest that I, in general, abstain from touching upon these matters in my letters to you; but I am fearful, if I were to do so, to change our present delightful and familiar correspondence into a formal and stiff discussion upon political matters, which would not be agreeable to either of us, and which I should deeply regret."

Even this did not make him give up hope of political success but the next reply was unquestionably final : " Though you seem not to dislike my political sparks, I think it is better not to increase them as they might finally take fire, particularly as I see with regret that upon this one subject we cannot agree. I shall, therefore, limit myself to my expressions of very sincere wishes for the welfare and prosperity of Belgium."

Henceforth King Leopold's letters were more subdued and his enthusiasm seemed to have deserted him. The determined, imperious nature of Victoria's real character was beginning to show itself.

3

Early in the young Queen's reign her wilfulness and inexperience were evident when she failed to control an extremely difficult situation.

At her Coronation in June, 1838, it was noted that she ignored her mother and looked for reassurance to Baroness Lehzen. The bitterness caused by the quarrels at Kensington had not dissolved and her feelings towards her mother had not softened. Acrimony was still present and Lady Flora Hastings still vented her spite in malicious remarks about the Baroness. The hostilities culminated in a scandal that swept the country.

In March 1839 Lady Flora was returning from a holiday in Scotland in a carriage with Sir John Conroy when an injudicious joke was made about her figure. The unseemly remark was repeated and ceased to be a joke; it was believed that she was pregnant. The fact that at the time Lady Flora was feeling ill seemed to confirm the suspicion and Sir James Clark the Court Physician, whom she consulted about her indisposition, unethically confirmed the rumour of her pregnancy. Immediately the situation became a scandal and eventually reached the ears of the Queen.

It was an opportunity to strike a blow for her beloved Lehzen and misguidedly Victoria agreed that Lady Flora should submit to a medical examination. Sir James and another doctor performed the examination, conducted, Lady Flora said, with unnecessary crudeness by Sir James. The rumour proved to be unfounded and the two physicians signed a certificate exonerating the unfortunate lady.

The Hastings family, supported by the Duchess, demanded the dismissal of Sir James as a salve to their outraged pride. Lord Hastings demanded audience with the Queen and spread the affair in the newpapers. At this stage the Queen's obstinacy caused her to make a grave error. In private she expressed her regret to Lady Flora, as though that ended the matter, but she did not dismiss the guilty Sir James.

The Court was at fault in allowing Victoria's inexperience to involve herself in a situation that made a palace quarrel public gossip. And Melbourne was to blame for permitting his judgement to be over-ridden by the obstinacy of the Queen. But at the beginning the old cynic must have been secretly amused by Lady Flora's predicament, particularly when he thought of his own escapades. Society was outraged by the vindictiveness of the royal quarrel and public opinion was solidly behhind the injured innocence of Lady Flora. The young Queen, who had begun her reign in a blaze of popularity, suddenly found herself unpopular.

The Hastings family were staunch Tories and the Tory Press attacked the Queen, the Court, Lord Melbourne and the Whigs in unbridled language. The Whigs were in a precarious position. In the General Election of 1837 they had obtained only a small majority and now in 1839 they were not able to withstand criticism. Early in May they could only gain a majority of five on the Jamaican Constitution Bill and were obliged to resign.

To Victoria the news was shattering and she burst into tears. The prospect of losing Lord M. was terrifying. She hated the Tories and did not view the political crisis from a point of view of the nation's welfare but solely from her own personal position. She sent for Lord Melbourne: " The Queen thinks Lord Melbourne may possibly wish to know how she is this morning; the Queen is somewhat calmer; she was in a wretched state till nine o'clock last night, when she tried to occupy herself and try to think less gloomily of this dreadful change, and she succeeded in calming herself till she went to bed at twelve, and she slept well; but on waking this morning all—all that had happened in one short eventful day came most forcibly to her mind, and brought back her grief; the Queen, however, feels better now; but she couldn't touch a morsel of food last night, nor can she this morning. The Queen trusts Lord Melbourne slept well, and is well this morning; and that he will come precisely at eleven o'clock."

Their meeting was a mournful one and she was reluctant to

end it. There was no other alternative but to send for Sir Robert Peel, whom, with his awkward manners, she disliked intensely.

At the first interview with the apprehensive Peel, Victoria was hostile but he survived the audience without upset. There had been a disagreement when she insisted that she must retain her present Ladies-in-Waiting after he had recommended that they should be replaced with ladies of his own Party. The matter was left in abeyance and he withdrew to form his Cabinet.

The next morning Sir Robert again had an audience with the Queen. After some discussion they reached agreement on the constitution of his Ministry, but when the vexed question of the Ladies-in-Waiting was raised he ran into trouble. The Queen was adamant and said that she could not give up any of her Ladies and had never imagined such a thing. Peel asked if she meant to retain *all* her Ladies. " *All*," she said and when he again queried the point she replied " *All*," quite definitely. Immediately after the interview she wrote to Lord Melbourne telling him to hold himself in readiness—" for you may soon be wanted."

It was a crisis. Peel returned and said that unless the Queen would agree to the appointment of at least some of the Tory ladies he could not form a Government.

The recent Whig Cabinet met hurriedly and advised the Queen to accept Peel's proposal. But it was no use, Victoria had made up her mind and nothing could change it. Negotiations were broken off with Sir Robert Peel and she sent him a categoric refusal to his demands. The Queen had triumphed. She had acted unconstitutionally, but her dear Lord Melbourne would again be in office and she was happy.

At dinner during the evening following the dissolution of Parliament Melbourne was in a jovial mood and allowed his sardonic humour, well-known to his friends but rarely exercised in the royal presence, to show itself. The Queen had recounted the difficulty experienced by one of her Ladies-in-Waiting in detaching the crown from her hair after the ceremony of prorogation in the House of Lords and added : " To be sure it was very nervous for poor Lady —— to do it before so many people, all looking at her, and never having done it before." Melbourne said cynically, " Your Majesty might have said as Mary,

Queen of Scots did on the scaffold, ' I am not accustomed to be undressed before so many people nor by such attendants!' "

In the meantime Victoria had reported the behaviour of Peel and her own action to King Leopold and in his reply he said: *" I approve very highly of the whole mode in which you have proceeded;* you acted with great *good faith and fairness,* and when finally propositions were made which you considered you could not submit to, you were very right to resist them. The march of the whole affair is very clear and fair and does you great *credit."*

In the eyes of the nation the affair did not reflect credit upon her conduct and the spell of happiness caused by the resumption of her association with Lord Melbourne was marred by the veiled hostility of the people outside the Palace.

Suddenly her unpopularity was forced into the open by a tragic turn of events. Lady Flora Hastings died. She had been suffering from an internal complaint, overlooked during the medical examination.

The carriage of the Queen's representatives at Lady Flora's funeral was stoned and on several occasions the Queen herself was insulted. Public feeling was expressed when " Mrs. Melbourne " was shouted at her as she drove past. Now it was noticed that there was a change in the Queen. Her expression had hardened and no longer was she the gay, happy young person who had created such a delightful impression when she began her reign.

4

On Queen Victoria's accession the Salic Law, excluding females from dynastic succession, precluded her from succeeding to the throne of Hanover, which British sovereigns had occupied since George the Elector of Hanover became George I of England in 1714. At the Congress of Vienna in 1814 Hanover had been elevated from an electorate to a kingdom and the kingdom passed in 1837 to Ernest, Duke of Cumberland, the next in succession to the British throne. That he was out of England was a matter of general satisfaction, but the fact that he would succeed to the throne in the events of Victoria's death was a very disturbing thought. There was therefore a strong desire that she should marry and have children to avoid the unpleasant possibility.

Cumberland was not fond of his niece, and she in turn fully sympathized with the unanimous trepidation with which his possible succession was viewed. But she was enjoying the feeling of autocratic isolation which sovereignty gave her and was in no hurry to rush into marriage. " At present," she said to Lord Melbourne in 1839, " *my* feeling is quite against ever marrying."

Her Uncle Leopold had other ideas. For years he had nurtured his plan for a marriage between Victoria and his nephew Albert and the visit to England in 1836 of Albert and his brother had been a preliminary move. The two youths had stayed with their uncle in Brussels for almost a year before going to Bonn University where they studied for eighteen months. As the next step in their education they were sent on a tour of Switzerland and Northern Italy in the capable charge of Baron Stockmar, whose services had been borrowed by King Leopold.

Apart from acting as guide and mentor to the young princes Stockmar had another duty. He was to report to King Leopold his opinions on the suitability of Albert as a husband for Victoria and also for the elevated position of Prince Consort to the Queen of England. Two years earlier he had been asked to express his opinion of Albert by King Leopold and with characteristic caution had been guarded in his reply. He wrote that Albert was a young man of good physique with a kindly and amiable disposition, adding: " Thus, externally, he possesses all that pleases the sex, and at all times and in all countries must please." But before passing an opinion on his mental qualities he said he would prefer to withhold judgement until he had had the opportunity of closer observation—" The young man ought to have not merely great ability, but a *right* ambition, and a great force of will as well. To pursue for a lifetime a political career so arduous demands more than energy and inclination—it demands also that earnest frame of mind which is ready of its own accord to sacrifice mere pleasure to real usefulness. If he is not satisfied hereafter with the consciousness of having achieved one of the most influential positions in Europe, how often will he feel tempted to repeat his adventure!" Thus Stockmar's presence on the tour was to give him the opportunity of making his final decision.

Stockmar's report, however, when they returned to Germany was still not unqualified. Whilst conceding that Albert was amiable and intelligent he considered that his manners could be improved and that he was shy and retiring, particularly so in the presence of the opposite sex. In addition, he appeared to show no interest whatsoever in politics or current events and never read a newspaper. His main interests were in art, museums, philosophy, and other learned subjects and he seemed happiest when engaged in conversations with scholars and professors.

In consequence despite his handsome appearance he was not attractive to women. The Grand Duke of Tuscany after observing Albert's conduct at a ball said to Stockmar: "Here is a Prince of whom we can be proud. Surrounded by beautiful dancing partners he occupies his time talking to the savants."

It was disappointing also that he avoided physical exercise as his constitution did not appear to be very strong, but any form of exertion was repugnant to him. However, despite these shortcomings, the Baron considered that on the whole he would make a suitable bridegroom.

The next step in Leopold's marriage plan was a visit of the princes to England in 1839, the year when Victoria herself was disinclined to marry. The memory of her previous meeting with Albert had apparently faded, for as the arrangements for the visit were being made she began to feel panicky and protested to her uncle in a letter sent by special courier: "I am anxious to put several questions to you and mention some feelings of my own upon the subject of my cousins' visit, which I am desirous should not transpire. First of all, I wish to know if Albert is aware of the wish of his *Father* and *you* relative to *me*? Secondly, if he knows that there is *no engagement* between us? I am anxious that you should acquaint Uncle Ernest, that if I should like Albert, that I can make *no final promise this year,* for, at the *very earliest,* any such event could not take place *till two or three years hence* . . . Though all the reports of Albert are most favourable, and though I have little doubt I shall like him, still one can never answer beforehand for *feelings,* and I may not

333

have the *feeling* for him which is requisite to ensure happiness. I *may* like him as a friend, and as a *cousin,* and as a *brother,* but not *more*; and should this be the case (which is not likely), I am *very* anxious that it should be understood that I am not guilty of any breach of promise, for I *never gave any*."

Victoria's attitude caused Leopold some perturbation for on the one hand he had his niece reluctant to marry and on the other his nephew impatient at the delay. Indeed some months previously Albert had expressed his dissatisfaction at the news that Victoria was not keen to go ahead with the project. Leopold had had a long conversation with him and in a letter to Stockmar he had quoted Albert as saying: " I am ready to submit to this delay, if I have only some assurance to go upon. But if, after waiting, perhaps, for three years, I should find that the Queen no longer desired the marriage, it would place me in a very ridiculous position and would, to a certain extent, ruin all the prospects of my future life."

Both Albert and his father continued to object to the proposed delay and in another letter to Baron Stockmar Leopold said : " I have spoken to Albert and what his father says upon the subject of the marriage is true. Albert is now passed eighteen. If he waits until he is in his twenty-first, twenty-second, or twenty-third year, it will be impossible to begin any new career, and his whole life would be marred if the Queen changed her mind."

The 21st of June 1839 was Prince Ernest's twenty-first birthday and by a Government patent the eighteen year old Albert was also declared to have become of full age. It was now deemed expedient for Albert and his brother to make their visit to England. The date of their departure was to be the 30th of September, but Victoria wrote, putting off their visit for a few days. They sailed on the 8th of October armed with a short letter from their uncle in which he recommended them as being " good and honest creatures deserving your kindness " and concluded with : " I am sure if you have anything to recommend to them they will be most happy to learn it from you." After an extremely unpleasant crossing from Antwerp, during which Albert lost his luggage, they arrived in England two days later. They immediately drove to Windsor where Victoria was giving a reception in their honour.

The Queen was waiting at the top of the staircase to greet them, and suddenly, as they stood before her and she looked up into the face of Albert, in one swallow-wing flash of emotion her objections vanished. She was in love.

Two days later she wrote to her uncle: "The dear cousins arrived at half past seven on Thursday, after a very bad and almost dangerous passage, but looking both very well, and much improved. Ernest is grown quite handsome; Albert's beauty is *most striking* and he is so amiable and unaffected—in short *very fascinating.*"

For Victoria the remainder of the week passed in a blaze of happiness and on the Sunday she again wrote to King Leopold: " My mind is quite made up—and I told Albert this morning of it; the warm affection he showed me on learning this gave me *great* pleasure. He seems *perfection,* and I think I have the prospect of very great happiness before me. I *love* him more than I can say, and I shall do everything in my power to render the sacrifice he has made (for a *sacrifice* in my opinion it is) as small as I can. He seems to have very great tact—a very necessary thing in his position. These last few days have passed like a dream to me, and I am so much bewildered by it all that I hardly know how to write; but I *do* feel *very, very* happy . . . and indeed loving Albert as I do, I cannot wish it should be delayed. My feelings are a *little* changed, I must say since last Spring, when I said I couldn't *think* of marrying for *three* or *four* years; but seeing Albert has changed all this."

The fortunate suitor's reactions were somewhat different. The realization that he had almost achieved his ambition overwhelmed him at first, for the next day he wrote to Stockmar describing what had taken place and ended by saying: " More, or more seriously, I cannot write to you; for that, at this moment, I am too bewildered."

Albert then wrote to his stepmother: " My future position will have its dark sides and the sky will not always be blue and unclouded. But life has its thorns in every position, and the consciousness of having used one's powers and endeavours for an object so great as that of promoting the good of so many, will surely be sufficient to support me."

He also wrote a further letter to Stockmar and this time he

dealt entirely with his future position in relation to the advice the Baron had given him—"individuality, the ground-work of my position, prudent, conduct, courage, resolution, zeal". The letter was crowded with such expressions; but not a word of love.

To his grandmother the Dowager Duchess of Gotha his letter naturally was mainly concerned with his sadness at having to take leave of his "dear, dear home and of you." He said "The subject which has occupied us so much of late is at last settled . . . Whilst I shall be untiring in my efforts and labours for the country to which I shall in future belong, and where I am called to so high a position, I shall never cease to be a true *German,* a true *Coburg* and *Gotha* man (*ein treuer Deutscher, Coburger, Gothaner zu sein*)". Again no word of love.

During the tour Albert had written of the impending separation from his brother Ernest. They were completely different in character and habits but there was a very strong feeling of brotherly attachment between them. Now that the parting had become inevitable they consoled each other by always being together. They sat at the piano and to the nostalgic music of Haydn returned in thought to their beloved homeland.

Albert wrote to Prince Löwenstein: "The separation will be frightfully painful to us. Up to this moment we have never, as far as we can recollect, been a single day away from each other. I cannot bear to think of this moment . . . I must now give up the custom of saying "We" and use "I", which sounds so egotistical and cold."

The two brothers returned to Germany and for a few months Albert resumed his old life whilst he settled his affairs.

But the date of the wedding had been arranged and after an emotional farewell he set sail for England and his destiny. His father and his brother accompanied him and after a very rough crossing during which the princes were "in an almost hopeless state" they landed at Dover, where a large crowd was assembled to welcome them.

In the meanwhile Victoria was in a feverish state of agitation, plagued by indecision. Sir James Clark, who diagnosed the Queen's condition as measles, was wrong again—she was terrified at the prospect of losing her freedom.

The happy association with Lord Melbourne had been resumed but the Tories were still a problem and now in connection with the wedding they found an opportunity of crossing the will of the Queen. Victoria wished her future husband's rank to be fixed by statute but the Tories were against the suggestion. They also opposed Victoria's wish that Albert should receive an allowance of £50,000 a year; the sum that had been granted to Leopold on the occasion of his marriage to Princess Charlotte. Instead they suggested £30,000 and pointed out that in fact this amount equalled the entire revenue of Coburg.

Sir Robert Peel had proposed the lesser amount and in retaliation the Queen said that there would be no Tory guest at the wedding. She relented in the case of her old friend Lord Liverpool but she would not agree to the Duke of Wellington's also being made an exception. When his name was mentioned, she said: "What! That old rebel. I won't have him." Lord Melbourne eventually persuaded her to change her mind but she made no secret of her resentment. She began to find fault with everyone and even her uncle King Leopold felt the sharpness of her irritation.

The marriage seemed to be in danger. But when Albert appeared, impeccably handsome in his dark green uniform, Victoria's doubts dissolved into adoration.

They were married on the 10th of February 1840 and on the morning of the wedding she wrote a short note to the bridegroom : " Dearest, How are you today, and have you slept well? I have rested very well, and feel very comfortable today. What weather! I believe, however, the rain will cease. Send one word when you, my most dearly loved bridegroom, will be ready. Thy ever-faithful, Victoria R."

The next day *The Times* devoted almost the entire issue to a description of the wedding. Beginning with : " This most important and national event took place yesterday at noon, at the Chapel Royal, St. James's; and since the marriage of her Royal Highness, the late Princess Charlotte of Wales, there has been no occurrence connected with the Royal Family of England which excited so great an interest," it then went on to describe in minute detail the ceremony, the procession, the dresses, the uniforms, the guests, the interiors of the Chapel Royal, Buckingham Palace,

St. James's Palace, the crowd at the various points on the route; every smile and cheer in fact was faithfully recorded. Of the Queen it was said " her countenance was extremely pale, and appeared to betoken considerable anxiety ". But when the happy, twenty-year-old pair drove off with their suites to Windsor at a quarter to four Victoria was radiant with happiness. The entry in her journal that evening was simple. She wrote " I and Albert alone."

The same day she sent a letter to her uncle in Belgium saying that she was " the happiest Being that ever existed," adding ecstatically : " Really, I do not think it is *possible* for anyone in the world to be *happier,* or as happy as I am. He is an Angel, and his kindness and affection for me is really touching. To look into those dear eyes, and that dear sunny face, is enough to make me adore him. What I can do to make him happy will be my greatest delight."

The letter gave King Leopold tremendous satisfaction for it betokened the success of his plans, and to keep him informed of the train of events his emissary Baron Stockmar was now firmly established in the royal household.

5

When Prince Ernest returned to Coburg on the 8th of May Albert felt the separation from his " beloved brother and dearest friend " very deeply. They had been inseparable and the parting brought tears to his eyes. The last link with his homeland seemed to have been severed.

He was not in love with his wife, although he greatly admired her and was very fond of her. But the warmth of his affection could never match Victoria's worshipping adoration. In future he was determined to devote himself to the fulfilling of his destiny in the high estate to which he had been elevated.

Victoria, however, although in love did not intend to share her power; not even with her husband. " The English," she said to her husband, " are very jealous of any foreigner interfering in the government of this country, and have already in some of the papers expressed a hope that you would not interfere." Albert's loneliness was increased by this enforced isolation. His ship of ambition appeared to have sailed into a quiet backwater and he was unable to pursue his policy, to use his own words, " of making his position entirely a part of the Queen's, continually and anxiously to watch every part of the public business, in order to be able to advise and assist her at any moment in any of the multifarious and difficult questions brought before her —sometimes political, or social, or personal : as the natural head of her family, superintendent of her household, manager of her private affairs; her sole confidential adviser in politics, and only assistant in her communications with the officers of the Government."

In May 1840 he wrote to his friend Prince Löwenstein : " I am very happy and contented; but the difficulty in filling my place with the proper dignity is, that I am only the husband, not the master in the house."

Even the appointment of the members of the Prince's household caused friction particularly when it came to choosing his private secretary. Albert wished to appoint a German but it was not considered desirable that a foreigner should be given this confidential post. The Prince did not want an Englishman, and the situation appeared to be a deadlock. Melbourne solved the problem, however, by nominating his own private secretary, George Anson, with whom Albert was already on good terms. Anson was a perfectly straightforward individual, utterly incapable of intrigue and he won the complete confidence of the Prince*.

Lord Melbourne was not only the Prime Minister but the personal confidant of the Queen and, in effect, acted as her Private Secretary. With him Victoria discussed the political affairs and all her decisions were channelled through him. In State affairs, therefore, there was no place for Albert.

But it was not only in political matters that the Prince found himself thwarted, for the Queen's private life was even more closely superintended. Baroness Lehzen, who had been the major influence in Victoria's life since she was five years old, had become even more powerful since the accession. Now she was in

---

* After Anson's death in 1849 the Prince said to the Queen: " He was my only intimate friend. We went through everything together since I came here. He was almost like a brother to me."

complete charge of the Royal Household, the Privy Purse, and even the Queen's private correspondence. Every detail of their life was controlled and Victoria welcomed the supervision of their affairs by her " dear Melbourne " and her " adored Lehzen ".

When Albert tackled his wife on the subject he also found Victoria had not forgotten the advice given to her by King Leopold to change the subject if it was one in which she was not interested.

In his social life he fared no better. To everyone but Victoria he was a foreigner, handsome perhaps, but in an un-English way; he was stiff, formal and too correct; too Germanic. In English eyes his aversion to physical exertions and lack of interest in sport, particularly fox-hunting, made him seem rather odd and certainly unmanly.

His attitude to life and his temperament were out of place amongst the easy habitual levity of the English aristocracy, whose habits were those of the Regency. To them he lacked a sense of humour; he disliked late hours; he enjoyed the pursuits that were best left to women and weaklings; but worse still he appeared to have no vices.

Albert was an intellectual and he was denied the conversation and interchange of ideas and opinions that were so essential to his happiness. His quiet tastes were not those of his boisterous, high-spirited young wife and to his grandmother he wrote " the late hours are what I find it most difficult to bear ".

Lord Melbourne commented that the Prince " would like to bring literary and scientific people about the Court, vary the society, and impose a more useful tendency into it. The Queen, however, has no fancy to encourage such people. This arises from a feeling on her part that her education has not fitted her to take part in such conversation; she would not like conversation to be going on in which she could not take her fair share and she is far too open and candid in her nature to pretend to an atom more knowledge than she really possesses."

But Victoria adored her husband with all the passion of a young wife and revelled in the intimacies of their private life. To her, this was part of a world to be kept separate from their official existence, but to Albert, duty was all-important and everything else was secondary. Inevitably there were times when these opposing elements of passion and duty caused a clash of wills. Albert found that almost invariably he was the victor; for she was madly in love with him. Often, even the redoubtable Lehzen was over-ruled; a foretaste of things to come. Gradually the well-intentioned Prince was asserting his authority and he even went so far as to effect some sort of a reconciliation between Victoria and her mother, whom he had always liked.

King Leopold's influence was also being brought to bear on the situation, for in a letter dated May 1840 discussing a proposed visit by Victoria and Albert to Claremont, he wrote : " I found several times that some people had given you the impression that poor Charlotte had been hasty and violent even to imperiousness and *rudeness.* I can assure you that it was *not so;* she was quick, and even violent, but I have never seen anybody so open to conviction, and so fair and candid when wrong. The proverb says, and not without some truth, that ladies come always back to the first words, to avoid any symptom of having been convinced. Generous minds, however, do not do this; they fight courageously their battles, but when they clearly see that they are wrong, and that the reasons and arguments submitted to them are *true,* they frankly admit the truth. Charlotte had eminently this disposition; besides, she was so anxious to please me, that often she would say : ' Let it be as it may, provided you wish it, I will do it.' I always answered : ' I never want anything for myself; when I press something on you, it is from a conviction that it is for your interest and for your good.' I know that you have been told that she ordered everything in the house, and liked to show that she was the mistress. It was not so. On the contrary, her pride was to make me appear to my best advantage, and even to display respect and obedience, when I least wanted it from her. She would almost exaggerate the feeling, to show very clearly that she considered me as her lord and master."

The Queen was still unpopular for the Hastings affair rankled but on the 10th of June 1840 an incident occurred which roused the entire nation in her favour.

The royal couple were taking their usual afternoon drive when an attempt was made on her life. The next day Albert sent an account of the affair to his grandmother: " We had hardly proceeded a hundred yards from the palace when I noticed on the footpath on my side a little mean-looking man holding something towards us; and before I could distinguish what it was, a shot was fired which almost stunned us both it was so loud, and fired barely six paces from us. Victoria had just turned to the left to look at a horse, and could not therefore understand why her ears were ringing, as from its being so very near she could hardly distinguish that it proceeded from a shot having been fired. The horses started and the carriage stopped. I seized Victoria's hands, and asked if the fright had not shaken her, but she laughed at the thing.

" I then looked again at the man, who was still standing in the same place, his arms crossed, and a pistol in each hand. His attitude was so affected and theatrical it quite amused me. Suddenly he again pointed his pistol and fired a second time. The ball must have passed just above her head, to judge from the place where it was found sticking in an opposite wall. The many people who stood round us and the man, and were at first petrified with fright on seeing what happened, now rushed upon him.* I called to the postilion to go on and we arrived safely at Aunt Kent's. From thence we took a short drive through the Park, partly to give Victoria a little air, partly also to show the public that we had not, on account of what had happened, lost all confidence in them."

For days after the occurrence the Queen and the Prince were cheered whenever they appeared in public, and when they went to the Opera " the whole house rose and cheered, waved hats and handkerchiefs and went on so for some time . . . and Albert was called for separately and much cheered."

The Prince's position had improved, due mainly to the unfailing support of Stockmar, the astute and influential Baron, who twenty years before had devoted his energies to the support of Leopold and now as whole-heartedly supported the nephew. He was the friend, confidant and mentor to the lonely prince; guiding, urging and encouraging.

With the co-operation of the helpful Anson, he arranged an interview with Lord Melbourne to persuade him to use his in-

---

* He was Edward Oxford, a seventeen year old potman at an inn and at his trial he was declared to be insane.

fluence with the Queen to take Albert into her confidence in matters of State. According to the Memorandum by Mr. Anson of the conversation Melbourne said: " I have spoken to the Queen, who says the Prince complains of a want of confidence on trivial matters, and on all matters connected with the politics of the country. She said it proceeded entirely from indolence, she knew it was wrong, but when she was with the Prince she preferred talking upon other subjects."

Stockmar was successful and in August Albert wrote to his father: "Victoria allows me to take part in Foreign Affairs, and I think I have already done some good. I always commit my views to paper and then communicate them to Lord Melbourne. He seldom answers me, but I have often had the satisfaction of seeing him act entirely in accordance with what I have said."

Next the Baron began to work for the removal of Baroness Lehzen whom he considered an obstacle in the path of the Prince. He had won the confidence of Lord Melbourne and said to him: " The Queen is influenced more than she is aware of by the Baroness. In consequence of that influence she is not so ingenuous as she was two years ago. I do not think that the withholding of her confidence does proceed wholly from indolence . . ." He made no secret of the fact that Lehzen was the cause of the trouble. Soon afterwards the Queen and the Prince made a tour of the country and for the first time Baroness Lehzen did not accompany them.

A month later the astute Stockmar was again successful when the Regency Bill was passed. The approaching birth of an heir to the throne had been announced and the Bill was proposed by the Queen. In the event of Victoria's death the Prince was to become Regent—alone, without a Council, provided he did not remarry a Catholic and remained in England. On the 24th of July the now happy Prince wrote to his father: " An affair of the greatest importance to me will be settled in a few days. I mean the Regency Bill, which will be read for the third time in the House of Lords, after which it will be brought before the House of Commons. There has been much trouble to carry the matter through, for all sorts of intrigues were at work, and had not Stockmar gained the Opposition for Ministers, it might well have ended, as did the £50,000. There was not a word of opposition in the House of Lords, except from the Duke of Sussex.*

Stockmar, whose intervention with the Tories had won the day, felt he deserved a rest and returned to his wife and family in Coburg but even on holiday his mind was still occupied with affairs in England and he sent a constant stream of letters to Albert, proffering advice and encouragement—"be patient courageous, never relax"—the theme was always the same.

After a few weeks the Baron returned, for a General Election was pending and his presence would be needed. It seemed certain the Tories would come into power and probably with a large majority. It was essential therefore that he should be at his pupil's elbow. Albert, after long discussions with Baron Stockmar, acted with an eye to the future. Through Anson he opened secret negotiations with Sir Robert Peel and reached complete agreement on the vexed question of the Ladies-of-the-Bedchamber. This time the constitutional issue would not be raised. Instead it was agreed that when the Tories came into power the Whig ladies would retire, and Sir Robert would then be free to appoint their successors, after first submitting their names to the Queen. Thus the Prince had established friendly relations with the probable new Prime Minister and the situation had been handled with diplomacy and tact. Victoria herself was grateful, for she was in the closing months of pregnancy and was also faced with the unhappy prospect of having her dear Lord M. replaced by the hateful Peel. She was not in the mood for disturbances. Her "dearest Angel", she wrote to King Leopold, "is indeed a comfort to me . . . and his judgment is as you say, good and mild."

The baby, a girl, was born on the 21st of November 1840 at Buckingham Palace and the birth of the Princess Royal raised Victoria's opinion of Albert to nothing less than perfection. The child was a bond between them and the influence of Baroness Lehzen was fading rapidly as the Queen became more and more absorbed in her husband and child.

* According to the Queen's Journal the Duke of Sussex had previously written to Lord Melbourne to say that he must oppose the Bill in the House of Lords and that he must not allow the rights of the Family to be passed over."

The Whig Ministry resigned in September 1841, but even the loss of Melbourne did not now seem important. Albert was quite capable of handling Peel, and the burden of Queenship was lighter.

Albert had at last achieved a complete reconciliation between mother and daughter and they lunched and dined together almost every day. The sinister Cumberland, now King of Hanover, and as unco-operative as ever, refused to give up the apartments he never used in St. James's Palace and Victoria rented Ingestre House in Belgrave Square, at £2,000 a year, for her mother. On the death of Princess Augusta in September, however, she made over to her mother Clarence House, St. James's Palace, and Frogmore Lodge, Windsor. Albert, the family man, was widening his circle.

In November 1841 a second child was born the Prince of Wales, and some months later another baby was expected. Albert was now supreme and it meant the eclipse of Baroness Lehzen. She left England in October 1842 and returned to Hanover where she took a small house at Bückeburg; there to dream of her past glories, for the walls were completely covered with portraits of Victoria. Stockmar had won. Melbourne had gone and Lehzen had been removed, so now he was the sole confidential attendant of Victoria and Albert, his pupil.

Melbourne had gone unwillingly for he found it hard to give up the pleasure of his privileged position as counsellor to the twenty-one year old Victoria. For some time afterwards he continued to correspond with the Queen and often discussed State affairs in private with her. But when it became known that the Queen was often taking his advice Stockmar immediately pointed out the unconstitutional nature of this behaviour in a memorandum. Reluctantly Melbourne was forced to accept the inevitable.

It was the final curtain for Melbourne. Twelve months later he was struck with a paralytic seizure. He recovered, but he was never the same again. The Queen was kind to her old friend, but it was kindness prompted by pity. He tottered around his old haunts, tolerated, but never taken seriously. For two years he lingered in this state of decline until he sank into a condition of imbecility. When he was in his last stages the Queen wrote to her uncle: "You will grieve to hear that our good dear, old

345

friend Melbourne is dying. One cannot forget how good and kind and amiable he was, and it brings back so many recollections to my mind, though God knows! I never wish that time back again."

The tide of events, of Albert and her children, of Stockmar, was driving her forward into the channel of duty and domesticity. Childbirth dominated her life, the Prince of Wales was followed by Princess Alice, a year later by Prince Alfred, then Princess Helena, and two years later by Princess Louise.

The ever-growing family needed wider fields and Windsor and London became insufficient. Osborne, an estate in the Isle of Wight was purchased on Peel's recommendation. Victoria's income was an annuity of £385,000, plus the revenues of the Duchy of Lancaster which provided an additional £27,000 and they were well able to afford the £200,000 they spent on building a new house and furnishing it. Here they lived the life the middle-class admired; calm, decorous and uneventful, a life governed by the noble Albert's sense of strict morality. Victorianism had taken the place of Regency immorality.

6

The fact that she lived in an atmosphere of domesticity did not prevent the Queen from enjoying her royal duties. Indeed, she entered into them with even greater enthusiasm and always Albert was by her side.

At the end of August, 1843, Victoria and Albert voiced their intention of crossing the Channel to pay a visit to the King of the French, whose family were related to Victoria's by marriage. The Queen's Ministers for the most part did not favour the idea. The proposed journey was a significant one for it was the first time for nearly a century that an English sovereign had left the British dominions. In addition it was the first time an English sovereign had visited a French sovereign since Henry VIII in 1520, and then Calais was an English possession. There was discussion of forming a regency during the Queen's intended absence but the Crown lawyers decided that this step might be dispensed with.

The visit lasted only from the 2nd of September to the 7th but a tremendous amount of entertainment was crammed into these few days and the Queen thoroughly enjoyed herself. It is noteworthy that Peel encouraged the visit and contended strongly that it would cement the peaceful relations between the two countries.*

With the advent of Peel the Prince began to play an active part in affairs of State, for Peel readily acquiesced with Stockmar's recommendation that the young man should be brought forward in public life. Albert, who had once regretted his enforced idleness, found himself involved in multitudinous duties; and he was satisfied.

The youth who had shown no interest whatsoever in politics had become a man obsessed with the affairs of State. From morning till night he toiled laboriously over the business of government. The royal nursery was expanding and the consequent absences of Victoria thrust Albert into greater responsibilities. Before the rest of the household were awake the Prince would be seated at his writing-table pouring over State documents, never relaxing, always driving himself relentlessly to greater industry, until far into the night.

Victoria rose early too but when she sat at her own writing-table next to Albert's she always found a heap of documents ready for her signature. His word was final and Victoria took delight in listening to his explanations and the reasons for his decisions. The rest of the day, beginning with a study of the newspapers, continued in unremitting application to work as they dealt with the never-ceasing flow of correspondence and interviews.

The Prince still devoted himself to his intellectual interests, with the result that the demands of society were neglected and less and less time was left for pleasure and exercise. The once handsome and energetic young man was gradually becoming flabby and stooping as he sacrificed his youth on the altar of duty. Only in matters of State did he show enthusiasm and alertness—making speeches, laying foundation stones, attending meetings, opening museums and art galleries, these were his only outlets for recreation. And always looking up at him with adora-

---

* In October, 1844, Louis Phillippe returned the visit and became the first French sovereign to land peaceably on English soil.

tion was Victoria, who seemed to thrive on duty and mother-
hood, for as he deteriorated physically she became more robust
and energetic.

But even his State and family duties were not enough and he
still found time to reorganize the Royal Household, which was
certainly in need of reform. Three years before, Stockmar had
prepared a comprehensive report on the unsatisfactory situation
and after examining the document Albert decided to do something about it.

Apparently there was a confusion of responsibilities with the
result that several authorities were responsible for very similar
tasks. In consequence, there was a great deal of inefficiency,
extravagance, malpractices and waste. Attendants and servants
were being paid and yet had no duties, and naturally the holders
of these sinecures objected strongly to what they called " the
Prince's meddling ". But he was not to be deterred and succeeded in establishing order out of chaos, placing the reorganized
household in the hands of a single official, who was responsible
for the entire management and was known as the Master of the
Household.

No one could accuse Albert of not being a worker and Stockmar was delighted to note that " the Prince has improved very
much lately. He has evidently a head for politics. He has become
too, far more independent. His mental activity is constantly on
the increase, and he gives the greater part of his time to business."
The Prince Consort had, in effect, become the King of England
and from 1843 onwards the Queen always used the plural " we "
instead of the singular pronoun " I " when announcing decisions
to her Ministers.

The antagonism towards the Prince was less marked and even
the critics of his lack of interest in fox-hunting were surprised
and mollified to discover when he hunted with the Belvoir hounds
on the 5th of December 1843 that he was a good horseman.
Victoria wrote to her uncle on the 12th of December : " One can
hardly credit the absurdity of people here, but Albert's riding so
boldly and hard has made such a sensation that it has been
written all over the country, and they make much more of it
than if he had done some great act !"

To Victoria life was an idyll and she was surrounded by happiness. In February 1843 she wrote to her uncle referring to " the present *great* happiness I now enjoy, and which is much greater than I deserve, though certainly my Kensington life for the last six or seven years had been one of great misery and oppression, and I may expect some little retribution, and, indeed *after* my accession, there was a great deal of worry. Indeed I *am* grateful for *possessing* (*really without* vanity or flattery or *blindness*) the *most perfect* being as a husband in existence, or who ever did exist; and I doubt whether anybody *ever* did love or respect as I do my dear Angel! And indeed Providence has ever mercifully protected us, through manifold dangers and trials, and I feel confident will continue to do so."

In this last remark Victoria was referring to two further attempts on her life. In May 1842, a man named John Francis, fired a pistol at her whilst she was driving with the Prince. The man escaped and to arrange his capture the Queen and her husband drove out again the next afternoon past the same spot in Green Park with the two equerries riding close to the carriage. A shot was fired at them from a few yards and the Prince wrote afterwards: " It was the fellow with the same pistol—a little, swarthy, ill-looking rascal. The shot must have passed under the carriage." The ruse succeeded, for Francis was captured and deported for life. Victoria and Albert undoubtedly displayed great courage, to a point of foolhardiness, and when they appeared in public they were cheered wildly.

Two months later, on July 3rd Victoria was driving in the Mall with the King of the Belgians when a crippled lad, John William Bean, attempted to fire at them. The pistol misfired and as there was no actual attempt to inflict injury, the offender was only sentenced to eighteen months imprisonment.

Assassination seemed to be a common risk for a few months later Peel's secretary, Edward Drummond, was fired on and killed, having been mistaken for his master.

The Queen's feelings towards Peel had undergone a change for she was pleased by his acknowledgment of Albert's position, particularly when Peel nominated Albert as the President of the Royal Commission, appointed in connection with the rebuilding of the Houses of Parliament which had been burnt down in 1834.

In private the Queen indignantly criticized the jury's verdict of insanity at the trial of MacNaghten, Drummond's assassin, and in a letter to Peel she wrote : " The law may be perfect, but how is that whenever a case for its application rises, it proves to be of no avail ? We have seen the trials of Oxford and MacNaghten conducted by the ablest lawyers of the day—and they *allow* and *advise* the Jury to pronounce the verdict of Not Guilty on account of *Insanity*—whilst *everybody* is morally *convinced* that both malefactors were perfectly conscious and aware of what they did !"

Now the Queen spoke of Sir Robert Peel as " our worthy Peel ", for whom she said she had " an *extreme* admiration " and that he was " a man of unbounded *loyalty, courage,* patriotism and *high-mindedness* ". His removal from office, she added, " would be a *great calamity.*"

7

During the summer of 1842 the Queen decided that she would like to take a holiday in Scotland and instructed Peel to make the necessary arrangements. The idea was greeted with doubts by her Ministers who said they feared for her safety in the disturbed districts of the North of England. As a compromise Peel recommended that the journey to Scotland should be made by sea. The first part of the journey, from Slough to Padding-ton, was made by rail and it was the second time the Queen had been in this new mechanical invention for she had travelled over the same route in June.* The royal party travelled to Woolwich in the normal way and sailed in the *Royal George* on the 29th of August. They reached Granton pier after a three day voyage, where they were met by Sir Robert Peel.

It was the Queen's first visit to Scotland and she was en-chanted. The scenery she found delightful and indeed she loved everything about Scotland during the fortnight she stayed there. On the 15th of September they returned, again by sea, and

* The first railway was opened in 1825 and was between Stockton and Darlington. In 1830 the line between Manchester and Liverpool was opened and in 1838 the first line entered London from Birmingham, although in 1842 a great deal of hostility was still being shown to this new form of transport.

arrived at Windsor on the 17th; but the happiness she had found in Scotland made the Queen determined to pay further visits in the future.

The decision to avoid passing through the Midlands and Northern England was a wise one for the trade depression was having its worst effects in these areas. The distress was widespread and the entire country was in a state of unrest, marked by the stark contrast between the happiness of the leisured classes and the abject misery of the workers.

The House of Commons had failed to solve the problem of the economic distress since the war, with the result that there had been a succession of riots and attacks upon the police and upon wealthy members of the middle-classes; particularly in the Midlands and the Northern counties. They were known as the Chartist riots.

The advantages of the Reform Act were, in fact, only enjoyed by the middle-classes and to the working man the situation was worse than ever.

Largely owing to Robert Owen's personal efforts unions had been formed during the years 1829 to 1834, resulting in the Grand National Consolidated Trades Union with half a million members. The feeling of employers was strongly against the unions and in 1834 six Dorchester labourers* who had tried to form an agricultural labourers' Union were charged with conspiracy and sentenced to transportation for seven years. This brought about the failure of direct industrial action by the unions.

The " People's Charter " drafted by Francis Place in 1838, which comprised the six points of the radical reformers, " manhood suffrage, the ballot, equal electoral districts, payment of Members of Parliament, abolition of property qualifications, and annual Parliaments," revived the political agitation of the labour movement. Revolutionary as these points seemed to be at the time all save the last one are now the law of the land.

Both the Tories and the Whigs, however, refused to treat the Charter seriously and the agitators took violent action. The Queen recommended that decisive measures for peace should be taken, but she did not regard the riots as being serious.

The country was in a terrible state. Bad trade filled the work-

* " The Tolpuddle Martyrs."

houses, millions existed at starvation level, and the workers were living in dreadful sanitary and housing conditions. They were treated like animals by their employers, who declared that only long hours could enable England to compete with foreign manufacture.

Owen said: " We had founded our wealth and our power on a system which for the first time had treated children not as human beings but as machines, and subjected all employed persons to dangers and evils unknown in earlier times."

There were 200,000 persons employed in the cotton industry, of whom more than a third were under eighteen years of age and a fifth under fourteen.

The deaths in coal mines were so frequent that inquests were not held and the conditions in the mines were nothing less than tragic. In every industry the story was the same, and even in agriculture families were forced to send mothers and children into the fields to labour under the " gang system."

These " agricultural gangs " averaged about twenty persons, usually women and children, and they were hired by a gang master who in turn hired them out as a gang to the farmers. Often children of six or seven years of age were included in the party* and they marched with the rest anything up to ten miles to the scene of their labours. They began work at six o'clock in the morning and seldom returned home before nine in the evening after a day of back-breaking tasks and vicious ill-treatment. The gang masters were brutal task-masters and the women and children were flogged with sticks or spade handles and kicked to make them work better. The wages were a few pence a week.

There were an enlightened few who saw the existing dreadful social order as the result of man's inhumanity to man. Chief among whom was the Earl of Shaftesbury who fought a life-crusade against the horrifying conditions of misery and squalor in which the oppressed classes existed. Born in 1801, Anthony Ashley Cooper, was inspired by the noble efforts of the puritanical John Wesley who in the previous century had awakened the conscience of the English-speaking world to religious activity.

Whilst Shaftesbury was in sympathy with the agitation of the

---

* Some parents when hiring out the older children made it conditional that the young ones should also be included in the gang.

period : in fact, he and Shaftesbury were close personal friends. The author said that the Earl's measures to improve the lodging-houses constituted " the best Act ever passed by our English Legislature ". On the other hand one can recognize how Dicken's graphic word-picture lent colour to Shafesbury's speeches. Another heart-rending problem was the large number of deserted or orphaned children who were destitute. In a moving speech Shaftesbury said that " after careful investigation, he was driven to conclude that naked, filthy, lawless, deserted children in the *metropolis* exceeded thirty thousands."

The Ragged Schools Movement, which had been pioneered by such men as John Pounds, Thomas Cranfield and Dr. Thomas Guthrie, was another cause to which Shafesbury gave his support. Dickens described one of these schools off Holborn Hill, which was London's worst district : " I found my first Ragged School in an obscene place called West Street, Saffron Hill, pitifully struggling for life under every disadvantage. It had no means; it had no suitable rooms; it derived no power or protection from being recognized by any authority; it attracted within its walls a fluctuating swarm of faces—young in years, but youthful in nothing else—that scowled Hope out of countenance. It was held in a low-roofed den, in a sickening atmosphere, in the midst of taint, dirt and pestilence; with all the deadly sins let loose, howling and shrieking at the doors. Zeal did not supply the place of method and training; the teachers knew little of their office; the pupils, with an evil sharpness, found them out, got the better of them, derided them, made blasphemous answers to Scriptural questions, sang, fought, danced, robbed each other —seemed possessed by a legion of devils. The place was stormed and carried over and over again; the lights were blown out, the books strewn in the gutters, and the female scholars carried off triumphantly to their old wickedness."

Ten years later Shaftesbury had effected a transformation and Holborn Hill Institution was a well-run, orderly school, attended by children during the day and by youths and adults in the evening. At night it was a place of refuge for the destitute, supplying food, clothes and washing facilities.

The Ragged Schools were the forerunners of Board Schools, although it was not until 1871 that the Elementary Education

Act came into force and refuted for ever the superstitious dogma that popular ignorance is the surest guarantee of national tranquillity.* In 1859, Shaftesbury had said: "A few years ago there was a great repugnance to the education of the people. We found men in this country—men who passed for wise statesmen —who thought that nothing was more perilous to the public peace than the knowledge of reading and writing among the people." It has been estimated that in London alone the Ragged Schools rescued 300,000 children from a life of crime.

The part played by Shaftesbury in the passing of the Ten Hours Bill was one of his greatest achievements. The conditions in the factories when he began his campaign were horrifying. The workers, including a large number of children, slaved for sixteen hours a day; they were a treadmill army, strapped and beaten into cowering submission. It was an ever-growing problem. In the cotton industry alone from 344 in 1819 the number of mills had grown to nearly 2,000 in 1840, and the conditions became worse as the demand for labour increased. Hand labour could not compete with steam-manufacture and the weaver in the face of economic pressure was forced to send his children into mechanical servitude—or starve.

Shafesbury, the reforming puritan, entered the field in 1833, but before that date Robert Arnot said "that he had seen boys when too late in the mornings, dragged naked out of their beds by the overseers, and even by the master, with their clothes in their hands, to the mill, where they put them on; that he had seen this done oftener than he can tell; and the boys were strapped naked as they got out of bed." The same treatment was applied to girls.

Michael Sadler, Tory M.P. for Southwark, had already submitted a report in 1831, printed in 1832, agitating against the conditions of labour. But after the General Election in 1832 he was not present. The cause was without a leader and Shaftesbury took up the challenge. In February 1833 he renewed the cause and a Commission was appointed to investigate the conditions. It was claimed that the report was prejudiced in favour of

---

* In 1844 for example the total amount allocated to all recognized institutions of public education was £40,000 out of a total budget of £55,000,000 whilst the Government grant to the Royal Stables was £70,000.

the workers and a new Commission was appointed. Years of struggle were ahead for Shaftesbury, years of opposition and heated debates before victory was achieved and the workers enjoyed the protection of national legislation, and ten hours a day became the period of work, with six and a half hours a day as the limit for children under thirteen.

Although industrial conditions were continually improving it was not until almost the end of the century that a standard was reached that would not horrify present day sensibilities.

In 1844, a Report on Factory Conditions revealed that in the North weavers worked for fourteen or fifteen hours a day for six days for eight or nine shillings a week, whilst children under thirteen earned five shillings for the same hours. They stood all day at the loom amidst the dust and noise with the knowledge that if they sat down for a rest they would be fined sixpence. In the Potteries they slaved in a similar manner, except that their labours entailed the dipping of the finished pottery into liquid containing arsenic and lead, with the consequent erosion of the skin. In London, fifteen thousand seamstresses worked at their exacting task, ruining their eyesight and health by long arduous hours of work. Everywhere, one could find terrible conditions, long hours and little leisure, on the treadmill of Industrial Britain.

Among the social atrocities that lingered on was the treatment of chimney-sweep boys. These boys were recruited from the orphanages and poor-house institutions and no value, whatsoever, was placed on their lives. Naked, they were prodded up the chimneys and if they were hesitant straw was burned in the grate to encourage them to climb. On occasions the boys were forced up the flues to extinguish fires and naturally there were many deaths caused; either by roasting or suffocation. The boys, and sometimes girls, were sold into a seven years' apprenticeship for as little as thirty shillings, during which time they experienced unspeakable brutalities in their tuition.

The Royal Commission's report on Trades and Manufactures in 1842 was horrifying, but the report on the conditions in the coalmines in the same year was blood-chilling in its savagery, and early Victorian England was shocked by the revelations. It revealed that in every mining district children under thirteen years of age were employed in the most arduous tasks and that there was no discrimination between the sexes.

The worst of the tasks was that of a " hurrier " or " wagoner ". For this work the children were naked, or at best wore a shift. A leather girdle was worn around the waist to which was fastened a chain, passing between the child's legs. Then on all fours like dogs they pulled coal sleds containing up to 2½ cwts. of coal along narrow tunnels no more than 2 feet high, with the floors usually covered with mud. When two children " hurried " together the load was increased to as much as 9 cwts. and sometimes one child hauled whilst the other pushed. When their strength failed them they were whipped to perform greater exertions.

The other duties in which children were employed in the mines were almost as bad; hewers, coal-carriers, fillers, donkey-drivers and " trappers ", the least arduous being the holding of candles whilst the fathers worked. The duty of the " trappers " was simple but vital, for it meant the opening and closing of doors in the ventilation system at regular intervals. Yet sitting in the dank darkness, listening to the sound of dripping water, and often beset by rats could be terrifying to a small child. Another duty was the pumping away of water, with the realization that to fall asleep would sometimes result in the victim becoming submerged by the rising water.

The hours were long and the brutality unbelievable, and for months some of the children never saw the daylight. Living underground like animals it was inevitable that they should develop bestial habits and the girls were as bad as the boys. Working as they did, half naked alongside the colliers who were usually completely naked, the circumstances provoked bestial conduct so that rape and bastardy were rife.

The bad conditions, foul air, dampness, and long hours extorted their toll and the mortality rate was high, or if not death, then stunted growth, premature old age, heart, lung and skin diseases were the result of colliery work.

The Home Office attempted to withhold the Report but were forced to make the findings public, and Shaftesbury had won. On the 14th of May a week after the Report was published Shaftesbury obtained from the Government permission to introduce his Bill on the 26th. In the meanwhile public indignation had been roused and Peel tried to postpone the Bill until the anger had subsided. The Earl was insistent that the Bill should be presented without delay and a new date was fixed, the 31st of May.

But again Shaftesbury was disappointed, for in the interim two attempts were made on the life of the Queen and Parliament was adjourned. The new date was the 7th of June and the Earl duly made his speech, an historic speech that lasted for two hours, delivered with fanatical eloquence.

Included in the widespread reforms he demanded were the three vital points: the withdrawing of female labour from the mines; the minimum age of boys to be thirteen; the abolition of the apprenticing of pauper children. Wisely he avoided the questions of hours of work so as not to antagonize the men workers whose earnings would have been affected.

Whilst the Bill was being debated Shaftesbury received a letter dated June 23rd from Prince Albert which said: " I have been horror-stricken by the statements which you have brought before the country. I know you do not want praise, and I therefore withhold it, but God's best blessing will rest with and support you in your arduous but glorious task. It is with real gratification I see in the papers the progress which you made last night. I have no doubt but that the whole country must be with you— at all events I can assure you that the Queen is, whom your statements have filled with the deepest sympathy. It would give me much pleasure to see you any day that you would call on me, at twelve o'clock, and to converse with you on the subject."

On the 25th of June Shaftesbury called on the Prince and they discussed the situation at length. There was no doubt in Shaftesbury's mind after the meeting that his reform measures had royal support. He found the Prince " kind, sensible and zealous ".

In Parliament the Bill met violent opposition and amendment followed amendment. But in the main Shaftesbury was successful and on the 10th of August 1842 an " Act to Prohibit the Employment of Women and Girls in the Mines and Collieries, to regulate the employment of Boys, and to make other Provisions relating to Persons working therein ", became law.

Although Shaftesbury had been busy on the Mines and Collieries Bill he had never slackened his efforts to build up a mass of evidence in support of his Ten Hours Bill. In 1833 the Government had contended that from the age of thirteen protection was not needed, and as a compromise Althorp supported by Shaftesbury introduced the Factory Bill of 1843, which limited the hours of work to forty-eight hours per week, whilst youths under eighteen were limited to twelve hours a day or sixty-nine hours a week. The real issue had been avoided by the Government and Shaftesbury bided his time for a further assault.

Five years later, he again spoke vehemently for the Ten Hours Cause in an attempt to shame the Government into action. He pointed out that although it was illegal to work children under thirteen more than forty-eight hours a week the law was being flaunted. Instead of the age limit condition, all children who had reached a height of 4 feet 3 inches were presumed to be thirteen and therefore eligible for the longer hours, and Shaftesbury produced evidence to support his contention. It was a constant tug-of-war, for Peel was adamant on a twelve-hour day whilst the Earl fought just as determinedly for the Ten Hours Amendment. In 1844 the controversy had reached a climax.

John Bright led the attack upon the Amendment and he was solidly backed by Peel. Indeed when the battle was at its height Peel tried to persuade Shaftesbury to withdraw the amendment by offering him the Lord-Lieutenancy of Ireland, for he feared that the reduction in hours would cause British trade to be ruined by foreign competition.

Shaftesbury rose to his greatest heights in conducting the debate, but Peel's threat to resign if the Amendment was passed swung the hesitant members against Shaftesbury. The Amendment was doomed and the Government Bill went up to the Lords, where despite the ranting of Brougham it was passed. But the 1844 Act, even without the Amendment, was a great step forward, for now women of all ages were protected as young persons.

The following year saw Shaftesbury busily occupied with the Lunacy Bill and also a Bill protecting women and children in calico-printing works. The next year was a momentous one, for it saw the Repeal of the Corn Laws, and, subsequently, the resignation of Peel the greatest opponent of the Ten Hours Bill. But ironically the Repeal also brought about the resignation of Shaftesbury himself.

The cause was taken up by John Fielding, Member for Oldham, who knew both sides of the situation, for he was also a mill-owner. In the meanwhile Shaftesbury rallied the supporters of the Ten Hours Amendment to tour the industrial districts awakening the public conscience, whilst he himself, conducted his campaign in the densely populated area of Lancashire. The reforming Earl was not in any way discouraged by not being able to lead the cause for he was concerned only with the result and not in personal glory.

Success crowned their united efforts for on July 1st 1847 the Bill was placed on the Statute Books. Even then complete victory was not won for certain mill-owners devised means of evading the law and their efforts had to be combatted. Nevertheless eventual enforcement was now merely a matter of time.

The Mines and Collieries Act and the Ten Hours Act were Shaftesbury's greatest achievements, but these successes were only part of his endeavours and they increased his zeal for reform in other directions. In Prince Albert he had found a kindred spirit and soon afterwards he conducted the Prince on his first tour of London's East End slums. Albert was an excellent recruit to the campaign for social reform, for always he devoted himself unsparingly to any cause he took up.

8

Sir Robert Peel, the Prime Minister whose retirement Victoria had said would be " a great calamity ", resigned on the 29th of June 1846 and his place was taken by Lord John Russell.

Lord John was fifty-three and in a long political career he had served the country well, having been Paymaster-General, Home Secretary and Secretary for War and the Colonies. Now to crown his career he had become Prime Minister, and as such he was quite acceptable to the Queen and her husband, for they knew he was amenable to reason. His Foreign Secretary, Lord Palmerston, was not.

Palmerston was sixty-one and had been a Minister since he

was twenty-two. He had first been Foreign Secretary in 1830 when Lord Grey's Ministry came into power and this was the third time he had held this important office. Now with the feel of the familiar reins in his hands, the forceful, self-opinionated Minister, was supremely confident. To him, the young Queen and her foreign husband did not present a problem. He would treat them as a stern father would deal with recalcitrant children.

Now that he was again in office he felt himself to be in control of the situation. His domineering personality and ability to capture the public imagination had already won him tremendous popularity and at times he even overshadowed the less forceful Prime Minister. The apprehension felt by the royal pair as the bombastic Palmerston appeared with a flourish on the political scene was therefore quite understandable; for here was a Minister who was never afraid to make a decision and to stand by it, right or wrong.

He was tall and angular, with a determined gaze, a long upper lip, an arrogant mouth, and dyed, bushy mutton-chop whiskers. His manner was jaunty and he had a somewhat tarnished reputation in his private life. He had moved in the gay Whig society at Melbourne House, and rather late in life had married Melbourne's sister, Lady Cowper, herself a prominent Whig hostess, thus consolidating his social position.

An incident is recorded by Lytton Strachey illustrating Palmerston's domineering, and at times reckless, attitude to life. After visiting Osborne he found he had missed the train back to London and ordered the station-master to put on a special train. The official pointed out that to do so at such short notice would be dangerous and that he could not take the responsibility. " On my responsibility then !" said Palmerston brushing aside his objections. The train was duly ordered and the Foreign Secretary travelled to London—fortunately without an accident.

This dictatorial attitude was typical of Palmerston and he had not been in office long before he demonstrated it again. Queen Isabella, a child of sixteen, occupied the throne of Spain and since 1841 her marriage had been a matter of interest to both England and France. Louis Philippe had ambitions of bringing Spain under French influence by marrying his fourth son the Duc d'Aumale to the Spanish Queen, whilst English politicians considered that such an alliance would be detrimental to England.

The French King wished to avoid antagonizing English opinion and announced that he was not interested in the marriage of Queen Isabella. But in 1843 he announced that his younger son, the Duc de Montpensier was to be affianced to the Spanish Queen's only sister.

In 1841, when the marriage of the Spanish Queen was first mooted the Regent Christina, mother of Isabella, suggested Prince Albert's elder brother Ernest as a desirable match for her daughter. When Ernest married the Grand Duchess Alexandrina of Baden in 1842 the Spanish Queen Mother designated Prince Leopold, the cousin of Albert and Ernest, as a suitable alternative son-in-law; particularly was this desirable as his brother was already Prince Consort of Portugal. The matter was discussed with Victoria and Albert, who on the advice of Stockmar decided that the marriage should be left in abeyance in view of the reluctance of English politicians to support Saxe-Coburg interests.

The French were against the marriage and Guizot the Prime Minister declared " that he would at all hazards preserve Spain from England's and Portugal's fate of a Saxe-Coburg ruler ". Consequently the idea was dropped.

In May 1846 the Spanish Queen Mother revived the proposition and wrote to Duke Ernst for his help. Immediately the Duke passed the letter to King Leopold, who decided that Victoria should be consulted.

In August King Leopold and Duke Ernst visited England and the matter was again discussed at length with Victoria and Albert. Between them they decided to stick to their original decision and Duke Ernst wrote to the Spanish Queen Mother accordingly, adding the recommendation that it would be better if Queen Isabella married a Spaniard.

In 1843 the English Foreign Secretary, Lord Aberdeen, had raised no objections to the proposed marriage of the Duc de Montpensier to Queen Isabella's young sister, provided that it was delayed until Isabella had herself married and had a child; it being agreed, of course, that she would not marry a member of the French royal family. This was the position when Palmerston became Foreign Secretary.

Without consulting the Queen and with only a vague knowledge of the recent Saxe-Coburg discussion he urged Queen Isabella to select a husband from a short list of three names he submitted. Prince Leopold of Saxe-Coburg was included among the candidates.

The French saw this move as a breach of faith and without more ado they arranged that the Duke of Cadiz, Isabella's cousin and already a Spanish suitor, should marry the Spanish Queen and that on the same day the Duc de Montpensier should marry her fourteen-year-old sister. In a private note to Victoria dated 8th September the French Queen gave the news of the impending marriages, and on the 10th Victoria replied expressing her surprise and regret. The marriages duly took place, although it was necessary to make Queen Isabella drunk at a wild party before she would consent to marry her cousin whom she hated.

The circle of correspondence increased; Louis Philippe wrote to his daughter the Queen of the Belgians, who wrote to Victoria. Stockmar was brought into it and his statement on the situation was read to the King of the French, but did little to soothe the acrimony. The rumour that the Duke of Cadiz was impotent and that the Spanish crown would descend to the children of Montpensier was taken as the French reason for the marriages.*

Although Palmerston by his precipitation had caused the upset, Victoria and Albert were in agreement with him on the main issue, but this was probably the only time they were in accord, and the future was a constant battle between the Crown and the Foreign Secretary. The tension mounted. Important Foreign Office despatches were not submitted to the Queen, or were submitted too late for them to be altered, or if they were altered, Palmerston changed them back again. Whenever Victoria remonstrated, Palmerston apologized, blamed his Staff, and continued to do as he wished. In 1847 he had almost broken off diplomatic relations with France entirely on his own initiative.

The Queen complained bitterly to her Prime Minister, but when Lord John raised the matter with Palmerston he received the same evasive answers—more than 20,000 despatches passed through the Foreign Office in a single year; if every one was to be submitted to the Queen the business of the department would

---

* This did not transpire for Queen Isabella became the mother of five children, ostensibly in wedlock.

come to a halt. Lord John would have been more in sympathy with this excuse if he himself was not being ignored by his Foreign Secretary. Palmerston was becoming a law unto himself, making important decisions without even consulting the Prime Minister or the Cabinet, and was even opening the Queen's private correspondence.

The unfortunate Russell was being badgered on one side by the Queen for the removal of Palmerston and thwarted on the other by the excuses and evasions of his Foreign Secretary. A crisis came with the visit in 1850 of the Austrian General Haynau, known already as General Hyaena, for his reputation arrived before him. He was notorious for the atrocities he had ordered in Italy and Hungary and particularly was he known as a flogger of women. Consequently when he visited the Barclay and Perkins's Brewery in London he was attacked by the draymen and only managed to escape with his life by bolting like a rabbit, but not before he had received a very rough handling. The Austrian Government demanded explanations and Palmerston, who was in sympathy with the draymen, sent a note to the Austrian Ambassador regretting the incident but qualifying it by criticizing the General for visiting England. A serious situation had arisen.

Prince Albert remonstrated with the Prime Minister and Palmerston was asked to withdraw his note. At first he refused, and to the delight of Albert he threatened to resign. Then suddenly with tears in his eyes he admitted his error and the note was withdrawn. The royal hopes were dashed.

In 1851 there were other crises and the most important one came towards the end of the year. The French Republic* without the support of England had become weak and unpopular and was ended on the 2nd of December by Louis Napoleon's *coup d'état*. Despite the English policy of complete neutrality towards France Palmerston told the French Ambassador in London that England approved and he repeated the opinion in a note to the British Ambassador in Paris. Neither the Queen nor the Prime Minister had seen the note and the patience of Lord John was at last exhausted. Palmerston was dismissed.

* Louis Philippe was overthrown in 1848.

Victoria and Albert were delighted and she wrote to her uncle: " I have the greatest pleasure in announcing to you a piece of news which I know will give you as much satisfaction and relief as it does to us, and will do to the *whole* world. *Lord Palmerston is no longer Foreign Secretary*—and Lord Granville is already named as his successor!" And Albert sent his brother Ernest the news " that the man who has embittered our whole life, by continually placing before us the shameful alternative of either sanctioning his misdeeds throughout Europe . . . or of bringing about an open conflict with the Crown, and thus plunging the only country where liberty, order, and lawfulness exist together into the general chaos—that this man has, as it were, cut his own throat." To make them happier still this was the year of Albert's greatest triumph—The Great Exhibition.

A civil servant in Whitehall, Henry Cole, a cultured man interested in the arts returned from the Paris Exhibition in 1849 with an idea for an even greater exhibition to be built in London. Prince Albert was delighted with the plan and took it up with enthusiasm. But unlike the French Exhibition he decided it was to be international in character. Its correct title was to be " The Great Exhibition of the Works of Industry of all Nations ", but whereas other previous Exhibitions had received Government support this one was to be financed by voluntary contributions. An executive committee of five members, including Henry Cole (later he was knighted), was set up under the personal direction of Prince Albert and the great undertaking began.

There were many objections to the tremendous project and the question of the site became the topic of the day. The Prince wanted one on the south side of Hyde Park but *The Times* and the Press in general attacked this suggestion and instead proposed Battersea. Sir Robert Peel supported the Prince and said " they must remain firm about Hyde Park or give up the Commission ". But on the day of the Parliamentary debate in June 1850 Peel was thrown from his horse on Constitution Hill and was killed. Albert said: " Peel was to have taken the lead in our defence, but now there is no one." The Hyde Park site motion was carried however.

Next came the problem of the design. No fewer than 245 designs were rejected, mainly due to the fact that nearly nineteen million bricks would be needed to build a solid structure of the size envisaged, before Joseph Paxton submitted a design of iron and glass that was accepted. It was in the form of a gigantic greenhouse; a fantastic palace of glass.

For two years the Prince devoted himself unsparingly to the work of construction and the collection of exhibits. His health was affected but following the earlier advice of Stockmar he never relaxed. Then came the obstacle of finance, and it seemed that the project was doomed owing to lack of support. But again Albert was not deterred and £200,000 was subscribed as a guarantee fund.

Crowds watched the construction of the fantastic crystal edifice as it rose higher and higher in the sky, enclosing towering elm-trees and acres of grass and shrubbery, until it dwarfed everything around it by its immensity. Still Albert toiled on, at committees and public meetings, whilst he was faced always with a constant flow of ever-increasing correspondence in connection with the project.

Victoria was almost delirious with excitement as the day of completion approached, but the royal couple had suffered a number of tragic blows caused by the deaths of relations and friends since the work on the Exhibition had begun.

Albert suffered a great loss when his secretary George Anson died in November 1849. A few days afterwards, on the 2nd of December, the good Queen Adelaide died and was buried beside her beloved William at Windsor. In the next year five days after the death of Peel, the Queen's uncle the Duke of Cambridge died, to be followed in August by the death of Louis Philippe who had been in exile at Claremont. In October his daughter, who was the wife of King Leopold, followed her father to the grave.

In addition anxiety had been caused by two fresh attacks on the Queen. On the 19th of May 1849 a pistol was fired at her near Constitution Hill by an Irishman named William Hamilton (later it was found to be a blank cartridge) and on the 27th of May 1850 Robert Pate a retired officer struck her forcibly on the head with his silver-knobbed cane as she was leaving Cambridge House in Piccadilly. The attacks excited a great deal of sympathy for the Queen particularly so as she was still recovering from the birth of her third son, Arthur, on the 1st of May. The two men were sentenced to seven years transportation.

But when the Exhibition was opened the tremendous excitement made Victoria forget her unhappiness and she wrote to her uncle: "I wish you could have witnessed the 1st May 1851 the *greatest* day in our history, the *most beautiful* and *imposing* and *touching* spectacle ever seen, and the triumph of my beloved Albert. Truly it was astonishing, a fairy scene. Many cried, and all felt touched and impressed with devotional feelings. It was the *happiest, proudest* day in my life, and I can think of nothing else. Albert's dearest name is immortalized with this *great* conception, *his* own, and my *own* dear country *showed* she was *worthy* of it."

The Great Exhibition was indeed a tremendous triumph. In the first six months more than six million visitors spent £500,000 in admission fees, refreshments and catalogues, yielding a profit of about £185,000. When the Exhibition ended in October, 1851, it was unanimously agreed to have been an unqualified success, and its object, the stimulation of British trade had been achieved.

Paxton proposed that the empty building should be turned into a permanent Winter Gardens, but the Commissioners decided to sell the building. It was therefore taken down and re-erected at Sydenham where it became the Crystal Palace.

Prince Albert decided that the profit should be used to buy land in South Kensington for the erection of a permanent National Museum. The results of his foresight and efforts would have delighted and gratified the industrious Albert for on the site have been built: the Victoria and Albert Museum, the Natural History Museum, the Science Museum, the Royal College of Science, the Royal College of Art, the Royal College of Music, the Imperial Institute, the India Museum, the Imperial College of Science and Technology, the Royal School of Mines, the City and Guilds College, the Meteorological Office, the Institute of Physics, the Entomological Society, Optical and Physical Societies, the Royal College of Organists, Royal School of Needlework, the Administrative Office of the British School in Rome, the Royal Albert Hall, and Queen Alexandra's House.

The dismissal of Palmerston brought respite to the royal pair for only a few weeks. Soon the jaunty, old reprobate was once again conspicuous on the floor of the House. Boldly and convincingly he denounced the Government's inadequate proposals for increasing the nation's defences against a possible attack by France. Thus, on the issue of the Militia Bill the Government was defeated and he had turned the tables on his former colleagues.

Lord Derby was instructed by the Queen to form a Conservative Government, and it is interesting to note that Disraeli entered official life for the first time. He was nominated as Chancellor of the Exchequer and Leader of the House of Commons. His stay in office, however, was precarious, for after a General Election in July the Conservatives were in a minority.

A few weeks later the Queen paid a visit to her Uncle Leopold, now a widower for the second time, and then Victoria and Albert spent a holiday in Scotland. Whilst they were here the Queen received the news that an old eccentric and miserly bachelor, Camden Neild, had left her almost his entire estate, which amounted to half a million pounds. As he was unmarried and had no relations, the Queen had no qualms about accepting the very large bequest.

The Highlands of Scotland had a tremendous fascination for Victoria, mainly because here Albert was happier than anywhere else. He seemed to throw off his cares amongst the glorious mountain scenery and his self-imposed burden of duty was laid aside. Since their first visit when newly-married they had returned again and again, and each visit had been more enjoyable than the last. In 1848 the Queen had taken a lease of "Balmoral", a small house near Braemar, in Aberdeenshire, where the tiny rooms were a novelty and as enchanting as a doll's house to a child. They loved the Highlanders too, their customs, their music, their dances, their dress—everything was fresh, delightful and truly idyllic in the clear, exhilarating mountain air. "The Highlanders," the Queen noted in her journal, "never make difficulties, but are cheerful, and happy, and merry, and ready to walk, and run, and do anything." And of her dear husband she said "Albert enjoys it so much! he is in ecstacies here."

But the planning mind of Albert was never completely at rest and when the Queen bought the house in 1852 he decided to demolish it and build in its place a splendid castle. Immediately the happy pair were launched into the excitement of examining and discussing the plans of the proposed building, the size and shape of the rooms, the interior decorations; everything down to the smallest detail was of tremendous interest for this was to be the castle of their dreams. The pleasure and excitement of the romantic project was to last for years for the castle was not completed until 1854. By then it was a magnificent sight; a granite building in the Scottish baronial style, with turrets and battlements and a tower a hundred feet high, with breath-taking views of the surrounding mountains and the River Dee. Inside, the walls of every room were covered with tartans, the carpets were of tartan patterns, and sometimes so was the linoleum. Predominant among the designs were the red and grey Balmoral tartan, designed by Albert, and the Victorian tartan, with a white stripe, designed by the Queen. Everything in Balmoral was of their own choosing and it was their nirvana.

Their stay in the autumn of 1852, however, was marred by the sad news of the death of the Duke of Wellington on the 14th of September. Victoria, who no longer regarded him as "that old rebel" wrote to her uncle: "I am sure you will mourn *with us* over the loss we and this whole nation have experienced in the death of the *dear* and great old Duke of Wellington . . . He was the GREATEST man this country ever produced, and the most *devoted* and *loyal* subject, and the staunchest supporter the Crown ever had. He was to us a true, kind friend and most valuable adviser."

The Queen opened Parliament on the 11th of November and Lord Derby was still the Prime Minister. Disraeli's budget was introduced on the 3rd of December but was rejected on the 17th. In consequence Lord Derby resigned and the Government fell. Next came a coalition Government under the leadership of Lord Aberdeen and with him returned the people's favourite, Palmerston. His appointment however was to the Home Office, where it was considered his conduct would be less irksome and Lord Clarendon became Foreign Secretary. Gladstone was appointed Chancellor of the Exchequer.

Palmerston, who had not liked Louis Philippe, was naturally in favour of his successor Napoleon III, but Victoria was openly against the usurper and she liked him even less because of Palmerston's partiality. Her Uncle Leopold realized the danger of antagonizing France, and early in 1853 he sent Duke Ernst of Saxe-Coburg on a friendly visit to Paris. He was received with great hospitality, and the Emperor and Empress lost no time in praising Queen Victoria. Their friendly attitude duly reached the ears of Victoria and she was somewhat mollified.

Encouraged by the improved relations with the Queen of England Napoleon next suggested a matrimonial alliance between the two countries. The proposed marriage was between Napoleon's cousin, Prince Jerome, and Victoria's cousin, Princess Mary of Cambridge, afterwards Duchess of Teck. Leopold and Palmerston were in favour of the idea, but when Victoria consulted her cousin, the Princess would not even consider the suggestion. Bold as ever, Palmerston said coolly " that Prince Jerome was at any rate preferable to a German princeling." But the shadow of war was looming over Europe and soon England was to ally herself with France against Russia.

In the autumn of 1853 Russia, with territorial ambitions, as a pretext objected with such violence to the ill-treatment of Christians within the Turkish Empire that Turkey was forced into a declaration of war. Public opinion in England was for an immediate intervention to protect Britain's ally, Turkey, and for months in Parliament the issue was debated. Aberdeen, the Prime Minister was for peace and in this he was supported by his colleagues; but Palmerston was for war to protect British interests in Turkey. Suddenly Palmerston resigned. The proof that he had correctly interpreted public opinion was soon evident. There was a national outcry of indignation. But unpredictably the abuse was not directed against the Government. Instead, the scapegoat was Prince Albert.

To some extent this was the fault of Palmerston himself. Indiscreetly he had implied that his resignation was due to foreign influence behind the throne. His words spread and were magnified. What began as a whispering campaign became open gossip and finally direct criticism, taken up even by the Press.

Undoubtedly there was a vein of truth in the rumour, for of course Albert was a foreigner, and behind him there was another, Baron Stockmar. Nevertheless, although the accusations were untrue, they continued to be magnified by the threat of war, until eventually the agitations for Palmerston's reinstatement became so violent that even the Government itself was jeopardized. Palmerston was recalled and the tumult died down to a resentful murmur. But the winter of 1853-4 produced only inertia on the part of the Government and the indignation burst out again with redoubled bitterness against the Prince and also against the Queen.

It was rumoured that they were in league with the Russians; and that the Prince was receiving instructions from the Czar through the Courts of Gotha and Brussels. It was even whispered that Palmerston the one Minister upon whom England relied, had arranged the arrest of the royal couple on a charge of high treason and that they were to be imprisoned in the Tower; around which crowds gathered expectantly to await their arrival.

Early in January 1854 the Prince wrote to his brother : " It is pretended that I whisper in Victoria's ear, she gets round old Aberdeen, and the voice of the only English Minister, Palmerston, is not listened to—ay, he is always intrigued against, at the Court and by the Court."

To attack Albert was to attack Victoria and she was very distressed by the wave of unpopularity, particularly after his tremendous success with the Exhibition. But the pacific ideals of three years before were forgotten and the nation was eager for action. At the time it was said " that what England wanted was not a good peace but a good war."

The Queen's Ministers realized that she had been hurt and when Parliament reassembled on January 31st the slanders were immediately repudiated in both Houses. Albert was vindicated and his right to advise the Queen was established.

Victoria was delighted and told Stockmar that " the position of my beloved lord and master had been defined for *once and all* and his merits have been acknowledged on all sides most duly." The criticism gradually petered out and the last remnants of hostility were swept aside a few weeks later when England and France formally declared war against Russia.

10

The nation was satisfied and gloried in the clangorous, flag-waving excitement of taking part in a war after forty years of peace. It was a great new adventure, stirring the emotions and capturing the imagination of everyone. Cheering crowds lined the streets as the proud, brave troops, in their gay uniforms marched past. Victoria wrote to the King of the Belgians on the 28th of February, 1854 : " The last battalion of the Guards (Scots Fusiliers) embarked today. They passed through the court-yard here at seven o'clock this morning. We stood on the balcony to see them—the morning fine, the sun rising over the towers of old Westminster Abbey—and an immense crowd collected to see these fine men, and cheering them immensely as they with difficulty marched along. They formed lines, presented arms, and they cheered us *very heartily,* and went off cheering. It was a *touching and beautiful* sight; many sorrowing friends were there, and one saw the shake of many a hand. My best wishes and prayers will be with them all . . ."

As events proved the prayers were needed. The flame of patriotism was to burn brightly in a terrible holocaust at Sebastopol. The 399 days siege of this port virtually comprised the entire war and 25,000 British troops were sacrificed in its capture.

At the beginning of the war efforts were made to induce Austria to become an ally. Austria refused to join us and Count Cavour, the Prime Minister to King Victor Emmanuel of Sardinia, and probably the greatest statesman in Europe, volunteered instead. The troops of this small state, with a population of only five million, fought at the side of the British and the French. In so doing and as a result of Austria's non-participation, Cavour paved the way for the future liberation of Italy.

The allied forces sailed for the Crimea on the 7th of September and the Queen received a telegram on the 21st saying that " 25,000 English, 25,000 French, and 8,000 Turkish troops have landed without meeting resistance and had begun the march to Sebastopol."

Sebastopol was the port from which the Russian fleet controlled the Black Sea and it could have been captured within a matter of weeks if a frontal attack from the north had been made. Instead, incompetent generalship dictated that an encirclement should be made from the south, and thousands of lives were thrown away unnecessarily. Time was lost, and Russian reinforcements arrived to outnumber the Allies heavily.

The British soldier was second to none in bravery as the two cavalry charges, made immortal by Tennyson, testify; but capable generalship and adequate supplies were sadly lacking. For this the Duke of Wellington was to blame. During his long term of duty as Commander-in-Chief he had always insisted that the army should remain unchanged; the weapons, the strategy and the methods of supply were those of Waterloo and the army chiefs were ingrained with the same out-dated ideas.

Britain was leading the world in industrial and mechanical developments yet, incredible as it now seems, was unable to maintain adequate supply lines between the port of Balaclava and her troops, a mere six miles away.

The base hospital at Scutari, a suburb of Constantinople, was a chaos of disease, filth and incompetence, and the ships carrying the wounded across the Black Sea were even worse. Instead of two or three days, the voyage was taking two or three weeks, and the wounded were thrown together in heaps like carcasses of meat, many of them bleeding to death from crude amputations.

Two forces saved England. The first was William Russell of *The Times,* the first war correspondent. He exposed the deplorable state of affairs in a vigorous series of despatches, with a complete disregard of security but also with a vigour that roused the nation to action. His disclosures brought about the resignation of Aberdeen, to whom the war was of secondary importance and the return of forceful Palmerston as Prime Minister in 1855.

The second was Florence Nightingale. In the light of Russell's revelations she was given sufficient support to allow her administrative genius full scope in time to save thousands of lives. Florence Nightingale herself estimated that of the 25,000 British deaths 16,000 were due to the terrible conditions.

Sidney Herbert, Secretary for War, and a personal friend of Florence Nightingale, devised the project of sending Miss Nightingale with a band of trained nurses to the Crimea. They sailed in November 1854 and established at Scutari a base hospital which was the first of its kind and a pattern for the future —with the help of her friend Sidney Herbert, Florence Nightingale remodelled the Army Medical Service in the early 'sixties.

On the 28th of November the Queen received a letter from Prince Edward of Saxe Weimar, a Lieut.-Colonel and A.D.C. to Lord Raglan, Commander-in-Chief in the Crimea, in which he said : " Never shall I forget the sight of the dead and dying Russians on the field. Some of these poor wretches had to lie on the field for sixty hours before they were removed to the hospital tents; the majority of course died. I am afraid this is one of the necessities of war, for we had to remove our own people first. I went round the hospitals the next morning. It was a horrid sight to see the bodies of the men who had died during the night stretched before the tents, and to see the heaps of arms and legs, with the trousers and boots still on, that had been cut off by the surgeons."

Florence Nightingale with her administrative genius and her devoted nurses reduced the death rate from 42 per cent to 22 per thousand, and the Red Cross Movement, which is now world-wide, began from the Geneva Convention of 1864, as a direct result of her efforts.

Little was won by anyone from the Crimean war, and the result of the work of the ministering angel, Florence Nightingale, was the greatest gain for everyone. As well as giving a great impetus to the advance of science in the cause of humanity she created a new conception of the place and capabilities of women in everyday life, which led to the founding by John Stuart Mill of the women's suffrage movement.

Sebastopol was captured on the 8th of September 1855 and in March 1856 the Treaty of Paris ended the war. In May the Queen personally presented medals to the returned Crimean heroes as they stood proudly to attention on the Horse Guards Parade and as Victoria herself wrote : " The rough hand of the brave and honest British soldier came for the first time in contact with their Sovereign and their Queen." In June, she

instituted a new medal for conspicuous valour, the Victoria
Cross, and she herself pinned it on the tunics of sixty-two men
at a review in Hyde Park. To Florence Nightingale she sent a
valuable jewel as a memento.

II

The royal couple spent their summer holiday of 1855 at Balmoral with their growing family, and here they received news
of the fall of Sebastopol. Albert unbent enough to light the
beacon on the top of a cairn and to join the jubilant Scotsmen,
enlivened by whisky, in a dance around the fire. Victoria
watched from a window. About three-quarters of an hour later
Albert came down and said "the scene had been wild and
exciting beyond everything. The people had been drinking
healths in whisky and were in great ecstasy." The sounds of the
pipes and of guns being fired into the air lingered on well into
the night.

With the end of the war in sight the family settled down with
their guests to enjoy their holiday. Among the visitors was the
Prince of Prussia's eldest son, Prince Frederick William (afterwards the Emperor Frederick), a presentable young man of
twenty-four. A romance developed between the Prince and the
Princess Royal, who was then almost fifteen. Despite her youth
he requested permission to propose marriage. Victoria liked him
and an engagement was made on the 29th of September; with
the stipulation that the official announcement was not to be made
until after the Princess's confirmation next year.

From England's point of view it was not a good match and
when the news inevitably leaked out it excited unfavourable
comment, particularly from *The Times,* which scathingly described the Prussians as " a paltry German dynasty ".

Albert was in favour of the proposed marriage for he believed
that a united Germany under the leadership of Prussia was the
pattern of the future, and consequently an alliance between the
two royal Houses would create a solid bloc. Palmerston was quite
uninterested in German politics but he was prepared to agree to
a scheme so strongly favoured by the Queen and the Prince.

During the Crimean War the royal pair had become reconciled with their Prime Minister, drawn together by their common hostility to Russia. With the attainment of his ultimate ambition the wayward Palmerston had become more reasonable and was pleasantly surprised to find that Albert was more intelligent than he had supposed. In addition, the enthusiastic industry and fanatical interest displayed by the Prince in the conduct of the war were highly commendable; particularly as some of his ideas were found to be worthy of adoption. One of his suggestions was the establishment of a depot at Malta; another was that troops should be concentrated for training in one place, which was the beginning of Aldershot; and yet another was that the Army should be divided into two Army Corps under separate commanders responsible to the Commander-in-Chief. In adopting the last suggestion Palmerston wrote: " I and all the other members of the Cabinet feel greatly obliged to your Royal Highness for having suggested an arrangement which had not occurred to any of us."

When the war was over the relations between the royal pair and Palmerston gradually reverted once again to antagonism. This was particularly so with regard to Italy. Albert disliked Cavour and Garibaldi, and the Court was never in favour of England's support of Italian unification, which was not to be achieved without a violent struggle. But, on the question of the marriage of the Princess Royal, Victoria and Albert had their way and the Prince immediately began to groom his daughter for her future position. This was an easy task and did not present any difficulties.

Vicky was an intelligent girl, solemn and thoughtful, with a great deal of her father's cold, analytical attitude to life in her nature. She was the favourite child, and there was no doubt that the blood of the calculating Coburgs flowed in her veins.

Bertie, the Prince of Wales, was different. He was a true descendant of the Hanoverians and the despair of his parents. Whilst he was still in the cradle, Prince Albert and Stockmar had worked out in great detail the possible hereditary tendencies he might have inherited, listing them so that they could be suppressed at the first sign of their emergence.

In consequence, the young Prince was subjected to a disciplinary upbringing of the utmost severity. He became virtually a prisoner, with his tutors as warders, in the White Lodge at Richmond. His life was planned in accordance with a long and detailed memorandum drawn up by his father. He was not allowed friends of his own age indeed any contact with persons outside the household of the White Lodge was strictly forbidden. The relentless unbending nature of Albert that had changed Victoria from a gay, happy and exuberant spirit into a severe and narrow-minded woman, was intent on producing a Prince in the same pattern. The fact that Bertie was backward and found any mental exertion distasteful only called for greater severity and a more rigid curriculum. But the young Prince was also wayward and determined and it became increasingly difficult to make him work at his studies. To his father Bertie was a great disappointment, and no longer could the Prince turn to Stockmar for solace and first hand discussion. The Baron had left England in March 1857 to spend the rest of his life in retirement at Coburg. He was seventy and he was finding the strain of Court and international affairs too much for him.

For years he had been a trusted friend and adviser to King Leopold, the Prince and Queen Victoria. In retirement he said : " I have worked as long as I had strength to work, and for a purpose no one can impugn. The consciousness of this is my reward—the only one which I desired to earn." Albert still corresponded with him and often sought his counsel, but the old man was in failing health and out of touch with current affairs. Sadly and dispiritedly the Prince realized that in future he alone must make the decisions.

The education of the other children in the family was also under the constantly vigilant eye of Albert, who took his parental responsibilities very seriously indeed, but the Prince of Wales received the brunt of his attentions, from which affection, tenderness and understanding were sadly missing.

But whilst the royal couple were about to lose a daughter they were also about to gain another, for on the 14th of April 1857 Princess Beatrice, the ninth and last child, was born.* The

* The nine children were—Victoria b. 1840, Edward b. 1841, Alice b. 1843, Alfred b. 1844, Helena b. 1846, Louise b. 1848, Arthur b. 1850, Leopold b. 1853, Beatrice b. 1857. On Lord Melbourne's advice Edward was not given the first name of Albert because of the public's animosity to Prince Albert. However, his father and mother always called him " Bertie ".

event does not appear to have stirred warm maternal feelings in Victoria, for in July when Albert was attending the wedding of King Leopold's daughter Charlotte to the Archduke Ferdinand Maximilian at Brussels she wrote to her uncle: " I wish I could be present—but my dearest *Half* being there makes me feel as I were there myself. I try to picture to myself how *all* will be. I could not give you a greater proof of my love for you all, and my anxiety to give you and dearest Charlotte pleasure, than urging my dearest Albert to go over—for I encouraged and *urged* him to go—though you cannot think *combien cela me coûte* or how completely *déroutée* I am and *feel* when he is away, or how I count the hours till he returns. *All* the numerous children are as *nothing* to me when *he is away*; it seems as if the whole life of the house and home are gone, when he is away."

At this time Victoria was in the midst of the preparations for her own daughter's wedding, and already the festivities had begun. On the 25th of May the Queen with some anxiety had asked Parliament for a provision for the Princess Royal. The amount proposed and agreed, after some outspoken objections, was a dowry of £40,000 and an annuity of £8,000. Victoria was quite happy with the result, although the daughters of George II and George III had each received £80,000 and an annuity of £5,000.

The palaces were crowded with foreign royalty and every day there was a ceremonial function, but always Albert seemed to stand apart from the gaiety. He was depressed, disconsolate and seemed to be feeling the strain of overworking himself. Even when, on the 25th of June, the Queen conferred on him by Royal Letters Patent the title of Prince Consort, he showed little enthusiasm. He wrote to his brother: " It was always a source of weakness for the Crown that the Queen always appeared before the people with her *foreign* husband." But to everyone in England the new name made no difference—he was still a foreigner.

Meanwhile the Indian Mutiny with its terrible atrocities occupied everyone's thoughts. The massacre at Cawnpore of English officers, women and children shocked the nation with its savagery. Battles were being fought and the casualties were heavy, for a quarter of a million Indian troops had risen against twenty-four thousand Britons. But troops were on the way, and happily on September the 30th Delhi, the stronghold of the mutineers, was captured; and Lucknow, where a thousand terror-stricken Europeans were beseiged, was about to be relieved. By December the Mutiny was nearing its end.

The Queen's depression during the Mutiny had been increased by the death at Claremont of her beloved cousin and friend Victoria, the Duchesse de Nemours. She was a first cousin on the Saxe-Coburg side of both Victoria and Albert, and the Queen said: " We were like sisters, bore the same name, married the same year, our children of the same age."

The Duchesse had been driven from France with her husband, the second son of Louis Philippe, on the overthrow of her father-in-law, and had been given refuge in England. Her death followed the birth of a child on the 28th of October. She was thirty-five and had been married at eighteen.

But soon the bustle of the approaching marriage dwarfed even the recent tragedy as the final arrangements were made. The festivities commenced on the 19th of January 1858 and the wedding took place on the 25th. Eight days later there was a tearful and emotional scene between mother and daughter as the young couple made their departure.

The Prince Consort was deeply touched. He seemed reluctant to let his daughter go and travelled with the newly-weds as far as Gravesend. It was cold and snowing hard but he stood alone on the wharf until the ship was out of sight. His heart was full, but his undemonstrative nature had prevented him from expressing his true feelings.

Practically every day afterwards he wrote to his daughter, pouring out advice and recommendations. His letters were full of nostalgia and in May he visited Coburg, alone. But things were very different from the days of his youth and he wrote to the Queen that he felt himself to be a stranger there.

In August he paid another visit, this time with Victoria, and the royal yacht was escorted by a large number of warships. They landed at Cherbourg, where they were welcomed by Emperor Napoleon III in the guise of friendship.

An attempt had been made on the life of Napoleon III in

January 1858, when several bombs were thrown at the Emperor and the Empress as their carriage approached the Opera House in Paris. They were unhurt, but 10 people were killed and 150 injured. Soon afterwards it was discovered that the attempt had been plotted in London and the bomb had been manufactured in England. The French Minister Walewski had demanded that steps should be taken to restrict French refugees in England, but Palmerston had ignored the note. However, the Bill he introduced as a conciliatory measure making conspiracy to murder a felony, instead of a misdemeanour, was defeated in the House of Commons and Palmerston resigned. He was succeeded by Lord Derby.

After the attempted assassination the relations between France and England were somewhat strained. Two of the assassins, Orsini and Pierri, were executed in Paris, but the trial in London of Dr. Bernard of Bayswater, who was accused of being an accomplice, produced an acquittal. The verdict was a reply to the antagonistic attitude of the French Ministers. Albert was very agitated in the presence of the Emperor and Empress, and the Queen in her diary recorded that watching his embarrassment made her hands shake so much that she could not drink her coffee.

Next they landed at Antwerp where they met King Leopold and at Aix-la-Chapelle they were joined by their daughter's father-in-law, the Prince of Prussia, who escorted them the rest of the way. After a very happy fortnight with their daughter, who was expecting a child in a few months time, they returned home and Albert resumed his arduous duties.

Not long after their return they received the news that the old King of Prussia had succumbed to growing insanity and his brother, their daughter's father-in-law, with whom Victoria and Albert were on very friendly terms, had taken his place. Their son-in-law, became Crown Prince and Albert's interest in Germany now became an obsession. He bombarded Frederick William with letters of advice. To Stockmar he wrote : " What an excellent turn all political matters have taken in Berlin."

On the 27th of January 1859 their first grandchild was born at Berlin. The birth was a difficult one and the new drug chloroform was used. Victoria wrote in her diary that " the doctors despaired at the first of the child's life." But the child survived and "Dear little William ", as he was called by the Queen was ultimately to become "The Kaiser", William 11, Emperor of Germany, and Albert's forecast of a united Germany was to come true.

12

The thirty-nine year old grandparents were pleased with their daughter, the Princess Royal, but the Prince of Wales was still causing anxiety. On November 9th 1858 he had attained his majority on his eighteenth birthday, but Sir James Clark, the Court physician, said he was "very backward for his age". Although legally he was now his own master the Prince Consort still exercised a rigid control over his life and at Oxford he was given " an entirely separate establishment with his governor and an equerry ", to restrict his activities.

In 1860 the discipline was relaxed, and arrangements were made for the Prince of Wales to visit Canada and the United States. After the Crimean War the Canadians had invited the Queen to visit their Colony but she declined saying that she did not feel well enough to undertake the long and fatiguing journey. Now she agreed that her eldest son should go instead, and soon after announcing the proposed visit an invitation was received from the American President, James Buchanan, for the Prince to visit Washington.

The Prince of Wales sailed for Canada on the 9th of July. He had said to his mother, " I will do my best " but the Prince Consort was not taking any risks and the Duke of Newcastle, Colonial Secretary, and General Bruce, who accompanied him were given strict instruction concerning his behaviour and speechmaking.

The fears were unfounded for the good-looking young Prince, exuberant in his freedom, was given an enthusiastic reception in Canada.

He opened the bridge across the St. Lawrence and this was one of the main reasons for his visit. Whilst he was in Canada the daring tightrope walker, Blondin, twice crossed Niagara Falls, first pushing a wheelbarrow and then on stilts. The Prince was entranced by this magnificent display of daring and skill, and when Blondin suggested that he might like to be a passenger in the wheelbarrow the Prince was quite willing. Naturally the nineteen-year-old heir to the Throne was not allowed to risk his life, but the story delighted the Canadians.

In America, the smiling Prince achieved a similar success and showed a distinct liking for the uninhibited American way of life. The representative of *The Times* who accompanied the royal party wrote of " an ovation such as has seldom been offered to any monarch in ancient or modern times It was not a reception; it was the grand impressive welcome of a mighty people." Undoubtedly Bertie's trip was a great success.

Whilst the Prince of Wales was away, Victoria and Albert again visited Coburg and the Queen saw her grandson for the first time. The holiday was clouded with sadness, however, for everyone was in mourning for the death of Albert's stepmother, and even the baby William had black bows on his white dress.

A further happening damped their spirits. Victoria became extremely agitated when she was told that Albert had been involved in an accident. Whilst he was travelling in a carriage the horses had bolted and he was forced to leap out. Fortunately he escaped with only minor scratches but he suffered a nervous depression as a result. In her thankfulness to Almighty Providence for saving her dear, precious Albert, Victoria endowed a Coburg charity with £1,000. They returned home to Windsor sooner than they had intended and were gratified to find letters from Bertie awaiting them, telling of his enthusiastic reception.

In November, the Queen wrote to her uncle: " Our poor Bertie is still on the Atlantic, detained by very contrary winds, which those large vessels, with only an auxilliary screw and only eight days coal cannot make any way against. Two powerful steamers have now gone out to look for him, and bring him back in . . ."

Victoria's anxiety was soon diverted from Bertie. He duly arrived safely and was sent to Cambridge University to continue his education; but her mother was seriously ill. A few weeks later there was a portent. The paralysed Frederick William IV died on the 2nd of January 1861 and was succeeded on the Prussian throne by his brother. Victoria's son-in-law and her daughter became the Crown Prince and Princess of Prussia, but

the good news was dampened by the sufferings of the Duchess
of Kent. On the 16th of March she died at Frogmore near
Windsor. She was seventy-four. The Duchess had had an operation for an abscess in the arm and appeared to be recovering.
The Queen was with her mother when she died.

It was the first time the Queen had been in the presence of
death and she was shocked by its dreadful finality. The previous
differences were forgotten and she poured her grief with morbid
intensity into her diary. To her uncle she wrote: " *On this, the*
most dreadful day of my life, does your poor broken-hearted child
write one line of love and devotion. *She* is gone! That precious,
dearly beloved tender Mother—whom I was never parted from
but for a few months—without whom I can't *imagine life*—has
been taken from us. I held her dear, dear hand in mine to the
very last, which I am truly thankful for! But the watching that
precious life going out was fearful!"

After the funeral she wrote again: " I had never been near a
coffin before, but dreadful and heart-rending as it was, it was so
beautifully arranged that it would have pleased *her*, and most
probably *she* looked down and blessed *us*—as we poor sorrowing
mortals knelt around, overwhelmed with grief!"

Months later she was still immersed in her sorrow, intensified
as she sorted out and turned over her mother's possessions, and
she wrote to Leopold: " You would, I think, find it soothing, and
it would painfully interest you to look over her letters and papers,
which make me *live* in times I heard her talk of when I was
a child. It is touching to find how she treasured up every little
flower, every bit of hair . . . All these notes show how very, very
much she and my beloved Father *loved* each other. Such *love*
and affection! I hardly knew it was *to that extent*. Then her
love for *me*—it is too touching! I have found some little books
with the accounts of my babyhood, and they show *such* unbounded tenderness. Oh! I am so wretched to think *how,* for a
time, *two people most* wickedly estranged us . . . But thank God!
that is all passed *long, long* ago, and she had forgotten it . . .
And all that was brought about by my good angel, dearest
Albert, whom *she* adored, and in whom *she* had such unbounded
confidence."

Superstition says that Death travels in threes, and the completion of the trinity was to deal Victoria a far more dreadful blow than she had ever known before, or would ever know again; the crowning sorrow of her life.

13

Gradually Victoria resumed public life and during the season hospitality was extended to the King of the Belgians, the Prince and Princess of Prussia and the King of Sweden and his son Prince Oscar.

The Prince of Wales was at the Curragh camp in Ireland for military training with the Second Battalion of the Grenadier Guards, and in August the royal family visited him and then made a tour of Ireland. At this time Bertie's marriage was being planned and a list of seven eligible princesses, prepared three years before by King Leopold and Stockmar, was scrutinized. Fifth on the list was the name of Princess Alexandra, the eldest daughter of Prince Christian of Schleswig-Holstein-Sonderburg-Glücksburg and of the heiress to the Danish throne. On the recommendation of the Princess Royal, who had met the Danish princess and found her " fascinating ", her name was promoted to the top of the list and arrangements were being discussed for the Prince of Wales to meet his future wife.

In the autumn the Queen and the Prince Consort spent their usual holiday at Balmoral and they returned to Windsor towards the end of October. The Prince Consort, however, did not appear to have derived any benefit from the holiday for he had not thrown off the nervous depression that had attacked him in Coburg. He suffered from insomnia and was in very low spirits. Victoria was in robust health and although she was continually solicitous she did not realize the seriousness of Albert's illness.

Despite his indisposition, the Prince drove to Sandhurst to inspect the new buildings of the Royal Military Academy and the Staff College. It was a cold, blustering day of continuous torrential downpour and when he returned in the early hours of the morning he was shivering and exhausted, but rheumatic pains again gave him a sleepless night. He was feeling thoroughly ill but still struggled to perform his duties.

Three days later he again ventured out into the dreadful weather to visit the Prince of Wales at Cambridge. A story had reached London that Bertie was having a love affair with a young woman in Cambridge and Albert was determined to put a stop to the escapade. His mission accomplished he stayed the night, but the next morning he was in such pain and felt so ill that he could barely board the train to Windsor. The doctors diagnosed his illness as rheumatism but then decided it was influenza. Yet he still continued to work.

A serious political crisis had arisen. The American Civil War had broken out in April and the Government had issued a proclamation of neutrality. Despite the statement, however, sides were being taken in England; the Crown favoured the North, but Palmerston, again Prime Minister, strongly supported the South. On the 27th of November, *Trent* a British Royal Mail packet docked at Southampton and the Captain reported that one day out from Havana a shot had been fired across her bows by the *San Jacinto,* an American warship. An armed party had boarded the *Trent* and four passengers had been taken off. Apparently they were two Southern envoys and their secretaries, who had run the Northern Federal's blockade to plead their cause in London and Paris.

On November 30th Palmerston sent to the Queen the draft of a despatch to Washington. It was couched in Palmerston's most peremptory language demanding redress for the flagrant breach of neutrality and the return of the four prisoners. The despatch was tantamount to an ultimatum.

Albert saw the danger signal and although barely able to hold a pen he redrafted the message, refuting any suggesting that the attack was a deliberate action on the part of the United States Government and wrote instead that it was believed to be due to the excessive zeal of a United States naval officer. The message added that the liberation of the four prisoners and their delivery into British hands with an apology would settle the affair.

The amended draft was sent to Palmerston with a note from the Prince Consort and it achieved the desired result. The prisoners were duly delivered to the British Embassy with an admission that reparation was due to Britain. The grave risk of war had been averted. The note was the last thing the Prince ever wrote.

Albert's condition was worse, but Victoria still did not realize that a terrible tragedy was near. On the 4th of December she wrote to the King of the Belgians: " I have many excuses to make for not writing yesterday, but I had a good deal to do, as my poor Albert's rheumatism has turned out to be a regular influenza which has pulled and lowered him very much. Since Monday he has been confined to his room . . . However, he is decidedly better today, and I hope in two or three days he will be quite himself again."

Still Albert continued to sink, but Sir James Clark was unperturbed and said there was no cause for alarm at this " feverish sort of influenza ".

Clark's report was sent to Leopold and he replied: " The medical advisers are, thank God! excellent and Clark knows Albert so well." But Clark did not know Albert's strange illness. He decided it was gastric fever and pooh-poohed the suggestion that another opinion should be sought.

Victoria wrote to her uncle on the 12th of December 1861 : " I can again report favourably, of our *most* precious invalid. He maintains his ground well—had another good night—takes plenty of nourishment, and shows surprising strength. I am constantly in and out of his room, but since the *first four dreadful nights,* last week—I do not sit up with him at night as I could be of no use; and there is nothing to cause alarm."

But now other doctors had been called in and the Queen wrote: " I cannot sufficiently praise the skill, attention, and devotion of Dr. Jenner, who is the *first fever* Doctor in Europe, one may say—and good old Clark is here every day; good Brown is also *most* useful . . . We have got Dr. Watson and Sir H. Holland. But I have kept clear of these two."

Albert's skin was like grey parchment, his eyes were wild and bright; he was irritable and feverish but at times lapsed into a torpor. Yet there were also times when he smiled faintly and stretched out a weak hand to touch his wife's cheek.

It was typhoid fever and Dr. Jenner knew that they had been called too late. On the 14th of December Victoria entered the sick room: " It was a bright morning, the sun just rising and shining brightly. The room had the sad look of night-watching, the candles burnt down to their sockets, the doctors looking anxious. I went in, and never can I forget how beautiful my darling looked, lying there with his face lit up by the rising sun, his eyes unusually bright, gazing as it were on unseen objects, and not taking notice of me."

During the day there was a relapse and as the awful, unspeakable possibility suddenly loomed before her she moaned in terrible apprehension.

The whole family filed silently into the room to gaze for the last time on the face of their father, whilst Victoria sat by his bedside immutably enduring the torments of a fearful nightmare.

In the evening the Queen left the room for a few moments but Sir James Clark sent someone to ask her to return. Albert was cold and grey. Victoria whispered her thoughts: "Oh, yes, this is death. I know it. I have seen this before." And as his face became rigid she broke down in wild, uncontrollable grief across the dead body.

14

Six days later she wrote to her uncle: "My *own* dearest, kindest Father—For as such have I *ever* loved you. The poor fatherless baby of eight months is now the utterly broken-hearted widow of forty-two! My *life* as a *happy* one is *ended*! the world is gone for *me*! If I *must live* on (and I will do nothing to make me worse than I am), it is henceforth for our poor fatherless children—as for my unhappy country, which has lost *all* in losing him—and in *only* doing what I know and *feel* he would wish, for he *is* near me—his spirit will guide and inspire me! But oh! to be cut off in the prime of life—to see our pure, happy, quiet, domestic life, which *alone* enabled me to bear my *much* disliked position, Cut Off at forty-two—when I *had* hoped with such instinctive certainty that God never *would* part us, and would let us grow old together (though *he* always talked of the shortness of life) is *too awful,* too cruel! His purity was too great, his aspiration *too high* for this poor, *miserable* world! His great soul is *now only* enjoying that for which it *was* worthy!"

Victoria was on the verge of a nervous breakdown and she was obsessed with the idea that her mind was about to break under the strain of her grief. Continually she held her hand to her head and in a wildly excited state declared that she was losing her reason. At other times she sank into a dark, dejected coma, withdrawing from reality to worship at the shrine in her heart with silent tears.

Four days after the tragedy she went with Princess Alice to the gardens at Frogmore to choose a site for a mausoleum.* Already she was contemplating death and it was here she wished to be buried with Albert. "It is but for a short time," she said, " and *then* I go—*never, never* to part! Oh! that blessed, blessed thought."

Great anxiety was felt for her welfare and the next day she was persuaded to leave Windsor, with its memories of her mad grandfather, for Osborne where it was hoped the sea air would benefit her health.

From Osborne, on the 24th of December, she wrote to her uncle again, and it was evident that she was determined to preserve for ever the memory and intentions of Albert. King Leopold was about to come to England and perhaps in anticipation of his possible influence, she wrote: "Though, please God! I am to see you so soon, I must write these few lines to prepare you for the trying, sad existence you will find it with your poor, forlorn, desolate child—who drags on a weary, pleasureless existence! I am also anxious to repeat *one* thing, and *that one* is *my firm* resolve, my *irrevocable decision,* viz. that *his* wishes—*his* plans —about everything, his views about *every* thing are to be *my law*! And *no human power* will make me swerve from *what* he decided and wished—and I look to *you* to *support* and *help* me in this. I apply this particularly as regards our children— Bertie etc.—for whose future he had traced everything *so* carefully. I am *also determined* that *no one* person, may he be ever so good, ever so devoted among my servants—is to lead or guide or dictate to *me*. I know *how* he would disapprove it. And I live *on* with him, for him; in fact I am only *outwardly* separated from him, and *only for a time* . . . Though miserably weak and utterly shattered, my spirit rises when I think *any* wish or plan of his is to be touched or changed or I am to be *made to do* any-

* It was built at a cost of £200,000 from her private purse.

thing." She ended her letter with a postscript—"What a Christmas! I won't think of it."

The image of Albert was everywhere and he was never out of her thoughts for a single moment. Everything she did and every word she spoke, however trivial, was associated with his memory. Morbidly she was determined that nothing was to be disturbed : the Blue Room at Windsor where he died, the rooms he had occupied at Buckingham Palace, Osborne and Balmoral, all were to remain exactly as he had left them. His clothes were laid out every day and even his papers and correspondence were left just as he had last touched them. Her world had stopped and his existence was lapidified.

For weeks she refused to see anyone except the intimate members of her household, and Princess Alice and Sir Charles Phipps, the Keeper of the Privy Purse, acted as intermediaries between the Queen and her Ministers. When it was necessary to hold a council she stayed in one room with the doors open whilst the members sat in the next room. She could be heard but not seen. On her desk was a white marble bust of Albert and so that his presence should be always near she hung his portrait on the bedhead above the vacant pillow.

She lived in almost complete seclusion, drawing a dark veil between herself and the outside world. Dressed in the deepest mourning she dolefully and silently dragged from one shrine to another, from Buckingham Palace to Windsor, to Osborne and to Balmoral.

The entire nation was stirred with sympathy for the Queen in her poignant grief, but although she was deeply touched by the wave of compassion she said sorrowfully : "They cannot tell what I have lost," and added bitterly : "Will they do him justice now?"

Victoria was determined that Albert should not be forgotten and statues and memorials made their appearance all over the country to remind the populace of the Prince Consort's goodness. In particular, she wished that a fitting memorial should be erected in Kensington Gardens as near as possible to the site of the Great Exhibition. The Queen assented to the suggestion that a Memorial Hall should be built, in which his statue would be erected in a dominant position, but unfortunately the sum of

£120,000 obtained by public subscription was insufficient and the Hall project had to be dropped. (Years later the Albert Hall was built as a private speculation).

For the statue a number of eminent architects were asked to submit designs. The one selected was by Gilbert Scott but it was not until May 1864 that the work of erection was begun. The architect himself said that " this taken as a whole, is perhaps one of the most laborious works of sculpture ever undertaken, consisting, as it does, of a continuous range of figure-sculpture of the most elaborate description, in the highest *alto-relievo* of life-size, of more than 200 feet in length, containing about 170 figures, and executed in the hardest marble which could be procured." The work was indeed long and laborious for the edifice which was to house the statue of the Prince Consort was not completed until 1872 and it was four years later before the central statue was in position. It was made of bronze-gilt and weighed nearly ten tons and was identified on the base by the single word " Albert ".

Victoria wrote: " I only lived through him, my heavenly Angel . . . Now I feel as though I am dead! I endeavour to do what is right and try at least to prevent anything which would not be according to his wishes but alas the vital power is finished. Disheartened, I continue my gloomy sorrowful life alone." Even her children did not divert her intense grief and she said: " The children are good and loving, but I do not find their company the same and it is no support."

As the months turned into years Victoria continued to dedicate her life to the dead and the tragedy revolved in her mind with an introversion that was pathological in its intensity. She still signed her letters to her children " your unhappy mama " and in every letter there was a reference to " your darling papa ".

Alone she wrestled with the problem of her eldest son, for whom she had developed " an unconquerable aversion ". She was convinced that her beloved husband had caught his chill as a result of his visit to their wayward son at Cambridge, and that this, combined with the worry over the episode, had contributed to the cause of his death. Lord Clarendon said her dislike of the Prince of Wales was " a positive monomania with her. She got quite excited while speaking of him, and it quite irritated her to see him in the room."

Nevertheless, the Queen was determined that the young Prince should undeviatingly follow the path chosen for him by the Prince Consort. She had no one to whom to turn for advice. Her Uncle Leopold, although willing, was now a doddering, old man, with a wig, darkened eyebrows and a painted face; Baron Stockmar was also decrepit and only a few months away from death;* whilst in England there was not one man upon whose counsel she could rely. But her isolation made her more determined than ever to follow the doctrines, plans and wishes of her beloved Albert.

The first step in the Prince's introduction to public life was that he should make a tour of the Holy Land and in February, 1862, he was sent on the expedition with Dr. Arthur Penrhyn Stanley, the late Prince's chaplain. Dr. Stanley was not enthusiastic about his task and said: "It is hardly possible to over-estimate the difficulty of producing any impression on a mind with no previous knowledge or interest to be awakened." But during the trip he altered his opinion somewhat and admitted that "there is more in him than I thought. I do not at all despair."

In June they returned to England and the good report received from the chaplain mollified the Queen's feelings; she began to allow her son a little more latitude. Nevertheless, she was not taking any chances with her unpredictable son and she instructed the sixty-five year old General Sir William Knollys to keep a watchful eye on his behaviour. In the meanwhile she went ahead with her plans for his marriage and also the marriage of Princess Alice.

The first wedding took place on the 1st of July 1862, when Princess Alice was married to Prince Louis of Hesse-Darmstadt at Osborne. The Queen was present at the ceremony but shut herself off so that she could not be seen by anyone in the congregation. Afterwards she lunched alone with the bride and bridegroom and was quite touched, for she felt acutely the loss of her daughter who had attended her so sympathetically during the worst period of her grief.

In September Victoria went abroad for the first time since

* He died in July 1863.

Albert's death and at Brussels she met her son's future wife also for the first time. Princess Alexandra's dignified appearance created a good impression and the Queen said she " looked lovely, in a black dress, nothing in her hair turned back off her beautiful forehead."

Bertie had only seen his future bride once before but he seemed to be happy, if a little cynical about the affair and a few days later the Queen, who had travelled on to Coburg, received a letter from her son in which he said : " Now I will take a walk with Princess Alexandra in the garden and in three-quarters of an hour I will take her into the grotto, and there I will propose, and I hope it will be to everybody's satisfaction."

It is impossible to please everyone and Prinz Otto von Bismarck, who had been appointed Minister-President of Prussia, was not happy about the proposed marriage. He had designs on the Danish duchies of Schleswig and Holstein and regarded the betrothal as proof of British sympathies with Denmark; particularly as the Crown Princess was known to have had a hand in the affair.

Prussian suspicions seemed to be confirmed when the Queen invited Princess Alexandra and the Crown Princess and her husband to visit Osborne. Unaccountably the Prince of Wales was sent on a cruise in the Mediterranean to be out of the way whilst the wedding plans were discussed.

The marriage took place on the 10th of March 1863 at St. George's Chapel Windsor and the Queen watched the ceremony, like a sombre blackbird in a tree, from a gallery overlooking the chancel. The ceremony below revived poignant memories of her own wedding and afterwards she retired alone to the mausoleum; there to commune with the dead.

For Bertie it was a happy occasion. When he had come of age in November 1858 he had inherited the estates of the Duchy of Cornwall with the revenues of £60,000 a year and the accumulated capital of £600,000; from which sum he was easily able to afford the purchase of Sandringham. Now on the occasion of his marriage Parliament granted him an additional annuity of £40,000, and they also gave his bride a wedding present of £10,000 a year, which was to be increased to £30,000 should she become a widow. Ahead of him there appeared to stretch a period of pleasure and in the bonds of matrimony he hoped to find freedom from his mother's domination.

Meanwhile, Victoria was determined to impress upon the nation the true greatness of her beloved Albert. Sir Arthur Helps was directed to prepare for publication a collection of his speeches and addresses, and her private secretary Lieutenant-General The Hon. Charles Grey was instructed to write *The Early Years of the Prince Consort*. But these were not enough and Mr. Theodore Martin (later he was knighted) was directed to write a full-length biography of the Prince. The first volume of this monumental work was published in 1874, to be followed by four others, which were not completed until 1880. Unfortunately the expected result was not achieved, for the volumes, due to the direct supervision of the Queen, were written in such a fulsome manner as to be cloying. The pages are liberally besprinkled with footnotes by the Queen and they bring to mind the picture of Victoria poring over the pages in a maudlin attempt to improve perfection, for as such was Albert presented. The figure presented was not of a man but of a plaster saint and the public never discovered the true Albert.

For twenty years the Prince Consort had virtually been the King of England and after the first numbing shock of his death had passed Victoria realized she had been left with a sacred trust—the furtherance of his plans. Before her, until she joined him, loomed the path of duty. She must work as he had worked, unsparingly in the cause of his ideals.

Her Ministers were relieved when direct contact was resumed, for the employment of intermediaries created an impossible situation. The Prime Minister, Lord Palmerston, visited the Queen at Osborne and although she resented the fact that he was not wearing mourning her previous antipathy had almost vanished. Indeed, the thought of any political change was abhorrent to her. The Government was in a precarious position and she sent a private note to the leader of the Opposition, Lord Derby, telling him that a change of Government might cause her to lose her reason.

But it was not long before there was again a clash of opinions between the Crown and the Government on the vital question of foreign policy. For years the conflicting claims of Denmark and

Germany to the duchies of Schleswig-Holstein had been a vital issue and now there were signs that violent measures were about to be taken. In 1852 at a conference in London arranged by the British Government the disputing parties had reached a compromise and peace had been guaranteed for eleven years. The time was almost up.

On the German side there were two parties, the Duke Frederick of Augustenburg and other lesser States, and the rulers of Prussia and Austria. Victoria had family connections with all of these, and of course with Denmark through her daughter-in-law, but her sympathies were with Prussia. To her Ministers she said: " I know that our dear angel Albert always regarded a strong Prussia as a necessity, for which, therefore, it is a sacred duty for *me* to work." Two of the claimants, the King of Denmark and Duke Frederick, were pressing for English intervention by force of arms in their support, and Palmerston and his Foreign Secretary, Lord John Russell, supported Denmark's claims.

The crisis came in January 1864, when Bismarck presented an ultimatum to the King of Denmark and followed it up by ordering Prussian and Austrian troops to invade the duchies in dispute. In England, there was a wave of anger against this high-handed action and it seemed likely that the country would go to war against Prussia. Victoria became frantic with anxiety and bombarded her Ministers with protests against intervention. She wrote: " The only chance of preserving peace for Europe is by not assisting Denmark, who has brought this entirely upon herself," and to her Foreign Secretary said that she could never allow the country " to be involved in a war in which no English interests were concerned."

England did not intervene, but whether this was due to a peaceful element in the Cabinet or to the Queen's demands is not clear. But non-intervention certainly made Victoria unpopular. She was attacked in the Press and criticized in the House of Lords by Lord Ellenborough; there were even rumours that she was about to abdicate. But though she was outraged by the abuse she was obdurate in her opinion.

The British Government took the opposite view and when the Prussian Government formally announced the joint occupation

by Prussia and Austria of Schleswig-Holstein a communication
was sent to Bismarck pointing out that the war was regarded as
" an act of unjust aggression and perfectly needless, and that the
British Government lamented the advantages that Austria and
Prussia had gained by their success in hostilities."

15

The marriage of the Prince of Wales had aroused tremendous
enthusiasm throughout the country and the birth of a son in
January 1864 was made the occasion for even wilder rejoicings.
The old Queen in her seclusion had become an unpopular figure
but now there was great agitation for her to appear again on the
public scene. *The Times* in a leading article gave credence to
the widespread rumours that she was about to re-enter social
life : " Her Majesty's loyal subjects will be very pleased to hear
that their sovereign is about to break her protracted seclusion."
It then went on to say that it would be futile on her part to
attempt to exert " an abiding influence on public affairs without
appearing as a factor of them. They who would isolate themselves from the world and its duties must cease to know and to
care, as well as to act, and be content to let things take their
course. This in effect they cannot do; this they never do; and the
only result is a struggle in which they neither live nor die—
neither live, as they wish, in the past, nor do their duty in the
' working world '."

The fact that her grief was not understood, surprising though it
was to the Queen, made her angry and five days later she wrote
a sorrowful and indignant letter to *The Times* denying that she
" is about to resume the place in society which she occupied
before her great affliction; that is, that she is about to hold *levées*
and drawing-rooms in person, and to appear as before at Court
Balls, concerts etc. This idea cannot be too explicitly contradicted.
The Queen appreciates the desire of her subjects to see her, and
whatever she can do to gratify them in this loyal and affectionate
wish she will do . . . Her Majesty will not shrink, as she has not
shrunk, from any personal sacrifice or exertion, however painful.
But there are other and higher duties than those of mere representation which are now thrown upon the Queen, alone and un-

assisted—duties which she cannot neglect without injury to the public service—which weigh unceasingly upon her, overwhelming her with work and anxiety. The Queen has laboured conscientiously to discharge these duties till her health and strength, already shaken by the bitter and abiding desolation which has taken the place of her former happiness, have been impaired." She then went on to say that she will " do what she can—in the manner least trying to her health, strength, and spirits—to meet the loyal wishes of her subjects . . . More the Queen cannot do; and more the kindness and good feeling of her people will surely not exact of her."

The Queen remained in seclusion and towards the end of the year *The Times* resumed its attack : " The living have their claims as well as the dead; and what claims can be more imperative than those of a great nation and the society of one of the first European capitals? It is impossible for a recluse to occupy the British throne without a gradual weakening of that authority which the Sovereign has been accustomed to exert. For the sake of the Crown as well as of the public we would, therefore, beseech her Majesty to return to the personal exercise of her exalted functions. It may be that in time London may accustom itself to do without the Palace, but it is not desirable that we should attain that point of Republican simplicity. For every reason we trust that now that these years have elapsed, and every honour that affection and gratitude could pay to the memory of the Prince Consort has been offered, her Majesty will think of her subjects' claims and the duties of her high station, and not postpone them longer to the indulgence of an unavailing grief."

Victoria persisted in her seclusion and the attacks continued, not only in the Press but also in the streets; a placard was hung outside Buckingham Palace saying : " To be let or sold in consequence of the late occupant declining business." *The Times* sarcastically reported that the workers at the Woolwich Arsenal had been warned that they would be arrested if they looked out of the windows whilst the Queen's carriage was passing.

In the Autumn of 1865 Victoria paid another visit to Coburg to unveil a statue of Albert and whilst there she arranged on the advice of her brother-in-law the Duke of Saxe-Coburg, the betrothal of her third daughter Princess Helena to Prince

Christian, the brother of Duke Frederick whose claim to the duchies of Schleswig and Holstein had cost him his territory and property. The match aroused indignation in Prussia where it was regarded as an act of political interference but the Queen was unperturbed and returned to England in good spirits. On the way home she met her uncle Leopold at Ostend and it was to be for the last time.

Troubles awaited the Queen in England. During the summer Parliament had been dissolved and the Liberals returned to office. But before the new Parliament met the Prime Minister, Lord Palmerston, died on the 18th of October two days before his eighty-first birthday. Victoria was at Balmoral when the news reached her and although she was touched by his death which severed one of the last links with the Georgian epoch she did not immediately return to London to deal with the emergency.

The seventy-three year old Lord John Russell was the obvious successor in Victoria's opinion and he was duly instructed to lead the Government with her friend Lord Clarendon as Foreign Secretary. Gladstone, the Chancellor of the Exchequer, became the leader of the House of Commons and although the Queen did not find him congenial she viewed his appointment with tolerance. Little did she know that in a few years' time he was to assume the aggravating role of the departed Palmerston.

On the 9th of December 1865 the Queen's strongest link with the happy past was broken when her uncle King Leopold, whom she had always regarded as a father, died at Laeken within a few days of his seventy-fifth birthday. Since her very early years she had always depended upon him for advice and with his death she felt her isolation was complete. Beside the tomb of his beloved Charlotte in St. George's Chapel Windsor, she placed his monument; and now she was alone on her pinnacle.

But the living had demands upon her. Her daughter Princess Helena was soon to be married and her second son Prince Alfred was nearing his coming of age. Victoria was anxious that they should receive grants from Parliament but she realized that the public resentment felt towards her retirement was not conducive to Parliamentary generosity. Reluctantly she agreed to open Parliament in person, the first time for five years, and on the

10th of February, 1866, she came to London from Windsor. But the ancient ceremony was conducted like a funeral. The Queen was dressed in black and the royal robes of state were placed on a chair by her side. She did not read the speech herself, but sat motionless, with unseeing eyes, during the ceremony. This was to be the procedure for the six subsequent openings of the Legislature during her reign. But her object had been achieved for Parliament duly made the grants to her children; Princess Helena received a dowry of £30,000 and an annuity of £6,000, while Prince Alfred was given an annuity of £15,000 to be increased to £25,000 on his marriage.

Victoria was satisfied with her domestic affairs and during the summer two marriages brightened her life. Her cousin, Princess Mary of Cambridge, married the Duke of Teck on June the 12th, and on the 5th of July Princess Helena married Prince Christian of Schleswig-Holstein. The marriage of the Duke and Duchess of Teck was of particular significance for Destiny had a prize in store for their future daughter, Princess May. One day she was to become the Queen of England through marrying the Prince of Wales's second son, George, who was then two years old.

Abroad, affairs were giving the Queen cause for anxiety. In America, 1865 had marked the end of the four-year struggle of the Civil War and Victoria's sympathies had been with the losers. A few days before the end Abraham Lincoln had been assassinated and Victoria had written a letter of deepest sympathy to Mrs. Lincoln, likening the tragedy to her own bereavement; and to Victoria widowhood was the greatest tragedy that life could hold.

But though Victoria had been disturbed by the affairs of America in 1865, they were completely forgotten when she contemplated the situation on the Continent in 1866. Events were moving rapidly towards a climax that would affect many members of her own family.

Her opinion of Prussia had changed, for Bismarck, having achieved possession of the Danish duchies, turned against Austria, and his ambitions were revealed. He was determined to dominate the other German states by force of arms and the danger of war was imminent; a war in which many relatives of Victoria would be the protagonists. Her son-in-law, the Crown Prince of Prussia, was opposed in the struggle for supremacy by her son-in-law of Hesse, her cousin of Hanover, and her brother-in-law, the Duke of Saxe-Coburg, who were on the side of Austria. The Queen was almost frantic in her efforts to maintain peace and her Ministry proposed to the King of Prussia that she should act as mediator. The proposal was rejected by Prussia and the tension mounted. Bismarck asserted that the Queen was exercising an unwarranted influence in Prussian affairs through her daughter, whilst at the same time urging the Duke of Saxe-Coburg to intrigue against Prussia.

In England the verbal battle for the second Reform Act was at full blast, but to Victoria this domestic issue was of secondary importance to the terrible consequences of war on the Continent and even the possible defeat of the Government did not affect her attitude.

The storm broke in June 1866 when, as Victoria had feared, Prussia went to war with Austria; and at home Lord Russell's Government was defeated in the House of Commons. Lord John resigned and after a few days Lord Derby was instructed to form a new Ministry.

The Austro-Prussian war lasted only seven weeks and Prussia emerged victorious with the leadership of the whole of Western Germany. The kingdom of Hanover, ruled by Victoria's blind cousin George, was abolished, Hanover becoming a Prussian province. This was a bitter blow to Victoria for Hanover had for 150 years been closely associated with England and but for the Salic law she would have been the Queen.

There was also a reduction in the power and prestige of the other states which had supported Austria and with which she was lineally connected. Judiciously the Duke of Saxe-Coburg, although opposed to Bismarck's designs, had remained neutral and his duchy was left intact. Italy had supported Prussia and as a result Austria lost her last hold on the Italian peninsula. The union of Italy under King Victor Emanuel thus virtually came into being, which was an additional disappointment to Victoria for she had always opposed the unification.

Albert's forecast of a united Germany under Prussian domination was coming true, but it gave Victoria little cause for jubilation, and even this modicum of satisfaction was dissipated by the contempt which Bismarck showed towards the Crown Prince and her daughter, the Crown Princess. But Victoria was still determined to impress upon the public the true greatness of Albert and with this end in view she herself launched into authorship. She issued in 1867, for private circulation, extracts from her diary entitled *Leaves from a Journal of our life in the Highlands from 1848 to 1861*, and in 1868 she made it available to the general public. In her journal she had revealed many intimate details of her private life and the favourable reception given to the publication by press and public alike quite touched her and gave her tremendous satisfaction.

16

" We authors, Ma'am . . ." was an expression often used by Benjamin Disraeli, England's new Prime Minister. He was adept at weaving intricate patterns on the thin ice of flattery and he knew that this reference to her literary efforts always evoked a smile on the Queen's face. To Matthew Arnold he once said : " Everyone likes flattery; and when you come to royalty you should lay it on with a trowel !" He did.

The Queen's gracious and warm reception of Disraeli as her First Minister had been quite unexpected for it was against the opinion Albert had expressed of him. He had said that the Jew Disraeli " had not one single element of a gentleman in his composition." Another important factor against Disraeli was that he had been a devastating critic of Sir Robert Peel and indeed had brought about his downfall. Yet by subtlety, whether sincere or contrived, he won his way into the Queen's esteem. His greatest asset was that he understood women, and they were attracted by his embroidered speech, his epigrams, his cynicism and his exaggerated courtesy. At sixty-four he was no longer handsome for time had channelled deep furrows in his face; a face that was sombre in repose, almost satanic; and all that remained of his long black ringlets was a single curl, dyed black, pressed upon his high forehead; yet his brillant eloquence, bizarre personality, and the sorcery of his intelligence remained undimmed.

The Conservatives came into office in 1866, but two years later

Lord Derby's frequent attacks of gout forced him into retirement. Disraeli, who since 1850 had been the leader of the Conservatives in the House of Commons, urged his Chief to remain in office and himself offered to undertake additional duties. But Derby had made up his mind. He tendered his resignation and at the same time he recommended to the Queen that Disraeli should be appointed as his successor. Victoria was happy to give her assent.

Since her husband's death Victoria's opinion of Disraeli had changed considerably. After the first numbing shock of Albert's death had passed she found great solace in Disraeli's condolences. His sympathies had been expressed in beautiful epistles, in which he had elevated the character of the Prince Consort to idealistic sublimity, indeed his opinions often soared into those flights of perfection, which Victoria had felt, but had herself been unable to express in words. " The Prince," he wrote, " is the only person whom Mr. Disraeli has ever known who realized the Ideal. None with whom he is acquainted have ever approached it. There was in him an union of the manly grace and sublime simplicity, of chivalry with the intellectual splendour of the Attic Academe. The only character in English history that would, in some respects, draw near to him is Sir Philip Sidney; the same high tone, the same universal accomplishments, the same blended tenderness and vigour, the same rare combination of romantic energy and classic repose." Expressions like these sealed his favour with Victoria, but when he first knelt to kiss the Queen's small, white, plump hand his thoughts might well have turned back to the long struggle behind him; his sardonic reply when his colleagues congratulated him was: " Yes, I have climbed to the top of the greasy pole."

His struggle had indeed been long and he had certainly had his ups and downs. His grandfather Benjamin D'Israeli arrived in London from Italy in 1748 with his second wife who had brought him a handsome dowry. D'Israeli was astute and considerably increased their fortune on the London Stock Exchange. They were Jews but kept themselves apart from other Jews; for Mrs. D'Israeli was embittered by the fact that being a Jewess precluded her from entering London's highest social circles.

They had an only son, Isaac, who was a great disappointment

to his parents, for he showed no interest whatsoever in business and devoted himself to the quiet world of books. He was a bibliophile to his dying day and spent his life in the compilation of literary anecdotes. When he was thirty-five he married a gentle, quiet woman who was also of Italian-Jewish descent. Their first child was a girl, Sarah, and their second a boy, born on the 21st of December 1804, was named Benjamin after his grandfather. The children saw little of their father for he spent long periods in seclusion, engrossed in his literary occupation, and they fondly believed him to be a very great writer. When he died he had completed three volumes of his projected *Amenities of Literature* and had been made a D.C.L. of Oxford for his *Commentaries on the Life of Charles I.*

The London Jewish Community also credited him with literary eminence and in 1813 he was nominated as Warden of their Congregation. But Isaac D'Israeli was indifferent to the Jewish rituals and refused the honour in an indignant letter. A fine was levied upon him which he refused to pay, and when the old Benjamin died three years later Isaac dissociated his family from the Jewish religion. His children were baptized as Protestants, for in England Jews and Catholics alike were precluded from many careers and were denied certain civic rights. Thus his son, who was then thirteen, was faced throughout the formative years of his education with the problem of being a Jew with a Christian belief.

But the spirit of ambition that was so lacking in the father burned feverishly in the heart of the son. The solicitor's office in which he began his career soon palled and he began to speculate in stocks and shares. In the meantime, he had met John Murray, the publisher of Sir Walter Scott, through his father's friendship with Murray.

The young Benjamin's next venture was the founding of a daily newspaper and he used Murray's name and prestige to further his plans. But a fall in the Stock Market brought an untimely end to this ambitious undertaking for he suddenly found himself saddled with £7,000 of debts. He was then only twenty years of age.

Next he turned to writing a novel and through the influence of the wife of a barrister named Austen, who was a neighbour of the D'Israeli's, the book was placed with Colburn, a well-known publisher. Unfortunately the novel, *Vivian Grey,* was launched as the anonymous work of an eminent author and despite its early success, when the true identity of the author came to light, it was subjected to a storm of critical abuse and ridicule. To the young Disraeli it appeared to be the end of his ambitions, for twice he had failed, and he had fallen into the hands of moneylenders in order to pay his debts. After a period of semi-retirement, however, he again occupied himself with his writing and with extensive travels in the Near East.

When he next appeared on the London scene he was twenty-five, a handsome, tall young man, elegant, amusing, extravagantly dressed and attractive to women, with something of a literary reputation, a brilliant talker, with an inexhaustible fund of strange stories. The doors of Society were opened to him and the drawing-rooms he found to be the very portals of Parliament. Soon he was the favourite of influential hostesses and through them he met the important political figures of the day. But his first three attempts to enter Parliament as an Independent met with failure.

Benjamin Disraeli, for he had dropped the apostrophe as being too foreign-looking, had made two invaluable friends and they were to bring him success. The first was Mrs. Wyndham Lewis, the wife of a Tory Member of Parliament. She was to become the most devoted friend he had in his life and his worshipping wife. Yet when he had first been introduced to her by a friend of his own age, also a writer, Edward Bulwer Lytton, he had written to his sister, Sarah : " I was introduced ' by particular desire ' to Mrs. Wyndham Lewis, a pretty little woman, a flirt, and a rattle; indeed gifted with a volubility I should think unequalled, and of which I can convey no idea. She told me that she liked ' silent, melancholy men.' I answered ' that I had no doubt of it.' "

The other friend was Lord Lyndhurst, the Tory Lord Chancellor. Despite the difference in their ages, for Lord Lyndhurst was sixty, they became firm friends and Lord Lyndhurst it was who encouraged him to become a Tory candidate. In 1835, Disraeli published his *Vindication of the English Constitution in a Letter to a Noble and Learned Lord* and the success of this work of political philosophy brought him recognition as a young man of great talent. Now his passage was easy for he was backed by Lyndhurst and the husband of Mrs. Wyndham Lewis, who suggested that he should become his fellow-member for Maidstone, a safe Conservative constituency with two seats. On the 27th of July 1837 Lewis and Disraeli were duly elected and Disraeli had gained, through the influence of a woman, the prize which had previously eluded his most determined efforts. His feet were firmly set on the ladder of ambition.

But the hopes he had of immediate acclaim were rudely shattered when he made his first speech. It had been carefully prepared beforehand and was liberally besprinkled with most elaborate phrases and as he rose like an actor before the House he felt confident of the tremendous impact he was about to make. Impact it was, but not the one he expected.

The Members examined with curiosity and astonishment the outlandish figure before them. He wore a bright green coat, a white waistcoat and a large black cravat which framed with his long black ringlets a face of unusual pallor; a most un-English face. They waited for the voice that went with this strange apparition. Hesitantly at first, then gathering confidence it came in a steady flow of ornate phrasing, unusual allegories and strange words. His listeners were dumbfounded, but as the first laugh sounded, they joined together in a chorus of laughter, growing louder and more uproarious as Disraeli struggled to make himself heard. The House was in a pandemonium of amusement with Members rolling in their seats as they struggled to shout " Question!" Then suddenly all was still, as Disraeli's voice rose above the rest, terrifying in its power, and he stood with uplifted arms and shouted : "Ay, sir, and though I sit down now, the time will come when you will hear me." Once again the taste of defeat was bitter and he sat down with his hands holding his head. The great moment had gone.

For a week the incident was the main topic of conversation but as the joke wore thin it was followed by a half shamefaced feeling that they had been shooting at a sitting bird; that perhaps on the whole they had been a little unsportsman-like and when Disraeli next stood up to speak the Members were prepared to give his extravagant sentences a tolerant hearing.

Again he surprised the House. But this time by the calm, quiet, completely commonplace manner in which he made his short speech. There were no frills, extravagances, or long words and as the speech concerned authors' rights he certainly knew what he was talking about—" perhaps the fellow was all right after all ?"

Disraeli had listened to advice and had not tried to dazzle his listeners with his brilliance. His speech had been precise and factual, mundane; the time for eloquence would come.

In the meantime, he was a frequent guest at the house of the Wyndham Lewis's and it was plain to see that Mrs. Wyndham Lewis admired him. Now he realized that she was not the empty-headed creature he had first supposed her to be. Whilst she was not brilliant, she was certainly not the rather stupid creature many said she was. He found that she had a very sane outlook on life and affairs and although she was forty-five, nearly thirteen years older than the aspiring young politician, the gap of years did not affect their relationship.

Six months after his election to Parliament tragedy entered the life of Mrs. Wyndham Lewis; her husband died, and Disraeli hurried to her side to console her in her grief. Gradually their friendship developed and soon they were addressing each other as Dizzy and Mary Anne. When they were together he felt relaxed and happy and he realized he was in love.

The difference in their ages and the fact that her husband had left her a large house at Grosvenor Gate and an income of £4,000 a year, whereas he was already saddled with considerable debts, caused a certain amount of unpleasant gossip. Therefore, when he made his declaration of love, Mary Anne felt that the situation required careful thought and she did not give him her answer immediately. She asked for a year in which to make up her mind.

To the impulsive Disraeli this was tantamount to a refusal and he wrote her a letter in which he repudiated the suggestion that he was interested in her money and ended by saying : " Farewell I will not affect to wish you happiness, for it is not in your nature to obtain it. For a few years you may flutter in some frivolous circle. But the time will come when you will sigh for any heart that could be fond, and despair of one that can be faithful. There will be the penal hour of retribution; then you will think of me with remorse, admiration and despair; then you will recall to your memory the passionate heart that you have forfeited, and the genius you have betrayed."

His letter brought an immediate reply : " For God's sake come to me. I am ill and almost distracted. I will answer all you wish. I never desired you to leave the house, or implied or thought a word of money . . ."

They were married at St. George's, Hanover Square, on the 28th of August 1839 and the flamboyant dandy who had admired Byron and Brummell sobered down to become a happily-married man with a house in Park Lane. The lonely individualist had found a partner whose loyalty was unsurpassed. Lively and gay, she brought happiness into his sombre ambition-filled life and, if on occasions she was apt to be ridiculous, laughter was never dared whilst Disraeli was there to defend her. Not once did he utter or allow a single word of criticism against his beloved Mary Anne and she repaid him with a devotion that was touching in its intensity.

An incident has been often quoted of Mary Anne accompanying her husband to the Commons. As he alighted her fingers were trapped in the carriage door, but although in great pain she did not utter a sound so that he would not be disturbed before entering the House. This action typified the unselfish devotion that remained constant to the end.

During the year of their marriage, which was also the year of Queen Victoria's wedding, another brilliant politician was married. His name was William Ewart Gladstone and a great future had been predicted for him; it was said that one day he was certain to become the Prime Minister. He met his future wife Catherine in Italy but theirs was not a tempestuous court-ship. She was the daughter of Lady Glynne and was already interested in politics for her brother the second Earl Spencer had formerly led the Liberal Party in the House of Commons as Lord Althorp. In addition, she had influence at Court for her sister was Lady Lyttelton, a Lady-in-Waiting who enjoyed the Queen's confidence (she was appointed governess to the royal children in 1842).

Catherine was travelling in Italy in a large family coach with her mother and sister when she first saw William Gladstone in Florence.

The handsome young statesman was introduced to the Glynne family and immediately formed an attachment to the pleasant and pious Catherine. Early in life he had wished to become a clergyman and he found the quiet, religious girl held very similar views on life to his own. When he returned to England he again sought the companionship of Catherine and duly proposed marriage. They were married in a quiet village church and on the afternoon of their wedding day they read the Bible together. This was to be the keynote of their life and even their cook was chosen only after a long discussion on religious matters.

William Ewart Gladstone was five years younger than Disraeli but had entered Parliament five years before him. He was the son of a wealthy Liverpool manufacturer and had been educated at Eton and Christchurch, Oxford. When he gave his maiden speech in 1833, his handsome, typically English face, grave demeanour, dark clothes and convincing oratory, had created exactly the right impression. Unlike Disraeli, he had been received with grave approbation and satisfied nods from the Members. The difference in their Parliamentary débuts was typical of the complete dissimilarity of their characters, personalties and opinions. They were destined to be life-long antagonists in the political arena. Both were brilliant leaders; but they always followed different paths.

For twenty years as they climbed in the esteem of their respective parties each watched the progress of the other with feelings of bitter rivalry. It was a battle of giants, for they towered above their contemporaries, who were spellbound as they watched the flashing interplay of the verbal rapiers wielded by two of the greatest statesmen that ever lived.

Disraeli had the greater genius, the more subtle intellect; but Gladstone was the greater orator, with more power and vigour in his attack. One was epigrammatic, flashy and brilliant, the other described his own method of fervent oratory when he gave the advice: " Collect facts and figures as accurately and conclusively as you can, and drive them home as if all the world must irresistibly take your own eager interest in them." Gladstone had a magnificent flow of eloquence, a wonderful voice, beautifully modulated, yet powerful and ringing. With the dramatic power and the flashing eyes of a great actor he held his audience enthralled; often suddenly startling his listeners from their immobility by crashing his fist down upon the table. His opponent was the perfect foil, for as the great voice thundered Disraeli's drooping figure would sink lower and lower, until at last with dramatic slowness he would rise to his feet, indolently confident as he carefully re-arranged the objects disturbed by the forceful fist. Then, with a smile, he would make his courteous, yet barbed reply. Always, whenever they clashed, the drama of the House was heightened as expectantly the Members waited for the inevitable display of fireworks. They were never disappointed. Disraeli and Gladstone were bitter antagonists, but posterity has forever linked their names together.

17

Soon after Disraeli became Prime Minister the Queen wrote to the Queen of Prussia: " Mr. Disraeli has achieved his present high position entirely by his ability, his wonderful, happy disposition, and the astounding way in which he carried through the Reform Bill, and I have nothing but praise for him. One thing which has for some time *predisposed* me in his favour is his great admiration for my beloved Albert."

Under the warm rays of his enthusiasm Victoria shed some of her grief and made occasional public appearances. On March the 10th she held a Drawing-Room at Buckingham Palace and on the 20th of June she reviewed 27,000 volunteers in Windsor Great Park. Two days later she gave a garden party (or " breakfast " as a garden party was called in those days) in the gardens of Buckingham Palace.

She was enlivened by his letters, " written in his best novel style," and delighted when he presented her with a specially bound set of his novels. In return she gave him a copy of *Leaves from the Journal of Our Life in the Highlands* and the phrase, " We authors Ma'am ", still brought a smile of appreciation to her stern face.

But the happy association lasted for only ten months. Ireland was in a state of unrest and violence was rife. The solution,

Gladstone insisted, was the disestablishment of the Protestant Irish Church. It was wrong, he said, that the Catholics should be forced to maintain a State Protestant Church and he proposed the separation of Church and State in Ireland. The General Election in December was fought on this religious issue and resulted in an overwhelming victory for the Liberal Party. Disraeli resigned and his brief tenure of office was ended without waiting for Parliament to meet. Reluctantly the Queen accepted Gladstone as her new First Minister.

Although Disraeli was already feeling the weight of his years and was suffering from asthma and rheumatism he was unwilling to withdraw from the struggle. He declined the Queen's offer of a peerage and an honourable retirement. Instead, he requested that his wife should be given the honour he was unable to accept, and the Queen, who was well aware of the devotion between them, was happy to assent. Thus, on the 30th of November 1868, Mary Anne became a peeress in her own right as Viscountess Beaconsfield whilst her husband remained Mr. Disraeli.

Judiciously he decided to bide his time before again doing battle with the doughty Gladstone, who was ready and willing to resist any attacks on his newly-won glory, fortified as he was by a huge majority of 128. Dizzy sank into an apparent torpor, but behind his bored, indolent expression his brain was alert, patiently waiting for the time when the fiery Gladstone would have expended his energy. In the meantime his leisure was spent at Hughenden Manor, a huge red-brick house set in beautiful grounds, two miles from High Wycombe. The Manor had been his castle since a few years after his marriage. Although saddled with £20,000 worth of debts at the time he had pledged his inheritance and borrowed from his friend Lord George Bentinck to raise the £35,000 purchase price. It had been a gamble and a struggle, but he had been able to welcome Mary Anne to their country home with: " It is done. You are now the lady of Hughenden." Here there was peace and he settled down quietly to the writing of a new novel. It was published under the title of *Lothair* and it became a tremendous success; the literary topic of the day. To his colleagues the novel was a bitter pill, for they would have preferred that their Leader devoted his energies to the unseating of the triumphant Gladstone.

Victoria, too, might well have preferred it for she was not happy with her Prime Minister; indeed she was most unhappy. Although Gladstone was sixty he was driven by what seemed boundless energy and even his arduous duties as Prime Minister were not sufficient to diminish his vigour. His leisure was spent in walking, sometimes thirty miles in a day, or felling trees. With the axe in his hands he was happy, as men are today with their golf clubs. But his greatest energies were reserved for his political duties and the Queen found herself in the position of a tree being attacked by the axe of reform; finance, education, the Services, parliamentary elections, Ireland, religion, justice; each blow was something different. Drafts, papers, documents, proposals, flooded upon her until she became too burdened to object. How she must have longed for the quiet, efficient, industrious Albert to unravel and explain the bewildering mass of documents.

Mr. Gladstone she could never ask. She even dreaded the thought of his involved, punctilious explanations. And his very manner roused her antagonism, particularly his attitude towards herself. He made her feel like a disembodied spirit, for he treated her with reverence and awe as though she was not of this world. Her oft-quoted statement: "He speaks to me as if I were a public meeting," has the epigrammatic ring of Disraeli, who often said: "Gladstone treats the Queen like a public department; I treat her like a woman."

Victoria wanted to be treated like a Queen, but also like a woman, and this Gladstone never understood, with the result that dislike turned into positive antipathy and the more obsequious he became the more distasteful did she find his presence. The Queen was a problem Gladstone could never solve, but although disappointed, even mortified, by her animosity he never relaxed the perfect correctness of his attitude. And Victoria's feelings towards him never softened; not even when he gallantly fought in her defence against the anti-royalist attacks upon the size of her income and expenditure.

In 1871 Radical opinion was stimulated by the flight of Napoleon III and the formation of a republic in France and it was openly prophesied that Queen Victoria would be the last monarch of England. Her seclusion lent force to the argument that the monarchy was too expensive, for her people were denied the pageantry they expected. A pamphlet entitled *Tracts for the Times, What does she do with it?* by Solomon Temple, which had a widespread circulation, professed to be a revealing estimate of her income and expenditure. The writer asserted that only a small proportion of her income was used " to defray the expenses of her royal household and to support the honour and dignity of the Crown." The remainder was being used to swell her private fortune, which was estimated to be £5,000,000. The facts were grossly misrepresented but when Sir Charles Dilke, M.P. for Chelsea, revealed that she paid no income tax the agitation seemed justified and " What does she do with it?" became the question on everyone's lips.

At this time the Queen's fourth daughter, Princess Louise, was about to be married to the Marquis of Lorne, the Duke of Argyll's eldest son, and the Queen asked Parliament to give the bride a dowry of £30,000 with an annuity of £6,000. To conciliate public feeling Victoria again opened Parliament in person and the manœuvre was again successful—Princess Louise's dowry and annuity were granted. Two months later, the Queen asked for an annuity of £15,000 for Prince Arthur, who had recently come of age. This amount was also granted, but only after attempts had been made in Parliament to reduce the amount to £10,000. Those financial discussions came at an unfortunate time for everyone wanted to know what the Queen did with her money. In Parliament questions were being asked and twice Gladstone spoke in her defence, insisting vehemently that the Queen's entire income was at her own disposal.

But the agitators were not silenced and on March 19th 1872 Sir Charles Dilke pressed for a full enquiry into the Queen's expenditure. Gladstone exerted the full force of eloquence in her defence and the proposal was rejected by a huge majority of 274. The republican storm died down, but the grievance still remained and the tide of the Queen's unpopularity was at its flood.

Public feeling had earlier been roused against the royal family in 1870, when the Prince of Wales appeared in court as a witness in a divorce case. Two of the Prince's friends had been cited as co-respondents by Sir Charles Mordaunt in a petition for divorce against his wife. Allegations were also made against the Prince for he had written a number of letters to Lady Mordaunt.

Although his innocence in the affair was proved beyond doubt (his letters were described in court as " stupidly honest letters ") it was evident that as a member of the royal family he had been mixing with the wrong people and after the trial he was publicly hissed.

Victoria escaped from the unhappiness of the public's vituperation for a few weeks during the March and April of 1872 when she visited her stepsister the Princess Féodore at Baden-Baden. The visit however was a sad one for Féodore was seriously ill. They were very fond of each other and Victoria was shocked a few months later when she received the sad news that her stepsister had died in September. In June Victoria had lost another friend when Dr. Norman Macleod her Scottish chaplain died. He had been a trusted confidant and she felt that another strong link with her " dearest angel " and his beloved Scotland had been severed.

In Scotland the Queen had spent the happiest days of her life and her regular visits to Balmoral still provided her greatest pleasure in life; for there she was surrounded by sacred memories. But even this solace became the subject of criticism and malicious gossip. John Brown, who had been the Prince Consort's gillie had now become the Queen's personal attendant and in Scotland he was always by her side, even sleeping in a bedroom next to hers. It was even suggested that a secret marriage had taken place. The rumours arose because of the Queen's peculiar devotion to one who had shared her beloved Albert's brief periods of recreation. The bluff, rugged Brown had a kind heart beneath a rough exterior and he had been the Prince's favourite servant. To Victoria he was a constant reminder of Albert, a spiritual link between the living and the dead, and the extreme tolerance with which she regarded him encouraged familiarity and liberty of speech. The simple Highlander treated the Queen like a father treats a wayward child, bullying her for her own good; and meekly she obeyed his commands to put on her shawl, change her damp footwear, or go indoors because it was raining. She found relief in depending upon someone whose loyalty was beyond question, and allowed this trusted servant to adopt an attitude of authority which as Queen she denied even her closest friends; until they too accepted the peculiar associa-

tion of personalties, realizing that old family retainers do sometimes become a part of their masters or mistresses. In 1874, Lord
Cairns, the Lord Chancellor, said: " What a coarse animal that
Brown is. Oh yes, I know the Ball could not go on without him.
But I did not conceive it possible that anyone could behave so
roughly as he does to the Queen." To quarrel with Brown,
however, was very dangerous. Prince Alfred, the Duke of Edinburgh, on one occasion was annoyed with Brown and for days
completely ignored him. The Queen's Private Secretary realized
that the Queen would take Brown's side and wisely patched up
the quarrel with apologies on both sides.

John Brown, who had been a stable-boy employed by Sir
Robert Gordon the previous owner of Balmoral, first became a
royal servant in 1849 and in the twelve years prior to Albert's
death he had reached a position of unique trust. When Victoria
was inconsolable at Osborne a few weeks after her husband
died, John Brown brought her favourite pony from Balmoral to
induce her to take exercise. The manœuvre was successful and
at the time when the Queen was unable to face the world she
found solace in being led through the peaceful grounds at
Osborne by this rugged, honest retainer, who shared her silences.
This in itself was an unforgettable memory. The years had not
dimmed the comforting thought of his presence and he accompanied the Queen on her travels abroad. In Germany and France
the unusual relationship was not understood and he was treated
almost as a state personage.

Victoria had an admirable trait in her character in that she
was particularly solicitous concerning her servants' welfare and
always tolerant when their misdemeanours were reported to her.
Consequently she ignored Brown's over-fondness for whisky and
she allowed the same latitude to other servants. Her only comment when she was told that a footman at Windsor had been
drunk and had dropped a lighted lamp on a carpet was: " Poor
man."

The Queen in her *Journal of the Highlands* made many references to John Brown and in 1866 she wrote of him: " His attention, care, and faithfulness cannot be exceeded; and the state of
my health, which of late years has been sorely tried and
weakened, renders such qualifications most valuable, and indeed

most needful in a constant attendant upon all occasions."

In 1872, John Brown proved his worth when Arthur O'Connor, a seventeen-year-old youth, attempted to fire a pistol at the Queen outside Buckingham Palace. O'Connor was roughly seized by John Brown and it was found that the pistol was not loaded. He was sentenced to twelve months' imprisonment and twenty strokes of the birch.

That the Queen's association with John Brown was perfectly innocent, although perhaps unwise, was obvious to anyone who knew of her rigid, moral integrity; but she was attacked in Scottish newspapers and there were dozens of ribald jokes bandied around the dinner tables in London. The insults and criticisms hurt Victoria but did not in the least lessen her friendship with Brown. She had no intention of hiding it from the world and instead in her second Highland Journal his name appeared on almost every page. John Brown died in 1883, the year before her second journal was published, and she dedicated it : " To my loyal Highlanders and especially to the memory of my devoted personal attendant and faithful friend John Brown ". At Balmoral the Queen erected a statue to her " devoted personal servant and faithful friend ".

18

For another faithful friend, Benjamin Disraeli, 1872 was also an unhappy year. Indeed, it was the unhappiest year of his life. On the 15th of September, the being he loved most in all the world, his beloved Mary Anne, died. She was eighty-one. Theirs had been a long and happy marriage. Mary Anne had often said : " He married me for my money, but now he would marry me for love "—and it was true.

For six years Mary Anne had known that she had a cancer of the stomach, but although she was often in great pain she tried to hide the awful truth from her husband. But Dizzy also knew and thought he was hiding his knowledge from her. Sometimes they were both ill and then they sent letters to each other and always there was love. One letter was : " Dizzy to Mrs. Dizzy : I have nothing to tell you except that I love you, which I fear, you will find rather dull."

Throughout their long marriage Mary Anne had cared for Dizzy with a thoughtfulness that spared him the petty worries of life. She was wife and mother in one. He had been her knight-errant, whilst his true feelings were expressed on the flyleaf of his novel *Sybil*: " I would inscribe these volumes to one whose noble spirit and gentle nature ever prompt her to sympathize with the suffering; to one whose sweet voice has often encouraged, and whose taste and judgment have ever guided, their pages; the most severe of critics but—a perfect wife."

Mary Anne's death was a terrible blow, and for many months the normally impassive face of Disraeli was torn with grief and he sought only the company of a few intimate friends. Life seemed to have lost its purpose and he was constantly moved to tears as odd incidents reminded him of the tender devotion he had lost. For more than thirty years Mary Anne had cut Dizzy's hair and as he sorted through the papers and old letters at Hughenden he came across a bundle of small envelopes in each of which was a lock of his hair. He was never to forget her and for the rest of his life his letters were edged with black. Even his opponent Gladstone felt sympathy for him in his grief and sent him a letter offering his sincere condolences; truly sincere, because he realized how tragic would have been his own grief if he had lost Catherine.

It was expected that his bereavement would bring about Disraeli's retirement, but instead the old statesman sought escape from his sorrow in political activity. As it happened the time was propitious. Gladstone's plan for the pacification of Ireland had failed, trade was bad and the enthusiasm for Liberalism was waning. In 1874, there was a General Election and the Conservatives were returned to office with a clear majority of fifty seats. Disraeli, the actor, was welcomed back on the stage with all the warm applause given to the return of an old favourite. The Queen was more pleased than anyone and made no attempt to conceal her delight and gratification.

The seventy-year-old Prime Minister, with his great capacity for affection, now turned all the warmth of his feelings upon Victoria, his Sovereign Lady. Tragedy was a bond between them and in each other they found consolation and happiness. After the cold, obsequious attitude of Gladstone the Queen found Dis-

raeli's adulation revitalizing and she smiled whenever he entered
the room. He was fascinating, witty, eloquent, charming, and
the tedious documents became pleasant subjects for discussion.
Gradually she began to emerge from the shell of her seclusion.
Her countenance became less forbidding and the imperious
hauteur softened. He even persuaded her to make semi-state
appearances and she attended a concert at the Royal Albert
Hall; reviewed troops at Aldershot; distributed medals at Gos-
port to heroes of the Ashanti War; presented colours to her
father's regiment, the Royal Scots, at Balmoral; opened a wing
at the London Hospital; and inspected the Albert Memorial in
Kensington Gardens. Under the influence of Disraeli's charm
she began to live again.

But her greatest happiness was during his hours of audience,
then his flattering remarks delicately embroidered with
romanticism made her feel like a girl again and she moved
flutteringly about the room with all the elation of youth. To
Disraeli, carried away by his own imaginings she became " The
Faery " and the Spenserian allusion enchanted him. She was the
centre of a world of phantasy, surrounded by his poetic imagery
and dreams. For a gift of snowdrops he thanked her in a letter
full of flowery phrases : " Yesterday eve, there appeared in
Whitehall Gardens, a delicate-looking case, with a royal inscription, which, when he opened, he thought, at first, that your
Majesty had graciously bestowed upon him the stars of your
Majesty's principal orders. And, indeed, he was so much impressed with this graceful illusion, that, having a banquet, where
there were many stars and ribbons, he could not resist the
temptation, by placing some snowdrops on his breast, of showing that he, too, was decorated by a gracious Sovereign.

" Then, in the middle of the night, it occurred to him, that it
might all be enchantment, and that, perhaps it was a Faery gift
and came from another monarch : Queen Titania, gathering
flowers, with her Court, in a soft and seagirt isle, and sending
magic blossoms, which, they say turn the heads of those who
receive them."

A dream it might be, but the Constitution was real; the
Queen's slightest wishes became his commands; unless they did
not coincide with the Government's policy, then, by tact and

gentle persuasion, he reconciled her views to his own. If sometimes he failed, then his graceful, humble acceptance of the inevitable made her forget his opposition. Fortunately the Government's policy was usually in line with her own.

But Disraeli was no idle dreamer, he was a man of action and he paid his tributes not only in words but in deeds. In November 1875 he learned from the editor of the *Pall Mall Gazette* that the Khedive of Egypt was short of money and was about to pledge his shares in the Suez Canal. An option had been given to a French syndicate for £3,680,000 and only a few days remained before it expired. Disraeli realized that the canal was vital to Britain's overseas trade particularly with India, Australia and New Zealand. But a payment of £4,000,000 needed Government sanction and Parliament was not in session. It was a race against time, but the day before the option expired he found the money.

He had told the Queen of his plans and now he implied that he had done it for her benefit and hers alone. He wrote : " It is just settled. You have it, Madam . . . Four millions sterling! and almost immediately. There was only one firm that could do it— Rothschild's. They behaved admirably; advanced the money at a low rate, and the entire interest of the Khedive is now yours, Madam."

The coup was a tremendous triumph for Disraeli and Victoria was delighted, but carried away by his own enthusiasm Dizzy suggested that the Queen ought to become the Empress of India. The suggestion captured her imagination and in the following year her Prime Minister was forced to introduce what he knew would be an unpopular Bill for the change of Royal Title. The name Empress sounded foreign to English ears and the change aroused bitter antagonism. There was a public outcry against the adoption of the proposed title and it was angrily opposed in both Houses.

Every stage of the Bill was a battle but Disraeli fought with tireless energy and his persuasive eloquence wore down the opposition. Victoria became the Empress of India and she was delighted. As a conciliatory measure Disraeli had agreed that the title would follow " Defender of the Faith " and would only apply to acts concerning India. The Queen's letter of gratitude to her Prime Minister, however, was signed " Victoria Regina et Imperatrix."

Disraeli was seventy-two and in failing health. He was finding his arduous duties a heavy burden and he contemplated retirement. The prospect of losing her Prime Minister and friend dismayed Victoria and as a counter-measure she suggested that he should enter the House of Lords, " where the fatigue would be *far less* and where he would be able to *direct* everything." So, in August 1876, Benjamin Disraeli became the Earl of Beaconsfield, Viscount Hughenden of Hughenden, and the fantastic dreams of a young man turned into reality.

But the new Earl's period of respite was brief for in the following December the dangerous Eastern Question, which had remained dormant since the Crimean War, suddenly threatened the safety of British interests in the Mediterranean. The Turkish subject races in the Balkans had risen in revolt and Russia was preparing to intervene on their behalf.

Beaconsfield was strongly in favour of supporting Turkey, but whilst the Turks strove to suppress the rebellion Gladstone reappeared on the political scene denouncing the Turkish barbarities. The two giants of English politics again came to grips.

In the meantime, whilst Beaconsfield was playing a hazardous game of bluff in attempting to prevent Russia going to war with Turkey by a threat of British intervention, he was faced on one side with the Queen who demanded in no uncertain terms that Britain should go to war with Russia and on the other side with the Foreign Secretary, Lord Derby,* who strongly advocated peace. The Prime Minister endeavoured to play off one against the other and received recriminations from both sides.

In April 1877 Russia declared war on Turkey and before the end of the year had emerged victorious. The Queen was disgusted and once again Beaconsfield contemplated retirement. He attended the Congress of Berlin which was held to determine the peace terms and succeeded in restoring Britain's prestige. When he returned to England with the news of his diplomatic success the Queen was mollified, and Lord Salisbury who had accompanied him replaced Lord Derby as Foreign Secretary.

* The fifteenth Earl of Derby.

But more important was the fact that a war between Britain and Russia had been averted.

Beaconsfield's popularity was at its height, but Parliament still had two more years to run and the public memory is short. At the General Election in 1880 Gladstone's storming oratory won the day; the Liberals were returned to office.

After Disraeli's defeat the Queen sent him a letter in which she said that in future they would not use the formal third person " when we correspond—which I hope we shall on many a private subject and without anyone being astonished or offended, and even more without anyone knowing about it." The correspondence which delighted them both was not to be continued however for more than a few months since Disraeli was very ill.

His long and eventful life was drawing to a close and he died on the 19th of April 1881. His death was a grievous blow to Victoria and from Osborne she wrote: " His devotion and kindness to me, his wise counsels, his great gentleness combined with firmness, his one thought of the honour and glory of the country, and his unswerving loyalty to the throne make the death of my dear Lord Beaconsfield a national calamity. My grief is great and lasting."

For his funeral Victoria sent a magnificent wreath of primroses with the inscription " *His* favourite flower ". From this arose the legend that Beaconsfield had especially liked the primrose—in fact he had never cared at all for such a humble wild flower—and the subsequent naming of the Primrose League. By " His " Victoria had meant the Prince Consort's! He was buried beside his wife at Hughenden and in the church there a tablet was placed bearing the Queen's inscription: " To the dear and honoured memory of Benjamin, Earl of Beaconsfield, this memorial is placed by his grateful sovereign and friend Victoria R.I. *Kings love him that speaketh right—Proverbs xvi. 13. February 27, 1882.*"

Queen Victoria viewed Gladstone's return to office with distaste. She received him with " perfect courtesy " but with her customary candour made no pretence of hiding her lack of enthusiasm. Her fears were justified, for Gladstone's second administration was a succession of alarms and failures; with disturbances in Egypt, Afghanistan, India, Ireland and South Africa.

Before twelve months had passed the Government was involved in troubles with Egypt. The Khedive's War Minister, Arabi Pasha, led a revolt against the Khedive's authority and by the summer of 1882 he was in control of the Egyptian Government. Since 1878 England and France to protect their interests had made themselves jointly responsible for maintaining order in Egypt. In 1882 France declined to intervene on the Khedive's behalf but Victoria had formed her own opinion. She was determined that England should suppress the revolt and immediately she reached her decision she began to agitate for action. Gladstone was reluctant to take violent steps, but the Queen was adamant and he was forced to yield to her demands.

Even then Victoria would not rest until the expeditionary force was on its way and she bombarded the Minister of War with advice and suggestions concerning equipment and supplies. By September victory was won and the Queen celebrated the good news by ordering a bonfire to be lit on the same cairn around which Albert had danced to celebrate the fall of Sebastopol.

The Queen's joy was a little premature for in the following year there was again trouble in Egypt. The Sudanese, in the southern province of Egypt, led by the Mahdi (the Guide), a fanatical mystic, rose in revolt against the Egyptian troops policing their territory. Two British expeditions failed to restore order and towards the end of 1883 the Mahdi's followers were threatening the Suez Canal. Victoria, belligerent as ever, demanded vigorous action, and early in 1884 a strong British force under the command of Sir Gerald Graham was moved south from Cairo. The Mahdi's troops were put to flight in the battles of El Teb and Tamar, but Gladstone made the mistake of withdrawing the British troops to Cairo leaving the isolated Egyptian garrisons in the Sudan at the mercy of the rebels. Again Victoria demonstrated her foresight by recommending that immediate action be taken to relieve the loyal Egyptian troops. But it was months later before the Government moved and then only because of the clamour of the Press. General Gordon, by reason of his previous influence with the Sudanese, was sent out to parley with the rebels for the relief of the garrisons.

Gordon realized soon after his arrival in Khartoum, the capital of the insurgent territory, that he had little chance of success and he recommended the appointment of an Egyptian as Governor-General of the Sudan to placate the rebels. The man suggested for the post was Zobeir, a rebel chieftan whom Gordon believed possessed the influence and following to supplant the Mahdi. Zobier was a villainous character and even Gordon, his sponsor, described him as " the greatest slave-hunter who ever existed."

Unfortunately this description reached London and the Anti-Slavery Society agitated against his appointment. The Queen was in favour of Gordon's recommendation and she was backed by expert opinion, but in the Cabinet there was dissension and finally they rejected Zobeir.

In the meantime Gordon's position became desperate. In April 1884 Khartoum was beseiged.

General Gordon himself was not unduly perturbed. There was about six months' supply of food and a force of 8,000 men in the garrison. He was confident that they could hold out for many months against " a feeble lot of stinking Dervishes."

The Queen was among the first to realize the true gravity of the situation and in March she telegraphed Lord Hartington, the Secretary of War: "It is alarming. General Gordon is in danger; you are bound to try to save him. You have incurred fearful responsibilities."

The telegraph wires between Khartoum and Cairo had been cut and soon the only news that reached England was based on alarming rumours. Public feeling was aroused and the alarm spread throughout the country. Mass meetings were held denouncing the Government for not taking action and the Prime Minister had to bear the brunt of the attack.

At this time Gladstone was at the peak of his popularity. His old rival had gone and he towered above his contemporaries with not one to challenge his supremacy. He stood alone; a dedicated, religious man of unimpeachable virtue and undeviating principles. But his very rigidity prevented him from understanding the situation. In the first place he had opposed Gordon's appointment and had eventually agreed only in the belief that Gordon's duties would not consist of much more than making a report.

As Gladstone saw the situation, Gordon was an agitator who

was remaining in Khartoum in order to incite the British Government to send forces to the Sudan and so bring about the downfall of the Mahdi. That there had been a breakdown in communications between Khartoum and Cairo, Gladstone contended, was insufficient reason to believe that Gordon was unable to escape; in any case there was no desperate need for relief as Gordon could hold out for months. Having decided that there was no urgency Gladstone was determined to investigate every angle of the situation and to consider each step before making a move. The wild clamour of public agitation and abuse left him quite unmoved.

The months passed whilst the Government vacillated and it was September before the relief expedition left England. It did not reach Khartoum until the 28th of January 1885, and then it was too late. General Gordon had been killed two days before.

The news of the tragedy shocked the country and anger mingled with grief. Victoria was furious and openly denounced the Government for not following her advice. But her greatest indignation was directed against Gladstone and she sent him a telegram blaming him for General Gordon's death. The whole nation was behind the Queen in discrediting the Government and Gladstone's removal from office seem imminent. About this time the Queen expressed her feelings in a letter to her Private Secretary :

" Mr. Gladstone never once has told her the different views of his colleagues. She is kept completely in the dark—and when they have quarrelled over it and decided amongst themselves he comes and tries to *force* this on her. The Queen feels greatly aggrieved at the utter ignorance in which she is kept. It is very wrong and Mr. Gladstone cannot expect the Queen to have any confidence in a Minister who never tells her the different views of the different people in the Cabinet. He speaks of the result, of ' one or two members,' etc., and she stands alone and unsupported and unable to know what goes on ! The Queen has never been treated so badly by any Minister or Ministers in this respect as the *present*. Sir Henry cannot wonder if the Queen would not be sorry if Mr. Gladstone retired."

On June 8 1885 the Liberals were defeated on their budget proposals and the following day Gladstone resigned. The Queen made no attempt to conceal her delight and invited Lord Salisbury, Beaconsfield's successor as leader of the Conservative Party, to form a Government. He took office on the 24th of June. The Queen opened Parliament in January 1886 (it was the last time she took part in the ceremony) but her pleasure was short-lived, for five days later Lord Salisbury's Government was unpredictably defeated and Gladstone returned to office for the third time. The Irish Nationalists supported the Liberals and the Conservatives were left in a hopeless minority.

The battle between the Queen and Gladstone began almost immediately. He was intent upon giving Home Rule to Ireland, a measure which the Queen had always opposed from the day of her coronation, when she had taken the oath to preserve the union of the two kingdoms. Their views were irreconcilable. Whilst the Government was being formed the Queen forcibly expressed her opinion against the separation to her Prime Minister and she was surprised and bitterly angry when the Bill was introduced by Gladstone. His speech lasted three and a half hours and was stirring in its eloquence. At every opportunity, to everyone she met, Victoria freely expressed her views and denounced Mr. Gladstone's action as a breach of faith. She was in a constant state of trepidation but at the General Election of 1886, to her intense relief, the majority of the nation agreed with her political views.

Of his farewell audience with the Queen, Gladstone wrote in his diary: " The Queen was in good spirits; her manners altogether pleasant. She made me sit at once. Asked after my wife as we began, and sent a kind message to her as we ended. About me personally, I think, her single remark was that I should require some rest. I remember that on a closing audience in 1874, she said she felt sure I might be reckoned upon to support the throne. She did not say anything of the sort today. Her mind and opinions have been seriously warped, and I respect her for the scrupulous avoidance of anything which could have seemed to indicate a desire on her part to claim anything in common with me."

With thankful relief the Queen welcomed the return of Lord Salisbury, the colleague of her faithful friend, and the new association brought back a flood of happy memories.

Suddenly she came out of the seclusion to which she had returned after Disraeli's death and made a number of public appearances, sometimes driving through the streets in an open carriage in the rain on her way to take part in official ceremonies.

An interesting anecdote of this period is given by the Queen's Private Secretary, Sir Henry Ponsonby, concerning the ceremony of opening the new Parliament in 1886. At that time the Controller in the Lord Chamberlain's Department was Sir Spencer Ponsonby-Fane and he was responsible for the safe conduct of the crown from the Tower to the House of Lords. He complained " that all the protection he had in the royal carriage was two ' puffing Beefeaters ' who walked on either side as fast as they could manage." On a previous occasion he put the crown in a hat-box and travelled in an ordinary four-wheeler. This, he said, was the safest method, but if it was to be taken by coach then he wanted an escort of Life Guards. Otherwise with the two Beefeaters " half-a-dozen determined men could make short work of it and carry off the whole thing before my friends recovered their wind." In future a cavalry escort was supplied.

19

Meanwhile, great changes had taken place in the Queen's private life. The marriages of her children and the resultant grandchildren had extended her family circle and now domestic interests demanded more and more of her attentions. She had even become tolerant in her attitude towards her youngest daughter Princess Beatrice.

Throughout her life the shy young Princess had been the constant companion of her mother and the prop upon which the Queen's sorrow had always leaned. On the night of Albert's death Victoria, nearly demented with grief, had carried the four-year-old Beatrice from her cot to her own bed, seeking solace by holding the sleeping child in her arms. It was a solace that was to last for years.

When Beatrice came of marriageable age the Queen had been horrified by the prospect of losing her and, when the Princess wished to marry Prince Henry of Battenberg, Victoria refused to speak to her daughter for six months. Victoria frowned on the introduction of a subject of conversation by anyone other than herself, but in particular she absolutely forbade any mention of marriage when Princess Beatrice was present. Never again did she permit Beatrice to be alone with a member of the male sex; but in 1885 the Queen relented and gave permission for Princess Beatrice to marry the man she loved, Prince Henry. The wedding took place on the 23rd of July and the Princess was granted the usual dowry of £30,000 and an annuity of £6,000. She was the last of the Queen's nine children to marry, but the Queen was still reluctant to part with her and insisted that the Princess and her husband must remain at her side. Fortunately it was a happy association for the family circle was enlivened by Prince Henry's genial manner and gay disposition.

The Royal Family now numbered more than fifty persons ruled by the matriarchal presence of Queen Victoria, sedate, yet domineering. But the old Queen, as is often the way with grandmothers, was now more tolerant towards her grandchildren than she had ever been towards her own children.

The blot on her domestic happiness was the conduct and behaviour of her eldest son Albert Edward, the Prince of Wales. To him she was unrelenting and he in consequence was always in tremendous awe of his mother. He had had an unhappy childhood for neither of his parents had shown him any affection. They had branded him, quite openly, as stupid and lazy, and they increased his sense of isolation by denying him the companionship of friends of his own age. In 1861, following the Prince Consort's death, the Queen's lack of interest turned to dislike and she became determined that her son should not be allowed to play any part in political affairs.

He idled his time away in pleasure, and when he gained his freedom by marrying Princes Alexandra of Denmark he immediately began to enjoy life to the full. Around him at Marlborough House he collected a circle of frivolous, care-free, dissolute companions and beautiful women—mainly actresses, free-and-easy society ladies and demi-mondaines (harlots who rode in Hyde Park and were known as " pretty horse-breakers ").

Princess Alexandra occupied herself with her children and turned a blind eye on her husband's peccadilloes. The Queen, however, was very annoyed and disturbed by her son's behaviour;

but she realized that it was a code of conduct prevalent throughout society and she wrote an indignant letter to *The Times*
condemning the dangers and evils of the general laxity of
behaviour. Strangely enough the letter was not published in *The
Times* until five years later, and certainly had little effect.

Victorian morality is a myth, created mainly by the Victorian
novelists and biographers who wrote their books for a section of
the middle-classes who represented Nonconformity and hypocrisy. At the beginning of Victoria's reign the religious revival
which had taken place during the last years of George III's
reign, followed by the preachings of the Evangelists during the
reign of George IV, began to take effect. A few years later there
was a reaction against Puritanism resulting in the standard of
morals in England becoming worse than anywhere else in the
civilized world. For almost the whole of Victoria's reign, certainly
until the 'eighties, England was a hot-bed of immorality. The gas-
lit streets of London were flesh-markets; brothels and night-
houses abounded on all sides, and even *The Times* carried adver-
tisements of cures for venereal diseases.

During the eighteenth century the night-life of London was
centred in the Covent Garden area, where the taverns, coffee-
houses, and brothels were situated, but with the installation of
gas lighting in 1807 there was a migration by the majority of
the harlots to the West End. Burlington Arcade became the
whores' paradise and they soon overflowed into Regent Street,
where Nash's magnificent covered promenade along both sides
of the street provided excellent shelter. In 1848 the prostitutes in
Regent Street were so numerous that the shopkeepers objected
to the continual parade past their windows as they believed it
was affecting their sales. In consequence, London's most beautiful thoroughfare was despoiled when the 270 iron colonnades
were removed. But the harlots continued to throng Regent Street
and the Victorian prostitutes' approach of " Are you good-
natured, dear?" was still a familiar sound. Poverty and hunger
ensured a never-ending flow of recruits to the ranks of prostitution, and for a young man to be a virgin was considered a sign
of weakness or as showing lack of spirit.

Puritanism had only nibbled at the edges of the public
morality and an interesting example of the general lack of in-

hibitions concerned sea-bathing. During the eighteenth century, when the new habit of bathing in the sea began, men and women bathed together in the nude and according to contemporary prints the bystanders appear to have been unaffected by the spectacle, particularly the women who seem quite unmoved. This practice of nude bathing was continued well into the Victorian age before women began to wear heavy flannel bathing costumes, but the men still went into the sea as naked as they were born. Feminine interest seems to have been aroused during the 'sixties and 'seventies for in prints of this period young ladies are depicted peering through telescopes at the naked men on the beach.

Undoubtedly during the Victorian age everyone showed an active interest in sex, and apart from generous marital indulgence (when ten children was quite a normal sized family) there was also a devouring appetite for illicit enjoyment. It was an essentially masculine world and the men did not neglect their opportunities. The lower classes had their whores costing a few pence, the middle classes their mistresses, and the upper classes their demi-mondaines. The Victorians had a lusty, bawdy appetite and drink was their aphrodisiac. Debauchery was dispensed throughout the day and night until dawn, and newspapers and books fed the public taste for pornography.

Henry Mayhew, a man with a social conscience, embarked upon a massive and detailed survey of the deplorable conditions in London. His work was titled *London Labour and the London Poor*. The first volume was published in 1851 and the fourth volume *Those That Will Not Work* dealing with prostitutes of all kinds. thieves and swindlers, beggars and cheats, appeared in 1861. It presented a staggering picture of lust and depravity in London, but, of course, similar conditions existed on a smaller scale in all the other large towns.

Mayhew estimated that there were more than 80,000 prostitutes in London and he based his figure upon reports and statistics from the Metropolitan Police, the Society for the Suppression of Vice, the Society for the Prevention of Juvenile Prostitution, the Returns of the Registrar-General, various estimates by other investigators, and his own extensive researches. The Metropolitan Police Returns revealed that the number of disorderly prostitutes taken into custody during the years 1850 to 1860 varied each year between 2,502 and 5,178, giving an average of nearly 4,200 a year. But these, Mr. Mayhew pointed out, were only the women who were charged with drunkenness or violent behaviour in the streets, and therefore mainly concerned the whores of the dockside area and the East End. The figure of 4,000 when related to the total number represented only a small percentage.

In 1857 the *Lancet* stated that in London one house in every sixty was a brothel and one female in every sixteen, *and this applied to all ages,* was a whore. This estimate agreed with Mayhew's figure of 80,000 prostitutes and showed 6,000 brothels against the police records of 2,825. The Bishop of Exeter also asserted the number of prostitutes in London to be 80,000, and Mayhew stated that: " About the year 1793 Mr. Colquhoun, a police magistrate, concluded after tedious investigations, that there were 50,000 prostitutes in the metropolis. At that period the population was one million, and as it is now more than double we may form some idea of the extensive ramifications of this insidious vice. In 1857, according to the best authorities, there were 8,600 prostitutes known to the police, but this is far from being an even approximate return of the number of loose women in the metropolis. It scarcely does more than record the circulating harlotry of the Haymarket and Regent Street."

Another investigator, Dr. William Acton, confirmed these findings in a huge volume *Prostitution considered in its Moral, Social, and Sanitary Aspects in London and Other Large Cities and Garrison Towns.* It was first published in 1857 and appeared in a revised and enlarged edition in 1869. In it he quoted a passage from an article in *Household Words,* that evokes a picture of the centre of London :

" About the top of this thoroughfare is diffused, every night, a very large part of what is blackguard, ruffianly, and deeply dangerous in London. If Piccadilly may be termed an artery of the metropolis, most assuredly that strip of pavement between the top of the Haymarket and the Regent Circus is one of its ulcers . . . It is always an offensive place to pass, even in the daytime; but at night it is absolutely hideous, with its sparring snobs, and flashing satins, and sporting gents, and painted cheeks, and brandy-sparkling eyes, and bad tobacco, and hoarse horse-laughs, and loud indecency . . . From an extensive continental experience of cities I can take personally from three-quarters of the globe; but I have never anywhere witnessed such open ruffianism and wretched profligacy as rings along those Piccadilly flagstones any time after the gas is lighted."

Mayhew also gave a description of the Haymarket and Regent Street. "A stranger on his coming to London, after visiting the Crystal Palace, British Museum, St. James's Palace, and Buckingham Palace, and other public buildings, seldom leaves the capital before he makes an evening visit to the Haymarket and Regent Street. Struck as he is with the dense throng of people who crowd along London Bridge, Fleet Street, Cheapside, Holborn, Oxford Street, and the Strand, perhaps no sight makes a more striking impression on his mind than the brilliant gaiety of Regent Street and the Haymarket. It is not only the architectural splendour of the aristocratic streets in that neighbourhood, but the brilliant illumination of the shops, cafés, Turkish divans, assembly halls, and concert rooms, and the troops of elegantly dressed courtesans, rustling in silks and satins, and waving in laces, promenading along these superb streets among the throngs of fashionable people, and persons apparently of every order and pursuit, from the ragged crossing sweeper and tattered shoe-black to the highbred gentleman of fashion and scion of nobility.

"Not to speak of the first class of kept women, who are supported by men of opulence and rank in the privacy of their own dwellings, the whole of the other classes are to be found in the Haymarket, from the beautiful girl with fresh blooming cheeks, newly arrived from the provinces, and the pale elegant, young lady from a milliner's shop in the aristocratic West End, to the old, bloated women who have grown grey in prostitution, or become invalid through venereal disease.

"We shall first advert to the highest class who walk the Haymarket, which in our general classification we have termed the second class of prostitutes.

"They consist of the better educated and more genteel girls, some of them connected with respectable middle-class families. We do not say that they are well-educated and genteel, but either well-educated or genteel. Some of these girls have a fine appearance, and are dressed in high style, yet are poorly educated, and have sprung from an humble origin. Others, who are more plainly dressed, have had a lady's education, and some are not so brilliant in their style, who have come from a middle-class home. Many of these girls have at one time been milliners or sewing girls in genteel houses in the West End, and have been seduced by shopmen, or by gentlemen of the town, and after being ruined in character, or having quarrelled with their relatives, may have taken to a life of prostitution; others have been waiting-maids in hotels, or in service in good families, and have been seduced by servants in the family, or by gentlemen in the house, and betaken themselves to a wild life of pleasure. A considerable number have come from the provinces to London, with unprincipled young men of their acquaintance, who after a short time have deserted them, and some of them have been enticed by gay gentlemen of the West End, when on their provincial tours. Others have come to the metropolis in search of work, and been disappointed. After spending the money they had with them, they have resorted to the career of a common prostitute. Others have come from provincial towns, who had not a happy home with a stepfather or stepmother. Some are young milliners and dressmakers at one time in business in town, but being unfortunate, are now walking the Haymarket. In addition to these, many of them are seclusives turned away or abandoned by the persons who supported them, who have recourse to a gay life in the West End. There are also a number of French girls, a few Belgian and German prostitutes, who promenade this locality. You see many of them walking along in black silk cloaks or light grey mantles—many with silk paletots and wide skirts, extended by an ample crinoline, looking almost like a pyramid, with the apex terminating at the black or white satin bonnet trimmed with waving ribbons and gay flowers. Some are to be seen with their cheeks ruddy with rouge, and here and there a few rosy with health. Many of them looking cold and heartless; others with an interesting appearance. We observe them walking up and down Regent Street and the Haymarket, often by themselves, one or more in company, sometimes with a gallant they have picked up, calling at the wine-vaults, or restaurants to get a glass of wine or gin, or sitting down in the brilliant coffee-rooms, adorned with large mirrors, to a cup of good bohea or coffee. Many of the faded prostitutes of this class frequent the Pavilion to meet gentlemen and enjoy the vocal and instrumental music over some liquor. Others of the higher style proceed to the Alhambra Music Hall, or to the Argyle Rooms, rustling in splendid dresses, to spend the time till midnight, when they accompany the gentlemen they have met to the expensive supper rooms and night houses which abound in the neighbourhood.

" In the course of the evening, we see many of the girls proceeding with young, middle-aged, and sometimes silverheaded frail old men to Oxenden Street, Panton Street, and James Street, near the Haymarket, where they enter houses of accommodation, which they prefer to going with them to their lodgings . . .

" The second class of prostitutes, who walk the Haymarket— the third class in our classification—generally come from the lower orders of society. They consist of domestic servants of a plainer order, the daughters of labouring people, and some of a still lower class. Some of these girls are of a very tender age— from thirteen years and upwards. You see them wandering along Leicester Square, and about the Haymarket, Tichborne Street, and Regent Street. Many of them are dressed in a light cotton or merino gown, and ill-suited crinoline, with light grey, or brown cloak, or mantle. Some with pork-pie hat, and waving feather— white, blue, or red; others with a slouched straw-hat. Some of them walk with a timid look of artless innocence and ingenuousness, others very pert, callous, and artful. Some have good features and fine figures, others are coarse-looking and dumpy, their features and accent indicating that they are Irish cockneys. They prostitute themselves for a lower price, and haunt those disreputable coffee-shops in the neighbourhood of the Haymarket and Leicester Square, where you may see the blinds drawn down, and the lights burning dimly within, with notices over the door that " beds are to be had within ".

" Many of these young girls—some of them good-looking— cohabit with young pickpockets about Drury Lane, St. Giles's, Gray's Inn Lane, Holborn, and other localities—young lads from fourteen to eighteen, groups of whom may be seen loitering about the Haymarket, and often speaking to them. Numbers of these girls are artful and adroit thieves. They follow persons into the dark by-streets of these localities, and are apt to pick his pockets, or they rifle his person when in the bedroom with him in low coffee-houses and brothels.

" The third and lowest class of prostitutes in the Haymarket— the fourth in our classification—are worn-out prostitutes or other degraded women, some of them married, yet equally degraded in character.

" These faded and miserable wretches skulk about the Haymarket, Regent Street, Leicester Square, Coventry Street, Panton Street, and Piccadilly, cadging from the fashionable people in the street and from the prostitutes passing along, and sometimes retire for prostitution into dirty low courts near St. James's Street, Coventry Court, Long's Court, Eary's Court, and Cranbourne Passage, with shopboys, errand lads, petty thieves, and labouring men, for a few paltry coppers. Most of them steal when they get an opportunity . . .

" Numbers of the women kept by the wealthy and the titled may occasionally be seen in the Haymarket, which is the only centre in the metropolis where all the various classes of prostitutes meet. They attend the Argyle Rooms and the Alhambra, and frequently indulge in the gaieties of the supper-rooms, where their broughams are often seen drawing up at the doors. In the more respectable circles they may be regarded with aversion, but they here reign as prima-donnas over the fast life of the West End.

" Occasionally genteel and beautiful girls in shops and workrooms in the West End, milliners, dressmakers, and shop girls, may be seen flitting along Regent Street and Pall Mall, like bright birds of passage, to meet with some gentleman on the sly, and to obtain a few quickly-earned guineas to add to their scanty salaries. Sometimes a fashionable young widow, or beautiful young married woman, will find her way in those dark evenings to meet with some rickety silver-headed old captain loitering about Pall Mall. Such things are not wondered at by those acquainted with high life in London."

This was the London into which the Prince emerged when he escaped from the bondage of his mother.

When the Prince of Wales was in his 'teens he was more interested in attending race meetings, presiding at prize-fights, watching dogs killing rats and practical joking than in the opposite sex. He was game for anything. A few years later, however, he became interested in the parade of demi-mondaines in Hyde Park and at this time particularly he annoyed his mother by smoking in Rotten Row. Even during the Regency period smoking in public had not been considered good manners and Victoria never permitted smoking in her presence or in the palaces. Guests who were unable to resist the urge to smoke were therefore forced to do so secretly in the privacy of their bedrooms. Following the example of the Prince people now began to smoke in the Row and one of the old social traditions of the Park was ended.

For many years Hyde Park had been the social centre of fashionable life during the summer months, a place where people watched the society pageant of carriages, coaches, and horseriders passing by. During the 'fifties the demi-mondaines first made their appearance in the parade and with their pretty looks and stylish glitter lent an air of glamour to the scene. Inevitably they captured rich and influential admirers and sponsors, so that by the 'sixties the demi-mondaines had become a recognized part of society.

The gay young prince was the richest prize and soon became on intimate terms with Catherine Walters, nicknamed " Skittles ". She was the most celebrated harlot of the sixties; the " Queen of Prostitution." This " pretty horsebreaker " became a social celebrity and the most acclaimed artist in England, Sir Edwin Landseer, painted her portrait. His picture *The Taming of the Shrew* was exhibited at the Royal Academy and caused a tremendous stir. It was the most discussed picture of the year. Soon afterwards the infatuated young Marquis of Hartington,* who later became the eighth Duke of Devonshire, gave Catherine a beautiful Mayfair house with servants and £2,000 a year for life. But

* He was the same Lord Hartington who was the Secretary of War during the General Gordon episode.

she always remained an intimate friend of the Prince of Wales.

When the pleasure-loving Prince visited Paris he surrounded himself with harlots and actresses. His reputation as a roué was well-earned and the Prince flung himself into the delights of debauchery; titilated by the daring new dance " the can-can ". When he returned to London the round of pleasure was continued and he became a well-known figure on the London scene. His gay abandon and pleasant, aimiable disposition won him popularity, for his social activities were an antidote to the dismal seclusion of the Queen.

In November 1871 the extent of his popularity was shown by the wave of public anxiety which greeted the news that the Prince of Wales was seriously ill. He was suffering from typhoid fever. Victoria was recovering from the effects of a poisoned arm, but she immediately hurried to Sandringham, full of misgivings and with the dreadful memories of ten years ago tormenting her thoughts. From behind a screen she looked at her son sleeping in the darkened room but as she was told there did not appear to be any immediate danger she returned to her duties. The alarming news of a relapse, however, brought her back again on the 8th of December. The Prince's condition was critical and for days his life hung in the balance. The 14th of December was the tenth anniversary of Albert's death and to Victoria, it had a fateful significance; she expected her son to die. But on this day the Prince showed signs of recovery and five days later the danger had passed. The Queen returned to Windsor and issued a letter thanking her people for the sympathy they had shown during " those painful terrible days ".

Victoria had suffered great anxiety during the Prince's illness, but when he had fully recovered, she soon made it evident that the worry had not lessened her resolve to deny him participation in any form of Government affairs. Once again Bertie resumed his life of idle pleasure.

The years passed by and his indulgence became a habit. He still chased pretty women with all the ardour of his youth, but now he had become a balding, heavy-paunched, middle-aged voluptuary. To his mother he was still a stupid, indolent boy and despite his mature years he still felt the same awe and trepidation whenever he was in her presence. Once he was late for a dinner party at Osborne and stood behind a pillar wiping his brow in nervous apprehension. As he peered round cautiously he caught the imperious eye of the Queen. She shook her head reprovingly and he dodged back quickly out of sight; there he stayed until the end of the dinner.

But the passing of time began to dim the memory of Albert and gradually the years softened Victoria's implacability. The conduct of the Prince of Wales seemed to be less reprehensible and her attitude towards him softened.

In 1886 with Lord Salisbury in office, her duties became less arduous. She believed that he had inherited the wisdom of Disraeli and she had confidence in his diplomacy. His policy was her policy and she was content to devote most of her time to family and domestic affairs. Her eyesight was failing and no longer did she pore over state documents. Instead the important papers were read out aloud to her as she sat upright at her desk—as rigid as the bust of Albert in front of her. Then after a few moments pause would come in a monotone the single word : " Approved."

Victoria was old. Her grey hair had whitened, her plump figure had become heavy and because of rheumatism she walked with the aid of a stick. But the harsh lines in her face had softened and the look of hardness had been replaced by an air of gentleness.

The next year was the fiftieth of her reign and it marked a complete change in the nation's attitude towards her. During the space of a few years she had suffered many bereavements and the people's hearts warmed in sympathy to the old lady who so resolutely withstood many grievous blows. When she had wept for the death of her youngest son, Prince Leopold, who died in 1884 shortly after his marriage, many had wept for her.

The change of public opinion had been gradual but an indication had been markedly evident in 1882, when the last of the seven attempts on her life took place. At Windsor as she walked from the train to her carriage a youth named MacClean had pointed a pistol at her. Fortunately an Eton schoolboy had knocked up MacClean's arm with his umbrella before the pistol was fired. The would-be assassin was tried and found guilty, but insane. The attempt stirred up a tremendous outcry of indignation and the national sympathy drew the Queen and her people closer together. She was given new heart and her public appearances and attendances at ceremonials became more frequent. But these were not the only reasons for the Queen's increasing popularity. As her own family had grown so had the colonies of the mother-country and Victoria had become the symbol linking together the members of the family of the British Empire.

The Prince of Wales had been playing a part in this union by organizing a Colonial and Indian Exhibition at South Kensington and it was opened in 1886. The ceremonial opening was magnificent and the Queen officiated, advancing to the front of the platform so that she could be seen, and she made a speech; the first in public for many, many years.

21

In 1887 the celebration ceremony of the jubilee of her accession was performed with great pomp and it was a tremendous success. On the 20th of June the Queen arrived from Balmoral to take part in the chief ceremonial on the following day at Westminster Abbey. As the magnificent procession made its way along the gaily-decorated streets to the Abbey the tumultuous applause of the crowd brought tears to her eyes and she was almost overwhelmed with the warmth of her feelings. At last, after a long day, she returned to Buckingham Palace and as she sat down she said to her old aunt, the Duchess of Cambridge: " I am very tired, but very happy."

The Jubilee was celebrated all over the country and for the next few weeks the public's enthusiasm was tremendous. Victoria played a prominent part in the celebrations and attended dinners, receptions, ceremonials, reviews and a garden party. A personal gift of £75,000, subscribed by three million women, was made to the Queen and she used this further demonstration of the nation's esteem to erect a bronze equestrian statute of the Prince Consort at Windsor, and with the bulk of the money to found a sick nurses' institute.

After the Jubilee the Queen entered the golden years of her reign. England was prosperous and the national complacency elevated Victoria to the pinnacle of her Sovereignty. Her omnipotence was tempered with benignity and her smile, so rarely seen before, now became a natural part of her expression. The ladies of her household loved her for the keen interest she showed in their affairs and she was charming to everyone she met. But the influence spread far beyond the walls of the Palace. The nation's attitude towards her had undergone a tremendous change and now in the eyes of her subjects she was enveloped in an aura of goodness. The old lady was a character and they loved her for it. She was the living symbol of Britain's greatness; the nation's ideal conception of a queen.

Old age had increased her regality and royal etiquette was even more rigidly observed, with the result that when occasionally severity was relaxed she gained greater esteem. But the relaxation was her prerogative and any deviation evoked a cold, quelling stare, whilst an indelicate joke brought forth the famous annihilating remark: " We are not amused "—and shuddering silence resulted.

Her interests and ideas remained the same for hers was a nature that abhorred change and she surrounded herself with the bric-à-brac and paraphernalia of the past to keep alive her memories. She could never bear to part with any item from her vast collection of possessions. Nothing was thrown away and everything was carefully catalogued; the dolls and dresses of her childhood, photographs, letters, paintings, statuettes, china-ware, until her palaces were vast depositories. The furniture, the carpets, the curtains, all remained exactly the same and when wear and tear made this impracticable, the particular article was replaced by another of identical shape and pattern.

The rooms which had been Albert's remained exactly as he had left them and the routine of laying out his clothes and changing the water in his basin still continued. It was a ritual that was strictly observed for forty years. Her daily routine and her visits to Balmoral and Osborne followed the same rigid timetable. Every day she worshipped at the great mausoleum at Frogmore or at one of Albert's shrines; but the memory was becoming blurred and the poignancy had become dulled. With Lord Salisbury at the helm the ship of state sailed into peaceful waters and Victoria was lulled by the gentle waves of domesticity.

In 1891 the proposed marriage of her grandson, the Duke of

Clarence, elder son of the Prince of Wales, to Princess May (Mary), the daughter of her cousin the Duchess of Teck, gave her great pleasure, for the line of succession was further established. Tragically, however, death prevented the marriage. The Duke died on the 14th of January, 1892, and the Queen was overwhelmed with grief. To Tennyson she wrote: " Was there ever a more terrible contrast? . . . a wedding night with bright hopes turned in a funeral!"

The next heir to the Throne after his father was now George, Duke of York, and he in turn became betrothed to Princess May. They were married in the Chapel Royal at St. James's Palace on the 6th of July 1893. Victoria was delighted and she issued an address of gratitude to her people.

In the meanwhile in 1892 the Queen's life suffered another disturbance. Gladstone's plan for Irish Home Rule received support and Lord Salisbury was forced to resign. This was a grievous blow and Victoria defied precedent by publicly expressing her disappointment; she accepted his resignation " with much regret." There was no alternative but to recall the hated Gladstone. The Home Rule Bill passed through the House of Commons in July 1893, but to the Queen's relief it was rejected by the House of Lords in September. Early in the next year Gladstone began to bow under the burden of his eighty-two years. Almost deaf and with his sight failing, he tendered his resignation in March. During his last official interview the Queen's manner was cold and detached and the old statesman retired from the political scene to the weary satisfaction of the sovereign whom he had served, after his fashion, so conscientiously throughout his long career. They met again in 1897 when they were both wintering at Cimiez and for the first and last time she gave him her hand. On the 19th of May 1898 Gladstone died.

When Gladstone retired in 1894 the Queen appointed the Earl of Rosebery as his successor, but his Ministry lasted only until 1895. Lord Salisbury returned for his third term of office and once again the Queen's peace of mind was restored.

On the 23rd of September 1896 Queen Victoria's reign exceeded by one day George III's reign of fifty-nine years and ninety-six days; and thus became the longest reign in English history. But within a few weeks plans were being discussed and preparations were being made to celebrate the completion of her sixtieth year of sovereignty by a Diamond Jubilee in the following year.

The emphasis was to be placed on the Empire and Prime Ministers, delegates, representatives and troops from all the British colonies and dependencies were to be invited to take part. It was to be the greatest celebration in Britain's history.

On the 20th of June 1897, the Queen wrote in her journal: "This eventful day, 1897, has opened, and I pray God to help and protect me as He has hitherto done during these sixty long eventful years." It was the climax of her long life.

Two days later a magnificent procession proceeded from Buckingham Palace to St. Paul's Cathedral, where a service was held, and returned by a circuitous route to the Palace. Millions thronged the streets and London echoed with the tumultuous cheers of her people. As the tiny, old lady bowed to the right and to the left, tears streamed down her cheeks and repeatedly she whispered, "How kind they are to me! How kind they are to me!"

Queen Victoria had received an acclamation of loyalty and affection which in its intensity had no precedent in history. She was very touched and that same evening a telegraphic greeting was sent to every corner of the Empire: "From my heart I thank them my beloved people. May God bless them!"

As the Queen entered the deepening twilight of her life she still retained a remarkably active interest in the country's affairs. Her troops were fighting a grim frontier war in India and Kitchener was conducting a campaign in Egypt to crush the rebellion which had started in 1883. The welfare of the troops was her main concern and she made a regular practice of visiting the wounded soldiers in hospital.

On the 2nd of September 1898 Kitchener won the battle of Omdurman and his telegram saying: "This morning the British and Egyptian flags were hoisted on the walls of Gordon's palace at Khartoum," gave the Queen immense satisfaction.

But the campaigns in India and Egypt were overshadowed by troubles in South Africa and in the October of 1899 the country became engaged in the Boer War. Suddenly calling upon hidden reserves of energy the Queen became vitally interested in every detail of the conflict. The disasters at the beginning of the war distressed her, but they also stirred her fighting spirit and she urged her Ministers to increase their efforts.

In December 1899 huge reinforcements were sent out under the command of Lord Roberts, with Kitchener, who had been recalled from the Sudan, as his Chief of Staff. The tide turned and early in 1900 gratifying news arrived of British victories. The Queen drove through the London streets and the public's enthusiasm was roused to fever pitch; cheering crowds greeted her everywhere.

Irish troops had played a gallant part in the British victories and the Queen visited Ireland for three weeks as a mark of appreciation. In Dublin, despite the warnings of her Ministers, she drove through the streets in an open carriage and was delighted with the loyal and enthusiastic reception she received.

In the late summer the war swung the other way and the British death list was mounting alarmingly. Gloom settled over the country, but although the news of deaths and casualties caused the Queen acute distress, she was still confident of final victory : " All will come right," she said.

But for Victoria the end was near. The strain and anxieties of the war began to take their toll on a constitution racked with rheumatism and the debilities of old age. Her strength was ebbing, but her strong determination made her weak body perform her duties. At the end of the year little but her spirit remained; she was very feeble and her memory, of which she had always been proud, was failing.

She spent Christmas at Osborne and was greatly distressed on Christmas morning by the sudden death of her Lady-in-Waiting and life-long friend, Jane Lady Churchill. On the 2nd of January she received Lord Roberts who had returned with good news from South Africa but it required a great effort of will to discuss the war with him. The news was of vital interest to her and she struggled through the interview. She then conferred on Lord Roberts an earldom and the Order of the Garter.

On the 14th Roberts again visited the Queen at Osborne and they talked for an hour. He said afterwards that the Queen seemed stronger than she had been at the previous interview; but when he had gone the Queen collapsed. The next day she had recovered and went for a drive with the widowed Duchess of Saxe-Coburg-Gotha. When they returned the Queen collapsed again and her doctors realized that her condition was hopeless. Her brain was failing and she was suffering attacks of aphasia.

Her children in England were summoned to Osborne. The Queen was in a coma and the next day, at half-past six in the evening, she died.

The Prince of Wales, the Duke of Connaught, his three daughters, Helena, Louise and Beatrice, and her grandson, the German Emperor, were at her bedside when she died. She was eighty-one. Her reign had lasted sixty-three years, seven months, and two days, exceeding by nearly four years the reign of George III, who had been England's longest-lived sovereign.

When the news of Queen Victoria's death was announced, a storm of genuine grief swept the country. Despite her advanced age there was a feeling of national incredulity, as though the impossible had happened, and as though some integral part of everyone's life had been taken away. There were not many of her subjects who could remember the time when Victoria had not been the Queen. She had become an institution, and in later years a loved one.

The Queen had left instructions that she was to be given a military funeral and as her white coffin, aboard the royal yacht *Alberta,* passed between eleven miles of warships, a last salute was fired. The coffin was borne on a gun-carriage through London to Paddington station and thence to Windsor for the funeral service in St. George's Chapel.

On Monday, the 4th of February, the coffin was carried to the Frogmore mausoleum and placed in the sarcophagus which held the remains of the Prince Consort. At last in death, as she had always prayed, Victoria was reunited with her beloved Albert.

The House of Hanover was ended. On the 24th of January 1901, the Prince of Wales was proclaimed King as Edward VII and the reign of the House of Saxe-Coburg had begun.*

---

* During the First World War, on July 17, 1917, George V issued a proclamation declaring that: "Henceforth Our House and Family shall be styled and known as the House and Family of Windsor."

SELECTED BIBLIOGRAPHY

Many more books have been consulted than those shown below and this bibliography makes no attempt to be a comprehensive list of sources. It is designed to provide a selection of reading matter to illustrate the text.

AIKIN, John : *Annals of the Reign of George III* (1816).

ALBERMARLE, Earl of : *Memoirs of Rockingham* (1852).

Anonymous : *A Biographical Memoir of the Public and Private Life of the much lamented Princess Charlotte Augusta of Wales and Saxe-Coburg* (1817).

An Historical Account of the Public and Domestic Life and Reign of his late Majesty, George the Fourth, with a variety of Anecdotes, obtained from the most authentic sources (1830).

Diaries of a Lady of Quality (1864).

George the Third, His Court and Family (1824).

The Authentic Memoirs of the Life of Princess Charlotte (1817).

ASHBOURNE, Lord : *Pitt* (1898).

ASHTON, John : *Old Times:* A Picture of Social Life at the End of the Eighteenth Century (1885).

Florizel's Folly (1899).

BALFOUR-MELVILLE, E. W. M. : *The Growth of the Constitution* (1925).

BARING, Lord Cromer : *Disraeli* (1912).

BARRINGTON, E. : *The Exquisite Perdita* (1926).

BASS, Robert D. : *The Green Dragoon.* The Lives of Banastre Tarleton and Mary Robinson (1958).

BAUER, Karoline : *Memoirs of Karoline Bauer* (1885).

BESANT, Sir Walter : *London in the Eighteenth Century* (1902).

443

BLEACKLEY, Horace : *Life of John Wilkes* (1917).

BOLITHO, Hector : *Albert the Good* (1932).
Victoria the Widow, and Her Son (1934).
The Reign of Queen Victoria (1949).

BREADY, J. Wesley : *Lord Shaftesbury and Social-Industrial Progress* (1926).

BROUGHAM, Lord Henry : *The Life and Times of Henry Lord Brougham* (1871).

BUCKINGHAM and CHANDOS, The Duke of : *Memoirs of the Court of England during the Regency 1811-1820* (1856).
Memoirs of the Court and Cabinets of William IV (1861).

BURKE, Edmund : *Reflections on the Revolution in France* (1790).

BURY, Charlotte : *The Diary of a Lady-in-Waiting* by *Lady* Charlotte Bury (1908).

BUTTERFIELD, Herbert : *George III, Lord North and the People* 1779-1780 (1949).

CARLYLE, T. : *The French Revolution* (1837).

CASTLE, E. Egerton : (Editor) *The Jerningham Letters 1780-1843* (1896).

CASTLEREAGH, Viscount : *Memoirs and Correspondence* (1848-53).

CASTRO, J. Paul de : *The Gordon Riots* (1926).

CHAMIER, Frederick : *The Life of a Sailor* (1832).

CHANNING, E. : *History of the United States* (1912).

CHURCHILL, Winston : *Marlborough: His Life and Times* (1933-8).

CLARKE, Mary Anne : *The Rival Princes* (1810).

CLARKE, J S. and MACARTHUR, J. : *Life of Lord Nelson* (1809).

CLAYDEN, P. W. : *England under Lord Beaconsfield* (1890).

CLERICI, Graziano Paolo : *A Queen of Indiscretions.* The tragedy of Caroline of Brunswick, Queen of England (from the Italian) (1907).

COBBETT, William : *History of the Regency and Reign of King George the Fourth* (1830).

COLLINGWOOD, Lord : *Memoir and Correspondence* (1828).

COLSON, Percy : *White's, 1693-1950* (1951).

CORTI, Caesar : *Leopold I of Belgium* (from the Italian) (1923).

CREEVEY, Thomas : *The Creevey Papers* (1903).

CROKER, John Wilson : *The Correspondence and Diaries of the late Right Honourable John Wilson Croker, LL.D., F.R.S.,* Secretary to the Admiralty from 1809 to 1813 (1884).

DICKENS, Charles : *Oliver Twist* (1838).
Nicholas Nickleby (1839).

Bibliography

Dictionary of National Biography

DISRAELI, Benjamin : *Coningsby* (1844).
  Sybil (1845).

D'ISRAELI, Isaac : *The Works with a Memoir by His Son* (1858).

DOBREE, E. : *Letters of George III* (1935).

DONNE, W. Boham : (Editor) *The Correspondence of King George III and Lord North*, 1768-1783 (1867).

DORAN, Dr. : *Lives of the Queens of England of the House of Hanover* (1855).

DRUID, The : *The Post and The Paddock.* With recollections of George IV, Sam Chifney and other Turf Celebrities (1895).

EASTMAN, R. M. : *Life of Robert Raikes* (1880).

ENGELS, Friedrich : *The Condition of the Working Class in England in 1844.*

ESCOTT, T. H. Sweet : *England. Its People, Polity, and Pursuits* (1885).
  Great Victorians (1916).

EVERSLEY, Lord : *Gladstone and Ireland* (1912).

FISKE, J. : *The American Revolution* (1905).

FITZGERALD, Percy : *The Good Queen Charlotte* (1899).

FRANCIS, C. H. : *The Late Sir Robert Peel* (1852).

FRANKLIN, Benjamin : *Memoirs of the Life and Writings of Benjamin Franklin* (1833).

FRANZERO, Carlo Maria : *The Life and Times of Beau Brummell* (1958).

FULWOOD, Roger : *The Royal Dukes* (1933).
  George IV (1935).

GARRATT, C. P. : *Life of Lord Brougham* (1935).

GEORGE, D. M. : *London Life in the Eighteenth Century* (1925).

GREENWOOD, Alice Drayton : *Lives of the Hanoverian Queens of England* (1909 and 1911).

Grenville Papers (1852-3).

GREVILLE, Charles C. F. : *The Greville Memoirs: A Journal of the Reign of Queen Victoria* (1887).

GREY, Lieut-General the Hon. C. : *The Early Years of His Royal Highness The Prince Consort*, compiled under the direction of Her Majesty The Queen (1867).

GUEPALLA, Philip : *Palmerston* (1926), *The Duke* (1931).

GUIZOT, F. : *Memoirs of Sir Robert Peel* (1856-7).

GURNEY, Mrs. Gerald : *Childhood of Queen Victoria* (1901).

HARCOURT, Earl of : *The Harcourt Papers* (privately printed 1876-1891).

HECTOR, A. F. : *Mrs. Norton* (1897).

HERVEY, Lord J. : *Memoirs of George II* (1848).

HIBBERT, Christopher : *King Mob* (1958).

HODDEX, Edwin : *Life of the Seventh Earl of Shaftesbury* (1887).
Lord Shaftesbury as Social Reformer (1897).

HOLMES, Richard R. (Librarian to the Queen) : *Queen Victoria* (1897).

HUISH, Robert : *The Public and Private Life of George III* (1821). *Memoirs of George IV* (1831).

JERROLD, Claire : *Story of Dorothy Jordan* (1914).

JERROLD, Walter B. : *A Day with Disraeli* (1872).

JESSE, J. H. : *Memoirs of Life and Reign of George III* (1867). *George Selwyn and his Contemporaries* (1882).

KEBBEL, T. E. : *Life of Lord Beaconsfield* (1888).

LANGDALE, Charles : *Memoirs of Mrs. Fitzherbert with an account of her marriage with H.R.H. The Prince of Wales, afterwards King George the Fourth* (1856).

LEE, E. : *Wives of Prime Ministers* (1918).

LEE, Sidney : *Queen Victoria*, a biography (1902). *King Edward VII* (1927).

LEOPOLD I, King of the Belgians : *Reminiscences of King Leopold* (1862).

LESLIE, Shane : *George the Fourth* (1926).

LLOYD, H. E. : *George IV, Memoirs of his Life and Reign,* interspersed with numerous personal anecdotes; to which is prefixed an historical account of the House of Brunswick from the earliest period (1830).

LUCAS, R. J. : *George II* (1910).

MCCARTHY, Justin : *A History of the Four Georges and William IV* (1884-1901).

MAITLAND, F. W. : *The Constitutional History of England,* edited by H. L. L. Fisher (1910).

MARRIOTT, Sir J. A. R. : *Queen Victoria and Her Ministers* (1933).

MARSHALL, D. : *The English Poor in the Eighteenth Century* (1926).

MARTIN, Sir Theodore : *Life of the Prince Consort* (1880).

MARVIN, F. S. : *The Century of Hope* (1919).

MARX, Karl : *Capital: Revolution and Counter Revolution* (1867).

Bibliography

MAUROIS, André : *Disraeli. A Picture of the Victorian Age* (from the French) (1927).

MAYHEW, Henry : *London Labour and the London Poor* (1861).

MAXWELL, Sir Herbert : *Life of Lord Clarendon, 4th Earl.*

MELVILLE, Lewis : *The First Gentleman of Europe* (1906).

MEYNELL, W. : *Benjamin Disraeli* (1903).

MILL, John Stuart : *The Subjection of Women* (1869).
Autobiography (1873).

MOLLOY, Fitzgerald : *The Sailor King* (1903).

MONVEL, Roger Boutet de : *Beau Brummell and His Times* (1908).

MORLEY, Lord : *The Life of William Ewart Gladstone* (1903).

NAMIER, L. B. : *England in the Age of the American Revolution* (1930).

NEALE, Erskine : *The Life of Field-Marshall His Royal Highness, Edward, Duke of Kent* (1850).

NEVILL, Ralph : *The Gay Victorians* (1930).

OWEN, Robert : *Life written by himself* (1857-8).

PANAM, Pauline : *The Memoirs of Madame Panam.* Translated by W. H. Ireland (1823).

PAPENDICK, Mrs. : *Court and Private Life in the Times of Queen Charlotte* (1887).

PARRY, Sir Edward : *Queen Caroline* (1930).

PITT LENNOX, Lord William : *Celebrities I have known; with Episodes, Political, Social, Sporting ,and Theatrical* (1877).

PLUMB, J. H. : *England in the Eighteenth Century* (1950).
The First Four Georges (1956).

PONSONBY, Lord Arthur : *Henry Ponsonby, Queen Victoria's Private Secretary.* His Life from his Letters by his son (1942).

PONSONBY, Sir F. : *Sidelights on Queen Victoria* (1930).

POSTGATE, Raymond : *That Devil Wilkes* (1930).

RAIKES, Thomas : *A Portion of the Journal kept by Thomas Raikes Esquire,* from 1831 to 1847 (1856).

Records of the Commissioners of Works and Public Buildings

REES, J. F. : *A Social and Industrial History of England 1815-1918*

ROBERTS, Henry D. : *The Story of the Royal Pavilion, Brighton* (1915).

ROBERTSON, C. Grant : *England under the Hanoverians* (1911).

ROBINSON, Mary : *Memoirs of the Late Mrs. Robinson.* Written by herself (1801).

RUSSELL, Lord J. : *Life and Times of C. F. Fox* (1859-1866).

SHERRARD, O. A. : *John Wilkes* (1930).

STANHOPE, Hester : *Memoirs of the Lady Hester Stanhope* as related by herself in conversations with her physician, comprising her opinions and anecdotes (1845).

STAPLETON, A. G. : *George Canning and His Times* (1859).

STEEGMAN, John : *Consort of Taste* (1950).

STEUART, Francis : (Editor) *The Last Journals of Horace Walpole* (1910).

STOCKMAR, E. von : *Memoirs of Baron Stockmar.* (Translated from the German 1872).

STRACHEY, Lytton : *Five Victorians*—combining Queen Victoria (1921) and Eminent Victorians (1918).

SYDNEY, W. C. : *England and the English in the Eighteenth Century* (1892).

TAYLOR, G. S. : *Robert Walpole* (1931).

TAYLOR, H. C. : *The Factory System* (1844).

TERRY, Sir H. M. I. : *Life of George I* (1927).

THACKERAY, W. M. : *The Four Georges* (1869).
    Vanity Fair (1847).

THOMPSON, Grace E. : *The Patriot King* (1932).

TILBY, A. W. : *Lord John Russell* (1930).

TOYNBEE, Arnold : *Industrial Revolution in England* (1906).

TREVELYAN, George Macaulay : *British History in the Nineteenth Century* 1782-1901 (1922).
    Lord Grey of the Reform Bill (1920).
    History of England (1926).

TREVELYAN, Sir G. O. : *George III and Charles Fox* (1912-1914).
    A History of the American Revolution (1909).

TUBERVILLE, A. S. : (Editor) *Johnson's England* (1933).

VICTORIA, Queen : *Letters of Queen Victoria.* A Selection from Her Majesty's correspondence between the years 1837 and 1861. Published by authority of His Majesty the King. Edited by Arthur Christopher Benson M.A., and Viscount Esher, G.C.V.O., K.C.B. (1907).
    Letters of Queen Victoria, edited by George Earle Buckle (1926-8 and 1930-2).
    Leaves from the Journal of our Life in the Highlands 1848-1861 (1868).
    More Leaves from the Journal of our Life in the Highlands 1862-1882 (1884).

Bibliography

VINCENT, William : *A Plain and Succinct Narrative of the Late Riots and Disturbances* (1780).

VULLIAMY, C. E. : *Royal George* (1937).
John Wesley (1931).

WALDEGRAVE, Earl : *Memoirs* (1821).

WALLACE, W. : *History of George IV* (pub. anon. 1831).

WALLAS, Graham : *Francis Place* (1898).

WALPOLE, Horace : *Memoirs of the Reign of George the Second* (1846).
Memoirs of the Reign of King George the Third, by Horace Walpole, Youngest son of Sir Robert Walpole, Earl of Orford (1845).
Journal of the Reign of King George the Third from the year 1771 to 1783 (1859).

WASHINGTON, George : *Washington's Writings*. Edited by Jared Sparks (1833-7).

WRAXALL, Sir Nathaniel William : *Historical Memoirs of My Own Time* (1815).

WEBB, Beatrice and Sidney : *The History of Trade Unionism* (1894).

WILKES, John : *Correspondence and Memoirs* (1805).

WILKINS, W. H. : *Mrs. Fitzherbert and George IV* (1905).

WILLIAMS, Robert Folkestone : *Memoirs of Sophia Dorothea* (1845).

WILSON, Harriette : *Memoirs* (1825).

YOUNG, G. M. : *Victorian England: Portrait of an Age* (1936).

PERIODICALS

Edinburgh Review, European Magazine, Gentleman's Magazine, The London Gazette, The Monthly Magazine, The Morning Chronicle, The Morning Herald, The Morning Post, The National Review, Pall Mall Gazette, Public Advertiser, The Times.

INDEX

Index

Index

Index

St. James's Chapel, 153
St. James's Palace, 72, 73, 82, 306; George III at, 107; Duke of Cumberland's rooms at, 345
St. Laurent, Mme. (*Duke of Kent's mistress*), 240, 241, 242-3
St. Lawrence River, Canada, 382
St. Leger, Col., 214, 215
St. Vincent, Cape, naval action off, 1780, 230
Salem, Mass., 121
Salic Law, 331, 400
Salisbury, Bishop of, 178
Salisbury, 3rd Marquess of, 419; Prime Minister, 1885-6, 424; —1886-92, 424, 436, 438, 439; —1895-1902, 439
San Jacinto, Federal warship, 386
Sandringham House, 393
Sandwich, naval action off, 230
Saratoga, Battle of, 1777, 125
Saxe-Coburg, Dowager Duchess of, *see* Augusta, Duchess
Saxe-Coburg, Dukes of, *see* Francis Frederick-Antoine *and* Ernst *and* Ernest
Saxe-Coburg, House of, 442
Saxe-Coburg dynasty, the, 180-208
Saxe-Meiningen, Dowager Duchess of, 238
Saxe-Weimar, Ida, Duchess of, 238, 290
Schleswig-Holstein, Duchies of, 393, 395
Schulenburg, Melusina von, 23, 41, 46; created Duchess of Kendal, 41, 46; Walpole approaches George I through, 56
Schwellenberg, Madame, 99, 103, 105
Scotland, Q. Victoria in, 350-1, 369, 413
Scott, Sir George Gilbert (*architect*), 391
Scutari Hospital, 374, 375
Sebastopol, Siege of, 1854-5, 373, 374, 375, 376
Sellis, (*valet*), 164
Settlement, Act of, 1701, 34, 40, 46, 55, 144
Seymour, Lady Horatio, 158
Seymour, Minnie, 158, 160
Shaftesbury, 7th Earl of, 352-61; quoted, 356, 359; Prince Albert's interest in his work, 359, 361
Shakespeare, William: *The Winter's Tale,* 140; *Othelo* and *Richard III,* 257

Shelburne, Lord (*Prime Minister*), 126
Shelley, Percy Bysshe: *Masque of Anarchy,* 260
Sheridan, Richard Brinsley (*playwright*), 140, 143, 155, 236; in Parliament, 146, 166, 166-7, 224
Siccard, (*Princess Caroline's steward*), 214, 250
Sidmouth, D. of Kent's death at, 250
Sidney, Sir Philip, Prince Consort likened to, 402
Siebold, Mme. (*midwife*), 245
"Six Acts, the," 1819, 260
Skerratt, Molly (*Walpole's mistress*), 70
Slavery, abolition of, 1834, 305-6, 315
Smith, Adam (*economist*), 262
Smith, Col. Francis, 123
Smith, Canon Sydney, quoted, 147 *n*
Smith, Sir Sydney, 161
Soane, Sir John (*architect*), 268
Somerset, Duke of, 89
Somerset House, 107, 142
"Sons of Liberty," (American), 119
Sophia, Electress of Hanover, 22, 36-7; succession to British throne and, 16, 40; her account of Königsmarck mystery, 30; guardian of George Augustus, 32, 34; Sophia Dorothea's appeal to, 33; her death, 1714, 37
Sophia, Princess (*dau. of George III*), 106 *n*
Sophia Charlotte of Hanover, 21, 34
Sophia Dorothea (*dau. of George I*), 23, 31, 51, 59; marriage to Duke of Gloucester proposed, 32; married to Frederick William I of Prussia, 36; plans for children's marriages, 66
Sophia Dorothea (*wife of George I*), 17-23; marriage, 17, 20; relations with husband, 23, 26, 27, 33; affair with von Königsmarck, 24-5, 26, 27-9; becomes Electoral Princess, 28; confesses to indiscretion, 30; divorce and imprisonment, 30-1; death, 1726, 31; George II and, 32
South Sea Company, the, 57-9
Spa Fields riots, 260, 261
Späth, Mme. de (*Victoria's preceptress*), 294
Spencer, 2nd Earl, 407

467